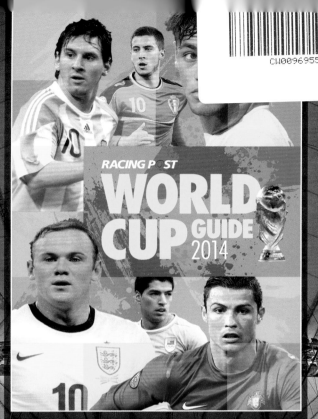

RACING P○ST

WORLD
CUP GUIDE 2014

Edited by Paul Charlton

Contributors Paul Charlton, Dan Childs, Michael Cox, Steve Davies, Ed Malyon, Kevin Pullein, Dan Sait

Stats editor Chris Mann (www.soccerbase.com)

Published in 2014 by Racing Post Books
High Street, Compton, Newbury, Berkshire, RG20 6NL

Cover designed by Jay Vincent
Graphics by David Penzer
Designed by Paul Charlton

A catalogue record for this book is available from the British Library.

ISBN 978-1-909471-54-2

Printed in Great Britain by Buxton Press

CONTENTS

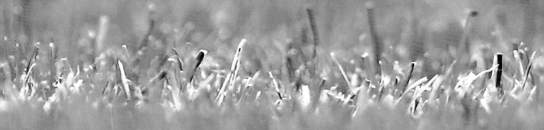

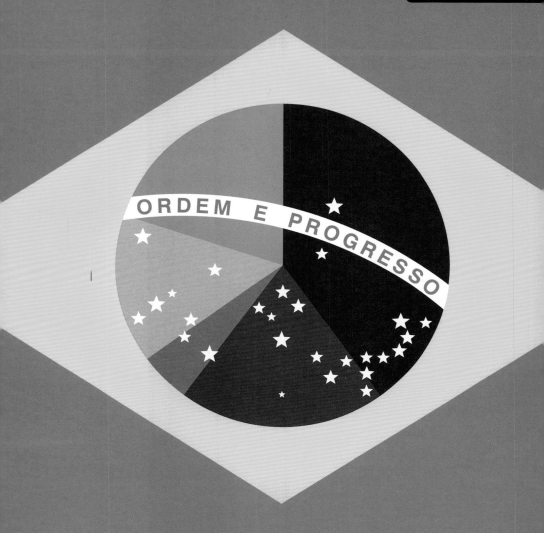

INTRODUCTION

With protests a certainty in Brazil, controversy over the costs, stadiums running late, and questions over the travelling and the climate, the build-up to Brazil 2014 hasn't exactly gone smoothly, **writes Paul Charlton**.

But this certainly isn't the first World Cup to kick off under a cloud, and it won't be the last either, with Russia 2018 and Qatar 2022 already the subject of more than their fair share of controversy.

We shouldn't forget about any of that but there's something that's just inherently exciting about the World Cup being held in Brazil. And wherever it takes place, a World Cup delivers thrills and excitement like no other sporting event. But let's face it, no matter how exciting a sporting event might be, it's more exciting when you've got some money on it.

You're in good hands here. Regular readers of the Racing Post will know that Mark Langdon, who has profiled all 32 teams and previewed all eight groups in this book, is recognised by the bookmakers as one of the most feared football tipsters in the game. Four years ago he tipped a Spain v Holland final in South Africa and he gives you his idea of how to profit from every team in Brazil.

Our other contributors are also hugely respected figures – Kevin Pullein's tips have finished in profit in each of the last 17 full seasons and, as we went to press, he was ahead for 2013-14 too. Dan Childs has a proven track record of finding tournament winners. Michael Cox runs the massively popular Zonal Marking website.

With their guidance and a superb array of stats from soccerbase.com, you should have all the ammunition you need to make this World Cup a profitable one.

Don't forget to buy the Racing Post and our sister paper, the Racing & Football Outlook, out every Tuesday, during the tournament for the latest odds, stats, facts, analysis and tips but, above all, enjoy the World Cup.

OUTRIGHT WINNER

Hosts hold solid claims but Spain have what it takes to defend the trophy

Key members of Spain's golden generation are approaching the twilight of their careers but there is enough left in the tank for a successful World Cup defence in Brazil, **writes Dan Childs**. But while France are the only host nation to triumph in the last eight World Cups, it is hard to ignore Brazil, who won the 2013 Confederations Cup in good style and are 3-1 favourites this summer.

The Selecao's modest Fifa ranking (ninth as we go to press) has been hit by a lack of competitive football in recent years but they have a strong squad, especially in defence and midfield.

Their problem could be an over-reliance on Neymar in attack because the 22-year-old has had a fairly modest impact at Barcelona and spent almost a month on the sidelines after an ankle injury sustained in a Copa Del Rey clash at Getafe on January 16.

Neymar will be keen to make up for lost time before the end of the campaign but if he fails to rediscover his best form Brazil's chances will be reduced.

None of their back-up forwards can be placed in the elite bracket and a lack of match winners could be a real problem for a side who look like being plunged into a massive last-16 encounter with either holders Spain or Holland, who beat them 2-1 in the 2010 quarter-finals.

Second favourites Argentina are another team with a superstar – Lionel Messi – in their ranks. They have much greater depth to their attacking resources than Brazil, with Carlos Tevez behind Sergio Aguero and Gonzalo Higuain in the pecking order.

They were impressive enough in qualification, finishing top of a strong Conmebol section, and their draw, alongside makeweights Bosnia, Iran and Nigeria in Group F, is about as good as is gets.

They have obvious claims but the main worry is a habit of falling short in big tournaments after going home in the quarter-finals or earlier at the last five World Cups and failing to win any of the last seven Copa Americas.

Germany are expected to lead the European challenge after qualifying in superb style, dropping just two points in their ten games.

Their squad is packed with individual flair and an abundance of quality attacking midfielders and wingers. But Germany have no obvious out-and-out striker to take the competition by storm and question marks are being raised over the defence after Joachim Low's team conceded three goals in three of their last eight matches of 2013.

None of the contenders tick every box but Spain go the closest. Like Germany, their defence looks far from rock-solid, but they keep the ball so well that it will be difficult for opposition teams to put them under sustained pressure.

It has been suggested that Xavi and Andres Iniesta are fading forces but they remain important members of a Barcelona side who are, as we go to press, challenging strongly on three fronts – La Liga, the Champions League and the Copa Del Rey.

La Roja have lacked a world class striker

Xavi might be getting on but he is still an influential figure for Spain and Barcelona

in recent years but that situation seems to have been resolved by the emergence of Atletico Madrid's Diego Costa and the impressive form of Alvaro Negredo, who seems revitalised by his move to Manchester City.

Ending up in the same group as Holland wasn't ideal but Spain look capable of beating anyone they come across and that marks them down as obvious contenders.

Spain's toughest match at Euro 2012 was their semi-final against Portugal, which they won on penalties.

It was the second time in six years that the Portuguese have graced the last four of a major tournament – they lost 1-0 to France at World Cup 2006 – and their chances of success in Brazil may have been overlooked.

Cristiano Ronaldo deservedly collected the 2013 Ballon d'Or after a succession of superb performances for Real Madrid and his wonderful display against Sweden that saw Portugal win their qualification play-off. If he can reproduce that sort of form on the World Cup stage, the Portuguese could be tough to stop. The back-up to Ronaldo isn't spectacular but the same could have been said of Argentina's 1986 team, who were dragged to glory by Diego Maradona, the world's best player at the time.

France, boosted by the continued brilliance of Franck Ribery and the emergence of Juventus midfielder Paul Pogba, are another dark horse who could go close and Belgium (full of talented individuals) and Italy (used to major tournament success) cannot be discounted in an open looking tournament.

It's Spain though, who have by far the best recent form in international tournaments and they can make it four major titles in a row.

Recommendation
Spain, Portugal each-way

ROUTE TO THE FINAL

Group A

Brazil v Croatia	12 June 9pm, Sao Paulo, ITV
Mexico v Cameroon	13 June 5pm, Natal, ITV
Brazil v Mexico	17 June 8pm, Fortaleza, BBC
Cameroon v Croatia	18 June 11pm, Manaus, ITV
Cameroon v Brazil	23 June 9pm, Brasilia, ITV
Croatia v Mexico	23 June 9pm, Recife, ITV

Group B

Spain v Holland	13 June 8pm, Salvador, BBC
Chile v Australia	13 June 11pm, Cuiaba, ITV
Australia v Holland	18 June 5pm, Porto Alegre, ITV
Spain v Chile	18 June 8pm, Rio, BBC
Australia v Spain	23 June 5pm, Curitiba, ITV
Holland v Chile	23 June 5pm, Sao Paulo, ITV

Group C

Colombia v Greece	14 June 5pm, Belo Horizonte, BBC
Ivory Coast v Japan	15 June 2am, Recife, ITV
Colombia v Ivory Coast	19 June 5pm, Brasilia, BBC
Japan v Greece	19 June 11pm, Natal, BBC
Japan v Colombia	24 June 9pm, Cuiaba, BBC
Greece v Ivory Coast	24 June 9pm, Fortaleza, BBC

Group D

Uruguay v Costa Rica	14 June 8pm, Fortaleza, ITV
England v Italy	14 June 11pm, Manaus, BBC
Uruguay v England	19 June 8pm, Sao Paulo, ITV
Italy v Costa Rica	20 June 5pm, Recife, BBC
Italy v Uruguay	24 June 5pm, Natal, ITV
Costa Rica v England	24 June 5pm, Belo Horizonte, ITV

Group E

Switzerland v Ecuador	15 June 5pm, Brasilia, ITV
France v Honduras	15 June 8pm, Porto Alegre, BBC
Switzerland v France	20 June 8pm, Salvador, ITV
Honduras v Ecuador	20 June 11pm, Curitiba, ITV
Honduras v Switzerland	25 June 9pm, Manaus, BBC
Ecuador v France	25 June 9pm, Rio, BBC

Group F

Argentina v Bosnia-Hz	15 June 11pm, Rio, BBC
Iran v Nigeria	16 June 8pm, Curitiba, BBC
Argentina v Iran	21 June 5pm, Belo Horizonte, ITV
Nigeria v Bosnia-Hz	21 June 11pm, Cuiaba, BBC
Nigeria v Argentina	25 June 5pm, Porto Alegre, ITV
Bosnia-Hz v Iran	25 June 5pm, Salvador, ITV

Group G

Germany v Portugal	16 June 5pm, Salvador, ITV
Ghana v USA	16 June 11pm, Natal, BBC
Germany v Ghana	21 June 8pm, Fortaleza, BBC
USA v Portugal	22 June 11pm, Manaus, BBC
USA v Germany	26 June 5pm, Recife, BBC
Portugal v Ghana	26 June 5pm, Brasilia, BBC

Group H

Belgium v Algeria	17 June 5pm, Belo Horizonte, ITV
Russia v South Korea	17 June 11pm, Cuiaba, BBC
Belgium v Russia	22 June 5pm, Rio, BBC
South Korea v Algeria	22 June 8pm, Porto Alegre, ITV
South Korea v Belgium	26 June 9pm, Sao Paulo, ITV
Algeria v Russia	26 June 9pm, Curitiba, ITV

Groups are decided as follows 1 Points **2** Goal difference **3** Goals scored. **If teams are still level: 4** Points in games between teams concerned **5** Goal difference in games between teams concerned **6** Goals scored in games between teams concerned **7** Lots are drawn

MARK LANGDON'S FIVE GOLDEN RULES FOR IN-PLAY BETTING

1 Check your bets
It seems obvious, but is really important in-play because the fastest-finger first mentality means we are rushing to place bets. It's happened to me twice where I have bet on the wrong in-play market and on both occasions, as if the gambling gods were punishing me, the bet I wanted to place won and the ones I did erroneously lost.

2 Think like a coach
There are many who use spreadsheets but my favourite part of in-play is trying to get into the mind of a coach. What happens at half-time? Will the manager change system? Might he go for a more direct style so should I be backing corners? Is he going to ask for more aggression, is there a bookings market to play? Could he ask the team to sit back and is now the time to start swimming against the tide as far as goals are concerned?

3 Work out injury time
This becomes more important for the second half and it is quite easy to forget injuries or over compensate for stoppages so writing down the important moments could give you a slight edge.

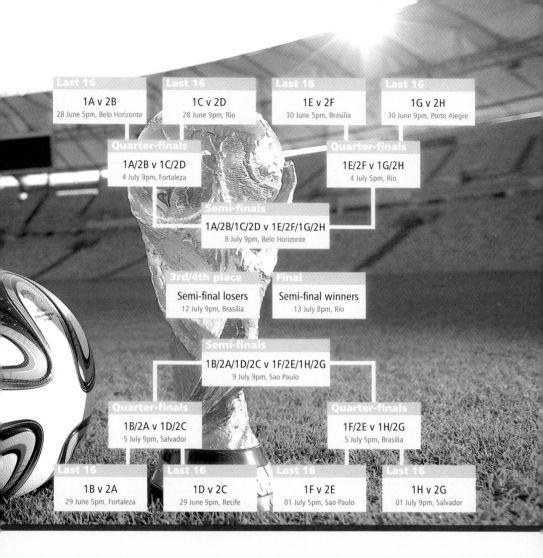

Last 16
1A v 2B
28 June 5pm, Belo Horizonte

Last 16
1C v 2D
28 June 9pm, Rio

Last 16
1E v 2F
30 June 5pm, Brasilia

Last 16
1G v 2H
30 June 9pm, Porto Alegre

Quarter-finals
1A/2B v 1C/2D
4 July 9pm, Fortaleza

Quarter-finals
1E/2F v 1G/2H
4 July 5pm, Rio

Semi-finals
1A/2B/1C/2D v 1E/2F/1G/2H
8 July 9pm, Belo Horizonte

3rd/4th place
Semi-final losers
12 July 9pm, Brasilia

Final
Semi-final winners
13 July 8pm, Rio

Semi-finals
1B/2A/1D/2C v 1F/2E/1H/2G
9 July 9pm, Sao Paulo

Quarter-finals
1B/2A v 1D/2C
5 July 9pm, Salvador

Quarter-finals
1F/2E v 1H/2G
5 July 5pm, Brasilia

Last 16
1B v 2A
29 June 5pm, Fortaleza

Last 16
1D v 2C
29 June 9pm, Recife

Last 16
1F v 2E
01 July 5pm, Sao Paulo

Last 16
1H v 2G
01 July 9pm, Salvador

On this subject it is worth pointing out as a general rule referees in the Premier League tend to allow more injury time than in most other countries and it is not uncommon for a continental match to finish the first half with no added on time.

4 Study pre-match
It's no good researching the teams once a game has kicked off – it needs to be done long before the pre-match handshakes. As a brief guide always try to evaluate the referee and both teams' records along with any characteristics of the two sides which could come in handy.

5 Don't get disheartened by a loser
It's a marathon not a sprint and there will be times where it goes wrong. As with all forms of betting decisions, rather than results make it pay over the long term. Losers are bound to happen during the World Cup but enjoy the experience – whether you are in it for fun or a serious punter, there are many opportunities to back winners if you can keep your discipline. If all else fails you could just back Ray Winstone's selections in the half-time adverts!

RISING STARS

There's no better place to make an impression than on the biggest stage of all

There are players at every World Cup who enjoy a breakthrough tournament – Pele in 1958, Franz Beckenbauer in 1966 or even Paul Gascoigne at Italia 90. They might be well known at home but there's no better opportunity for an ambitious youngster to stake a claim to international fame and fortune than a World Cup. **Mark Langdon** looks at the deadly half-dozen most likely to make a name for themselves in Brazil.

Ricardo Rodriguez (Switzerland)

This marauding left-back first came to prominence in the 2009 Under-17 World Cup, scoring three goals – the same number as Mario Gotze and Isco – to help Switzerland to a shock success in Nigeria.

Those performances put Rodriguez on the radar of Europe's bigger clubs and he eventually left FC Zurich for Wolfsburg in 2012, where his performances in the Bundesliga this season have apparently attracted interested from Manchester City and Chelsea.

The 21-year-old is a set-piece specialist capable not only of creating opportunities for team-mates thanks to his wicked delivery but also of popping up with vital goals, so punters should keep him in the first scorer notebook.

Heung-Min Son (South Korea)

There must have been something in the water during that youth World Cup in Nigeria because another potential star to come out of the finals was Heung-Min Son of South Korea.

Son shone as his country made the last eight but it's in the Bundesliga where his career has really taken off and the majority of his goals, first at Hamburg and now for Bayer Leverkusen, can only be filed under the 'wow' category.

This speedy 21-year-old winger can play on both flanks and is comfortable shooting off either foot. That makes him a nightmare for opposition full-backs but at the same time a joy for those who love to watch players with individual flair.

Paul Pogba (France)

Never ignore the obvious. Some of the names here are potentially exciting but Paul Pogba is already a world-class talent and he's ready to blossom on the biggest stage of the lot having been voted the best player as France won the Under-20 World Cup last year.

That tournament was like watching men against boys, with Pogba clearly in a class of his own. The Juventus superstar has got everything in his locker – something Sir Alex Ferguson failed to recognise, with the 21-year-old leaving Old Trafford after making just three Manchester United appearances.

Pogba, who looks to be closing in on a second Serie A winner's medal with Juve as we go to press, can score goals, create opportunities for team-mates, uses the ball wisely and is strong and quick. What's more, his tremendous engine means he can do all of the above for the entire 90 minutes.

William Carvalho (Portugal)

The rapid rise of the Angolan-born defensive midfielder has been sensational – he finished

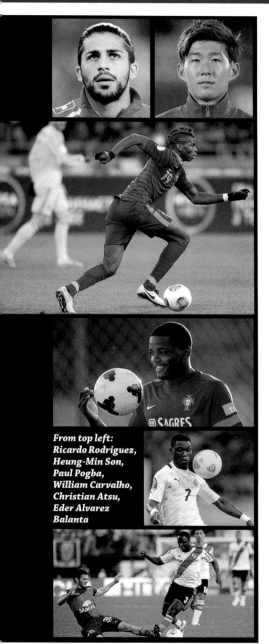

From top left:
Ricardo Rodriguez,
Heung-Min Son,
Paul Pogba,
William Carvalho,
Christian Atsu,
Eder Alvarez
Balanta

last season on loan in Belgium – but he will go to the World Cup with Europe's biggest clubs chasing his signature.

Scouts have been flocking to Lisbon to watch the Sporting spoiler and must have been impressed with a player who has been compared to Patrick Vieira, only with more technical ability.

Portugal boss Paulo Bento knows he can't hold Carvalho back any longer. He made his international debut as a substitute in the second leg of the dramatic play-off win in Sweden and played 75 minutes against Cameroon in a 5-1 friendly win in March.

Christian Atsu (Ghana)

There was a queue of Premier League clubs trying to prise Christian Atsu from Porto last summer before Chelsea beat rumoured interest from Liverpool and Tottenham for the Ghanaian's signature, who has rather lazily and absurdly been dubbed in some quarters as the African Lionel Messi.

Atsu is no Messi – who is? – but he could still be a player who can turn matches in Ghana's favour this summer, and is currently benefiting from a loan spell at Chelsea's unofficial Dutch feeder club Vitesse.

Black Stars forward Asamoah Gyan says Atsu is "going to be a star" and the winger knows where his strengths are.

"For anyone to dribble, the first touch has to be perfect," Atsu told the BBC website. "I think that is my biggest quality."

Eder Alvarez Balanta (Colombia)

It would be a gamble to take this cultured centre-back to Brazil – he only turned 21 in February – but it would be a much bigger risk to leave Eder Alvarez Balanta out of Colombia's World Cup squad given his rapid rise at River Plate.

Barcelona and Monaco have been linked with Balanta, who has already earned comparisons with Daniel Passarella, which is high praise indeed.

Passarella himself said: "Balanta is worth a lot and will be worth much more. He could cost €50m."

GOLDEN BOOT

Fred plays in the right place at the right price

L et past World Cups be your guide when you're looking for the profile of the top goalscorer in Brazil, **writes Mark Langdon**, as the winner usually plays for one of the main contenders.

Since the World Cup reverted to a straight knockout tournament after one group stage in 1986, Oleg Salenko is the only man to have finished at least joint-top of the pile without having reached at least the quarter-final stage after the Russian scored five goals against Cameroon.

Salenko scored six times at USA 94 – the same amount as Hristo Stoichkov – but they were the only goals he ever bagged at international level, a fact that serves to highlight the randomness which will probably happen only once in our lifetime.

Making the semi-finals is usually crucial because you are then guaranteed the third-place play-off fixture. It's hardly rocket science – the more games you play the more likely you are to find the leading goalscorer so we are looking for a team who are going to go deep in the tournament rather than a star striker who is a dangerman for a smaller nation.

They don't come any bigger than Brazil and their central striker Fred looks an enormous price in excess of 33-1 considering the hosts are seen as the favourites to win the competition.

The Fluminense forward has had a difficult time with two different injuries, which elongated a six-month goalscoring drought, but Fred hit the ground running on his latest return to fitness in February and he should benefit from the attacking midfield wizardry of Neymar and Oscar.

Fred was level with Fernando Torres on five goals at the Confederations Cup and would have been a clear winner had the Spaniard not helped himself to a four-goal haul against tiny Tahiti. He is by no means the best striker at the finals but being the focal point of Brazil's forward play means Fred will naturally get opportunities.

Lionel Messi heads the market but the Argentinian may find himself sharing the goals with Sergio Aguero and Gonzalo Higuain, while the likes of Luis Suarez and Mario Balotelli should find themselves involved in a tight scrap for points in a group containing Uruguay, England and Italy, and Robin van Persie's Holland could easily be on the first plane home with Spain and Chile for company in Group B.

Neymar has an obvious chance with Brazil

facing weak opponents Croatia, Mexico and Cameroon in the group stage but Fred is faced with the same defences and is a much bigger price so the value is clearly with the older man.

The draw worked out beautifully for France – if the market is correct Les Bleus will face Nigeria or Bosnia in the second round following a group of Ecuador, Honduras and Switzerland – so there is serious potential for Didier Deschamps' side to make at least the last eight.

Karim Benzema had a shocking European Championship in 2012 but he seems to have rebuilt his confidence at Real Madrid and should be boosted by scoring one of the goals which helped France to overcome Ukraine in the World Cup play-offs.

Spain don't have an easy passage but Holland's and Chile's weakness is defensively and Diego Costa could come alive playing in his homeland after controversially snubbing an offer from the hosts to play for the world and European champions.

Costa has been sensational for for Atletico Madrid, both in Europe and in La Liga and is the man to add a finishing touch to Spain's outstanding approach play.

Germany boss Joachim Low must be tempted to play one of Thomas Muller (joint-winner in 2010), Mario Gotze or Marco Reus as a false number nine given his lack of forward options. All three attacking midfielders would bring something different to the role – Gotze skill, Reus pace and Muller power – but too much guesswork is needed at this stage to see who will get the nod.

However, keep an eye on German plans nearer to the time and be prepared to stick a few quid on any of the trio if it looks like they will be used in an advanced position.

Finally, note that while the Golden Shoe award handed out by Fifa includes a variety of countback options to determine a winner, for betting purposes the top scorer market will be considered a dead-heat in the event of a tie.

Recommendations

Fred, Karim Benzema, Diego Costa

Hodgson's safety-first style can be an asset for England against top teams

England's recent record at major tournaments is about meeting expectations in a mediocre manner, **writes Michael Cox**. It is rare for the Three Lions suffer a shock loss to a minnow, but it's equally unusual to see them prevail against true giants in the knockout stages. In general, they collect the results we all anticipate. However, this might change under Roy Hodgson.

The England manager's cautious, defensive-minded approach inhibits his team when attempting to break down weaker sides, but provides them with great defensive shape against stronger opposition. Two friendlies last summer summed it up – within the space of a week, England drew to an inferior Ireland side, then drew to a superior Brazil side. Hodgson's system acts as a leveller.

While England's draw in Group D is very tough, perhaps they have the right coach for the challenge, and the order of the three group matches suits them, too.

The first fixture is against Italy, who are traditionally slow starters. Cesare Prandelli's side eliminated England at Euro 2012 on penalties, were dominant in normal time, and should have won the match convincingly.

The major lesson is simple: England must shut down Andrea Pirlo. Wayne Rooney's lack of positional discipline in the Euro 2012 contest was shocking, and prompted both Hodgson and Joe Hart to scream at him, reminding him of his tactical responsibilities. Prandelli uses a midfield diamond, and other players can create, but Pirlo is the key man to stop.

England's previous ten debut matches in major tournaments have produced two wins, six draws and two defeats – another draw would suit Hodgson.

The challenge of Uruguay will be very different. Whereas Italy are a possession-based side who will dominate the contest, Uruguay are more defensive and functional, so England might see more of the ball, and must use it intelligently and efficiently. An ageing backline means Oscar Tabarez protects his defence with two holding midfielders and functional, hard-working wide players – the type of system Hodgson is often associated with, although England

SPAIN HAVE THE SQUAD TO DEFEND THEIR CROWN

Recent history suggests successful World Cup sides boast excellent full-backs, a fine defensive record and a plethora of tactically different attacking options. Both Marcello Lippi and Vicente del Bosque used their squads excellently throughout their successes in 2006 and 2010 respectively, and it's important to look beyond each nation's starting XI.

Argentina and Germany both have great attacking options but also a significant weakness at full-back, while Brazil have the competition's best full-backs, but lack quality and variety in the final third.

Spain, however, continue to tick all the boxes. Their defence looks shakier than usual, but their excellent possession play means they generally

have moved away from two banks of four in recent months.

The attacking is almost solely the responsibility of the front two. Luis Suarez usually plays on the shoulder of the last defender, while Edinson Cavani plays a supporting role, trying to connect Suarez and the rest. This should be more of a counter-attacking match, and decision-making on the break will be crucial.

The final group game, against Costa Rica, is theoretically the easiest clash. It suits England to face the minnows in the final game, especially if qualification comes down to goal difference.

Costa Rica manager Jorge Luis Pinto is a meticulous planner, studies opponents in detail, and could adjust his strategy significantly throughout the tournament. However, he's likely to use a 5-4-1 formation, which will be tough to break down.

Costa Rica depend upon good performances from their fine goalkeeper, Keylor Navas of Spanish side Levante, and have an impressive midfield base with Christian Bolanos, who has impressed in the Champions League with Copenhagen, and home-based youngster Yeltsin Tejeda. Further forward, the guile of Bryan Ruiz and the pace of Joel Campbell can cause problems on the break.

Overall, England should progress. A draw against Italy is achievable with both sides likely to be cautious, while Uruguay are certainly beatable – past Suarez and Cavani, they've declined significantly since 2010. Qualification could be about breaking down Costa Rica.

Michael Cox runs the tactics website zonalmarking.net

keep clean sheets — astonishingly, they haven't conceded a goal in their ten last knockout matches across Euro 2008, World Cup 2010 and Euro 2012.

Diego Costa (left) is a different type of centre-forward who completes the attacking section of the side and, as fourth favourites, they seem the best value.

WORLD CUP JURY

Michael Brear
Racing Post tipster
BACK ARGENTINA

Why Argentina? A cracking draw, the best player, increasingly balanced tactics and a leisurely travel schedule round southern Brazil work heavily in their favour. I'm only worried about their keeper

Which of the market leaders is most vulnerable? I don't want to take on any of the top four but though Brazil have proved me wrong so far, the pressure could get to them. They'll rue missing out on Diego Costa

And the Golden Boot winner is... My outright fancy makes this predictable, so I'll go for someone other than Messi. Germans are perennially underrated in this market and that's the case with Marco Reus

What's the best bet in the eight groups? France look value to win a straightforward group. They're clearly on the up at the moment

Dan Childs
Racing Post tipster
BACK SPAIN

Why Spain? They have shown they have the ability and mental strength to win the big tournaments and can become the first European side to win the World Cup in South America

Which of the market leaders is most vulnerable? Brazil look like favourites to avoid. They should get out of their group but a last-16 clash against Spain, Holland or Chile is fraught with danger

And the Golden Boot winner is... France could have a decent tournament and that would mean plenty of opportunities for Karim Benzema, who is playing well for Real Madrid

What's the best bet in the eight groups? Group C looks like being wide open if Colombia striker Radamel Falcao is not fully fit. I like the look of 5-1 shots Japan, who are an underrated side

Steve Davies
Racing Post tipster
BACK ARGENTINA

Why Argentina? Germany could challenge Brazil, but the most obvious threat to the favourites is likely to come from a Messi-inspired Argentina, who look a formidable unit

Which of the market leaders is most vulnerable? Spain's failure to score in either knockout game at last year's Confederations Cup suggests that even if they get through a tough group, they can be shackled

And the Golden Boot winner is... No one has won the Golden Boot twice, but since Germany are sure to score plenty of goals, Thomas Muller is a contender to make history

What's the best bet in the eight groups? Brazil to win all three games in Group A, a bet pipped by the mightily impressive Chileans to qualify ahead of either Spain or Holland in Group B

JAMES MILTON'S GUIDE TO BETTING JARGON

Like Steve McClaren's Dutch accent, football-betting jargon can be both confusing and distressing. Don't fret, though – just study our guide to the key terminology and soon you'll be telling anybody who's interested (and plenty who aren't) about landing a coup on the Asian cards market or having your yankee sunk by a complete skinner.

Correct score
Roughly 68 per cent of tweets sent during the World Cup will be bullish correct-score predictions so why not put your money where your big, stupid mouth is? Accurately predicting the score of a football match is deceptively difficult but the rewards on offer mean it's a hugely popular bet. To take one random example from the 2010 World Cup, Germany 4 England 1 was a 100-1 shot. Looks obvious now, doesn't it?

First goalscorer
You guessed it – a bet on which player will score the first goal of the match. Play it safe by backing Lionel Messi or aim for the jackpot with a bet on Costa Rica's left-back at massive odds. Keep an eye out for any crazy South American goalkeepers who moonlight as free-kick specialists and remember – if the first goal is an own goal then whoever scores second is settled as a winner. So if Jamie Carragher receives a shock England recall, we could be in for a long wait.

Over/under
Most punters are familiar with backing over or

James Milton
Racing Post tipster

BACK ARGENTINA

Why Argentina? They have an incredible array of attackers and may be more comfortable in the conditions than the Europeans. France should go well at a bigger price

Which of the market leaders is most vulnerable? Layers may be slightly overestimating Brazil's home advantage and I can't see why Germany are trading shorter than tournament specialists Spain

And the Golden Boot winner is... France's Karim Benzema endured a long international goal drought but he has looked rejuvenated at Real Madrid this season and could fill his boots in a straightforward group

What's the best bet in the eight groups? Spain and Chile to qualify from Group B. Australia are out of their depth and Holland finished bottom of their group at Euro 2012

Sean O'Sullevan
Paddy Power odds compiler

BACK BRAZIL

Why Brazil? It's the obvious answer. A brilliant starting XI, and if they keep key men fit in the run-up to the finals they will take an incredible amount of stopping

Which of the market leaders is most vulnerable? Belgium look far too short. Despite Hazard's run of form, other notable first-teamers are drastically out of form and there is a lack of big-game experience

And the Golden Boot winner is... You need a player playing for a team you expect to go far in the competition. Messi has obvious appeal, but I will go with the star man of likely winners Brazil – Neymar

What's the best bet in the eight groups? Chile to qualify. Impressed against Germany last time out and should have earned at least a draw. With Sanchez leading the ranks they could surprise the ageing Dutch

Ian Wilkerson
Racing Post tipster

BACK SPAIN

Why Spain? They are such a well-linked group of outstanding players who still have a big tournament in them. And Diego Costa gives them the attacking dominance they've lacked

Which of the market leaders is most vulnerable? Brazil. There's a massive expectation and South Americans should not enjoy that big an advantage with most of their top players now playing in Europe

And the Golden Boot winner is... Luis Suarez has been in such great form for Liverpool that he can shine again, especially if Uruguay build on their experience of reaching the last four last time

What's the best bet in the eight groups? England to get four points in Group D. The Three Lions should beat Costa Rica but Uruguay and Italy are a different kettle of fish

---

under 2.5 goals in a match but that's just the start of the over-or-under fun. Those generous bookies will price up a line on everything from how many points Ecuador take in Group E to total penalties scored in the tournament or the number of times Cristiano Ronaldo pouts at the television camera in the first ten minutes of Portugal's opening game. Then punters must decide whether the bookies' estimate is too high or too low. Over the moon or w-under-ful? It's up to you.

Double result
Sounds like a phrase uttered by a smug mate who's just got a free pint and the barmaid's number but it's actually a market in which punters predict the result at half-time and at full-time. It's a good way of supporting a short-priced

favourite – the Belgium-Belgium double result against Algeria looks a solid bet, for instance – or opposing a team you expect to start strongly before wilting in the second half (mentioning no names, England against Italy in the 99 per cent humidity of Manaus...)

Accumulator
Put as many teams as you like in an accumulator but be warned: all of them must win in order for you to get your grubby hands on the bookies' dough. Accas are where the betting gods are at their most mischievous so if Australia (13-2), Costa Rica (10-1), Honduras (12-1) and Bosnia (8-1) have already done the business, it's almost certain that 1-5 shots Argentina will let you down against Iran. That's why we love the game.

HOW THEY BET

World Cup 2014 winner odds

	bet365	Betfred	Boylesports	Coral	Ladbrokes	P Power	Will Hill
Brazil	3	3	3	3	3	3	3
Argentina	4	9-2	9-2	5	9-2	5	9-2
Germany	11-2	11-2	11-2	11-2	11-2	11-2	11-2
Spain	7	7	7	7	6	7	7
Belgium	14	14	14	14	14	14	14
France	22	20	22	22	18	22	20
Italy	26	25	25	25	22	25	25
Colombia	28	20	22	22	22	25	22
Uruguay	25	28	25	28	28	25	28
Holland	30	25	33	33	25	22	28
Portugal	33	33	33	33	25	33	33
England	30	33	28	28	33	25	33
Chile	45	40	40	33	50	40	50
Russia	80	50	80	66	80	66	66
Switzerland	100	100	100	80	100	100	100
Mexico	100	100	125	150	125	125	150
Ivory Coast	125	100	150	125	150	100	150
Ecuador	125	125	150	125	150	125	150
Japan	150	150	150	100	175	150	125
Croatia	150	150	150	125	150	125	200
USA	150	125	200	150	200	150	150
Bosnia-Hz	150	150	150	125	200	150	150
Ghana	250	150	200	150	250	150	200
Nigeria	250	200	250	200	200	200	250
Greece	300	200	250	200	250	200	250
South Korea	300	250	350	250	400	300	250
Australia	500	500	400	750	500	500	750
Cameroon	500	500	500	500	750	500	750
Iran	1500	1500	1000	1500	1500	1500	750
Algeria	1500	1000	1000	750	750	2000	1000
Costa Rica	2500	1000	1000	1000	1000	2000	2500
Honduras	2000	2000	1000	1500	1500	3000	2500

Win or each-way. See individual bookmakers for terms. Prices correct March 28 2014

REFEREES

Africa Alioum (Cameroon), Daniel Bennett (South Africa), Noumandiez Doue (Ivory Coast), Bakary Gassama (Gambia), Djamel Haimoudi (Algeria)

Europe Felix Brych (Germany), Cuneyt Cakir (Turkey), Jonas Eriksson (Sweden), Bjorn Kuipers (Holland), Milorad Mazic (Serbia), Svein Oddvar Moen (Norway), Pedro Proenca (Portugal), Nicola Rizzoli (Italy), Carlos Velasco Carballo (Spain), Howard Webb (England)

South America Victor Carrillo (Peru), Enrique Osses (Chile), Nestor Pittana (Argentina), Sandro Ricci (Brazil), Wilmar Roldan (Colombia), Carlos Alfredo Vera (Ecuador)

Concacaf Joel Aguilar (El Salvador), Mark Geiger (USA), Walter Lopez (Guatemala), Roberto Moreno Salazar (Panama), Marco Rodriguez (Mexico)

Asia Alireza Faghani (Iran), Ravshan Irmatov (Uzbekistan), Yuichi Nishimura (Japan), Nawaf Shukralla (Bahrain), Ben Williams (Australia)

Oceania Norbert Hauata (Tahiti), Peter O'Leary (New Zealand)

Brazil's testing conditions could be a decisive factor

I t wouldn't be a World Cup without controversy and chaos in the run-up and Brazil 2014 has been no different, **writes Steve Davies**. The race to build or refurbish 12 stadiums has veered between the incompetent and the shambolic, with riots over the amount of money the tournament was costing, and constant questions over ticket and accommodation prices. As we go to press, stadium building and work on infrastructure projects is still frantically underway.

It's made for an entertaining seven-year frenzy since Rio was awarded the competition but the burning questions occupying the minds of players and staff of the 32 competing nations should be: how hot is it going to be and how much travelling is there to do?

And once we, like they, have sifted through average daily temperatures, humidity levels and air miles, it's clear some countries have done far better than others.

Italy keeper Gianluigi Buffon already knows how hot it can be in Brazil in their mid-winter. Buffon was the skipper of the Italian team which finished third at last summer's Confederations Cup in Brazil, a tournament which acted as the ideal barometer for what to expect at the big one.

Italy signed off from the competition with two games in four days in draining heat and humidity in Fortaleza and Salvador, in the tropical north, and Buffon was fiercely critical of the scheduling, especially the 1pm kick-off time against Uruguay. That match was played in front of swathes of empty seats as it was deemed too hot to sit in, never mind play in.

Spain, the other European entrant, went on to reach the final, but defender Alvaro Arbeloa demanded no 1pm local time kick-offs at the finals. Brazilian physiologist Turibio Leite de Barros added weight to the argument, saying: "It is an insanity to have games kicking off at 1pm. It is very dangerous. There is a real risk." It's a plea

that has fallen on deaf ears.

Fifa, in its infinite wisdom, has pencilled in 18 group games for 1pm starts (5pm UK time), including half-a-dozen in the sweltering heat of the north-east. Germany, for example, have lunchtime kick-offs against Portugal in Salvador and the United States in Recife while their second game – against Ghana – is at 4pm in fiery Fortaleza, where temperatures, even in June, can comfortably clear 30 degrees with 80 per cent humidity.

Italy, who kick off their Group D campaign against England in the jungle heat and humidity of Manaus, then have 1pm kick-offs against Costa Rica in Recife and Uruguay in Natal.

Buffon, however, is clinging to the positives, saying: "Playing in a hot, humid climate now might be an advantage for the World Cup, because if we remember what it was like, it might help our staff prepare us."

Clearly it's not simply where you are playing and when, but who the opponents are. England against Italy in breathless Manaus will be no fun for either side; Honduras versus Switzerland at the same venue, however, climatically ought to play into the hands of the Central Americans.

For the record, teams with two 1pm kick-offs are Australia and Holland in Group B, Colombia in Group C, Group D rivals Italy and Costa Rica, Argentina and Iran in F, Germany and Portugal in G and Belgium, favourites in Group H.

That said, a 1pm start in Curitiba, for

Estadio do Maracana, Rio
(76,804) Peak temp: 25°C
No. of games: 7

Estadio Nacional, Brasilia
(68,009) Peak temp: 25°C
No. of games: 7

Estadio Mineirao, Belo
Horizonte (62,547) Peak temp:
25°C No. of games: 6

Estadio Castelao, Fortaleza
(64,846) Peak temp: 30°C
No. of games: 6

Arena de Sao Paulo, Sao
Paulo (65,807) Peak temp:
20°C No. of games: 6

Arena Fonte Nova, Salvador
(48,747) Peak temp: 26°C
No. of games: 6

Arena Pernambuco, Recife
(44,248) Peak temp: 28°C
No. of games: 5

Estadio Beira-Rio, Porto
Alegre (48,849) Peak temp:
20°C No. of games: 5

Estadio das Dunas, Natal
(42,086) Peak temp: 25°C
No. of games: 4

Arena Pantanal, Cuiaba
(42,968) Peak temp: 30°C
No. of games: 4

Arena da Baixada, Curitiba
(41,456) Peak temp: 20°C
No. of games: 4

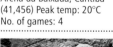

Arena Amazonia, Manaus
(42,374) Peak temp: 30°C
No. of games: 4

1 Rio, 2 Brasilia, 3 Belo
Horizonte, 4 Fortaleza, 5 Sao
Paulo, 6 Salvador, 7 Recife,
8 Porto Alegre, 9 Natal,
10 Cuiaba, 11 Curitiba,
12 Manaus

example, can't compare to starting at a similar time in, say, Fortaleza. It can be warm in Curitiba but it is also the coldest of Brazil's 26 state capitals so Spain and Australia won't be fazed by their lunchtime start at the Arena da Baixada.

There's also the issue of travelling which, in sapping heat and humidity, you'd probably want to keep to a minimum. Like Argentina, who will chalk up just 3,500km of air miles in their three group games. Belgium not only have the cushiest group, they are also travelling just under 2,500km.

Compare that to Italy who will travel more than 13,000km going to and from base camp to matches while the United States, almost inexplicably, play all three games in the north yet have based themselves in southern Sao Paulo and will therefore spend over 20 hours in the air covering more than 15,000km. Mexico, similarly, have a trio of games on the north-east coast but are also housed near Sao Paulo.

Rest between games and travelling will be important and that's another area in which Argentina have done well. They and Group F rivals Bosnia play their three group games over 11 days, Iran and Nigeria play them in ten. It's a quirk of the schedule and one which will please Albiceleste supporters.

Brazil, even in winter, can be hot. And, as last year's Confederations Cup highlighted, it can be exceptionally hot. You can get cooler days around Porto Alegre and Curitiba, you can get cooling breezes off the sea in Salvador. But this is basically a country where extreme heat and humidity will test out the best footballers in the world and the teams who are more familiar with those conditions will surely enjoy a considerable edge.

LOCAL HEROES

Argentina a real danger but Brazil look the best hope for the home continent

S outh America's great hopes for this World Cup are as familiar as ever, but there is something magical and different about the two Conmebol superpowers going for glory in their own backyard, **writes Ed Malyon**. Hosts Brazil are the obvious and undoubted favourites. Winners on home soil at the Confederations Cup, the slaying of Spain showed that they can mix it with the best.

Luiz Felipe Scolari's supremely confident bunch of players have proven thus far that the weight of expectation isn't too heavy for some young shoulders.

Mano Menezes was sacked just when he appeared to have found the right shape for his team, but in Scolari they have a manager with experience and the respect of his squad, ably assisted by another World Cup-winning coach, Carlos Alberto Parreira. You feel that they will get by on sheer force of personality and will power where Menezes would have needed an impeccable approach.

Argentina's claim is strong, and it's not just about a certain 5'7" forward from Rosario. Alejandro Sabella has evolved this side over his three-year reign and the arch-pragmatist has created a squad comfortable in a variety of systems, something that could prove crucial in a tournament environment.

Capable of playing with a three-, four- or five-man defence, the most important thing for Sabella was finding the right personnel to play there and once he had settled on Ezequiel Garay and Federico Fernandez at the heart of his backline, he stuck with them.

The result has been a developing partnership at the base of a dynamic, exciting team. The first-choice shape is a lop-sided 4-3-3 which, even if you can deal with Lionel Messi, leaves you with the not inconsiderable threat of Gonzalo Higuain, Angel Di Maria

and Sergio Aguero. And that's without even mentioning the bench.

Solid behind the firepower, the weaknesses in this team remain at left-back and in goal but given an easyish group and more time to gel there is something ominous about what Sabella is creating.

Colombia were once the big dark horses, but Radamel Falcao's injury has somewhat dampened the excitement about the Cafeteros. However, there is plenty in reserve, especially up front, Jose Pekerman is one of the best coaches at the tournament and his first XI is exceptional even without the Monaco forward. Let everyone go cold on them and they could well regain their value.

The team to replace them as the outsiders are Chile, whose brilliant manager Jorge Sampaoli has performed wonders with a side that were dour and ill-disciplined under Claudio Borghi. If they get through the group of death, which they are more than capable of doing, La Roja are a side that have beaten top nations over the last 12 months and could easily be a semi-finalist or better.

Ecuador will only make up the numbers, but Uruguay's ageing yet feisty unit could have one last hurrah with their golden generation. Just don't expect a repeat of the third place we saw in South Africa.

Ed Malyon is a Daily Mirror writer and South American football expert

Brazil showed they can compete with anyone in last summer's Confederations Cup final

The easiest way to boost success in penalty shootouts is simply to kick first

On average three of the 16 knockout ties at a World Cup are decided on penalties, **writes Kevin Pullein**. In previous tournaments there were never fewer than two shootouts or more than four. Twice the final was settled by spot kicks from 12 yards: in 1994 Brazil beat Italy and in 2006 Italy beat France.

In the absence of any other information, your best guess of the winner of a penalty shootout is the team who kick first. Professor Ignacio Palacios-Huerta of the London School of Economics studied 269 shootouts and found that in 159 of them the team who kicked first won. That's 59 per cent.

I was so startled by his findings that I tried to double-check them as best I could. From my sample of 76 penalty shootouts at neutral venues in major international and club competitions I found 44 in which the team who kicked first won. That's 58 per cent. At the World Cup 13 out of 22 shootouts were won by the team who kicked first. That's 59 per cent.

Fabio Grosso scores Italy's winning penalty in 2006, the most recent final to be decided from the spot

Palacios-Huerta argues that the team who kick first are more likely than not to score, and if they do there is stronger pressure on the team kicking second. He proposes a change to the order in which penalties are taken, replacing the present arrangement (AB/AB/AB/AB/AB) with one that would distribute pressure more evenly between the teams (AB/BA/AB/BA/AB).

It is used in tennis tiebreaks. It is simple and sensible. And there is no indication that governing body Fifa has any interest in it whatsoever.

The first penalty shootout at a World Cup was in the 1982 semi-final when West Germany beat France. The game is more often remembered for another reason, the notorious tackle by West German goalkeeper Harald Schumacher on French defender Patrick Battiston. England have contested three World Cup shootouts and lost them all: their 1990 semi-final against West Germany, a 1998 round of 16 tie against Argentina and a 2006 quarter-final against Portugal.

Altogether there have been 22 shootouts at the World Cup. A total of 204 penalties were taken, of which 144 were scored, 71 per cent. The conversion rate is lower than for other international tournaments such as the European Championship and Copa America. In Brazil it is more likely to rise than to fall.

Only two shootouts required more than the originally scheduled ten kicks, five per side. Twelve penalties were taken in that 1982 semi-final between West Germany and France and also in a 1994 quarter-final when Sweden beat Romania.

No shootout can be completed with fewer than six kicks. Seven were taken at the World Cup in a 1986 quarter-final between West Germany and Mexico and a 2006 round of 16 game between Ukraine and Switzerland. West Germany beat Mexico 4-1 (Mexico missed twice) and Ukraine beat Switzerland 3-0 (Ukraine missed once and Switzerland missed three times). The average number of penalties taken in a World Cup penalty shootout is nine.

Depleted Croatia may be struggling from the first whistle of the World Cup

This should be a stroll for hosts Brazil and they look a safe team to put in group multiples, but the most attractive betting heat from this section comes in focusing on the three nations behind the long odds-on favourites, **writes Mark Langdon**.

Croatia could be on the back foot from the opening night of the tournament as they take on the hosts minus the services of the suspended Mario Mandzukic.

Backing the Europeans to suffer a group-stage exit is the value punt. Mandzukic will return from a one-match ban to face Cameroon and Mexico but Croatia are short on quality outside of the Bayern Munich centre forward and Real Madrid midfielder Luka Modric, and the schedule could have been much kinder to novice boss Niko Kovac.

Trips to Recife and Manaus were not what the doctor ordered for an industrious team and you would have to imagine the conditions will favour opponents Cameroon and Mexico respectively.

Mexico, like Croatia, will have to put a poor qualifying campaign behind them to get involved but on paper there is much to like about El Tri, particularly as manager Miguel Herrera seems to have restored order to a squad that was on the brink of crisis.

Carlos Vela's absence is a blow but it was only two years ago that Mexico were walking away with Olympic gold at London 2012, beating a strong Brazil team which included Oscar, Thiago Silva and Neymar.

Mexico also did reasonably well in last summer's Confederations Cup when they lost to heavyweights Italy (2-1) and Brazil (2-0) before beating Japan 2-1. A similar level of performance could easily be enough to see them eliminate Croatia.

However, Cameroon also have the potential to take points off teams if the squad's equilibrium is not disrupted by Samuel Eto'o's dressing-room influence.

Mandzukic sees red

Eto'o and Alex Song are two difference-makers within the Cameroon squad and the Indomitable Lions' inconsistent ways makes it more sensible to oppose Croatia with a couple of teams rather than a straight bet on anyone to go through with Brazil.

Talking of the Samba Stars, it should be a nine-point haul for the hosts.

Recommendation
Croatia not to qualify

	bet365	Coral	Lads	Power	W Hill
Brazil	**1-4**	1-5	1-6	2-9	**1-4**
Mexico	8	8	**17-2**	8	7
Croatia	6	7	**9**	8	11-2
Cameroon	**25**	25	25	20	**25**

Straight forecast

	Power
Brazil/Croatia	**9-5**
Brazil/Mexico	**9-5**
Brazil/Cameroon	**9-2**
Croatia/Brazil	**10**
Mexico/Brazil	**10**
Cameroon/Brazil	**25**
Mexico/Croatia	**40**
Croatia/Mexico	**40**
Croatia/Cameroon	**80**
Mexico/Cameroon	**80**
Cameroon/Mexico	**100**
Cameroon/Croatia	**100**

To qualify odds **Finish bottom**

	Lads	Power	W Hill	Power	W Hill
Brazil	1-40	**1-33**	1-40	**66**	50
Croatia	5-6	**11-10**	5-6	3	**4**
Mexico	**11-10**	**11-10**	**11-10**	3	5-2
Cameroon	**5**	9-2	**5**	**4-6**	8-13

All group betting markets are win only

Group matches **World Cup history** **Head-to-head record** **Last meeting**

Brazil v Croatia Thursday June 12, 9pm (GMT), Sao Paulo	A 1-0 win for Brazil in their first match of 2006 World Cup	A 1-1 draw in 2005 followed by the 1-0 win for Brazil in Germany	It was at Germany 2006 and Kaka got the only goal of the game
Mexico v Cameroon Friday June 13, 5pm, Natal	No previous World Cup meetings	Played once before, when Mexico won 1-0	Daniel Guzman scored the only goal in Los Angeles back in 1993
Brazil v Mexico Tuesday June 17, 8pm, Fortaleza	Wins for Brazil, in 1950, 54 and 62, by an aggregate score of 11-0	22 wins for Brazil, ten for Mexico, six draws	Neymar and Jo scored in Brazil's 2-0 Confederations Cup win last year
Cameroon v Croatia Wednesday June 18, 11pm, Manaus	No previous World Cup meetings	No previous meetings	
Cameroon v Brazil Monday June 23, 9pm, Brasilia	A 3-0 win for Brazil in the group stage of USA 94	Four meetings, three wins for Brazil, one for Cameroon	Samuel Eto'o got the only goal in the Confederations Cup 2003
Croatia v Mexico, Monday June 23, 9pm, Recife	A 1-0 win for Mexico in the group stage at Korea/Japan 2002	Three meetings in total, two wins for Croatia, one for Mexico	Cuauhtemoc Blanco scored from the penalty spot at World Cup 2002

Route to the final

Group winners

Round of 16 June 28 Belo Horizonte
2B Spain, Holland, Chile, Australia

Quarter-finals July 4 Fortaleza
1C Colombia, Greece, Ivory Coast, Japan
2D Uruguay, Costa Rica, England, Italy

Semi-finals July 8 Belo Horizonte
1E Switzerland, Ecuador, France, Honduras
2F Argentina, Bosnia-Herzegovina, Iran, Nigeria
1G Germany, Portugal, Ghana, USA
2H Belgium, Algeria, Russia, South Korea

Final July 13 Rio

Group runners-up

Round of 16 June 29 Fortaleza
1B Spain, Holland, Chile, Australia

Quarter-finals July 5 Salvador
1D Uruguay, Costa Rica, England, Italy
2C Colombia, Greece, Ivory Coast, Japan

Semi-finals July 9 Sao Paulo
1F Argentina, Bosnia-Herzegovina, Iran, Nigeria
2E Switzerland, Ecuador, France, Honduras
1H Belgium, Algeria, Russia, South Korea
2G Germany, Portugal, Ghana, USA

BRAZIL

The question is whether favourites crumble under the weight of expectation

D ealing with pressure doesn't come easy to the Brazilian national football team and the manner in which the squad handles the intense demand for success could be the key to whether the host nation will lift the World Cup for a sixth time at the Maracana on July 13. The bookmakers rate the Samba Stars favourites for glory but will they be able to deliver the dream to over 200 million home supporters?

How they qualified

As hosts, Brazil did not have to qualify. Instead they used two tournaments as preparation for the real thing with the London Olympics of 2012 and 2013 Confederations Cup on home soil targeted.

Mano Menezes was sacked soon after Brazil missed out on gold in London – they surprisingly lost the final to Mexico – and he was replaced by Luiz Felipe Scolari, who led the team to success in the Confederations Cup when the hosts beat Japan, Mexico, Italy and Uruguay before smashing Spain 3-0 in the final.

Interestingly, anyone who backed Brazil-Brazil on the double result market last summer was in clover with Scolari's side leading at the interval in all five of those tournament victories.

The manager

The 65-year-old has had a colourful coaching career which has taken him all around the world from Kuwait to the Premier League with Chelsea to Bunyodkor in Uzbekistan and he has won a couple of Copa Libertadores titles with different Brazilian clubs.

However, he is best known for his first spell as Brazil's manager when he won the 2002 World Cup, and he so nearly repeated the trick with Portugal. Big Phil took them to the 2006 semi-finals two years after losing

Country factfile

FA founded 1914
www cbf.com.br
Head coach Luiz Felipe Scolari
National league Serie A
System of government Federal republic
Population 200 million
Capital city Brasilia
Currency Real
Official language Portuguese

Strengths
☑ Scolari has course and distance form
☑ Neymar showed at the Confederations Cup he is the real deal
☑ Good defensive options with David Luiz or Dante partnering Thiago Silva

Weaknesses
☒ Midfield lacks creativity in central areas
☒ No world-class striker in the squad
☒ Huge pressure

Base Teresopolis

Fixtures
1 Croatia, June 12, Sao Paulo
2 Mexico, June 17, Fortaleza
3 Cameroon, June 23, Brasilia

the final of the European Championship to Greece in a huge upset on home soil.

Match winners

Neymar is the poster boy of this World Cup and the Brazilian crowd is whipped into a frenzy every time he goes on one of those mesmeric dribbles. The 22-year-old was voted player of the tournament at the Confederations Cup and he has since settled in at Barcelona. In Thiago Silva Brazil have the best centre-back on the planet.

Scolari shrewdly used marauding full-backs in 2002 with Cafu and Roberto Carlos basically fielded as wingers – expect more of the same from Dani Alves and Marcelo.

Question marks

The biggest is whether they crumble under the weight of expectation. It happened, albeit a long time ago, when Brazil last hosted the World Cup in 1950, and we see it every four years when they try (and fail) to win Olympic gold, which is a massive deal for them.

Scolari is incredibly loyal to certain players so the erratic Hulk continues to be selected ahead of more popular performers along with goalkeeper Julio Cesar, who barely played for Championship side QPR this season and was loaned out to MLS side Toronto.

How to back them

Brazil are going to have their backers to win the World Cup but if they do go all the way Neymar will have to come up big. Backing him to be crowned player of the tournament may be a way of supporting the Samba Stars at a much bigger price.

A safer play is to back Brazil to qualify from Group A with maximum points. They are unlikely to be troubled by Mexico, Cameroon and Croatia and will be determined to secure top spot, as the runners-up are likely to meet Spain in the last 16.

Brazil need Neymar (left) to reprise last summer's Confederations Cup performance

BRAZIL

Their distinctive style makes Brazil football's favourite team

Brazil has a population of 200 million, **writes Kevin Pullein**. It is the fifth most populous country in the world. None of the lands with more inhabitants has fallen in love with football.

It is not surprising that Brazil has become the most successful nation in the history of international football, winning the World Cup five times. It was not inevitable that Brazil would also become the best loved. The reason it has is its distinctive style: bends of the body and bends of the ball.

The best Brazilian teams have found a framework in which they were able to express their individual brilliance to the most devastating and delightful effect. My favourites are those that became world champions in 2002, 1970 and 1958.

Brazil won the World Cup in 1958 with some exceptional talents – among them right winger Garrincha and a teenage inside left called Pele – plus a new formation: 4-2-4. In possession it was actually 3-3-4; one of the centre backs stepped into midfield to help attack. Out of possession it was actually 4-3-3; left winger Mario Zagallo dropped

World Cup record

Uruguay 1930	Group stage
Italy 1934	First round
France 1938	Third place
Brazil 1950	Runners-up
Switzerland 1954	Quarter-finals
Sweden 1958	**Winners**
Chile 1962	**Winners**
England 1966	Group stage
Mexico 1970	**Winners**
Germany 1974	Fourth place
Argentina 1978	Third place
Spain 1982	Second round
Mexico 1986	Quarter-finals
Italy 1990	Round of 16
USA 1994	**Winners**
France 1998	Runners-up
Korea/Japan 2002	**Winners**
Germany 2006	Quarter-finals
South Africa 2010	Quarter-finals

Clockwise from main: Brazil's 1970 World Cup final XI, Garrincha and Pele, the 2002 vintage

Continental titles

Copa America (1919, 1922, 1949, 1989, 1997, 1999, 2004, 2007)

Legendary player

The list of legendary Brazilian footballers is a long one but all of them are eclipsed by **Pele**. The winner of three World Cups, scorer of a Brazilian record 77 international goals – 12 at the finals – and a world record 1,281 over the course of his career, for many people he is the best player of all time.

into midfield to help defend.

By 1970 Zagallo was coach. The strategy was essentially the same. Left winger Rivelino retreated into midfield on the rare occasions it was necessary to defend. Rather more often right back Carlos Alberto galloped into attack. The signature goal of perhaps the greatest international team of all time was the last: Pele, playing the ninth pass of an attack, rolled the ball to overlapping scorer Carlos Alberto.

Attacking full-backs are a Brazilian speciality. In 2002 there were two: Cafu and Roberto Carlos. To cover them – and a forward line of Ronaldo and Rivaldo, supported by Ronaldinho – coach Luiz Felipe Scolari added a third centre back and kept two stoppers in central midfield.

Did you know?

In seven World Cups held in the Americas, Brazil have reached at least the semi-finals five times and won it three times

BRAZIL

Players used since World Cup 2010

Pos		Club	Age	P	G	Pos		Club	Age	P	G
G	Jefferson	Botafogo	31	9	0	M	Hernanes	Inter	28	23	2
G	Victor	Atl. Mineiro	31	6	0	M	Jadson	Corinthians	30	8	1
G	Julio Cesar	Toronto	34	78	0	M	Fernandinho	Man City	28	6	1
D	Maxwell	Paris St-G.	32	7	0	M	Jean	Fluminense	27	6	0
D	Dante	Bayern Munich	30	11	2	M	Kaka	Milan	31	87	29
D	Dede	Cruzeiro	25	9	1	M	Lucas Moura	Paris St-G.	21	31	4
D	Filipe Luis	Atl Madrid	28	4	0	M	Luiz Gustavo	Wolfsburg	26	17	1
D	Maicon	Roma	32	69	7	M	Oscar	Chelsea	22	29	9
D	Marcelo	Real Madrid	25	29	4	M	Paulinho	Tottenham	25	25	5
D	Henrique	Napoli	27	4	0	M	Ralf	Corinthians	29	8	0
D	Marcos Rocha	Atl. Mineiro	25	2	0	M	Ramires	Chelsea	27	41	4
D	Marquinhos	Paris St-G.	19	1	0	F	Diego Costa	Atl Madrid	25	2	0
D	Rever	Atl. Mineiro	29	8	1	F	Fred	Fluminense	30	31	16
D	Andre Santos	Flamengo	31	24	0	F	Hulk	Zenit	27	33	8
D	Dani Alves	Barcelona	30	73	5	F	Jo	Atl. Mineiro	27	15	5
D	David Luiz	Chelsea	26	34	0	F	Leandro	Palmeiras	20	1	1
D	Thiago Silva	Paris St-G.	29	45	2	F	Leandro Damiao	Santos	24	17	3
M	Lucas	Liverpool	27	24	0	F	Neymar	Barcelona	22	47	30
M	Marcos Arouca	Santos	27	4	0	F	Osvaldo	Sao Paulo	26	2	0
M	Willian	Chelsea	25	5	1	F	Robinho	Milan	30	92	27
M	Bernard	Shakhtar	21	10	1	F	Ronaldinho	Atl. Mineiro	34	97	33
M	Fernando	Shakhtar	22	8	0	F	Alexandre Pato	Sao Paulo	24	27	10

KEY TO THE STATS

SOCCERBASE.COM

All stats cover competitive matches only since the 2010 World Cup unless otherwise stated. Brazil's stats include friendly matches.

Players used in qualifying Includes all-time caps and goals plus caps goals and cards during qualifying for Brazil 2014. Caps, goals, ages and clubs current as of March 28 2014.

Goal times Goals scored and conceded in competitive matches since the last World Cup. Goals scored in injury time at the end of each half are included within that time segment, ie: 37-45 and 82-90.

Correct scores Number of occurrences of every 90-minute scoreline in which one of the teams has scored up to four goals. Friendlies are included (but listed separately). The score of the team being profiled is given first.

Top scorers World Cup qualifying only. 'First' denotes the first goal of the game, 'anytime' is any scoring appearance, no matter when the goal was scored.

Unders & overs The percentage of competitive games in which the total number of goals scored fell either side of the popular goal betting lines.

Half-time/Full-time Occurrences of each listed half-time result followed by each list full-time result. For example, L/W or Lose/Win means losing at half-time, winning at full-time. Pie-charts show total 90-minute win/lose/draw percentages.

Clean sheets Number of times each team has conceded no goals and failed to score.

What happens if... Results of competitive games where each team has either scored or conceded the first goal. Percentages include all competitive games.

Penalty shootouts Includes the final tournaments of World Cup, European Championships, Copa America, Africa Cup of Nations, Asian Nations Cup and CONCACAF Gold Cup.

Goal times

For			Against
7		0-9	1
6		10-18	3
13		19-27	3
9		28-36	3
12		37-45	3
15		46-54	5
11		55-63	6
11		64-72	6
11		73-81	4
20		82-90	4

Brazil			Opponents	
47	39%	1st half	13	34%
68	60%	2nd half	25	66%

52 games since 2010 World Cup

Top scorers

	Total	First	%	Anytime
Neymar	21	5	24	16
Hulk	8	3	38	7
Oscar	8	3	38	7
A Pato	7	0	0	6
Fred	6	3	50	6
Jo	3	1	33	2
Leandro Damiao	3	3	100	3
Marcelo	3	1	33	3
Paulinho	3	1	33	3
Kaka	2	0	0	2
D Alves	2	2	100	2
Robinho	2	0	0	2
Lucas	2	1	50	2
Hernanes	2	0	0	2

Since 2010 World Cup

Correct scores

	Friendly	Comp
1-0	4	0
2-0	8	1
2-1	4	1
3-0	3	2
3-1	2	0
3-2	0	0
4-0	2	0
4-1	1	0
4-2	0	2
4-3	0	0
0-0	2	2
1-1	2	0
2-2	3	1
3-3	0	0
4-4	0	0
0-1	3	0
0-2	1	0
1-2	2	0
0-3	0	0
1-3	0	0
2-3	1	0
0-4	0	0
1-4	0	0
2-4	0	0
3-4	1	0
Other	5	0

53 games since 2010 World Cup

Unders & overs

1.5 goals		2.5 goals		3.5 goals		4.5 goals	
Under	Over	Under	Over	Under	Over	Under	Over
21%	79%	44%	56%	67%	33%	83%	17%

52 games since 2010 World Cup

Half-time/Full-time

Win/Win	25	48%
Draw/Win	8	15%
Lose/Win	1	2%
Win/Draw	1	2%
Draw/Draw	7	13%
Lose/Draw	2	4%
Win/Lose	0	0%
Draw/Lose	5	10%
Lose/Lose	3	6%

WIN 65%

52 games since 2010 World Cup

Penalty shootouts

Won	6	60%
Lost	4	40%

All-time record

Clean sheets

Brazil	28	54%
Opponents	8	15%

52 games since 2010 World Cup

What happens if ...

Brazil score first

Brazil win	31	60%
Draw	3	6%
Brazil lose	1	1%

52 games since 2010 World Cup

WIN 60%

Opponents score first

Brazil win	3	5%
Draw	3	5%
Brazil lose	7	13%

LOSE 13%

Schedule and suspensions leave Kovac's Croatia facing an uphill battle

N iko Kovac (pictured right) doesn't have fond memories of the World Cup – he was injured and missed out as Croatia memorably reached the semi-finals in 1998 and then played a full part when they suffered a group-stage elimination four years later. The former skipper will be hoping for better fortune in Brazil when he leads the country into action having replaced former team-mate Igor Stimac in the managerial hotseat.

How they qualified

Having taken charge of their group thanks to an early draw with Belgium, Croatia fell apart and had to qualify via the play-offs. They finished by collecting one point from a possible 12, losing home and away to Scotland in the process, and that was enough for Stimac to lose his job.

Kovac took control for the play-off success over Iceland. Being paired with Iceland was a slice of good fortune but Croatia still made heavy work of it, drawing 0-0 away in the first leg despite the opposition being reduced to ten men on 50 minutes.

The 2-0 win in the return was comfortable enough even though Mario Mandzukic was sent off but the big story came after the final whistle when experienced defender Josip Simunic was found guilty of chanting a pro-Nazi slogan and picked up a ten-match ban from Fifa, ruling him out of the World Cup.

The manager

This is Kovac's first managerial role and he will be assisted by his brother Robert. Discussing his managerial style, Kovac told Fifa.com: "I want to be human, open and honest. I was born and brought up in Germany and played most of my football there. I completely and totally embody the typical German virtues of thoroughness, orderliness, discipline and organisation."

Country factfile

FA founded 1912
www hns-cff.hr
Head coach Niko Kovac
National league Prva Liga
System of government Parliamentary democracy
Population 4.5 million
Capital city Zagreb
Currency Kuna
Official language Croatian
Strengths
- ☑ Modric conducts the orchestra beautifully in midfield
- ☑ Mandzukic a proven goalscorer at the highest level
- ☑ Kovac can't do worse than Stimac

Weaknesses
- ☒ Suspensions could hit hard
- ☒ Defence lacks pace
- ☒ Harsh schedule

Base Mata de Sao Joao

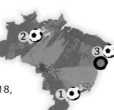

Fixtures
1 Brazil, June 12, Sao Paulo
2 Cameroon, June 18, Manaus
3 Mexico, June 23, Recife

Match winners

There are two players head and shoulders above the rest in this Croatian squad – Bayern Munich's Mandzukic and Real Madrid's Luka Modric.

Mandzukic is suspended for the opener against Brazil but the Champions League winner will be important once he returns. He was Croatia's top scorer in qualifying with four goals, and also notched three times in as many matches at Euro 2012.

Modric, after a poor start to life at Real Madrid, is now a key man at the Bernabeu and will dictate play from midfield, while captain Darijo Srna usually provides excellent delivery from his attacking right-back role.

Question marks

The central defence was unconvincing even before Simunic, who started nine matches in qualifying, disgraced himself and Croatia will have to defend deep with Vedran Corluka alongside Dejan Lovren.

It's not easy to see where the goals will come from outside of Mandzukic – Croatia did not score more than twice in any game during qualifying – and the emphasis will be on midfielders such as Ivan Rakitic and Ivan Perisic to help out in the attacking third.

Another concern is over the schedule, which sees Croatia facing trips to hot and humid Recife and Manaus after they have taken on hosts Brazil.

How to back them

The schedule is against Croatia and backing them for a group-stage exit looks smart.

They are unlikely to get anything first up against Brazil, particularly with Mandzukic sitting in the stands, and they appear to be a team on a downward spiral. Croatia may even struggle to see off Cameroon, never mind the superior Mexico.

CROATIA

World Cup record

Uruguay 1930	Fourth place*
Italy 1934	Did not qualify*
France 1938	Did not qualify*
Brazil 1950	Group stage*
Switzerland 1954	Quarter-finals*
Sweden 1958	Quarter-finals*
Chile 1962	Fourth place*
England 1966	Did not qualify*
Mexico 1970	Did not qualify*
Germany 1974	Second round*
Argentina 1978	Did not qualify*
Spain 1982	Group stage*
Mexico 1986	Did not qualify*
Italy 1990	Quarter-finals*
USA 1994	Did not enter
France 1998	Third place
Korea/Japan 2002	Group stage
Germany 2006	Group stage
South Africa 2010	Did not qualify

*Part of Yugoslavia until 1991, recognised by Fifa in 1992

Continental titles

None

Legendary player

Croatia finished third at France 98 and **Davor Suker** scored the goals that helped them do it. He got six in seven matches and picked up the Golden Shoe. Although he had a couple of seasons in England with Arsenal and West Ham, his best years were spent in Spain, where he won the Champions League with Real Madrid.

Did you know?

Croatia have won just one of their last six competitive matches

Luka Modric has become a key man for Real Madrid

Final group	P	W	D	L	F	A	GD	Pts
Belgium	10	8	2	0	18	4	14	26
Croatia	**10**	**5**	**2**	**3**	**12**	**9**	**3**	**17**
Serbia	10	4	2	4	18	11	7	14
Scotland	10	3	2	5	8	12	-4	11
Wales	10	3	1	6	9	20	-11	10
Macedonia	10	2	1	7	7	16	-9	7

Croatia ....(0) 1-0 (0)........ Macedonia
Croatia: Jelavic (69)

Belgium...........(1) 1-1 (1)............. Croatia
Belgium: Gillet (45) Croatia: Perisic (6)

Macedonia ......(1) 1-2 (1)............. Croatia
Macedonia: Ibraimi (16) Croatia: Corluka (33) Rakitic (60)

Croatia ....(1) 2-0 (0)............... Wales
Croatia: Mandzukic (27) Eduardo (58)

Croatia ....(2) 2-0 (0)...............Serbia
Croatia: Mandzukic (23) Olic (37)

Wales ....(1) 1-2 (0)............. Croatia
Wales: Bale (pen 21) Croatia: Lovren (77) Eduardo (87)

Croatia ....(0) 0-1 (1)............Scotland
Scotland: Snodgrass (26)

Serbia ....(0) 1-1 (0)............. Croatia
Serbia: Mitrovic (66) Croatia: Mandzukic (53)

Croatia ....(0) 1-2 (2)............Belgium
Croatia: Kranjcar (83) Belgium: Lukaku (15, 38)

Scotland ....(1) 2-0 (0)............. Croatia
Scotland: Snodgrass (28) Naismith (73)

Play-off
Iceland ....(0) 0-0 (0)............. Croatia
Croatia ....(1) 2-0 (0)............. Iceland
Croatia: Mandzukic (27) Srna (47)

Full qualifying results and tables on pages 234-256

CROATIA

Players used in qualifying		Career			Qualifying		
Pos	Club	Age	P	G	P	G	Y/R
G Stipe Pletikosa	R. Rostov	35	109	0	12	0	0
D Dejan Lovren	Southampton	24	24	2	7	1	2
D Domagoj Vida	Dynamo Kiev	24	21	1	6	0	0
D Gordon Schildenfeld	Panathinaikos	29	21	0	4	0	1
D Ivan Strinic	Dnipro	26	32	0	9	0	1
D Josip Simunic	Dynamo Zagreb	36	105	3	9	0	2/1
D Vedran Corluka	Loko Moscow	28	71	4	9	1	3
D Sime Vrsaljko	Genoa	22	5	0	1	0	1
D Dario Srna	Shakhtar	31	111	21	11	1	2
M Danijel Pranjic	Panathinaikos	32	49	0	2	0	0
M Ivan Perisic	Wolfsburg	24	27	1	10	1	0
M Ivan Rakitic	Seville	26	60	9	10	1	1
M Ivo Ilicevic	Hamburg	27	8	1	1	0	0
M Sammir	Getafe	26	4	0	3	0	0
M Josip Radosevic	Napoli	19	1	0	1	0	0
M Luka Modric	Real Madrid	28	73	8	11	0	3
M Mateo Kovacic	Inter	19	8	0	6	0	1
M Milan Badelj	Hamburg	25	9	1	3	0	0
M Niko Kranjcar	QPR	29	81	15	6	1	1
M Ognjen Vukojevic	Dynamo Kiev	30	54	4	7	0	4
F Ivica Olic	Wolfsburg	34	90	18	7	1	1
F Eduardo	Shakhtar	31	61	29	7	2	1
F Ante Rebic	Fiorentina	20	3	1	2	0	0
F Leon Benko	Dalian Aerbin	30	4	0	1	0	0
F Mario Mandzukic	Bayern Munich	27	48	13	12	4	1/1
F Nikica Jelavic	Hull	28	31	5	6	1	1
F Nikola Kalinic	Dnipro	26	20	6	5	0	0

Croatia celebrate reaching the finals

What happens if ...

Croatia score first

Croatia win	11	41%
Draw	2	7%
Croatia lose	0	0%

Opponents score first

Croatia win	4	15%
Draw	1	4%
Croatia lose	6	22%

27 games since 2010 World Cup

Goal times

For		Against
3	0-9	0
2	10-18	3
3	19-27	3
4	28-36	1
5	37-45	5
6	46-54	0
4	55-63	0
5	64-72	2
5	73-81	3
2	82-90	2

Croatia		Opponents	
17	44% 1st half	12	63%
22	56% 2nd half	7	37%

27 games since 2010 World Cup

Correct scores

	Friendly	Comp
1-0	0	1
2-0	0	4
2-1	2	4
3-0	0	3
3-1	1	3
3-2	1	0
4-0	1	0
4-1	0	0
4-2	1	0
4-3	0	0
0-0	2	3
1-1	2	3
2-2	1	0
3-3	0	0
4-4	0	0
0-1	1	3
0-2	0	2
1-2	0	1
0-3	0	0
1-3	1	0
2-3	0	0
0-4	0	0
1-4	0	0
2-4	1	0
3-4	0	0
Other	0	0

41 games since 2010 World Cup

Bookings

Yellow cards	26
Red cards	2
Avg make-up	25.8

In 2014 World Cup qualifying

Top scorers

	Total	First	%	Anytime	%
M Mandzukic	4	4	100	4	33
Eduardo	2	0	0	2	29

In World Cup 2014 qualification

Mario Mandzukic scores in the 2013 Champions League final

Unders & overs

1.5 goals		2.5 goals		3.5 goals		4.5 goals	
Under	Over	Under	Over	Under	Over	Under	Over
26%	74%	59%	41%	89%	11%	100%	0%

27 games since 2010 World Cup

Half-time/Full-time

Win/Win	9	33%
Draw/Win	3	11%
Lose/Win	3	11%
Win/Draw	0	0%
Draw/Draw	5	19%
Lose/Draw	1	4%
Win/Lose	0	0%
Draw/Lose	3	11%
Lose/Lose	3	11%

WIN 55%

27 games since 2010 World Cup

Penalty shootouts

Won	0	0%
Lost	1	100%

All-time record

Clean sheets

Croatia	11	41%
Opponents	8	30%

27 games since 2010 World Cup

Peralta is the man to fire El Tri into the knockout rounds behind the hosts

O nly Brazil, Argentina, Italy and Germany have made more World Cup appearances than Mexico. They have reached every finals since being banned from Italia 90 for the cachirules scandal that hit the country hard after they were found to have used several overage players for a youth tournament in 1988. There was nearly another scandal, this time on the pitch, as Mexico used up a lot of luck to make it to Brazil.

How they qualified

It started superbly with Mexico winning all six matches by an aggregate score of 15-2 to move into the final qualifying section but El Tricolor fell to pieces and the eventual 9-3 aggregate play-off triumph over a desperate New Zealand side does not even begin to tell the story.

Mexico won just two of their ten matches against their fellow Concacaf rivals in the fourth round, a six-team group stage known as the Hex. They scored a meagre seven goals and only made it into the play-off berth at the 11th hour, when the USA scored an injury-time goal away to Panama on the final matchday.

Their only away victory in the Hex came in Jamaica, while Costa Rica, Jamaica and the USA all gained goalless draws at the Azteca and Honduras took all three points at a venue that is usually a fortress for Mexico.

The manager

Miguel Herrera was Mexico's fourth boss during the woeful qualifying campaign. He combined the Club America job with the national side on a caretaker basis for the play-off with New Zealand when all the foreign-based squad members were ditched in favour of domestic players.

Herrera has managed five different clubs in Mexico but his only title came last year with

FA founded 1927
www femexfut.org.mx
Head coach Miguel Herrera
National league Liga MX
System of government Federal republic
Population 119 million
Capital city Mexico City
Currency Peso
Official language Spanish
Strengths
- ☑ Nice forward options
- ☑ Climate unlikely to be a problem
- ☑ Going well at youth level for a while

Weaknesses
- ☒ Influential centre-back Rafael Marquez lost his pace years ago
- ☒ Can Europe-based players be integrated with those in Mexico?
- ☒ Carlos Vela's absence

Base Santos

Fixtures
1 Cameroon, June 13, Natal
2 Brazil, June 17, Fortaleza
3 Croatia, June 23, Recife

America. However, he is now the permanent national team boss and the Mexican Football Federation have said they want to keep him in the role until after the 2018 World Cup in Russia.

Match winners

Herrera welcomed back the foreign stars in February so that means World Cup spots for the likes of forwards Javier Hernandez and Giovani dos Santos as well as utility man Andres Guardado, who left Valencia in January to play for Bayer Leverkusen.

Javier Aquino is another to watch out for, having impressed for La Liga's surprise package Villarreal.

Of the Mexican-based players, Oribe Peralta has been a regular source of goals for Santos Laguna and has also found the net in this season's Copa Libertadores, while 22-year-old Alan Pulido burst on to the scene with a hat-trick on his international debut against South Korea.

Question marks

No team can afford to be without their best players and Carlos Vela's refusal to play for his country is a dagger through the heart.

Hugo Sanchez described the Sociedad striker as "Mexico's Messi" and he is simply irreplaceable.

At the other end of the pitch, the ageing defence is vulnerable.

How to profit

A simple bet on Mexico to qualify for the last 16 looks the pick of the bunch and a straight forecast wager with El Tricolor finishing behind Brazil is another option.

They are better, on paper at least, than both Cameroon and Croatia assuming the problems Mexico had during qualification are in the past.

Peralta is the obvious place to look for the top Mexican goalscorer. He notched ten times in 11 games during the qualifying process and was the hero as his country won Olympic gold, scoring both goals against Brazil in the final at London 2012.

Oribe Peralta celebrates scoring against New Zealand

MEXICO

World Cup record

Uruguay 1930	Group stage
Italy 1934	Did not qualify
France 1938	Withdrew
Brazil 1950	Group stage
Switzerland 1954	Group stage
Sweden 1958	Group stage
Chile 1962	Group stage
England 1966	Group stage
Mexico 1970	Quarter-finals
Germany 1974	Did not qualify
Argentina 1978	Group stage
Spain 1982	Did not qualify
Mexico 1986	Quarter-finals
Italy 1990	Banned
USA 1994	Round of 16
France 1998	Round of 16
Korea/Japan 2002	Round of 16
Germany 2006	Round of 16
South Africa 2010	Round of 16

Continental titles

CONCACAF Championship (1965, 1971), CONCACAF Gold Cup (1993, 1996, 1998, 2003, 2009, 2011)

Legendary player

One goal in his three World Cups (1978, 1986 and 1994) isn't a great return but **Hugo Sanchez** was one of the greatest strikers of any era, with his 38 goals for Real Madrid in 1989-90 the highlight of an extraordinary career.

Did you know?

Uruguay are the only other finalists who can match Mexico's 18 qualifying games

How they qualified

Round 3

Mexico ....(2) 3-1 (0)............. Guyana
Mexico: Salcido (11) Dos Santos (15) Rodrigues (51 og) Guyana: Moreno (62 og)

El Salvador ......(0) 1-2 (0).............. Mexico
El Salvador: Pacheco (65) Mexico: Zavala (60) Moreno (82)

Costa Rica ....(0) 0-2 (1).............. Mexico
Mexico: Salcido (43) Zavala (52)

Mexico ....(0) 1-0 (0)......... Costa Rica
Mexico: Hernandez (61)

Guyana............(0) 0-5 (0)............. Mexico
Mexico: Guardado (78) Peralta (79) Pollard (82 og) Hernandez (84) Reyna (86)

Mexico ....(0) 2-0 (0)........ El Salvador
Mexico: Peralta (64) Hernandez (85)

Final group

	P	W	D	L	F	A	GD	Pts
USA	10	7	1	2	15	8	7	22
Costa Rica	10	5	3	2	13	7	6	18
Honduras	10	4	3	3	13	12	1	15
Mexico	**10**	**2**	**5**	**3**	**7**	**9**	**-2**	**11**
Panama	10	1	5	4	10	14	-4	8
Jamaica	10	0	5	5	5	13	-8	5

Mexico ....(0) 0-0 (0).............Jamaica

Honduras ....(0) 2-2 (1).............. Mexico
Honduras: Costly (77) Bengtson (80) Mexico: Hernandez (28, 54)

Mexico ....(0) 0-0 (0)...................USA

Jamaica ....(0) 0-1 (0).............. Mexico
Mexico: de Nigris (48)

Panama ....(0) 0-0 (0).............. Mexico

Mexico ....(0) 0-0 (0)......... Costa Rica

Mexico ....(1) 1-2 (0)......... Honduras
Mexico: Peralta (5) Honduras: Bengtson (63) Costly (66)

USA ....(0) 2-0 (0).............. Mexico
USA: Johnson (49) Donovan (78)

Mexico ....(1) 2-1 (0)............. Panama
Mexico: Peralta (40) Jimenez (85) Panama: Tejada (81)

Costa Rica ....(1) 2-1 (1).............. Mexico
Costa Rica: Ruiz (25) Saborio (64) Mexico: Peralta (29)

Intercontinental play-off

Mexico ....(2) 5-1 (0).....New Zealand
Mexico: Aguilar (32) Jimenez (40) Peralta (48, 80) Marquez (84) New Zealand: James (85)

New Zealand ...(0) 2-4 (3).............. Mexico
New Zealand: James (80) Fallon (84) Mexico: Peralta (14, 29, 33) Pena (87)

Full qualifying results and tables on pages 234-256

Unders & overs

<1.5	>1.5	<2.5	>2.5	<3.5	>3.5	<4.5	>4.5
26%	74%	43%	57%	71%	29%	80%	20%

25 competitive games since 2010 World Cup

Half-time/Full-time

W/W	9	26%	W/D	1	3%	W/L	2	6%
D/W	9	26%	D/D	5	14%	D/L	6	17%
L/W	1	3%	L/D	0	0%	L/L	2	6%

35 competitive games since 2010 World Cup

Bookings

Yellow cards	18
Red cards	0
Avg make-up	18.0

In 2014 World Cup qualifying

Penalty shootouts

Won	2	33%
Lost	4	67%

All-time record

What happens if ...

Mexico score first			Their opponents score first		
Mexico win	18	51%	Mexico win	2	6%
Draw	1	3%	Draw	0	0%
Mexico lose	2	6%	Mexico lose	8	23%

35 competitive games since 2010 World Cup

Top scorers

	Total	First	%	Anytime	%
O Peralta	10	4	40	7	64
J Hernandez	5	2	40	4	25
C Salcido	2	2	100	2	17
J Zavala	2	1	50	2	17
R Jimenez	2	0	0	2	29

In World Cup 2014 qualification

Goal times

For		Against
1	0-9	4
4	10-18	2
4	19-27	3
10	28-36	0
7	37-45	1
8	46-54	2
7	55-63	3
6	64-72	5
5	73-81	7
13	82-90	5

Mexico		Opponents	
26 40%	1st half	10	31%
39 60%	2nd half	22	68%

35 games since 2010 World Cup

Correct scores

	Friendly	Comp
1-0	2	3
2-0	4	4
2-1	1	4
3-0	1	0
3-1	2	2
3-2	0	0
4-0	1	0
4-1	1	1
4-2	1	2
4-3	0	0
0-0	2	4
1-1	6	0
2-2	2	1
3-3	0	0
4-4	0	0
0-1	1	2
0-2	1	2
1-2	2	6
0-3	0	0
1-3	0	0
2-3	0	0
0-4	0	0
1-4	0	0
2-4	0	0
3-4	0	0
Other	0	4

62 games since 2010 World Cup

Clean sheets

Mexico	14	40%
Opp	9	26%

35 competitive games since 2010 World Cup

Players used in qualifying

Pos		Club	Career			Qualifying		
			Age	P	G	P	G	Y/R
G	Alfredo Talavera	Toluca	31	12	0	1	0	0
G	Guillermo Ochoa	Ajaccio	28	56	0	4	0	0
G	Jonathan Orozco	Monterrey	27	6	0	1	0	0
G	Jose Corona	Cruz Azul	33	32	0	10	0	0
G	Moises Munoz	Club America	34	12	0	2	0	1
D	Carlos Salcido	Tigres	33	119	10	12	2	2
D	Francisco Rodriguez	Club America	32	90	1	13	0	2
D	Gerardo Flores	Cruz Azul	27	7	0	3	0	1
D	Hector Moreno	Espanyol	26	50	1	12	1	1
D	Hiram Mier	Monterrey	24	10	0	1	0	0
D	Hugo Ayala	Tigres	26	11	0	4	0	0
D	Joel Huiqui	Morelia	31	14	1	1	0	0
D	Israel Jimenez	Tigres	24	6	0	2	0	0
D	Juan Valenzuela	Club America	29	18	0	2	0	0
D	Jorge Torres	Tigres	26	38	1	10	0	2
D	Paul Aguilar	Club America	28	25	3	3	1	0
D	Rafael Marquez	Leon	35	119	14	4	1	1
D	Adrian Aldrete	Club America	25	14	0	1	0	0
D	Severo Meza	Monterrey	27	16	0	10	0	0
D	Diego Reyes	Porto	21	12	0	4	0	0
D	Jesus Molina	Club America	25	8	0	1	0	0
D	Miguel Layun	Club America	25	10	0	4	0	0
M	JA Guardado	Valencia	27	100	14	14	1	0
M	Angel Reyna	Veracruz	29	25	2	9	1	0
M	Zinha	Toluca	37	56	6	3	0	0
M	Carlos Pena	Leon	23	13	2	5	1	0
M	Christian Gimenez	Cruz Azul	33	5	0	4	0	0
M	Edgar Andrade	CF Pachuca	25	8	0	2	0	0
M	Elias Hernandez	Leon	25	11	1	3	0	0
M	Fernando Arce	Tijuana	33	47	7	3	0	0
M	Jesus Escoboza	Santos Laguna	21	3	1	2	0	0
M	Juan Medina	Club America	30	6	0	2	0	1
M	Luis Montes	Leon	27	10	2	2	0	1
M	Gerardo Torrado	Cruz Azul	34	146	6	5	0	2
M	Giovani Dos Santos	Villarreal	24	73	14	12	1	0
M	Hector Herrera	Porto	23	10	0	5	0	1
M	Isaac Brizuela	Toluca	23	4	0	1	0	0
M	Javier Aquino	Villarreal	24	21	0	11	0	0
M	Jesus Zavala	Monterrey	26	29	2	12	2	1
M	Jorge Enriquez	Guadalajara	23	8	0	2	0	0
M	Pablo Barrera	Cruz Azul	26	57	6	4	0	0
F	Aldo de Nigris	Guadalajara	30	28	9	6	1	0
F	Javier Hernandez	Man Utd	25	58	35	16	5	1
F	Marco Fabian	Cruz Azul	24	10	4	3	0	0
F	Omar Bravo	Guadalajara	34	67	15	2	0	0
F	Oribe Peralta	Santos Laguna	30	26	16	11	10	1
F	Raul Jimenez	Club America	22	21	4	7	2	0

Manager's toughest task might be keeping all his players pulling together

Volker Finke believes an African team could reach the semi-finals in Brazil but there are better placed outfits than his own Cameroon side to make that prediction come true. There's no doubt the Indomitable Lions are progressing after a spell in the doldrums and their group could have been tougher but there is still plenty of thinking for Finke to do if Cameroon are to stun the watching world.

How they qualified

Chaotic would have to the word. Cameroon got lucky when a 2-0 defeat to Togo was overturned after their opponents fielded the banned Alaixys Romao, although the Indomitable Lions were themselves suspended from Fifa at one stage because of "government interference."

Replacing Jean-Paul Akono with Finke eventually worked the oracle and Cameroon grew in stature as the campaign progressed, with the high point a comfortable 4-1 aggregate success over the higher-ranked Tunisia in the play-offs.

The manager

Finke spent 16 years in charge of Freiburg between 1991 and 2007 but you get the impression things won't be quite so stable with Cameroon, who have averaged a managerial change every year since 2000 and are never far away from off-field strife.

Match winners

Samuel Eto'o is the obvious name given that he is a multiple Champions League winner and back in a major championship with Chelsea following a spell boosting his pension fund at Anzhi.

However, Eto'o had previously refused to play for Cameroon – he announced his retirement from international football

Country factfile

FA founded 1959
www federationcamerounaisedefootball.com
Head coach Volker Finke
National league Elite ONE
System of government Republic
Population 23 million
Capital city Yaounde
Currency Central African Franc
Official languages French, English

Strengths

☑ Finished qualifying impressively
☑ Plenty of Champions League experience
☑ Solid enough at the back

Weaknesses

☒ Eto'o has been at war with his team-mates
☒ Midfield lacks creativity
☒ Team spirit has previously been questioned

Base Vitoria

Fixtures

1 Mexico, June 13, Natal
2 Croatia, June 18, Manaus
3 Brazil, June 23, Brasilia

Samuel Eto'o went back on his international retirement to help Cameroon qualify

last September. Eto'o returned following persuasion by Finke, only for the forward to complain he had to drop deep in to midfield against Tunisia after his team-mates refused to pass to him.

Finke denied there was a problem and Cameroon have experience elsewhere with five of the starters against Tunisia having played in this season's Champions League with Aurelien Chedjou (Galatasaray), Joel Matip (Schalke), Alex Song (Barcelona) and Nicolas N'Koulou (Marseille) joining Eto'o in Europe's premier club competition.

Question marks

Eto'o's ego casts a large spell over the nation and whether the camp will be happy stuck together for a lengthy period in Brazil remains to be seen.

Centre-back N'Koulou's form has dipped considerably over the last year, while Song gets little playing time at Barcelona. Finke needs his big hitters to be at their best from the first whistle.

How to back them

Much will depend on Cameroon's opening game against Mexico on June 13. If they start well then qualification is on but the most likely outcome is a defeat and that would provide a big test of Finke's ability to keep the camp pulling in the same direction.

Making a prediction on Cameroon's points tally is therefore far from easy and instead, it could be worth backing Pierre Webo to score the most goals for the Indomitable Lions.

As you'd expect, Eto'o's reputation means he goes off favourite in this market but he isn't flavour of the month with his own team-mates and the play-off victory over Tunisia hinted that the captain will have to play in a deeper role or even out wide to gain a spot in the starting XI.

Webo started both matches as the centre forward and, despite not being used on a regular basis at Fenerbahce, he has still chipped in with goals as an impact substitute to suggest there is still plenty of firepower in his 32-year-old legs.

CAMEROON

World Cup record

Uruguay 1930	Did not enter
Italy 1934	Did not enter
France 1938	Did not enter
Brazil 1950	Did not enter
Switzerland 1954	Did not enter
Sweden 1958	Did not enter
Chile 1962	Did not enter
England 1966	Withdrew
Mexico 1970	Did not qualify
Germany 1974	Did not qualify
Argentina 1978	Did not qualify
Spain 1982	Group stage
Mexico 1986	Did not qualify
Italy 1990	Quarter-finals
USA 1994	Group stage
France 1998	Group stage
Korea/Japan 2002	Group stage
Germany 2006	Did not qualify
South Africa 2010	Group stage

Continental titles

Africa Cup of Nations (1984, 1988, 2000, 2002)

Legendary player

Part of the Cameroon side that returned home unbeaten from Spain 1982, their first World Cup appearance, **Roger Milla** scored four at Italia 90 as they reached the quarter-finals. At USA 94, Milla set the record for the oldest scorer at a World Cup at the ripe old age of 42.

How they qualified

Final group	P	W	D	L	F	A	GD	Pts
Cameroon	**6**	**4**	**1**	**1**	**8**	**3**	**5**	**13**
Libya	6	2	3	1	5	3	2	9
DR Congo	6	1	3	2	3	3	0	6
Togo	6	1	1	4	4	11	-7	4

Cameroon ....(0) 1-0 (0)..........DR Congo
Cameroon: Choupo-Moting (pen 54)

Libya ....(1) 2-1 (1)......... Cameroon
Libya: Zuway (8) Snousi (90) Cameroon: Choupo-Moting (16)

Cameroon ....(1) 2-1 (1)...................Togo
Cameroon: Eto'o (pen 42, 82) Togo: Dove Wome (45)

Togo ....(0) 0-3 (0)......... Cameroon
Match awarded

DR Congo........(0) 0-0 (0)......... Cameroon

Cameroon ....(1) 1-0 (0)................. Libya
Cameroon: Chedjou (42)

Round 3

Tunisia ....(0) 0-0 (0)......... Cameroon

Cameroon ....(2) 4-1 (0)..............Tunisia
Cameroon: Webo (4) Moukandjo (30) Makoun (66, 86)
Tunisia: Akaichi (51)

Full qualifying results and tables on pages 234-256

Unders & overs

<1.5	>1.5	<2.5	>2.5	<3.5	>3.5	<4.5	>4.5
44%	56%	56%	44%	78%	22%	83%	17%

18 competitive games since 2010 World Cup

Half-time/Full-time

W/W	2	11%	W/D	0	0%	W/L	0	0%
D/W	8	44%	D/D	3	17%	D/L	2	11%
L/W	1	6%	L/D	1	6%	L/L	1	6%

18 competitive games since 2010 World Cup

Bookings

Yellow cards	13
Red cards	0
Avg make-up	16.3

In 2014 World Cup qualifying

Penalty shootouts

Won	3	50%
Lost	3	50%

All-time record

What happens if ...

Cameroon score first			Their opponents score first		
Cameroon win	8	44%	Cameroon win	2	11%
Draw	0	0%	Draw	1	6%
Cameroon lose	0	0%	Cameroon lose	3	17%

18 competitive games since 2010 World Cup

Did you know?

Cameroon averaged just 1.13 goals a game in qualifying

Top scorers

	Total	First	%	Anytime	%
S Eto'o	2	1	50	1	25
J Makoun	2	0	0	1	17
E C-Moting	2	1	50	2	40

In World Cup 2014 qualification

Goal times

For			Against
1		0-9	1
2		10-18	3
1		19-27	0
1		28-36	0
3		37-45	4
4		46-54	1
1		55-63	1
3		64-72	0
3		73-81	0
6		82-90	2

Cameroon			Opponents
5	20%	1st half	8	67%
20	80%	2nd half	4	33%

18 games since 2010 World Cup

Correct scores

	Friendly	Comp
1-0	1	4
2-0	0	0
2-1	1	2
3-0	1	1
3-1	1	1
3-2	0	1
4-0	0	0
4-1	0	1
4-2	0	0
4-3	0	0
0-0	5	3
1-1	3	1
2-2	0	0
3-3	0	0
4-4	0	0
0-1	2	1
0-2	0	1
1-2	1	1
0-3	1	0
1-3	1	0
2-3	0	0
0-4	0	0
1-4	0	0
2-4	0	0
3-4	0	0
Other	1	1

36 games since
2010 World Cup

Clean sheets

Cameroon	9	50%
Opp	5	28%

18 competitive games
since 2010 World Cup

Players used in qualifying

Pos		Club	Age	P	G	P	G	Y/R
G	Charles Itandje	Konyaspor	31	7	0	6	0	0
G	Idriss Kameni	Malaga	30	70	0	2	0	0
D	Allan-Romeo Nyom	Granada	25	6	0	1	0	1
D	Aurelian Chedjou	Galatasaray	28	30	1	7	1	0
D	Benoit Angbwa	Anzhi	32	19	1	1	0	0
D	Benoit Assou-Ekotto	QPR	30	20	0	2	0	1
D	Dany Nounkeu	Besiktas	27	13	0	6	0	0
D	Gaetan Bong	Olympiakos	25	11	0	1	0	0
D	Henri Bedimo	Lyon	29	27	0	4	0	2
D	Jean Armel Kana Biyik	Rennes	24	5	0	2	0	0
D	Joel Matip	Schalke	22	20	0	5	0	1
D	Nicolas N'koulou	Marseille	24	45	0	7	0	1
D	Alexandre Song	Barcelona	26	43	0	8	0	1
M	Stephane Mbia	Seville	27	50	3	7	0	1
M	Achille Emana	Cruz Azul	31	41	7	1	0	0
M	Edgar Salli	Lens	21	7	0	2	0	0
M	Eyong Enoh	Antalyaspor	28	33	2	5	0	1
M	Georges Mandjeck	Erciyesspor	25	18	0	2	0	0
M	Jean Makoun	Rennes	30	66	5	6	2	0
M	Landry N'Guemo	Bordeaux	28	35	3	4	0	1
M	Matthew Mbuta	Syrianska	28	6	3	1	0	0
F	Benjamin Moukandjo	Nancy	25	13	2	5	1	1
F	Eric Maxim C-Moting	Mainz	25	23	9	5	2	0
F	Fabrice Olinga	Waregem	17	5	1	1	0	0
F	Jacques Zoua	Hamburg	22	5	0	2	0	0
F	Leonard Kweuke	Rizespor	26	10	2	4	0	0
F	Mohamadou Idrissou	Kaiserslautern	33	36	6	1	0	0
F	Pierre Webo	Fenerbahce	32	51	18	2	1	0
F	Samuel Eto'o	Chelsea	33	117	56	4	2	1
F	Vincent Aboubakar	Lorient	22	23	2	3	0	0
F	Yannick N'Djeng	Esperance	24	5	0	3	0	0

GROUP B

GROUP B

Gutsy Chile can follow the world champions through to the knockout rounds

Holland failed to pass a difficult group stage in the last European Championship and they could once again be home before the postcards, with Spain and Chile fancied to go through, **writes Mark Langdon**.

Two years ago it was Germany and Portugal who did for the Dutch and things are promising to be just as tough in Brazil.

Spain have tended to start slowly themselves, despite winning every major tournament since 2008. They were beaten by Switzerland in the group stage of the 2010 World Cup and were held by Italy to a draw at Euro 2012 but the tough nature of this beast should mean Vicente del Bosque's side are at full concentration levels from the first whistle.

La Roja have proven themselves to be the strongest team on the planet with a complete domination of the international scene and the emergence of Diego Costa to the forward line will give the defending champions an added dimension to their attacking play.

Spain remain a joy to watch in midfield positions and are solid at the back, something which cannot be said of the Dutch.

Louis van Gaal seems to be putting his faith in a bunch of kids from the Eredivisie, a strategy which may easily backfire. They are not used to this level of ability and we've seen in Europe how Dutch club sides are beginning to be outclassed by even moderate opposition.

The Oranje will be relying on Robin van Persie for goals, although RVP has rarely been seen at his best in major finals. He scored the most goals in qualifying but managed

only one goal each at Euro 2012 and the 2010 World Cup, even though the Dutch reached the final. Going back further, Van Persie notched just twice at Euro 2008 and once in Germany '06 so it is asking a lot of the 30-year-old Manchester United forward to suddenly produce a personal best.

Chile are the team who can come through with Spain.

The South Americans, who are a fantastically courageous side, should get off to a flyer in their opener against potential whipping boys Australia and can call upon two world-class performers in Juventus's Arturo Vidal and Alexis Sanchez of Barcelona.

Australia appear nailed-on for the last spot, although it may be of interest to note that Holland have not beaten the Socceroos in any of their three friendly matches in 2006, 2008 and 2009.

Recommendation
Spain-Chile dual forecast

Spain and Chile drew 2-2 last year

48   Racing Post World Cup Guide

FOOTBALL
FEDERATION
AUSTRALIA

	bet365	Coral	Lads	Power	W Hill
Spain	8-11	4-6	7-10	8-11	8-11
Holland	5-2	9-4	12-5	5-2	2
Chile	4	9-2	9-2	9-2	9-2
Australia	33	66	33	33	66

	Power
Spain/Holland	2
Holland/Spain	10-3
Spain/Chile	7-2
Holland/Chile	8
Chile/Spain	8
Chile/Holland	11
Spain/Australia	16
Holland/Australia	35
Australia/Spain	70
Chile/Australia	80
Australia/Holland	100
Australia/Chile	150

	Lads	Power	W Hill	Power	W Hill
Spain	1-6	1-6	1-6	25	28
Holland	1-2	1-2	2-5	17-2	10
Chile	11-10	11-10	6-5	9-2	7-2
Australia	9	15-2	9	1-4	1-4

All group betting markets are win only

Group matches	World Cup history	Head-to-head record	Last meeting
Chile v Australia June 13, 5pm, Cuiaba	A goalless draw in the group stage of Germany 1974	Three wins for Chile and one draw	A 2-1 win for Chile in a February 2000 friendly
Spain v Holland June 13, 8pm, Salvador	One meeting in the last World Cup final – Spain won 1-0 after extra time	Four wins each and one draw	The World Cup final, which had 14 yellow cards and a red
Australia v Holland June 18, 5pm, Porto Alegre	No previous World Cup meetings	A win for the Socceroos and two draws since June 2006	A goalless draw in Sydney in October 2009
Spain v Chile June 18, 8pm, Rio de Janeiro	Group-stage meetings in 1950 and 2010 – Spain won them both	Ten meetings, eight wins for Spain, two draws	A 2-2 draw in Geneva in September 2013
Australia v Spain June 23, 5pm, Curitiba	No previous World Cup meetings	No previous meetings	
Holland v Chile June 23, 5pm, Sao Paulo	No previous World Cup meetings	No previous meetings	

Group winners

Round of 16 June 29 Fortaleza
2A Brazil, Croatia, Mexico, Cameroon

Quarter-finals July 5 Salvador
1D Uruguay, Costa Rica, England, Italy
2C Colombia, Greece, Ivory Coast, Japan

Semi-finals July 9 Sao Paulo
1F Argentina, Bosnia-Herzegovina, Iran, Nigeria
2E Switzerland, Ecuador, France, Honduras
1H Belgium, Algeria, Russia, South Korea
2G Germany, Portugal, Ghana, USA

Final July 13 Rio

Group runners-up

Round of 16 June 28 Belo Horizonte
1A Brazil, Croatia, Mexico, Cameroon

Quarter-finals July 4 Fortaleza
1C Colombia, Greece, Ivory Coast, Japan
2D Uruguay, Costa Rica, England, Italy

Semi-finals July 8 Belo Horizonte
1E Switzerland, Ecuador, France, Honduras
2F Argentina, Bosnia-Herzegovina, Iran, Nigeria
1G Germany, Portugal, Ghana, USA
2H Belgium, Algeria, Russia, South Korea

SPAIN

The greatest international team of all time must be on every punter's shortlist

George Best, Pele, Maradona, Zidane or Messi? Who is the world's best individual talent is the kind of pub chat which will continue long past last orders and can never truly be proven but there can be little doubt when it comes to deciding the greatest international football team of all time. Step forward Spain, the reigning World Cup holders and Euro 2008 and 2012 winners, who have dominated the international arena for six years.

How they qualified

It did not go how you would have imagined for all-conquering Spain, who dropped home points to France and Finland in surprise draws. A 4-0 success over Belarus was the only time in eight attempts that La Roja notched more than twice in a game.

However, when the pressure was on Spain responded in fine fashion and a 1-0 success in Paris via a Pedro goal put them in command and, overall, Vicente del Bosque's side conceded just three goals. Pedro was pivotal in the qualifying campaign and popped up with four goals, including a hat-trick away to Belarus.

The manager

Nobody can match Del Bosque's mind-boggling record and he has eclipsed his own playing career which saw him win Spain's Primera Liga five times and the Copa Del Rey four times.

As a manager he took Real Madrid to two La Liga crowns and two Champions League triumphs before being considered not good enough at the Bernabeu – a theory he has proven to be as spectacularly off target as a Chris Waddle penalty kick.

Del Bosque led Spain to the 2010 World Cup and Euro 2012 and on both occasions La Roja did not concede a goal in the knockout stages.

Country factfile

FA founded 1913
www rfef.es
Head coach Vicente Del Bosque
National league Primera Division
System of government Parliamentary monarchy
Population 47 million
Capital city Madrid
Currency Euro
Official language Spanish

Strengths
- ☑ Outstanding quality in all positions with tremendous cover too
- ☑ Fantastic recent winning mentality
- ☑ Won all three penalty shootouts in last six years

Weaknesses
- ☒ Difficult draw
- ☒ Struggled at Confederations Cup

Base Curitiba
Fixtures
1 Holland, June 13, Salvador
2 Chile, June 18, Rio
3 Australia, June 23, Curitiba

Match winners

The squad is ridiculously talented and even a Spanish B team would be better than most sides heading to Brazil.

Midfield possession has been the key to Spain's sustained success which is why Andres Iniesta, Xavi, Sergio Busquets and Xabi Alonso are so important. The bench isn't bad either with Cesc Fabregas, David Silva, Javi Martinez and too many others to mention able to come in to the fold.

Jesus Navas, Pedro, Santi Cazorla provide wide choices (although potential wild card Jese is ruled out because of injury) and up front, the nationalisation of Brazilian-born Diego Costa adds a new dimension, with Alvaro Negredo or Fernando Llorente offering beefier options.

The starting defence, including goalkeeper and captain Iker Casillas, is usually made up of Barcelona and Real Madrid players.

Question marks

Spain lost the Confederations Cup final 3-0 to Brazil last summer and were not that impressive in the semi-final shootout success over Italy either. However, there were similar concerns four years ago when Spain were poor in the warm-up tournament but went on to win the World Cup.

The fiery Costa needs to be integrated into the harmonious squad and influential 34-year-old Xavi is slowly on the downgrade.

How to back them

It's a tough group alongside Holland and Chile, and Brazil could be waiting in the last 16 but La Roja's recent tournament triumphs means they must be given enormous respect. It would be madness to write them off and Spain must be on the shortlist to become the first team since Brazil in 1962 to successfully defend the World Cup.

For a shorter-term investment consider snapping up odds-against quotes for Spain to start with a win against an inexperienced Holland side in a repeat of the 2010 final in Salvador on June 13.

SPAIN

World Cup record

Uruguay 1930	Did not enter
Italy 1934	Quarter-finals
France 1938	Withdrew
Brazil 1950	Fourth place
Switzerland 1954	Did not qualify
Sweden 1958	Did not qualify
Chile 1962	Group stage
England 1966	Group stage
Mexico 1970	Did not qualify
Germany 1974	Did not qualify
Argentina 1978	Group stage
Spain 1982	Second round
Mexico 1986	Quarter-finals
Italy 1990	Round of 16
USA 1994	Quarter-finals
France 1998	Group stage
Korea/Japan 2002	Quarter-finals
Germany 2006	Round of 16
South Africa 2010	**Winners**

Continental titles

European Championships (1964, 2008, 2012)

Legendary player

Andres Iniesta is still a key member of the Spanish team and with two European Championships and a World Cup winners medal, not to mention a host of honours won with Barcelona, he is one of the most decorated players in the history of the game. His skill, vision and versatility make him the complete footballer and scoring the only goal in his man-of-the-match perfomance in the 2010 World Cup final sealed his place in history.

Did you know?

Spain's defeat to Brazil in the Confederations Cup final last summer ended a record run of 29 competitive matches unbeaten

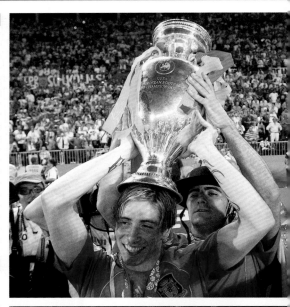

Serial winners (clockwise from above): Euro 2008, Euro 2012, World Cup 2010

How they qualified

Final group	P	W	D	L	F	A	GD	Pts
Spain	8	6	2	0	14	3	11	20
France	8	5	2	1	15	6	9	17
Finland	8	2	3	3	5	9	-4	9
Georgia	8	1	2	5	3	10	-7	5
Belarus	8	1	1	6	7	16	-9	4

Pedro celebrates a crucial goal against France

Georgia ....(0) 0-1 (0)................Spain
Spain: Soldado (86)

Belarus ....(0) 0-4 (2)................Spain
Spain: Alba (12) Pedro (20, 69, 72)

Spain..............(1) 1-1 (0)..............France
Spain: Ramos (25) France: Giroud (90)

Spain..............(0) 1-1 (0)..............Finland
Spain: Ramos (49) Finland: Pukki (79)

France ....(0) 0-1 (0)................Spain
Spain: Pedro (58)

Finland ....(0) 0-2 (1)................Spain
Spain: Alba (18) Negredo (86)

Spain...............(0) 2-1 (0).............Belarus
Spain: Xavi (61) Negredo (78) Belarus: Kornilenko (89)

Spain..............(1) 2-0 (0)............Georgia
Spain: Negredo (26) Mata (61)

Full qualifying results and tables on pages 234-256

SPAIN

Players used in qualifying		Career			Qualifying		
Pos		**Club**	**Age**	**P**	**G**	**P**	**G**	**Y/R**
G	Iker Casillas	Real Madrid	32	153	0	5	0	0
G	Victor Valdes	Barcelona	32	20	0	3	0	0
D	Alberto Moreno	Seville	21	2	0	1	0	0
D	Alvaro Arbeloa	Real Madrid	31	56	0	6	0	1
D	Gerard Pique	Barcelona	27	59	4	5	0	1
D	Jordi Alba	Barcelona	25	25	5	5	2	0
D	Nacho Monreal	Arsenal	28	16	0	2	0	0
D	Raul Albiol	Napoli	28	45	0	2	0	0
D	Sergio Ramos	Real Madrid	27	116	9	8	2	0
D	Juanfran	Atl Madrid	29	7	1	2	0	1
M	Isco	Real Madrid	21	2	0	1	0	0
M	Koke	Atl Madrid	22	7	0	3	0	0
M	Xavi	Barcelona	34	130	13	7	1	1
M	Andres Iniesta	Barcelona	29	95	11	8	0	0
M	Cesc Fabregas	Barcelona	26	87	13	7	0	1
M	David Silva	Man City	28	78	20	5	0	2
M	Jesus Navas	Man City	28	35	3	3	0	0
M	Juan Mata	Man Utd	25	32	9	3	1	0
M	Mario Suarez	Atl Madrid	27	2	0	1	0	1
M	Santi Cazorla	Arsenal	29	62	11	5	0	0
M	Sergi Busquets	Barcelona	25	64	0	7	0	0
M	Xabi Alonso	Real Madrid	32	110	15	4	0	0
F	Pedro	Barcelona	26	38	14	8	4	0
F	Michu	Swansea	28	1	0	1	0	0
F	Alvaro Negredo	Man City	28	21	10	4	3	0
F	David Villa	Atl Madrid	32	95	56	4	0	0
F	Fernando Torres	Chelsea	29	106	36	1	0	0
F	Roberto Soldado	Tottenham	28	12	7	1	1	0

What happens if ...

Spain score first		
Spain win	20	74%
Draw	2	7%
Spain lose	0	0%

27 games since 2010 World Cup

Opponents score first		
Spain win	1	4%
Draw	1	4%
Spain lose	1	4%

Goal times

For		Against
5	0-9	1
4	10-18	0
8	19-27	0
4	28-36	1
6	37-45	1
7	46-54	2
9	55-63	3
8	64-72	2
6	73-81	1
10	82-90	3

Spain			Opponents	
27	40%	1st half	3	21%
40	60%	2nd half	11	79%

27 games since 2010 World Cup

Correct scores

	Friendly	Comp
1-0	3	3
2-0	3	4
2-1	3	3
3-0	1	1
3-1	1	3
3-2	1	1
4-0	1	4
4-1	1	0
4-2	0	0
4-3	0	0
0-0	0	2
1-1	1	3
2-2	2	0
3-3	0	0
4-4	0	0
0-1	2	0
0-2	0	0
1-2	1	0
0-3	0	1
1-3	0	0
2-3	0	0
0-4	1	0
1-4	1	0
2-4	0	0
3-4	0	0
Other	3	2

52 games since 2010 World Cup

Bookings

Yellow cards	8
Red cards	0
Avg make-up	10.0

In 2014 World Cup qualifying

Top scorers

	Total	First	%	Anytime	%
Pedro	4	1	25	2	25
A Negredo	3	1	33	3	75
S Ramos	2	2	100	2	25
J Alba	2	2	100	2	40

In World Cup 2014 qualification

A midfield to die for:
Fabregas, Xavi and Iniesta

Unders & overs

1.5 goals		2.5 goals		3.5 goals		4.5 goals	
Under	Over	Under	Over	Under	Over	Under	Over
19%	81%	44%	56%	63%	37%	89%	11%

27 games since 2010 World Cup

Half-time/Full-time

Win/Win	15	56%
Draw/Win	5	19%
Lose/Win	1	4%
Win/Draw	1	4%
Draw/Draw	4	15%
Lose/Draw	0	0%
Win/Lose	0	0%
Draw/Lose	0	0%
Lose/Lose	1	4%

WIN 79%

27 games since 2010 World Cup

Penalty shootouts

Won	4	57%
Lost	3	43%

All-time record

Clean sheets

Spain	16	59%
Opponents	3	11%

27 games since 2010 World Cup

HOLLAND

The disappointment could come early in Brazil for 2010's beaten finalists

Four years ago Holland were beaten in extra-time of the World Cup final and two years later they crashed out of the European Championship at the first hurdle after losing all three matches, so they are among the more difficult teams to judge in Brazil this summer. The future is clearly bright for a young and brash Oranje but there are also reservations as to whether they are ready to shed the tag of being the best team never to win the World Cup.

How they qualified

This Dutch side is far more attractive than the 2010 version. They qualified with a goal difference of plus 29 having hammered a number of teams, including a brilliant 8-1 humbling of a Hungarian outfit who were aiming for second place at the time.

Unbeaten Holland, who were the first European team to qualify, scored at least two goals in every match and eight of their 34-goal tally came against second-placed Romania. Robin van Persie finished qualifying as Uefa's top scorer with 11 goals in just 688 minutes played.

However, perhaps even more pleasing were the home and away 2-0 successes over Turkey that started and ended qualifying. They showed that the defence can keep clean sheets, although a 2-2 draw away to Estonia highlighted that weakness.

The manager

Louis van Gaal is a straight-talker – would you expect anything else from the Dutch! – but also a great thinker. He made his name at Ajax, where victories in the Uefa Cup and Champions League plus three straight Eredivisie championships earned him a move to Barcelona, where he claimed two La Liga titles.

Van Gaal also won the Eredivisie with AZ and started the revolution at Bayern Munich,

Country factfile

FA founded 1889
www knvb.nl
Head coach Louis van Gaal
National league Eredivisie
System of government Constitutional monarchy
Population 17 million
Capital city Amsterdam
Currency Euro
Official language Dutch, Frisian

Strengths
☑ Van Persie and Robben can win matches on their own
☑ Goals all over the pitch
☑ Young players with scope to improve

Weaknesses
☒ Defence lacks experience at top level
☒ Difficult group with Spain up first
☒ Market anticipates meeting with Brazil in last 16

Base Rio

Fixtures
1 Spain, June 13, Salvador
2 Australia, June 18, Porto Alegre
3 Chile, June 23, Sao Paulo

With 36 players used in qualifying, there are doubts over whether Louis van Gaal knows his best team

where his innovations included moving Bastian Schweinsteiger from the wing to central midfield and David Alaba from the heart of the engine room to left-back.

However, Van Gaal also had plenty of arguments and failed to qualify for the World Cup when he was last in the Dutch dugout between 2000 and 2002.

Match winners

Van Persie and Arjen Robben are the two superstars and Van Gaal must decide which of Wesley Sneijder or Rafael van der Vaart is given the playmaking duties.

Question marks

Van Gaal will be hoping Van Persie and Robben arrive in prime fitness which cannot be taken for granted. It must also be debateable as to whether the coach knows his best team – 36 players were used in qualifying and five different goalkeepers started during the process.

The defence is mainly made up of Eredivisie youngsters and, while they all have potential, there is a mammoth gulf between taking on Dutch domestic opponents and Spain and Chile.

However, the World Cup-ending injury to Kevin Strootman is the biggest concern. The Roma midfielder has been excellent in Serie A and played the most minutes under Van Gaal – he is not easy to replace, even if long-term injury concern Marco van Ginkel recovers in time from his problems.

How to back them

It's worth bearing in mind what Van Gaal told the ANP: "Winning would be a surprise. I can count eight teams who have a better chance of becoming world champions than us."

That's not mind games from Van Gaal, just an honest assessment, but they will be one of the sides in contention if they can first get out of this group, which is no gimme.

It's going to be tight between them and Chile so the value is to back the early elimination.

HOLLAND

GROUP B

World Cup record

Uruguay 1930	Did not enter
Italy 1934	First round
France 1938	First round
Brazil 1950	Did not enter
Switzerland 1954	Did not enter
Sweden 1958	Did not qualify
Chile 1962	Did not qualify
England 1966	Did not qualify
Mexico 1970	Did not qualify
Germany 1974	Runners-up
Argentina 1978	Runners-up
Spain 1982	Did not qualify
Mexico 1986	Did not qualify
Italy 1990	Round of 16
USA 1994	Quarter-finals
France 1998	Fourth
Korea/Japan 2002	Did not qualify
Germany 2006	Round of 16
South Africa 2010	Runners-up

Continental titles

European Championships (1988)

Legendary player

He only played in one World Cup but **Johan Cruyff** is unquestionably one of football's all-time greats. In 48 games for the Oranje, he scored 33 times but he is remembered as much for his ability as a creator as for his own considerable goal threat.

Did you know?

Only Luis Suarez of Uruguay and Belize's Deon McCaulay could match Robin van Persie's 11 goals in qualification

Arjen Robben and Robin van Persie failed to fire in the 2010 World Cup Final

How they qualified

Final group	P	W	D	L	F	A	GD	Pts
Holland	**10**	**9**	**1**	**0**	**34**	**5**	**29**	**28**
Romania	10	6	1	3	19	12	7	19
Hungary	10	5	2	3	21	20	1	17
Turkey	10	5	1	4	16	9	7	16
Estonia	10	2	1	7	6	20	-14	7
Andorra	10	0	0	10	0	30	-30	0

Holland ....(1) 2-0 (0).............. Turkey
Holland: van Persie (16) Narsingh (90)

Hungary ....(1) 1-4 (2)............. Holland
Hungary: Dzsudzsak (pen 7) Holland: Lens (3, 53) Martins
Indi (19) Huntelaar (74)

Holland ....(2) 3-0 (0)............ Andorra
Holland: van der Vaart (7) Huntelaar (15) Schaken (50)

Romania..........(1) 1-4 (3).............. Holland
Romania: Marica (40) Holland: Lens (9) Martins Indi (29) van
der Vaart (pen 45) van Persie (86)

Holland ....(0) 3-0 (0).............. Estonia
Holland: van der Vaart (47) van Persie (72) Schaken (84)

Holland ....(1) 4-0 (0)...........Romania
Holland: van der Vaart (12) van Persie (56, pen 65) Lens (90)

Estonia ....(1) 2-2 (1)............. Holland
Estonia: Vassiljev (18, 57) Holland: Robben (2) van Persie
(pen 90)

Andorra...........(0) 0-2 (0)............. Holland
Holland: van Persie (50, 54)

Holland ....(4) 8-1 (0)............ Hungary
Holland: van Persie (16, 44, 53) Strootman (25) Lens (38)
Devecseri (65 og) van der Vaart (86) Robben (90) Hungary:
Dzsudzsak (pen 47)

Turkey..............(0) 0-2 (1)............. Holland
Holland: Robben (8) Sneijder (47)

Full qualifying results and tables on pages 234-256

HOLLAND

Top scorers

	Total	First	%	Anytime	%
R van Persie	11	3	27	7	77
R van der Vaart	5	3	60	5	100
J Lens	5	2	40	4	44
A Robben	3	2	67	3	50
K Huntelaar	2	0	0	2	100
B Martins	2	0	0	2	25
R Schaken	2	0	0	2	66

In World Cup 2014 qualification

Robin van Persie

Players used in qualifying

Pos		Club	Age	Career P	G	Qualifying P	G	Y/R
G	Jasper Cillessen	Ajax	24	5	0	1	0	0
G	Kenneth Vermeer	Ajax	28	4	0	2	0	0
G	Maarten Stekelenburg	Fulham	31	54	0	3	0	0
G	Michel Vorm	Swansea	30	14	0	3	0	0
G	Tim Krul	Newcastle	25	5	0	1	0	0
D	Bruno Martins Indi	Feyenoord	22	13	2	8	2	3
D	Darryl Janmaat	Feyenoord	24	13	0	8	0	2
D	Jeffrey Bruma	PSV Eindhoven	22	7	0	3	0	0
D	Jetro Willems	PSV Eindhoven	19	11	0	4	0	1
D	Johnny Heitinga	Fulham	30	87	7	3	0	0
D	Joris Mathijsen	Feyenoord	33	84	3	1	0	0
D	Ricardo van Rhijn	Ajax	22	7	0	3	0	0
D	Ron Vlaar	Aston Villa	29	22	1	7	0	1
D	Stefan de Vrij	Feyenoord	22	9	0	4	0	0
D	Urby Emanuelson	Milan	27	16	0	1	0	0
D	Daley Blind	Ajax	24	9	0	4	0	2
M	Adam Maher	PSV Eindhoven	20	5	0	3	0	1
M	Arjen Robben	Bayern Munich	30	73	22	6	3	2
M	Dirk Kuyt	Fenerbahce	33	97	24	5	0	0
M	Eljero Elia	W Bremen	26	28	2	1	0	0
M	Ibrahim Afellay	Barcelona	27	44	5	2	0	0
M	Jonathan de Guzman	Swansea	26	8	0	3	0	0
M	Jordy Clasie	Feyenoord	22	7	0	5	0	1
M	Kevin Strootman	Roma	24	25	3	9	1	1
M	Leroy Fer	Norwich	24	5	0	3	0	0
M	Nigel de Jong	Milan	29	69	1	3	0	2
M	Rafael van der Vaart	Hamburg	31	109	25	5	5	0
M	Siem de Jong	Ajax	25	6	2	1	0	0
M	Stijn Schaars	PSV Eindhoven	30	23	0	2	0	0
M	Ruben Schaken	Feyenoord	31	7	2	3	2	0
M	Wesley Sneijder	Galatasaray	29	97	26	6	1	0
M	Luciano Narsingh	PSV Eindhoven	23	7	2	3	1	0
F	Jeremain Lens	Dynamo Kiev	26	20	7	9	5	1
F	Klaas-Jan Huntelaar	Schalke	30	60	34	2	2	0
F	Memphis Depay	PSV Eindhoven	20	4	0	1	0	0
F	Robin van Persie	Man Utd	30	82	41	9	11	0

What happens if ...

Holland score first

Holland win	18	78%
Draw	1	4%
Holland lose	1	4%

Opponents score first

Holland win	0	0%
Draw	0	0%
Holland lose	3	13%

23 games since 2010 World Cup

Goal times

For		Against
9	0-9	1
10	10-18	3
3	19-27	2
2	28-36	1
8	37-45	2
11	46-54	5
6	55-63	1
7	64-72	1
6	73-81	2
11	82-90	0

Holland			Opponents	
32	44%	1st half	9	50%
41	56%	2nd half	9	50%

23 games since 2010 World Cup

Correct scores

	Friendly	Comp
1-0	1	2
2-0	2	4
2-1	0	1
3-0	1	2
3-1	1	0
3-2	1	0
4-0	0	2
4-1	0	3
4-2	0	0
4-3	0	0
0-0	4	0
1-1	4	0
2-2	1	1
3-3	0	0
4-4	0	0
0-1	0	1
0-2	1	0
1-2	1	2
0-3	1	0
1-3	0	0
2-3	0	1
0-4	0	0
1-4	0	0
2-4	1	0
3-4	0	0
Other	1	4

43 games since 2010 World Cup

Bookings

Yellow cards	18
Red cards	0
Avg make-up	18.0

In 2014 World Cup qualifying

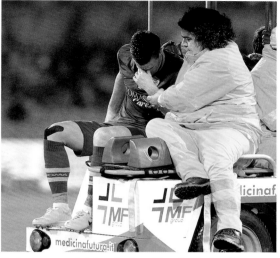

Kevin Strootman's injury is a huge blow for the Dutch

Unders & overs

1.5 goals		2.5 goals		3.5 goals		4.5 goals	
Under	Over	Under	Over	Under	Over	Under	Over
13%	87%	30%	70%	52%	48%	65%	35%

23 games since 2010 World Cup

Half-time/Full-time

Win/Win	16	70%
Draw/Win	2	9%
Lose/Win	0	0%
Win/Draw	0	0%
Draw/Draw	1	4%
Lose/Draw	0	0%
Win/Lose	0	0%
Draw/Lose	2	9%
Lose/Lose	2	9%

WIN 79%

23 games since 2010 World Cup

Penalty shootouts

Won	1	20%
Lost	4	80%

All-time record

Clean sheets

Holland	12	52%
Opponents	1	4%

23 games since 2010 World Cup

CHILE

GROUP B

Positive style means goals are almost guaranteed despite the difficult draw

C hile have qualified for successive World Cups for the first time in their history (although they played as hosts in 1962 and were in England in 1966) and many pundits were tipping them as tournament dark horses before a horror draw saw them in with 2010 finalists Spain and Holland. Even if they get through, Brazil could be waiting in the first knockout round, but Chile are capable of testing all of the title contenders this summer.

How they qualified

Chile eventually finished third behind Argentina and Colombia but it was a topsy-turvy Conmebol qualifying section. Only once Jorge Sampaoli had taken over the reins did they manage to kick on, with five wins and a draw in the last six matches.

That draw came in a bizarre match away to Colombia when Chile were red hot in the first half and raced into a 3-0 lead before being pegged back, but by the end of proceedings they looked a completely different side to the one that was beaten 4-1 by Argentina in their opening game.

The manager

Anyone who watched Sampaoli's gung-ho Universidad de Chile team blitz their way to Copa Sudamericana delight will know what to expect this summer and, as a disciple of Marcelo Bielsa, it will be attack, attack and then attack again.

They are a tactically flexible team capable of playing a number of different formations but the style remains the same with a high-energy pressing game and a fluidity which will be difficult to stop when executed correctly. Sampaoli won't move from his philosophy whoever the opposition.

Match winners

There are plenty in the attacking third and

Country factfile

FA founded 1895
www anfp.cl
Head coach Jorge Sampaoli
National league Primera Division
System of government Republic
Population 17 million
Capital city Santiago
Currency Peso
Official language Spanish

Strengths

☑ Sanchez and Vidal are undisputed world-class talents
☑ Scored at least two goals in their last six qualifiers

Weaknesses

☒ Attacking style leaves them open defensively
☒ A cruel draw

Base Belo Horizonte

Fixtures

1 Australia, June 13, Cuiaba
2 Spain, June 18, Rio
3 Holland, June 23, Sao Paulo

Jorge Sampaoli in action during Chile's international friendly against Germany

Alexis Sanchez has been in devastating goalscoring form for Barcelona this season.

The speed of Sanchez makes him dangerous whether he plays out wide or through the middle and there is not a better all-round box-to-box midfielder in the business than Juventus's Arturo Vidal. Both stars were part of the Chilean youth team which reached the semi-finals of the U20 World Cup in Canada in 2007.

Jorge Valdivia is the influential playmaker and Gary Medel is important from a defensive aspect.

Question marks

The clear issue is whether Medel and his mates can keep out the opposition, particularly against the attacking quality of Spain and Holland. They conceded 25 goals in qualifying – five more than Venezuela, who failed to even make the play-offs – and goals look guaranteed at both ends when Chile take to the pitch this summer.

Valdivia, described by Sampaoli as an "irreplaceable talent", has been struggling with injuries, although he did come off the bench during Chile's friendly defeat by Germany in March.

How to back them

The qualification prices look about right and it should be close between Holland and Chile to see who qualifies alongside Spain, but the South Americans could easily notch against both European powerhouses and taking them to score over 3.5 Group B goals is by far and away the best bet.

It's no exaggeration to say that Chile can cover that line in their opening match against Australia if the forward players click straight into gear, with Vidal and Sanchez capable of hurting the very best defences in this competition.

Chile notched twice against Spain in each of their last two meetings with the world and European champions and even with a weakened team they comfortably won 2-0 at Wembley in November.

CHILE

World Cup record

Uruguay 1930	Group stage
Italy 1934	Withdrew
France 1938	Withdrew
Brazil 1950	Group stage
Switzerland 1954	Did not qualify
Sweden 1958	Did not qualify
Chile 1962	Third place
England 1966	Group stage
Mexico 1970	Did not qualify
Germany 1974	Group stage
Argentina 1978	Did not qualify
Spain 1982	Group stage
Mexico 1986	Did not qualify
Italy 1990	Did not qualify
USA 1994	Banned
France 1998	Round of 16
Korea/Japan 2002	Did not qualify
Germany 2006	Did not qualify
South Africa 2010	Round of 16

Continental titles

None

Legendary player

He only featured at one World Cup, unlike legendary defender Elias Figueroa who made it to three, but **Ivan Zamorano** played in all four of Chile's matches at France 98 and was top scorer as Chile won Bronze at the 2000 Olympic games. At club level, he won trophies on two continents and, as part of Real Madrid's title winning side in 1994-95, finished as La Liga's top scorer. He also won the Uefa Cup with Inter.

Did you know?

Chile have only failed to score twice (against Peru and Germany) in 16 matches since the beginning of 2013

Alexis Sanchez in action during March's 1-0 friendly loss to Germany

How they qualified

Final group	P	W	D	L	F	A	GD	Pts
Argentina	16	9	5	2	35	15	20	32
Colombia	16	9	3	4	27	13	14	30
Chile	**16**	**9**	**1**	**6**	**29**	**25**	**4**	**28**
Ecuador	16	7	4	5	20	16	4	25
Uruguay	16	7	4	5	25	25	0	25
Venezuela	16	5	5	6	14	20	-6	20
Peru	16	4	3	9	17	26	-9	15
Bolivia	16	2	6	8	17	30	-13	12
Paraguay	16	3	3	10	17	31	-14	12

Argentina ....(2) 4-1 (0).................Chile
Argentina: Higuain (8, 52, 63) Messi (26) Chile: Fernandez (60)

Chile................(2) 4-2 (0)................. Peru
Chile: Ponce (2) Vargas (18) Medel (48) Suazo (pen 64) Peru: Pizarro (49) Farfan (mer) (60)

Uruguay ....(2) 4-0 (0)..................Chile
Uruguay: Suarez (42, 45, 68, 74)

Chile................(1) 2-0 (0)........... Paraguay
Chile: Contreras (27) Campos (85)

Bolivia ....(0) 0-2 (1)..................Chile
Chile: Aranguiz (45) Vidal (83)

Venezuela........(0) 0-2 (0)..................Chile
Chile: Fernandez (85) Aranguiz (90)

Chile................(1) 1-3 (0).......... Colombia
Chile: Fernandez (42) Colombia: Rodriguez (58) Falcao (73) Gutierrez (76)

Ecuador...........(1) 3-1 (1)..................Chile
Ecuador: Caicedo (33, 56) Castillo (90) Chile: Paredes (25 og)

Chile................(0) 1-2 (2).........Argentina
Chile: Gutierrez (90) Argentina: Messi (28) Higuain (31)

Peru................(0) 1-0 (0)..................Chile
Peru: Farfan (87)

Chile................(1) 2-0 (0)............ Uruguay
Chile: Paredes (10) Vargas (78)

Paraguay ....(0) 1-2 (1)..................Chile
Paraguay: Santa Cruz (87) Chile: Vargas (40) Vidal (55)

Chile................(2) 3-1 (1)............... Bolivia
Chile: Vargas (16) Sanchez (18) Vidal (90) Bolivia: Moreno (32)

Chile................(2) 3-0 (0)......... Venezuela
Chile: Vargas (10) Gonzalez (30) Vidal (85)

Colombia.........(0) 3-3 (3)..................Chile
Colombia: Gutierrez (69) Falcao (pen 75, pen 84) Chile: Vidal (pen 19) Sanchez (22, 29)

Chile................(2) 2-1 (0).............Ecuador
Chile: Sanchez (35) Medel (38) Ecuador: Caicedo (66)

Full qualifying results and tables on pages 234-256

CHILE

GROUP B

Players used in qualifying			Career			Qualifying		
Pos		Club	Age	P	G	P	G	Y/R
G	Claudio Bravo	Sociedad	30	78	0	14	0	1
G	Miguel Pinto	Correcaminos	30	21	0	2	0	1
D	Eugenio Mena	Santos	25	23	3	10	0	2
D	Gonzalo Jara	Nottm Forest	28	64	3	8	0	3
D	Jose Rojas	Univ de Chile	30	18	1	7	0	0
D	Luis-Pedro Figueroa	O'Higgins	30	16	1	2	0	0
D	Marcelo Diaz	Basle	27	19	0	11	0	3
D	Marcos Gonzalez	Flamengo	33	27	2	14	1	0
D	Osvaldo Gonzalez	Univ de Chile	29	12	0	3	0	2
D	Pablo Contreras	Melbourne Victory	35	66	2	5	1	3/1
D	Waldo Ponce	Cruz Azul	31	42	4	4	1	0
D	Braulio Leal	O'Higgins	32	7	0	1	0	0
D	Matias Campos	Union Espanola	24	6	1	2	1	0
M	Arturo Vidal	Juventus	26	53	8	11	5	1/1
M	Carlos Carmona	Atalanta	27	42	1	5	0	1/1
M	Charles Aranguiz	Internacional	24	19	2	7	2	2
M	Cristobal Jorquera	Eskisehirspor	25	4	0	1	0	0
M	David Pizarro	Fiorentina	34	40	2	2	0	0
M	Felipe Gutierrez	FC Twente	23	16	1	2	1	1
M	Felipe Seymour	Spezia	26	6	0	1	0	0
M	Francisco Silva	Osasuna	28	11	0	2	0	1
M	Gary Medel	Cardiff	26	59	5	12	2	1/1
M	Jean Beausejour	Wigan	29	58	5	10	0	3
M	Jorge Valdivia	Palmeiras	30	56	5	5	0	0
M	Mark Gonzalez	Uni. Catolica	29	49	4	2	0	0
M	Matias Fernandez	Fiorentina	27	60	14	12	3	0
M	Mauricio Isla	Juventus	25	45	2	13	0	3
M	Milovan Mirosevic	Uni. Catolica	33	24	4	2	0	0
F	Alexis Sanchez	Barcelona	25	64	22	12	4	3
F	Angelo Henriquez	Zaragoza	19	3	2	1	0	0
F	Eduardo Vargas	Valencia	24	27	10	14	5	1
F	Esteban Paredes	Colo Colo	33	33	9	6	1	0
F	Gustavo Canales	Union Espanola	31	1	0	1	0	0
F	Humberto Suazo	Monterrey	32	60	21	7	1	2
F	Junior Fernandes	Dyn. Zagreb	25	9	0	3	0	0
F	Mauricio Pinilla	Cagliari	30	25	4	3	0	1
F	Nicolas Castillo	Club Brugge	20	1	0	1	0	0
F	Sebastian Pinto	Bursaspor	28	5	3	4	0	0

What happens if ...

Chile score first		
Chile win	10	50%
Draw	1	5%
Chile lose	2	10%

WIN 50%

Opponents score first		
Chile win	1	5%
Draw	1	5%
Chile lose	5	25%

LOSE 25%

20 games since 2010 World Cup

Goal times

For		Against
1	0-9	1
5	10-18	0
4	19-27	1
3	28-36	5
4	37-45	3
1	46-54	3
2	55-63	4
4	64-72	3
2	73-81	5
8	82-90	4

Chile			Opponents
17	50%	1st half	10	34%
17	50%	2nd half	19	65%

20 games since 2010 World Cup

Correct scores

	Friendly	Comp
1-0	1	1
2-0	4	4
2-1	1	3
3-0	2	1
3-1	1	1
3-2	1	0
4-0	2	0
4-1	0	0
4-2	0	1
4-3	0	0
0-0	1	0
1-1	4	1
2-2	2	0
3-3	0	1
4-4	0	0
0-1	2	1
0-2	1	0
1-2	2	2
0-3	1	0
1-3	1	2
2-3	1	0
0-4	0	1
1-4	0	1
2-4	0	0
3-4	0	0
Other	1	0

48 games since 2010 World Cup

Bookings

Yellow cards	35
Red cards	4
Ave make-up	28.1

In 2014 World Cup qualifying

Top scorers

	Total	First	%	Anytime	%
A Vidal	5	1	20	5	45
E Vargas	5	3	60	5	36
A Sanchez	4	1	25	3	25
M Fernandez	3	2	66	3	25
C Aranguiz	2	1	50	2	29
G Medel	2	0	0	2	17

In World Cup 2014 qualification

Eduardo Vargas

Unders & overs

1.5 goals		2.5 goals		3.5 goals		4.5 goals	
Under	Over	Under	Over	Under	Over	Under	Over
10%	90%	35%	65%	65%	35%	85%	15%

20 competitive games since 2010 World Cup

Half-time/Full-time

Win/Win	8	40%
Draw/Win	2	10%
Lose/Win	1	5%
Win/Draw	1	5%
Draw/Draw	1	5%
Lose/Draw	0	0%
Win/Lose	1	5%
Draw/Lose	2	10%
Lose/Lose	4	20%

WIN 55%

20 games since 2010 World Cup

Penalty shootouts

Won	1	100%
Lost	0	0%

All-time record

Clean sheets

Chile	6	30%
Opponents	2	10%

20 games since 2010 World Cup

GROUP B

A nightmarish group draw means the Socceroos look likely to be out for a duck

Australia's cricket team managed to restore national pride with a whitewash of England in the latest Ashes series but the football team are unlikely to ride the wave of sporting success after being handed a nightmare draw. "We've got a chance to make some headlines when the World Cup comes around," was coach Ange Postecoglou's upbeat message but they are massive outsiders in a group containing Spain, Holland and Chile.

How they qualified
It started convincingly with Australia cruising to top spot in their first group effort but things got trickier in the final round as the Socceroos finished second to Japan. Defeats away to Oman (in the first group stage) and Jordan were the low points, although a 2-2 home draw with Oman was also shambolic.

The highs came in home and away draws with Japan but Australia still failed to win five of their eight qualifiers in the second group stage and German coach Holger Osieck was sacked after successive 6-0 friendly losses to Brazil and France in September and October.

The manager
Osieck was replaced by Postecoglou, a Greek-born Australian who has mopped up plenty of domestic A-League honours. The fact he has been given a five-year deal suggests the Socceroos have put the foundations in place for a better crack at the 2018 World Cup.

Postecoglou achieved relative success with Australia's U17 and U20 teams over a seven-year period and was the manager of South Melbourne when they lost all three matches, including a 2-0 defeat to Manchester United, at the 2000 Fifa Club World Championship.

Match winners
Postecoglou may well be tempted to push aside the ailing old guard – Mark Schwarzer

Country factfile

FA founded 1961
www footballaustralia.com.au
Head coach Ange Postecoglou
National league A-League
System of government Federal parliamentary democracy
Population 22 million
Capital city Canberra
Currency Australian dollar
Official language English

Strengths
- ☑ Postecoglou an upgrade on former coach Osieck
- ☑ They've never lost in three previous matches against Holland

Weaknesses
- ☒ Ageing side with problems in all areas
- ☒ Group looks ridiculously tough

Base Vitoria
Fixtures
1 Chile, June 13, Cuiaba
2 Holland, June 18, Porto Alegre
3 Spain, June 23, Curitiba

FOOTBALL
FEDERATION
AUSTRALIA

Tim Cahill and Co could be heading home pointless

has already retired from international football – but veteran forward Tim Cahill remains the Socceroos' best hope of delivering the kind of upset the coach was referring to.

Cahill notched 11 times for New York Red Bulls in the 2013 MLS campaign and became Australia's all-time leading goalscorer in February's 4-3 friendly loss to Ecuador.

Watch out for keeper Mitchell Langerak if he starts. He was sent off for a reckless challenge against Ecuador but the Borussia Dortmund reserve has looked top notch when called upon at club level.

Question marks

There are weaknesses all over the pitch. Most of the old crew are past their best but the youngsters are probably not quite ready to take over, and long-term injuries to Robbie Kruse and Rhys Williams are cruel blows.

Postecoglou came to England on a fact-finding mission and spent most of his time watching players in the Football League, while 33-year-old midfielder Mark Bresciano's four-month ban, which ended in March, following an "illegal transfer" is hardly ideal preparation for the biggest tournament on the planet.

How to back them

You won't get rich backing Australia to finish bottom of Group B although the Socceroos do look booked for last spot. A better value bet could come in taking them to leave the tournament without scoring, particularly with Bayer Leverkusen's Kruse crocked.

Josh Kennedy bagged five goals in qualifying and is favourite to top the Aussie charts but the giant striker was a flop when he came to Europe many moons ago and the 2011 Japanese Golden Boot winner can't be trusted to repeat his respectable Nagoya Grampus form.

Cahill's set-piece threat could come to the fore for those who don't fancy Australia to fire blanks, but either way the odds about Postecoglou's men finishing pointless are worth snapping up.

AUSTRALIA

World Cup record

Uruguay 1930	Did not enter
Italy 1934	Did not enter
France 1938	Did not enter
Brazil 1950	Did not enter
Switzerland 1954	Did not enter
Sweden 1958	Did not enter
Chile 1962	Did not enter
England 1966	Did not qualify
Mexico 1970	Did not qualify
Germany 1974	Group stage
Argentina 1978	Did not qualify
Spain 1982	Did not qualify
Mexico 1986	Did not qualify
Italy 1990	Did not qualify
USA 1994	Did not qualify
France 1998	Did not qualify
Korea/Japan 2002	Did not qualify
Germany 2006	Round of 16
South Africa 2010	Group stage

Continental titles

OFC Nations Cup (1980, 1995, 2000, 2004)

Legendary player

Harry Kewell scored some vital goals for the Socceroos, none more so than the equaliser against Croatia in Australia's final group game at Germany 2006 that saw them reach the last 16 for the first time in their history.

Did you know?

Australia have lost their last four matches against European nations

How they qualified

Round 3

Australia..........(0) 2-1 (1)...........Thailand
Australia: Kennedy (58) Brosque (86) Thailand: Dangda (15)

Saudi Arabia....(0) 1-3 (1)...........Australia
Saudi Arabia: Al-Shamrani (66) Australia: Kennedy (40, 56) Wilkshire (pen 77)

Australia..........(1) 3-0 (0)...............Oman
Australia: Holman (8) Kennedy (65) Jedinak (85)

Oman..............(1) 1-0 (0)...........Australia
Oman: Imad Al-Hosni (18)

Thailand ....(0) 0-1 (0)...........Australia
Australia: Holman (77)

Australia..........(1) 4-2 (2).....Saudi Arabia
Australia: Brosque (43, 75) Kewell (73) Emerton (76) Saudi Arabia: Al-Dossari (19) Al-Shamrani (45)

Final group	P	W	D	L	F	A	GD	Pts
Japan	8	5	2	1	16	5	11	17
Australia	**8**	**3**	**4**	**1**	**12**	**7**	**5**	**13**
Jordan	8	3	1	4	7	16	-9	10
Oman	8	2	3	3	7	10	-3	9
Iraq	8	1	2	5	4	8	-4	5

Oman ....(0) 0-0 (0)...........Australia

Australia..........(0) 1-1 (0)............Japan
Australia: Wilkshire (pen 70) Japan: Kurihara (65)

Jordan ....(0) 2-1 (0)...........Australia
Jordan: Hassan Abdel-Fat (pen 50) Deeb (73) Australia: Thompson (86)

Iraq ....(0) 1-2 (0)...........Australia
Iraq: Abdul-Zahra (72) Australia: Cahill (80) Thompson (84)

Australia..........(0) 2-2 (0)...............Oman
Australia: Cahill (52) Holman (85) Oman: Abdulaziz Al-Muq (6) Jedinak (49 og)

Japan ....(0) 1-1 (0)...........Australia
Japan: Honda (pen 90) Australia: Oar (82)

Australia..........(1) 4-0 (0)...............Jordan
Australia: Bresciano (16) Cahill (61) Kruse (76) Neill (84)

Australia..........(0) 1-0 (0)...................Iraq
Australia: Kennedy (83)

Full qualifying results and tables on pages 234-256

Full qualifying results and tables on pages 234-256

Unders & overs

<1.5	>1.5	<2.5	>2.5	<3.5	>3.5	<4.5	>4.5
35%	65%	50%	50%	70%	30%	90%	10%

20 competitive games since 2010 World Cup

Half-time/Full-time

W/W	6	30%	W/D	0	0%	W/L	0	0%
D/W	3	15%	D/D	6	30%	D/L	1	5%
L/W	2	10%	L/D	1	5%	L/L	1	5%

20 competitive games since 2010 World Cup

Bookings

Yellow cards	20
Red cards	1
Avg make-up	16.1

In 2014 World Cup qualifying

Penalty shootouts

Won	0	0%
Lost	1	100%

All-time record

FOOTBALL
FEDERATION
AUSTRALIA

What happens if ...

Australia score first			Their opponents score first		
Australia win	9	45%	Australia win	3	15%
Draw	1	5%	Draw	3	15%
Australia lose	0	0%	Australia lose	3	15%

20 competitive games since 2010 World Cup

Top scorers

	Total	First	%	Anytime	%
J Kennedy	5	2	40	4	67
B Holman	3	2	66	3	27
A Brosque	3	0	0	2	22
T Cahill	3	0	0	3	33
A Thompson	2	0	0	2	25
L Wilkshire	2	0	0	2	15

In World Cup 2014 qualification

Goal times

For			Against
2		0-9	1
2		10-18	2
1		19-27	2
1		28-36	0
4		37-45	1
1		46-54	2
4		55-63	0
4		64-72	3
8		73-81	1
11		82-90	2

Australia		Opponents	
10 26%	1st half	6	36%
28 74%	2nd half	8	64%

20 games since 2010 World Cup

Correct scores

	Friendly	Comp
1-0	3	3
2-0	0	0
2-1	4	2
3-0	3	1
3-1	0	1
3-2	0	0
4-0	0	2
4-1	0	0
4-2	0	1
4-3	0	0
0-0	3	3
1-1	1	3
2-2	0	1
3-3	0	0
4-4	0	0
0-1	0	1
0-2	2	0
1-2	0	1
0-3	1	0
1-3	1	0
2-3	2	0
0-4	0	0
1-4	0	0
2-4	0	0
3-4	2	0
Other	5	1

47 games since
2010 World Cup

Clean sheets

Australia	10	50%
Opp	4	20%

20 competitive games
since 2010 World Cup

Players used in qualifying

Pos		Club	Career			Qualifying		
			Age	P	G	P	G	Y/R
G	Adam Federici	Reading	28	8	0	1	0	0
G	Mark Schwarzer	Chelsea	41	109	0	13	0	0
D	David Carney	Newcastle Jets	30	48	6	4	0	0
D	Jade North	Brisbane Roar	32	41	0	3	0	0
D	Sasa Ognenovski	Sydney FC	34	22	1	8	0	2
D	Michael Thwaite	Perth Glory	30	13	0	1	0	0
D	Robert Cornthwaite	Chunnam Drag	28	8	3	1	0	1
D	Lucas Neill	Doncaster	36	96	1	13	1	2
D	Rhys Williams	Middlesbrough	25	14	0	2	0	0
D	Matthew Spiranovic	Western Sydney	25	17	0	7	0	0
D	Michael Zullo	Adelaide Utd	25	10	0	3	0	1
D	Mark Milligan	Melbourne Vic	28	27	2	6	0	1/1
M	Carl Valeri	Ternana	29	50	1	8	0	2
M	Brett Holman	Al Nassr	29	63	9	11	3	0
M	Neil Kilkenny	Preston	28	15	0	3	0	0
M	Brett Emerton	Retired	34	94	20	5	1	1
M	Harry Kewell	Melbourne H	35	58	17	3	1	0
M	Tom Rogic	Melbourne Vic	21	9	0	2	0	0
M	Luke Wilkshire	Din. Moscow	32	79	8	13	2	3
M	Dario Vidosic	FC Sion	26	21	2	2	0	0
M	Mile Jedinak	Crystal Palace	29	43	3	7	1	1
M	Thomas Oar	FC Utrecht	22	13	1	5	1	0
M	Nikita Rukavytsya	FSV Frankfurt	26	13	1	1	0	0
M	Tim Cahill	NY Red Bulls	34	67	31	9	3	1
M	Matt McKay	Brisbane Roar	31	45	1	13	0	3
M	James Holland	Aus. Vienna	24	12	0	2	0	0
M	Mark Bresciano	Al Gharafa	34	73	13	8	1	1
F	James Troisi	Melbourne V	25	9	1	2	0	0
F	Alex Brosque	Al-Ain	30	21	5	9	3	0
F	Archie Thompson	Melbourne Vic	35	54	28	8	2	0
F	Robbie Kruse	B Leverkusen	25	29	3	13	1	0
F	Joshua Kennedy	Nagoya Grampus	31	35	17	6	5	1

GROUP C

Despite the injury to Falcao, Colombia can make the most of a nice draw

Colombia have been uneasy in the Group C betting ever since the anterior cruciate ligament injury that Falcao suffered playing for Monaco threatened his participation in the World Cup but, with or without their star man, the South Americans can take top spot, **writes Mark Langdon**.

The draw, which pits them against Japan, Greece and Ivory Coast, has been relatively kind to Colombia and, assuming there is an advantage to the Conmebol qualifiers in Brazil, the odds-on favourites seem fair value.

Falcao scored nine times in qualifying and will be missed if he doesn't make the finals, but he is not their only striker scoring goals in a major European league. Whoever gets the nod from Jose Pekerman can rely on excellent service from James Rodriguez, while those who watch Fiorentina regularly will know exactly what Juan Cuadrado is capable of from the right flank.

Colombia have beaten Uruguay, Chile and Belgium and drawn against Brazil, Argentina and Holland since the start of the 2012-13 season, so this is clearly a team capable of going deep at the World Cup.

It would certainly be a surprise if Pekerman's boys came up short in this section, although there is a fascinating race for second spot which should mean all of the teams will drop points at some stage in the round-robin action.

In Gervinho, Salomon Kalou and Didier Drogba, Ivory Coast

have the forwards to be dangerous, not to mention marauding midfielder Yaya Toure, but defensively the Elephants can be sloppy which is an obvious concern.

Japan have similar issues. They conceded nine goals in three Confederations Cup matches last summer but in attacking positions Japan have the talent to make the last 16 with Keisuke Honda and Shinji Kagawa two of those with the ability to pick holes in Ivory Coast and Greece.

Bookmakers consider Greece to be the worst team in the pool but don't discount them entirely from the qualification picture. Fernando Santos's side enjoy performing as underdogs and were good enough to reach the Euro 2012 quarter-finals before their run was ended in an entertaining 4-2 loss to Germany. They must have a fair chance against Ivory Coast and Japan.

Recommendation
Colombia

	bet365	Coral	Lads	Power	W Hill
Colombia	4-5	8-11	**5-6**	**5-6**	4-5
Ivory Coast	7-2	**4**	10-3	7-2	7-2
Japan	4	4	**9-2**	**9-2**	4
Greece	**15-2**	7	6	11-2	6

	Power
Colombia/Ivory Coast	**7-2**
Colombia/Japan	**4**
Colombia/Greece	**5**
Ivory Coast/Colombia	**6**
Japan/Colombia	**15-2**
Greece/Colombia	**10**
Ivory Coast/Japan	**12**
Japan/Ivory Coast	**14**
Ivory Coast/Greece	**14**
Japan/Greece	**22**
Greece/Ivory Coast	**22**
Greece/Japan	**25**

	Lads	Power	W Hill	Power	W Hill
Colombia	2-7	**3-10**	2-7	17-2	**9**
Ivory Coast	**10-11**	10-11	**10-11**	5-2	9-4
Japan	**5-4**	6-5	11-10	**21-10**	2
Greece	7-4	7-4	**15-8**	7-5	**6-4**

All group betting markets are win only

Group matches	World Cup history	Head-to-head record	Last meeting
Colombia v Greece Saturday June 14, 5pm, Belo Horizonte	No previous World Cup meetings	A friendly win for Colombia in their only previous meeting	2-0 to Colombia in the build-up to USA 94
Ivory Coast v Japan Sunday June 15, 2am, Recife	No previous World Cup meetings	One win for Ivory Coast, two wins for Japan (the first after extra time)	Sven-Goran Eriksson's Elephants won a 2010 World Cup warm-up 2-0
Colombia v Ivory Coast Thursday June 19, 5pm, Brasilia	No previous World Cup meetings	No previous meetings	
Japan v Greece Thursday June 19, 11pm, Natal	No previous World Cup meetings	They've played once before, with Japan winning 1-0	A group-stage game at the 2005 Confederations Cup in Germany
Japan v Colombia Tuesday June 24, 9pm Cuiaba	No previous World Cup meetings	A win for Colombia in the 2003 Confederations Cup and a draw	Saitama staged a 0-0 draw between the pair in the 2007 Kirin Cup
Greece v Ivory Coast Tuesday June 24, 9pm, Fortaleza	No previous World Cup meetings	No previous meetings	

Group winners

Round of 16 June 28 Rio de Janeiro
2D Uruguay, Costa Rica, England, Italy

Quarter-finals July 4 Fortaleza
1A Brazil, Croatia, Mexico, Cameroon
2B Spain, Holland, Chile, Australia

Semi-finals July 8 Belo Horizonte
1E Switzerland, Ecuador, France, Honduras
2F Argentina, Bosnia-Herzegovina, Iran, Nigeria
1G Germany, Portugal, Ghana, USA
2H Belgium, Algeria, Russia, South Korea

Final July 13 Rio

Group runners-up

Round of 16 June 29 Recife
1D Uruguay, Costa Rica, England, Italy

Quarter-finals July 5 Salvador
1B Spain, Holland, Chile, Australia
2A Brazil, Croatia, Mexico, Cameroon

Semi-finals July 9 Sao Paulo
1F Argentina, Bosnia-Herzegovina, Iran, Nigeria
2E Switzerland, Ecuador, France, Honduras
1H Belgium, Algeria, Russia, South Korea
2G Germany, Portugal, Ghana, USA

COLOMBIA

Los Cafeteros have the depth and the quality to justify 'dark horses' tag

T hink of Colombia and the World Cup and it's almost impossible not to think of Andres Escobar, the player murdered for scoring the own goal which eliminated his team from the finals in the group stage of USA '94. It is all the more poignant 20 years on because – as in the States – Colombia are fancied to make their mark after a rapid rise in fortunes which has seen their odds contract considerably from an opening show of 300-1.

How they qualified

Colombia did so in style, conceding only 13 goals. It was the best defensive record in Conmebol and their four victories in eight road games bodes well for the trip to Brazil. Colombia won eight of their 13 matches once Jose Pekerman was appointed as the coach and a 4-0 thrashing of Uruguay and 0-0 draw away to Argentina showed everyone why Los Cafeteros are going into the finals as the official World Cup dark horses.

A deserved 1-1 draw with Brazil and win over Belgium in friendlies was further evidence of Colombia's ability to mix it in elite company – now they have to show that steel under the pressure of tournament football.

The manager

Pekerman had great success with Argentina's youth teams and is Colombia's first foreign coach since 1982, although he has not been immune from criticism despite leading the nation to their first World Cup in 16 years.

A flexible coach who is not afraid to make big calls, Pekerman was roundly criticised at the 2006 World Cup when, as Argentina's coach, he subbed off Juan Roman Riquelme in the quarter-finals against hosts Germany – Argentina were leading 1-0 only for his side to concede a late goal and suffer defeat on penalties. With hindsight, hooking Riquelme

Country factfile

FA founded 1924
www fcf.com.co
Head coach Jose Pekerman
National league Primera A
System of government Republic
Population 46 million
Capital city Bogota
Currency Peso
Official language Spanish

Strengths
- ☑ Balanced team with right mix of youth and experience
- ☑ Majority play at major clubs in Europe
- ☑ Loads of attacking firepower

Weaknesses
- ☒ Ageing defence may be a problem
- ☒ Falcao's injury is an obvious blow

Base Cotia

Fixtures
1 Greece, June 14, Belo Horizonte
2 Ivory Coast, June 19, Brasilia
3 Japan, June 24, Cuiaba

Teo Gutierrez got six goals in qualifying

and not using substitute Lionel Messi were major mistakes but until that point Argentina were easily the best and most attractive team in the tournament.

Match winners

Star striker Radamel Falcao is a major doubt with an ACL injury but Colombia are far from light on forward options. Porto's Jackson Martinez is highly regarded, Teo Gutierrez scored six times in qualifying, Luis Muriel is a speedy alternative and Carlos Bacca and Adrian Ramos have got themselves into contention after shooting the lights out at Seville and Hertha Berlin respectively this campaign.

Fredy Guarin is a hard-running midfielder, Macnelly Torres is the man to open up defences, while James Rodriguez brings a sprinkling of magic to proceedings from the left and Juan Cuadrado can do similar damage on the opposite flank.

Question marks

Falcao scored nine of Colombia's 27 goals in qualifying so the Monaco man will clearly be missed if he is ruled out.

However, of slightly more concern is the age of the current first-choice centre-backs, 38-year-old Mario Yepes and 35-year-old partner Luis Perea. The duo picked up 12 yellow cards between them in qualifying and are past their best.

How to back them

There are worse each-way bets to win the whole thing, while backing Pekerman's men to reach the quarter-finals is a punt for those looking to be conservative with the market predicting a last-eight clash with Brazil.

They should qualify from a group containing Japan, Greece and Ivory Coast and even if Falcao misses out on the finals, there is plenty of attacking quality to help them go deep.

COLOMBIA

World Cup record

Uruguay 1930	Did not enter
Italy 1934	Did not enter
France 1938	Withdrew
Brazil 1950	Did not enter
Switzerland 1954	Did not enter
Sweden 1958	Did not qualify
Chile 1962	Group stage
England 1966	Did not qualify
Mexico 1970	Did not qualify
Germany 1974	Did not qualify
Argentina 1978	Did not qualify
Spain 1982	Did not qualify
Mexico 1986	Did not qualify
Italy 1990	Round of 16
USA 1994	Group stage
France 1998	Group stage
Korea/Japan 2002	Did not qualify
Germany 2006	Did not qualify
South Africa 2010	Did not qualify

Continental titles

Copa America (2001)

Legendary player

Instantly recognisable with his massive blonde afro, **Carlos Valderrama** had the substance to match his style with imagination, great touch and the ability to find the perfect pass when it mattered – see the inch-perfect through ball that allowed Freddy Rincon to score a 93rd-minute equaliser against West Germany and send Colombia into the last 16 at Italia 90.

Did you know?

Colombia have only lost three of their 21 matches since Jose Pekerman took charge in January 2012

Final group	P	W	D	L	F	A	GD	Pts
Argentina	16	9	5	2	35	15	20	32
Colombia	**16**	**9**	**3**	**4**	**27**	**13**	**14**	**30**
Chile	16	9	1	6	29	25	4	28
Ecuador	16	7	4	5	20	16	4	25
Uruguay	16	7	4	5	25	25	0	25
Venezuela	16	5	5	6	14	20	-6	20
Peru	16	4	3	9	17	26	-9	15
Bolivia	16	2	6	8	17	30	-13	12
Paraguay	16	3	3	10	17	31	-14	12

Bolivia ....(0) 1-2 (0)......... Colombia
Bolivia: Flores (85) Colombia: Pabon (48) Falcao (90)

Colombia.........(1) 1-1 (0)......... Venezuela
Colombia: Guarin (11) Venezuela: Feltscher (79)

Colombia.........(1) 1-2 (0)..........Argentina
Colombia: Pabon (45) Argentina: Messi (61) Aguero (85)

Peru.................(0) 0-1 (0)......... Colombia
Colombia: Rodriguez (52)

Ecuador...........(0) 1-0 (0)......... Colombia
Ecuador: Benitez (54)

Colombia.........(2) 4-0 (0)............ Uruguay
Colombia: Falcao (2) Gutierrez (47, 52) Zuniga (90)

Chile................(1) 1-3 (0)......... Colombia
Chile: Fernandez (42) Colombia: Rodriguez (58) Falcao (73) Gutierrez (76)

Colombia.........(0) 2-0 (0)........... Paraguay
Colombia: Falcao (51, 89)

Colombia.........(1) 5-0 (0).............. Bolivia
Colombia: Torres (21) Valdes (50) Gutierrez (62) Falcao (87) Armero (90)

Venezuela........(1) 1-0 (0)......... Colombia
Venezuela: Rondon (13)

Argentina ....(0) 0-0 (0)......... Colombia

Colombia.........(2) 2-0 (0)................. Peru
Colombia: Falcao (12) Gutierrez (45)

Colombia.........(1) 1-0 (0).............Ecuador
Colombia: Rodriguez (30)

Uruguay ....(0) 2-0 (0)......... Colombia
Uruguay: Cavani (77) Stuani (81)

Colombia.........(0) 3-3 (3).................Chile
Colombia: Gutierrez (69) Falcao (pen 75, pen 84) Chile: Vidal (pen 19) Sanchez (22, 29)

Paraguay ....(1) 1-2 (1).......... Colombia
Paraguay: Rojas (8) Colombia: Yepes (38, 57)

Full qualifying results and tables on pages 234-256

Only Luis Suarez and Lionel Messi outscored Radamel Falcao in South American qualification

COLOMBIA

Top scorers

	Total	First	%	Anytime	%
R Falcao	9	3	33	7	54
T Gutierrez	6	0	0	5	45
J Rodriguez	3	2	66	3	20
M Yepes	2	0	0	1	8
D Pabon	2	2	100	2	40

In World Cup 2014 qualification

James Rodriguez

Players used in qualifying

Pos		Club	Age	Career P	G	Qualifying P	G	Y/R
G	David Ospina	Nice	25	43	0	16	0	1
D	Aquivaldo Mosquera	America	32	30	1	4	0	2
D	Carlos Valdes	San Lorenzo	28	12	2	5	1	1
D	Christian Zapata	Milan	27	20	0	2	0	0/1
D	Gerardo Vallejo	Itagui	37	21	0	1	0	0
D	Luis Perea	Cruz Azul	35	76	0	12	0	5
D	Mario Yepes	Atalanta	38	96	6	12	2	7
D	Pablo Armero	West Ham	27	51	1	15	1	3
D	Santiago Arias	PSV Eindhoven	22	4	0	1	0	0
D	Juan Cuadrado	Fiorentina	25	27	3	11	0	2
D	Steffan Medina	Nacional	21	2	0	2	0	1
D	Juan Zuniga	Napoli	28	51	1	12	1	1
M	Abel Aguilar	Toulouse	29	46	5	11	0	2/1
M	Aldo Ramirez	Morelia	32	28	1	9	0	2
M	Alexander Mejia	Nacional	25	7	0	5	0	0
M	Carlos Sanchez	Elche	28	42	0	12	0	2
M	Christian Marrugo	Deportivo Cali	28	11	0	1	0	0
M	Diego Arias	At. Nacional	28	1	0	1	0	0
M	Diego Chara	Portland Timbers	27	2	0	1	0	0
M	Edwin Valencia	Fluminense	28	15	0	5	0	2
M	Elkin Soto	Mainz	33	26	6	2	0	0
M	Freddy Guarin	Inter	27	48	3	9	1	2/1
M	Gustavo Bolivar	Deportivo Cali	28	6	0	2	0	0
M	James Rodriguez	Monaco	22	21	4	15	3	1
M	Juan Quintero	Porto	21	3	0	1	0	0
M	Macnelly Torres	Al-Shabab	29	38	3	9	1	0
F	Adrian Ramos	Hertha Berlin	28	24	2	1	0	0
F	Carlos Bacca	Seville	27	9	2	3	0	0
F	Carlos Quintero	Santos Laguna	26	14	1	3	0	0
F	Dayro Moreno	Millonarios	28	27	2	3	0	0
F	Dorlan Pabon	Sao Paulo	26	15	3	5	2	0
F	Jackson Martinez	Porto	27	26	8	7	0	0
F	Luis Muriel	Udinese	22	5	1	2	0	0
F	Radamel Falcao	Monaco	28	51	20	13	9	2
F	Teofilo Gutierrez	River Plate	28	29	11	11	6	1

What happens if ...

Colombia score first

Colombia win	9	45%
Draw	1	5%
Colombia lose	1	5%

20 games since 2010 World Cup

WIN
45%

Opponents score first

Colombia win	2	10%
Draw	1	5%
Colombia lose	4	20%

LOSE
20%

GROUP C

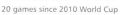

Goal times

For			Against
1	0-9		1
3	10-18		1
1	19-27		2
2	28-36		1
4	37-45		1
6	46-54		1
3	55-63		1
1	64-72		0
3	73-81		3
6	82-90		4

Colombia			Opponents
11	37%	1st half	6	40%
19	63%	2nd half	9	60%

20 games since 2010 World Cup

Correct scores

	Friendly	Comp
1-0	2	3
2-0	7	3
2-1	0	2
3-0	1	0
3-1	0	1
3-2	0	0
4-0	0	1
4-1	1	0
4-2	0	0
4-3	0	0
0-0	2	2
1-1	4	1
2-2	0	0
3-3	0	1
4-4	0	0
0-1	2	2
0-2	1	2
1-2	0	1
0-3	0	0
1-3	0	0
2-3	0	0
0-4	0	0
1-4	0	0
2-4	0	0
3-4	0	0
Other	0	1

40 games since 2010 World Cup

Jose Pekerman transformed Colombia's qualifying campaign

Unders & overs

1.5 goals		2.5 goals		3.5 goals		4.5 goals	
Under	Over	Under	Over	Under	Over	Under	Over
35%	65%	65%	35%	80%	20%	90%	10%

20 games since 2010 World Cup

Half-time/Full-time

Win/Win	6	30%
Draw/Win	4	20%
Lose/Win	1	5%
Win/Draw	1	5%
Draw/Draw	3	15%
Lose/Draw	1	5%
Win/Lose	1	5%
Draw/Lose	2	10%
Lose/Lose	1	5%

WIN 55%

20 games since 2010 World Cup

Bookings

Yellow cards	37
Red cards	3
Avg make-up	27.8

In 2014 World Cup qualifying

Penalty shootouts

Won	2	67%
Lost	1	33%

All-time record

Clean sheets

Colombia	10	50%
Opponents	6	30%

20 games since 2010 World Cup

GREECE

Team spirit and a strong work ethic offer best hope of reaching the last 16

G reece are not being given much chance in the betting but that's just the way they like it, having recorded one of the biggest sporting upsets in 2004 as they took down a host of supposedly superior nations to win the European Championship as 100-1 rank outsiders. A repeat of those heroics is even less likely ten years on and the first target is to make the second round after group-stage eliminations in their two previous World Cup attempts.

How they qualified

They missed out on automatic qualification on goal difference to Bosnia, taking one point from a possible six against the top dogs, who landed a 3-1 win in Zenica.

However, the Greeks recovered to beat Romania 4-2 on aggregate in the play-offs as Kostas Mitroglou helped himself to three goals. Perhaps critically, Romania were minus star defender Vlad Chiriches for the first match and that 3-1 success was the only time Greece notched more than twice in a qualifying fixture.

Eight of Greece's ten group matches produced under 2.5 goals, seven of their victories were to nil and five of those games were won 1-0.

The manager

Fernando Santos has been Greece's manager since 2010 and the Portuguese-born boss has worked extensively in the domestic Super League having taken charge of AEK Athens twice, Panathinaikos and PAOK as well as Porto and Benfica in Portugal.

He led Greece to the quarter-finals at Euro 2012 and his tactics are slightly more progressive than the defensive style which helped Otto Rehhagel land Euro 2004.

Match winners

Greece's main strength is their unity and

Country factfile

FA founded 1926

www epo.gr

Head coach Fernando Santos

National league Super League

System of government Parliamentary republic

Population 11 million

Capital city Athens

Currency Euro

Official language Greek

Strengths
- ☑ Difficult to break down and well organised all over the pitch
- ☑ Excellent work ethic

Weaknesses
- ☒ Reliance on Mitroglou to score goals
- ☒ Ageing midfield
- ☒ History of failure at the World Cup

Base Aracaju

Fixtures

1 Colombia, June 14, Belo Horizonte

2 Japan, June 19, Natal

3 Ivory Coast, June 24, Fortaleza

Greece celebrate their play-off win over Romania

defensive organisation.

Granada goalkeeper Orestis Karnezis was beaten just four times in their qualifying group – only Spain conceded fewer goals – and at the back Borussia Dortmund's Sokratis Papastathopoulos and Vassilis Torosidis of Roma are influential.

Mitroglou has burst on to the scene in recent campaigns, scoring 14 goals in 12 league games for Olympiakos and a hat-trick in the Champions League this season, before being snapped up by Premier League side Fulham. He is without question Greece's main danger.

Question marks

Greece scored only 16 times in their 12 qualifiers, even including their two play-off matches. There is going to be a huge emphasis on Mitroglou to carry a forward threat and he has struggled for fitness in 2014.

There has to be a doubt as to whether 37-year-old Giorgos Karagounis and Kostas Katsouranis, who turns 35 in June, can still

influence matches, particularly in the heat and humidity of Brazil – Greece have games in Natal and Fortaleza and an early start against Colombia in Belo Horizonte.

How to back them

A group-stage exit is seen as the most likely outcome but Greece relish the role of underdogs so they are not without a chance of getting out of the opening section for the first time in their history from a balanced group containing Colombia, Japan and Ivory Coast.

They would finish bottom on talent but football is a team game and individual skill is not the only factor. However, the scheduling could have been kinder for a side who will spend most of their time chasing opponents blessed with more technical ability.

The best bet is Mitroglou to justify favouritism in the top Greek goalscorer market. The Fulham forward finished one clear of the ever-willing Dimitrios Salpingidis in qualifying and has proven his talent in this season's Champions League.

GREECE

GROUP C

World Cup record

Uruguay 1930	Did not enter
Italy 1934	Did not qualify
France 1938	Did not qualify
Brazil 1950	Did not enter
Switzerland 1954	Did not qualify
Sweden 1958	Did not qualify
Chile 1962	Did not qualify
England 1966	Did not qualify
Mexico 1970	Did not qualify
Germany 1974	Did not qualify
Argentina 1978	Did not qualify
Spain 1982	Did not qualify
Mexico 1986	Did not qualify
Italy 1990	Did not qualify
USA 1994	Group stage
France 1998	Did not qualify
Korea/Japan 2002	Did not qualify
Germany 2006	Did not qualify
South Africa 2010	Group stage

Continental titles

European Championships (2004)

Legendary player

Greece pulled off one of the biggest sporting upsets of all time when they won Euro 2004 and **Theo Zagorakis** was key to the dogged displays that saw them go through the knockout rounds in Portugal without conceding a goal. The Greek captain was named player of the tournament.

Did you know?

Greece's 2-1 victory over Nigeria in South Africa was their only win at a World Cup finals and saw them score their only goals. They've lost their other five games to nil

How they qualified

Final group	P	W	D	L	F	A	GD	Pts
Bosnia-Hz	10	8	1	1	30	6	24	25
Greece	**10**	**8**	**1**	**1**	**12**	**4**	**8**	**25**
Slovakia	10	3	4	3	11	10	1	13
Lithuania	10	3	2	5	9	11	-2	11
Latvia	10	2	2	6	10	20	-10	8
Liechtenstein	10	0	2	8	4	25	-21	2

Latvia ....(1) 1-2 (0)...............Greece
Latvia: Cauna (pen 42) Greece: Spyropoulos (57) Gekas (69)

Greece.............(0) 2-0 (0)...........Lithuania
Greece: Ninis (55) Mitroglou (72)

Greece.............(0) 0-0 (0)........Bosnia-Hz.

Slovakia...........(0) 0-1 (0)..............Greece
Greece: Salpingidis (63)

Bosnia-Hz. ....(2) 3-1 (0)..............Greece
Bosnia-Hz.: Dzeko (29, 53) Ibisevic (36) Greece: Gekas (90)

Lithuania ....(0) 0-1 (1)..............Greece
Greece: Christodoulopoul (20)

Liechtenstein ...(0) 0-1 (0)..............Greece
Greece: Mitroglou (72)

Greece.............(0) 1-0 (0)............... Latvia
Greece: Salpingidis (58)

Greece.............(1) 1-0 (0)............Slovakia
Greece: Skrtel (44 og)

Greece.............(1) 2-0 (0).....Liechtenstein
Greece: Salpingidis (7) Karagounis (81)

Fernando Santos enjoying watching his team

Play-off

Greece.............(2) 3-1 (1)............Romania
Greece: Mitroglou (14, 66) Salpingidis (21) Romania: Stancu (19)

Romania..........(0) 1-1 (1)..............Greece
Romania: Torosidis (55 og) Greece: Mitroglou (23)

Full qualifying results and tables on pages 234-256

Kostas Mitroglou leaves the field after Greece's loss to the Czech Republic at Euro 2012 – their Euros bid looked over but they beat Russia in their final group game to reach the quarter-finals

GREECE

Players used in qualifying		Career			Qualifying		
Pos		Club	Age	P	G	P	G	Y/R
G	Orestis Karnezis	Granada	28	17	0	12	0	1
D	Avraam Papadopoulos	Olympiakos	29	36	0	1	0	0
D	Georgios Tzavellas	PAOK Salonika	26	12	0	3	0	1
D	Giannis Maniatis	Olympiakos	27	28	0	10	0	2
D	Jose Holebas	Olympiakos	29	20	1	9	0	3/1
D	Kostas Manolas	Olympiakos	22	6	0	3	0	0
D	Kyriakos Papadopoulos	Schalke	21	16	4	2	0	1
D	Loukas Vintra	Levante	33	47	0	2	0	0
D	Nikos Spyropoulos	PAOK Salonika	30	35	2	4	1	0
D	S Papastathopoulos	B Dortmund	25	46	0	11	0	0
D	Stelios Malezas	F Dusseldorf	28	3	0	1	0	0
D	Vassilis Torosidis	Roma	28	64	7	11	0	1
D	Dimitrios Siovas	Olympiakos	25	8	0	6	0	1
D	Kostas Katsouranis	PAOK Salonika	34	109	9	10	0	3/1
M	Alexandros Tziolis	Kayserispor	29	47	1	10	0	2
M	Andreas Samaris	Olympiakos	24	3	0	3	0	0
M	Charalampos Mavrias	Sunderland	20	2	0	1	0	0
M	Giannis Fetfatzidis	Genoa	23	16	3	2	0	0
M	Giorgios Karagounis	Fulham	36	132	10	10	1	1
M	Giorgos Fotakis	Atromitos	32	13	2	1	0	0
M	Kostas Fortounis	Kaiserslautern	21	12	0	3	0	1
M	L Christodoulopoulos	Bologna	27	16	1	6	1	0
M	Gkergki Kone	Bologna	26	14	0	2	0	2
M	Panagiotis Tachtsidis	Torino	23	4	0	1	0	0
M	Sotiris Ninis	PAOK Salonika	23	31	3	6	1	0
F	Dimi Papadopoulos	Atromitos	32	21	2	1	0	0
F	Dimitrios Salpingidis	PAOK Salonika	32	73	13	9	4	3
F	Georgios Samaras	Celtic	29	71	8	10	0	2
F	Kostas Mitroglou	Fulham	26	29	8	10	5	1
F	Stefanos Athanasiadis	PAOK Salonika	25	6	0	1	0	0
F	Theofanis Gekas	Konyaspor	33	69	24	7	2	0

What happens if ...

Greece score first

Greece win	15	58%
Draw	1	4%
Greece lose	0	0%

26 games since 2010 World Cup

WIN
58%

Opponents score first

Greece win	2	8%
Draw	3	12%
Greece lose	3	12%

LOSE
DRAW
12%

Goal times

For		Against
2	0-9	3
1	10-18	1
5	19-27	3
0	28-36	2
2	37-45	2
2	46-54	2
9	55-63	3
6	64-72	1
3	73-81	1
5	82-90	0

Greece			Opponents	
10	28%	1st half	11	61%
25	71%	2nd half	7	38%

26 games since 2010 World Cup

Correct scores

	Friendly	Comp
1-0	4	9
2-0	1	3
2-1	1	3
3-0	0	0
3-1	0	2
3-2	1	0
4-0	0	0
4-1	0	0
4-2	0	0
4-3	0	0
0-0	3	2
1-1	4	4
2-2	0	0
3-3	0	0
4-4	0	0
0-1	0	0
0-2	1	0
1-2	0	1
0-3	0	0
1-3	1	1
2-3	0	0
0-4	0	0
1-4	0	0
2-4	0	1
3-4	0	0
Other	0	0

42 games since 2010 World Cup

Bookings

Yellow cards	25
Red cards	2
Ave make-up	25.0

In 2014 World Cup qualifying

Top scorers

	Total	First	%	Anytime	%
K Mitroglou	5	3	60	4	40
D Salpingidis	4	3	75	4	44
T Gekas	2	0	0	2	29

In World Cup 2014 qualification

Dimitrios Salpingidis takes on Liechtenstein

Unders & overs

1.5 goals		2.5 goals		3.5 goals		4.5 goals	
Under	Over	Under	Over	Under	Over	Under	Over
42%	58%	69%	31%	85%	15%	96%	4%

26 competitive games since 2010 World Cup

Half-time/Full-time

Win/Win	7	27%
Draw/Win	8	31%
Lose/Win	2	8%
Win/Draw	1	4%
Draw/Draw	2	8%
Lose/Draw	3	12%
Win/Lose	0	0%
Draw/Lose	0	0%
Lose/Lose	3	12%

WIN 64%

26 games since 2010 World Cup

Penalty shootouts

Won	-	-
Lost	-	-

All-time record

Clean sheets

Greece	14	54%
Opponents	2	8%

26 games since 2010 World Cup

Finally a kind draw, but the Elephants do not shoulder expectation easily

I t's the last chance for Ivory Coast's ageing golden generation to finally impress at a World Cup following two straight group-stage eliminations but, unlike in previous tournaments, the Elephants have finally had some luck with the draw. Ivory Coast found themselves in with Argentina and Holland in 2006 and Brazil and Portugal in 2010 but there can be no group-of-death excuses this summer after landing a section containing Colombia, Greece and Japan.

How they qualified

Ivory Coast strolled through their group, finishing five points clear of Morocco and scoring 15 goals in six matches.

The Elephants were also on cruise control in their play-off with Senegal after racing into a 3-0 lead, but a last-minute away goal made life tricky for the reverse leg and Ivory Coast were hanging on for dear life in the return (played in neutral Morocco) before eventually wining 4-2 on aggregate, a margin of victory which sounds more comfortable than it was.

The manager

Former French international Sabri Lamouchi has been in the post – his first managerial position – since May 2012. He could easily have been sacked after the disappointing Africa Cup of Nations, when Ivory Coast were beaten by Nigeria in the quarter-finals, having been unimpressive in the group stage.

Match winners

Ivory Coast are seen as the strongest team in Africa and it's easy to see why.

Captain Didier Drogba still leads the line, while other forward options include rejuvenated duo Salomon Kalou and Gervinho, Wilfried Bony, Lacina Traore and CSKA Moscow's Seydou Doumbia, who is capable of playing at a much higher level

Country factfile

FA founded 1960
www fif-ci.com
Head coach Sabri Lamouchi
National league Ligue 1
System of government Republic
Population 22 million
Capital city Yamoussoukro
Currency West African Franc
Official language French

Strengths
- ☑ Forward line bristles with pace, power and depth
- ☑ Yaya Toure is a world-class operator

Weaknesses
- ☒ Coping with expectation and pressure – beaten on penalties in two of the last five Africa Cup of Nations finals
- ☒ Defence far weaker than the attack
- ☒ Ageing squad with little motivation to earn life-changing transfer

Base Aguas de Lindoia

Fixtures
1 Japan, June 15, Recife
2 Colombia, June 19, Brasilia
3 Greece, June 24, Fortaleza

It's party time as Salomon Kalou's last-minute goal makes sure of Ivory Coast's place in Brazil

than the Russian Premier League.

Yaya Toure is the lung-busting midfielder who has become the boss of Manchester City's midfield and he can turn a match in the blink of an eye.

Question marks

How Lamouchi would love to have the same kind of talent defensively. Lokeren goalkeeper Boubacar Barry has rarely convinced in top-level company and the heart of the defence could contain Trabzonspor duo Didier Zokora and Sol Bamba.

Neither is ultra-reliable at centre-back but the other option is Kolo Toure, inconsistent at best when asked to fill in for Liverpool.

It's also interesting to note what former manager Philippe Troussier told the BBC: "In the beginning, when they were young, the players were all hungry to prove themselves in Europe. However, they are not as hungry now, and physically the team is getting very old."

How to back them

If Ivory Coast start well – they open up against Asia's best side, Japan – then the Elephants should go furthest of the African teams in Brazil, but they have crumbled under the weight of expectation in the past.

A better bet comes in the top Ivorian goalscorer market where the bookmakers who rate Kalou as favourite have got things badly wrong.

Kalou scored five times in qualifying but is often asked to play out wide opposite Gervinho in a 4-2-3-1 formation, where Yaya Toure is used off penalty-taker Drogba.

Yaya and Drogba bagged four and three goals respectively in qualifying so don't have much to make up on Kalou, while the influential duo bring big-game mentality to the side. Yaya found goalscoring easy at City this season and Drogba performed with credit with Galatasaray in the Champions League after initially taking time to adjust to Turkish football following a spell in China.

IVORY COAST

World Cup record

Uruguay 1930	Did not enter
Italy 1934	Did not enter
France 1938	Did not enter
Brazil 1950	Did not enter
Switzerland 1954	Did not enter
Sweden 1958	Did not enter
Chile 1962	Did not enter
England 1966	Did not enter
Mexico 1970	Did not enter
Germany 1974	Did not qualify
Argentina 1978	Did not qualify
Spain 1982	Did not enter
Mexico 1986	Did not qualify
Italy 1990	Did not qualify
USA 1994	Did not qualify
France 1998	Did not qualify
Korea/Japan 2002	Did not qualify
Germany 2006	Group stage
South Africa 2010	Group stage

Continental titles

Africa Cup of Nations (1992)

Legendary player

Didier Drogba scored Ivory Coast's first goal at a World Cup, in a 2-1 defeat to Argentina at Germany 2006, and is the captain and record scorer for the national team. As well as leading his country to three World Cups, he has also played for them in two Africa Cup of Nations finals, in 2006 and 2012 – the Elephants lost both matches on penalties.

Did you know?

Following Ivory Coast's March friendly against Belgium, both sides had scored in nine of the Elephants' last ten matches

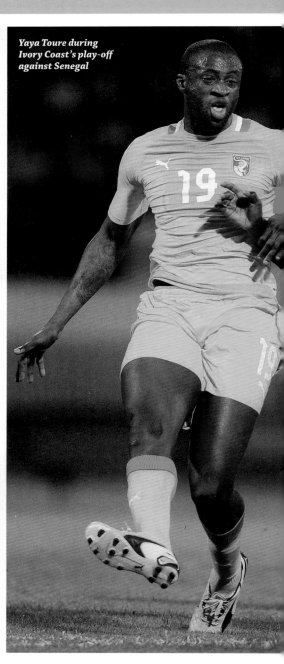

Yaya Toure during Ivory Coast's play-off against Senegal

How they qualified

Final group	P	W	D	L	F	A	GD	Pts
Ivory Coast	**6**	**4**	**2**	**0**	**15**	**5**	**10**	**14**
Morocco	6	2	3	1	9	8	1	9
Tanzania	6	2	0	4	8	12	-4	6
Gambia	6	1	1	4	4	11	-7	4

Ivory Coast ......(1) 2-0 (0)............Tanzania
Ivory Coast: Kalou (10) Drogba (71)

Morocco..........(1) 2-2 (1)........Ivory Coast
Morocco: Kharja (pen 42) Abourazzouk (89) Ivory Coast:
Kalou (8) Toure (60)

Ivory Coast ......(0) 3-0 (0).............Gambia
Ivory Coast: Bony (pen 51) Toure (57) Kalou (70)

Gambia ....(0) 0-3 (1)........Ivory Coast
Ivory Coast: Traore (12) Bony (62) Toure (90)

Tanzania ....(2) 2-4 (3)........Ivory Coast
Tanzania: Kiemba (2) Ulimwengu (34) Ivory Coast: Traore (13)
Toure (23, pen 43) Bony (90)

Ivory Coast ......(0) 1-1 (0)........... Morocco
Ivory Coast: Drogba (pen 83) Morocco: El Arabi (53)

Elephants coach Sabri Lamouchi looks on

Round 3

Ivory Coast ......(2) 3-1 (0).............Senegal
Ivory Coast: Drogba (pen 5) Sane (14 og) Kalou (49) Senegal:
Cisse (90)

Senegal ....(0) 1-1 (0)........Ivory Coast
Senegal: Sow (pen 77) Ivory Coast: Kalou (90)

Full qualifying results and tables on pages 234-256

IVORY COAST

Players used in qualifying

Pos		Club	Age	P	G	P	G	Y/R
				Career		**Qualifying**		
G	Boubacar Barry	Lokeren	34	76	0	8	0	1
D	Arthur Boka	Stuttgart	30	74	1	4	0	1
D	Benjamin Angoua	Valenciennes	27	17	1	3	0	1
D	Brice Dja Djedje	Marseille	23	3	0	1	0	0
D	Igor Lolo	R. Rostov	31	20	0	2	0	1
D	Kolo Toure	Liverpool	33	107	6	4	1	0
D	Ousmane Viera	Rizespor	27	1	0	1	0	0
D	Serge Aurier	Toulouse	21	7	0	5	0	0
D	Siaka Tiene	Montpellier	32	83	2	3	0	0
D	Souleymane Bamba	Trabzonspor	29	42	2	5	0	1
M	Romaric	Bastia	30	46	5	4	0	0
M	Cheick Tiote	Newcastle	27	41	1	6	0	4
M	Didier Zokora	Trabzonspor	33	116	1	5	0	1
M	Emmanuel Eboue	Galatasaray	30	75	3	1	0	0
M	Serey Die	Basle	29	5	0	4	0	2
M	Jean-Jacques Gosso	Genclerbirligi	30	23	0	4	0	2
M	Abdul Kader Keita	Al Sadd	32	73	11	2	0	0
M	Kafoumba Coulibaly	Kasimpasa	28	12	0	2	0	0
M	Mathis Bolly	Fortuna D.	23	2	0	1	0	0
M	Max Gradel	St-Etienne	26	24	3	3	0	0
M	Yaya Toure	Man City	30	79	16	6	4	2
F	Gervinho	Roma	26	51	13	7	0	3
F	Arouna Kone	Everton	30	37	9	1	0	0
F	Didier Drogba	Galatasaray	36	101	64	5	3	0
F	Didier Ya Konan	Hannover	30	24	7	4	0	0
F	Giovanni Sio	Basle	24	6	0	4	0	0
F	Lacina Traore	Everton	23	7	4	3	2	1
F	Salomon Kalou	Lille	28	63	21	7	5	0
F	Wilfried Bony	Swansea	25	23	9	5	3	0

What happens if ...

Ivory Coast score first

Ivory Coast win	17	63%
Draw	1	3%
Ivory Coast lose	0	0%

27 games since 2010 World Cup

Opponents score first

Ivory Coast win	3	11%
Draw	3	11%
Ivory Coast lose	2	7%

Goal times

For			Against
4	■	0-9	1
7	■	10-18	2
5	■	19-27	0
5	■	28-36	3
9	■	37-45	3
3	■	46-54	1
3	■	55-63	4
7	■	64-72	2
7	■	73-81	3
12	■	82-90	3

Ivory Coast			Opponents
30	48%	1st half	9	41%
32	52%	2nd half	13	59%

27 games since 2010 World Cup

Top scorers

	Total	First	%	Anytime	%
S Kalou	5	2	40	5	71
Y Toure	4	0	0	3	50
D Drogba	3	1	33	3	60
W Bony	3	1	33	3	60
L Traore	2	1	50	2	67

In World Cup 2014 qualification

Correct scores

	Friendly	Comp
1-0	3	3
2-0	2	4
2-1	0	3
3-0	1	5
3-1	0	1
3-2	0	0
4-0	0	0
4-1	0	0
4-2	1	2
4-3	1	0
0-0	1	1
1-1	2	2
2-2	1	2
3-3	0	0
4-4	0	0
0-1	0	0
0-2	0	0
1-2	2	1
0-3	0	0
1-3	1	0
2-3	0	0
0-4	0	0
1-4	1	1
2-4	0	0
3-4	0	0
Other	0	2

43 games since 2010 World Cup

Unders & overs

	1.5 goals		2.5 goals		3.5 goals		4.5 goals	
	Under	Over	Under	Over	Under	Over	Under	Over
	15%	85%	37%	63%	70%	30%	81%	19%

27 competitive games since 2010 World Cup

Half-time/Full-time

Win/Win	15	56%
Draw/Win	5	19%
Lose/Win	0	0%
Win/Draw	0	0%
Draw/Draw	5	19%
Lose/Draw	0	0%
Win/Lose	0	0%
Draw/Lose	0	0%
Lose/Lose	2	7%

WIN 75%

27 games since 2010 World Cup

Bookings

Yellow cards	20
Red cards	0
Avg make-up	25.0

In 2014 World Cup qualifying

Penalty shootouts

Won	4	40%
Lost	6	60%

All-time record

Clean sheets

Ivory Coast	14	52%
Opponents	1	4%

27 games since 2010 World Cup

JAPAN

Defence is a concern but Japan's Euro stars can help them cover goal line

T he Confederations Cup is rarely a reliable form guide – no team has ever won the warm-up competition and then gone on to land the main prize at the next World Cup – and Japan will be hoping they can leave last summer's miserable show behind them when the real thing begins. They lost all three games in Brazil despite being considered dark horses for that tournament.

How they qualified

Japan scored the joint-most goals (30) in Asian qualifying and Shinji Okazaki was the leading scorer on the continent. He got eight goals in 14 appearances as the Samurai Blue won their final group by four points from Australia, although it was not always plain sailing.

They had initially struggled to adapt to Alberto Zaccheroni's tactics and in the first group phase they finished a disappointing six points behind Uzbekistan, who beat them in Toyota in February 2012. And despite clearly being a better team than Australia, Japan also failed to beat the Socceroos home or away in the final group phase.

The manager

Zaccheroni made his name at Udinese with the trademark 3-4-3 formation that is his preferred shape, and won Serie A with Milan in 1999. However, that is his only honour, despite also managing Lazio, Inter, Torino and Juventus before taking over the Japan role in 2010.

At the Confederations Cup he started with a 4-2-3-1 formation for losses to Brazil (3-0) and Italy (4-3) but switched to 3-4-3 in the second half of the 2-1 defeat to Mexico.

Match winners

It's a squad based mainly in Europe. Fourteen

Country factfile

FA founded 1921
www jfa.or.jp
Head coach Alberto Zaccheroni
National league J.League
System of government Parliamentary government with constitutional monarchy
Population 127 million
Capital city Tokyo
Currency Yen
Official language Japanese

Strengths
☑ Most of the starting XI play in major European leagues
☑ Dynamic forward line

Weaknesses
☒ Kagawa's lack of minutes for United
☒ Conditions won't suit pressing game
☒ Defence exposed in Confederations Cup

Base Itu

Fixtures
1 Ivory Coast, June 15, Recife
2 Greece, June 19, Natal
3 Colombia, June 24, Cuiaba

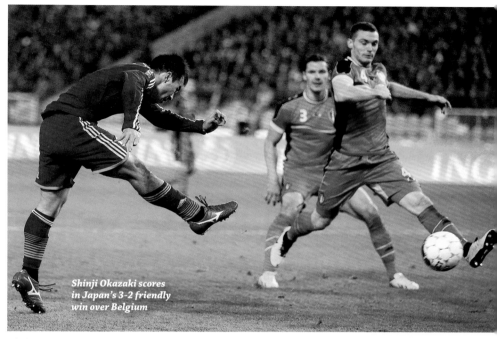

*Shinji Okazaki scores
in Japan's 3-2 friendly
win over Belgium*

of the 23 men chosen for Confederations Cup duty were with clubs across European leagues, with eight from the Bundesliga. There is plenty of attacking flair to select from, particularly as Okazaki has been magnificent for Mainz this term.

Milan's Keisuke Honda is a dynamic playmaker, Shinji Kagawa showed at Borussia Dortmund what a threat he can be, and attacking right-footed left-back Yuto Nagatomo is perfectly suited to a wing-back role if Zaccheroni reverts to a 3-4-3.

Question marks

The Confederations Cup was a real eye-opener. Japan played better than the results suggested but to concede nine goals is clearly a big problem, particularly as they deserved so much more from a blistering start against Italy, where they pressured the Azzurri relentlessly in the first period before getting tired. They also showed signs of fatigue against Mexico.

"We got tired but if you want to win at this level, you can't afford to be tired", said Honda after the tournament. "We've got to start addressing the defence on an individual basis." Nagatomo added: "We couldn't keep up with Mexico and that's the bottom line."

As well as the defensive concerns, Kagawa's unhappy stint at Manchester United is not ideal heading into the World Cup.

How to back them

Whether Japan defend well enough to qualify remains to be seen but they are a delight to watch in attacking areas and can cover the over/under 3.5 group-stage goal line just like they did at the Confederations Cup, despite losing all three matches.

The Samurai Blue scored three goals against Italy so they should not be afraid of Colombia, Ivory Coast and Greece. Even when firing blanks against Brazil last summer, Japan only lost the shot count 14-11 and the shots on target tally 9-7.

JAPAN

GROUP C

World Cup record

Uruguay 1930	Did not enter
Italy 1934	Did not enter
France 1938	Withdrew
Brazil 1950	Banned
Switzerland 1954	Did not qualify
Sweden 1958	Did not enter
Chile 1962	Did not qualify
England 1966	Did not enter
Mexico 1970	Did not qualify
Germany 1974	Did not qualify
Argentina 1978	Did not qualify
Spain 1982	Did not qualify
Mexico 1986	Did not qualify
Italy 1990	Did not qualify
USA 1994	Did not qualify
France 1998	Group stage
Korea/Japan 2002	Round of 16
Germany 2006	Group stage
South Africa 2010	Round of 16

Continental titles

Asian Nations Cup (1992, 2000, 2004, 2011)

Legendary player

There are plenty of Japanese players in Europe these days but **Hidetoshi Nakata** was a trailblazer when he left home for a career in Serie A. He played in the 1998, 2002 and 2006 World Cups.

Did you know?

Even as recently as 2010, 19 of Japan's World Cup squad played in the J.League

How they qualified

Round 3

Japan ....(0) 1-0 (0)...... North Korea
Japan: Yoshida (90)

Uzbekistan ......(1) 1-1 (0)............... Japan
Uzbekistan: Djeparov (8) Japan: Okazaki (66)

Japan ....(4) 8-0 (0)........... Tajikistan
Japan: Havenaar (11, 47) Okazaki (17, 74) Komano (35) Kagawa (41, 67) Nakamura (57)

Tajikistan ....(0) 0-4 (1)............... Japan
Japan: Konno (35) Okazaki (61, 90) Maeda (82)

North Korea.....(0) 1-0 (0)............... Japan
North Korea: Pak Nam—Chol (50)

Japan ....(0) 0-1 (0)........ Uzbekistan
Uzbekistan: Shadrin (54)

Final group	P	W	D	L	F	A	GD	Pts
Japan	8	5	2	1	16	5	11	17
Australia	8	3	4	1	12	7	5	13
Jordan	8	3	1	4	7	16	-9	10
Oman	8	2	3	3	7	10	-3	9
Iraq	8	1	2	5	4	8	-4	5

Japan ....(1) 3-0 (0)...............Oman
Japan: Honda (12) Maeda (52) Okazaki (55)

Japan ....(4) 6-0 (0)...............Jordan
Japan: Maeda (19) Honda (22, 31, pen 54) Kagawa (34) Kurihara (90)

Australia...........(0) 1-1 (0)............... Japan
Australia: Wilkshire (pen 70) Japan: Kurihara (65)

Japan ....(1) 1-0 (0)................... Iraq
Japan: Maeda (25)

Oman ....(0) 1-2 (1)............... Japan
Oman: Kano (77) Japan: Kiyotake (20) Okazaki (90)

Jordan ....(1) 2-1 (0)............... Japan
Jordan: Attiah (45) Hayel (60) Japan: Kagawa (69)

Japan ....(0) 1-1 (0)............Australia
Japan: Honda (pen 90) Australia: Oar (82)

Iraq ....(0) 0-1 (0)............... Japan
Japan: Okazaki (89)

Full qualifying results and tables on pages 234-256

Unders & overs

<1.5	>1.5	<2.5	>2.5	<3.5	>3.5	<4.5	>4.5
26%	74%	43%	57%	70%	30%	78%	22%

23 competitive games since 2010 World Cup

Half-time/Full-time

W/W	8	35%	W/D	0	0%	W/L	1	4%
D/W	3	13%	D/D	4	17%	D/L	3	13%
L/W	0	0%	L/D	2	9%	L/L	2	9%

23 competitive games since 2010 World Cup

Bookings

Yellow cards	9
Red cards	1
Avg make-up	8.2

In 2014 World Cup qualifying

Penalty shootouts

Won	3	60%
Lost	2	40%

All-time record

SOCCERBASE.COM
SMARTERBETTING

What happens if ...

Japan score first			Their opponents score first		
Japan win	11	48%	Japan win	1	4%
Draw	1	4%	Draw	4	17%
Japan lose	1	4%	Japan lose	5	22%

23 competitive games since 2010 World Cup

Top scorers

	Total	First	%	Anytime	%
S Okazaki	8	1	13	6	43
K Honda	5	1	20	3	50
R Maeda	4	2	50	4	40
S Kagawa	4	0	0	3	27
Y Kurihara	2	1	50	2	50
M Havenaar	2	1	50	1	10

In World Cup 2014 qualification

Goal times

For		Against
1	0-9	2
4	10-18	1
6	19-27	1
8	28-36	0
1	37-45	3
4	46-54	6
3	55-63	2
6	64-72	2
2	73-81	2
13	82-90	4

Japan			Opponents	
20	42%	1st half	7	30%
28	58%	2nd half	16	70%

23 games since 2010 World Cup

Correct scores

	Friendly	Comp
1-0	5	3
2-0	1	0
2-1	3	2
3-0	3	1
3-1	2	0
3-2	2	1
4-0	0	1
4-1	0	0
4-2	1	0
4-3	0	0
0-0	3	1
1-1	1	4
2-2	1	1
3-3	1	0
4-4	0	0
0-1	1	2
0-2	2	0
1-2	0	2
0-3	0	1
1-3	0	0
2-3	0	0
0-4	1	0
1-4	0	0
2-4	1	0
3-4	0	1
Other	0	3

51 games since 2010 World Cup

Clean sheets

Japan	9	39%
Opp	4	17%

23 competitive games since 2010 World Cup

Players used in qualifying

Pos		Club	Age	Career P	Career G	Qualifying P	Qualifying G	Y/R
G	Eiji Kawashima	Standard Liege	31	54	0	13	0	0
G	Shusaku Nishikawa	Urawa Reds	27	10	0	1	0	0
D	Atsuto Uchida	Schalke	26	65	1	10	0	2
D	Gotoku Sakai	Stuttgart	23	12	0	2	0	0
D	Hideto Takahashi	FC Tokyo	26	6	0	2	0	0
D	Hiroki Sakai	Hannover	23	15	0	4	0	0
D	Masahiko Inoha	Jubilo Iwata	28	21	1	6	0	0
D	Maya Yoshida	Southampton	25	37	2	11	1	0
D	Tomoaki Makino	Urawa Reds	26	12	1	1	0	0
D	Yuichi Komano	Jubilo Iwata	32	76	1	8	1	0
D	Yuto Nagatomo	Inter	27	67	3	9	0	0
D	Yuzo Kurihara	Yokohama M	30	20	3	4	2	1/1
M	Hiroshi Kiyotake	Nuremberg	24	24	1	11	1	0
M	Hajime Hosogai	Hertha Berlin	27	25	1	6	0	0
M	Jungo Fujimoto	Yokohama M	29	13	1	2	0	0
M	Keisuke Honda	Milan	27	53	20	6	5	1
M	Yasuyuki Konno	Gamba Osaka	31	78	1	13	1	2
M	Kengo Nakamura	Kawasaki F	33	68	6	5	1	0
M	Makoto Hasebe	Nuremberg	30	77	2	13	0	2
M	Shinji Kagawa	Man Utd	25	54	16	11	4	0
M	Takashi Inui	E. Frankfurt	25	12	0	2	0	0
M	Yasuhito Endo	Gamba Osaka	34	141	12	13	0	0
M	Yosuke Kashiwagi	Urawa Reds	26	4	0	1	0	0
M	Yuki Abe	Urawa Reds	32	53	3	1	0	0
F	Mike Havenaar	Vitesse Arn.	26	17	4	10	2	0
F	Ryoichi Maeda	Jubilo Iwata	32	33	10	10	4	1
F	Shinji Okazaki	Mainz	27	73	38	14	8	0
F	Tadanari Lee	Urawa Reds	28	11	2	5	0	0

Italy look the most reliable bet of the three former World Cup winners

Bookmakers consider this group the most difficult puzzle to solve and that assessment looks correct in a section where cases can be made for Italy, Uruguay and England, **writes Mark Langdon**.

The only outcome which looks certain is that Costa Rica will finish bottom and it could even come down to whichever of the nations does the worst against the minnows, with goal difference potentially needed to separate the three teams at the top of the betting.

However, despite the fact there is little between the trio, taking Italy to justify their slight tag of favourites is the shrewdest play.

Neither Italy nor England will enjoy the trip to Manaus for that opening fixture but if there is to be a winner then the Azzurri are the more likely.

They dominated the Euro 2012 quarter-final between the teams even though the Azzurri needed penalties to go through, and the fact Cesare Prandelli's outfit are better in possession means the clash in the Amazon jungle should suit Italy slightly more than England's 100mph approach.

Andrea Pirlo (pictured, talking to Prandelli) still pulls the strings in midfield and Mario Balotelli is capable of match-winning moments, while Italy scored ten goals in five Confederations Cup fixtures last season in matches against Brazil, Japan, Spain and Uruguay.

Uruguay have one of the most lethal forward lines at the World Cup with Luis Suarez in tandem with Edinson Cavani and if they click then Uruguay will be dangerous. However, the balance of the team is not quite right. There is a lack of midfielders capable of supplying the deadly double act and Uruguay often look disjointed.

They are a tricky side to judge and are set to battle it out with England for a spot in the last 16 alongside Italy, who are the most complete team of the three former world champions.

England will be hoping Daniel Sturridge and Wayne Rooney are firing on all cylinders to give them a reasonable chance but they don't have the midfield nous to slow matches down and could easily be running on empty by the time they face Costa Rica last time out in an early start in Belo Horizonte.

Recommendation
Italy

	bet365	Coral	Lads	Power	W Hill
Italy	13-8	13-8	7-5	**7-4**	11-8
Uruguay	13-8	7-4	9-5	**15-8**	7-4
England	9-4	2	**23-10**	21-10	9-4
Costa Rica	50	33	25	33	**66**

	Power
Italy/Uruguay	**4**
Uruguay/Italy	**9-2**
Italy/England	**9-2**
Uruguay/England	**5**
England/Italy	**5**
England/Uruguay	**11-2**
Italy/Costa Rica	**35**
Uruguay/Costa Rica	**45**
England/Costa Rica	**55**
Costa Rica/Italy	**125**
Costa Rica/England	**150**
Costa Rica/Uruguay	**150**

	Lads	Power	W Hill	Power	W Hill
Italy	2-5	**4-9**	1-3	12	**16**
Uruguay	**1-2**	**1-2**	4-9	**10**	**10**
England	**4-6**	4-7	**4-6**	17-2	**12**
Costa Rica	13-2	10	**12**	**1-7**	1-10

All group betting markets are win only

Uruguay v Costa Rica
Saturday June 14, 8pm, Fortaleza

First meeting in the finals but Uruguay beat Costa Rica in 2010 play-off

Six wins for Uruguay and two draws since first meeting in 1990

A 1-1 draw in Montevideo sent Uruguay to South Africa

England v Italy
Saturday June 14, 11pm, Manaus

Baggio and Schillaci scored as Italy won the 1990 third-place match

Eight wins for England, nine for Italy and seven draws since 1933

A 2-1 friendly win for England weeks after Euro 2012 penalty defeat

Uruguay v England
Thursday June 19, 8pm, Sao Paolo

A win for Uruguay in the 1954 quarters, a group-stage draw in 1966

Uruguay have won four, England three, three draws

Peter Crouch and Joe Cole scored in a 2-1 win at Anfield in 2006

Italy v Costa Rica
Friday June 20, 5pm, Recife

No previous World Cup meetings

They've played once and Italy won it

A 1-0 win for Italy ahead of USA 94

Italy v Uruguay
Tuesday June 24, 5pm, Natal

A 0-0 in the group stage in 1970, Italy won 2-0 in the last 16 in 1990

Italy have won two but Uruguay have won three, with four draws

Italy on pens for third at the Confederations Cup after a 2-2 draw

Costa Rica v England
Tuesday June 24, 5pm, Belo Horizonte

No previous World Cup meetings

No previous meetings

Group winners

Round of 16 June 29 Recife
2C Colombia, Greece, Ivory Coast, Japan

Quarter-finals July 5 Salvador
1B Spain, Holland, Chile, Australia
2A Brazil, Croatia, Mexico, Cameroon

Semi-finals July 9 Sao Paulo
1F Argentina, Bosnia-Herzegovina, Iran, Nigeria
2E Switzerland, Ecuador, France, Honduras
1H Belgium, Algeria, Russia, South Korea
2G Germany, Portugal, Ghana, USA

Final July 13 Rio

Group runners-up

Round of 16 June 28 Rio de Janeiro
1C Colombia, Greece, Ivory Coast, Japan

Quarter-finals July 4 Fortaleza
1A Brazil, Croatia, Mexico, Cameroon
2B Spain, Holland, Chile, Australia

Semi-finals July 8 Belo Horizonte
1E Switzerland, Ecuador, France, Honduras
2F Argentina, Bosnia-Herzegovina, Iran, Nigeria
1G Germany, Portugal, Ghana, USA
2H Belgium, Algeria, Russia, South Korea

URUGUAY

Suarez is the only sure thing when it comes to weighing up Uruguay

I f you want a course and distance winner on your side at the World Cup then there is only one team to consider. Unfortunately you have to go back to 1950 and the great upset when Uruguay shocked hosts Brazil to land a stunning victory which is known as the Maracanazo, a word which is now commonly used in reference to a giantkilling. Few teams love a Maracanazo quite like Uruguay and they will revel in the role of underdog once again this summer.

How they qualified
For a long time Uruguay looked in danger of missing out entirely but a strong finish secured a play-off berth, where Jordan were brushed aside 5-0 on aggregate.

At home Uruguay were unbeaten and 20 of their 25 Conmebol goals were scored in Montevideo, with Luis Suarez helping himself to 11 goals in 16 appearances overall.

The defence was not so solid, though, and Uruguay managed only three clean sheets in 16 matches against South American opponents. However, two of those came in convincing home successes over fellow qualifiers Colombia and Chile.

The manager
Oscar Tabarez has worked in a number of countries, including Italy and Spain, but had his biggest success at club level when leading Penarol to the Copa Libertadores in 1987.

The former teacher is in his second spell as Uruguay boss – the first saw him take La Celeste to the last 16 at Italia '90 – but this time Tabarez has produced miracles.

He guided Uruguay to the semi-finals of the 2010 World Cup and the 2013 Confederations Cup after winning the 2011 Copa America in Argentina.

Match winners
The obvious place to start is in the forward

Country factfile

FA founded 1900
www auf.org.uy
Head coach Oscar Tabarez
National league Primera Division
System of government Constitutional republic
Population 3 million
Capital city Montevideo
Currency Peso
Official language Spanish
Strengths
☑ Suarez and Cavani
☑ Excellent recent tournament record
☑ Godin and Muslera mean it's not all about the much-touted attack
Weaknesses
☒ Lack of technical talent in midfield
☒ Influential members of the dressing room are over the hill
☒ Tough group
Base Sete Lagoas
Fixtures
1 Costa Rica, June 14, Fortaleza
2 England, June 19, Sao Paulo
3 Italy, June 24, Natal

department where two of the world's best strikers are housed. Luis Suarez and Edinson Cavani would be worth an absolute fortune on the transfer market and will scare the living daylights out of Group D opponents England, Italy and Costa Rica.

Diego Godin has earned a reputation as one of the most reliable centre-backs in La Liga as Atletico Madrid have risen to prominence, Maxi Pereira can do damage from his position on the right and athletic keeper Fernando Muslera has proven himself in the Champions League with Galatasaray.

Question marks

Is this a World Cup too far for veterans like Diego Forlan, Diego Lugano, Diego Perez and Egidio Arevalo? They will have a combined age of 134 when the tournament begins and Lugano has struggled at West Brom this season, while Forlan had to move to Japan for competitive football.

Tabarez must wish this World Cup had come a couple of years ago, particularly as young hopes like Gaston Ramirez and Sebastian Coates haven't quite trained on and the Olympic team, which also featured Suarez and Cavani, went out at the first hurdle in 2012.

A lack of creativity to link the midfield and attack often means Uruguay defend with everyone bar Suarez and Cavani, who are asked to conjure up a moment of magic.

How to back them

Sometimes you have to admit you just don't know how a team will do. Uruguay have certain negative traits which could see them go out in the first round but they usually come alive in tournaments and have a formidable forward duo who could take them a long way.

Suarez comfortably outscored Cavani in qualifying (11-6) and the Liverpool man is a worthy odds-on favourite to be Uruguay's top scorer in the World Cup.

URUGUAY

World Cup record

Uruguay 1930	**Winners**
Italy 1934	Did not enter
France 1938	Did not enter
Brazil 1950	**Winners**
Switzerland 1954	Fourth place
Sweden 1958	Did not qualify
Chile 1962	Group stage
England 1966	Quarter-finals
Mexico 1970	Fourth place
Germany 1974	Group stage
Argentina 1978	Did not qualify
Spain 1982	Did not qualify
Mexico 1986	Round of 16
Italy 1990	Round of 16
USA 1994	Did not qualify
France 1998	Did not qualify
Korea/Japan 2002	Group stage
Germany 2006	Did not qualify
South Africa 2010	Fourth place

Continental titles

Copa America (1916, 1917, 1920, 1923, 1924, 1926, 1935, 1942, 1956, 1959, 1967, 1983, 1987, 1995, 2011)

Legendary player

The honour of captaining the first ever World Cup winning team went to **Jose Nasazzi**. He had already won Gold at the 1924 and 1928 Olympics and, with Uruguay trailing 2-1 to Argentina at the half-time in the final, Nasazzi was able to rally his team-mates in the break. Uruguay won 4-2 and he got to lift the trophy.

Did you know?

Uruguay's fourth place in 2010 equalled their best performance at the finals since they last won the trophy in Brazil in 1950

Edinson Cavani enjoys the moment after scoring what turned out to be the winner in Uruguay's 3-2 victory over Argentina

GROUP D

How they qualified

Final group	P	W	D	L	F	A	GD	Pts
Argentina	16	9	5	2	35	15	20	32
Colombia	16	9	3	4	27	13	14	30
Chile	16	9	1	6	29	25	4	28
Ecuador	16	7	4	5	20	16	4	25
Uruguay	**16**	**7**	**4**	**5**	**25**	**25**	**0**	**25**
Venezuela	16	5	5	6	14	20	-6	20
Peru	16	4	3	9	17	26	-9	15
Bolivia	16	2	6	8	17	30	-13	12
Paraguay	16	3	3	10	17	31	-14	12

Uruguay ....(3) 4-2 (1).............. Bolivia
Uruguay: Suarez (4) Lugano (26, 72) Cavani (35) Bolivia: Cardozo (18) Martins (pen 88)

Paraguay ....(0) 1-1 (0)............Uruguay
Paraguay: Ortiz (90) Uruguay: Forlan (68)

Uruguay ....(2) 4-0 (0).................Chile
Uruguay: Suarez (42, 45, 68, 74)

Uruguay ....(1) 1-1 (0)......... Venezuela
Uruguay: Forlan (38) Venezuela: Rondon (85)

Uruguay ....(2) 4-2 (1)................. Peru
Uruguay: Suarez (15) Pereira (30) Rodriguez (63) Eguren (90) Peru: Godin (40 og) Guerrero (48)

Colombia.........(2) 4-0 (0)............ Uruguay
Colombia: Falcao (2) Gutierrez (47, 52) Zuniga (90)

Uruguay ....(0) 1-1 (1).............Ecuador
Uruguay: Cavani (67) Ecuador: Caicedo (pen 8)

Argentina ....(0) 3-0 (0)............ Uruguay
Argentina: Messi (66, 80) Aguero (75)

Bolivia ....(2) 4-1 (0)............ Uruguay
Bolivia: Saucedo (5, 51, 55) Mojica (26) Uruguay: Suarez (80)

Uruguay ....(0) 1-1 (0)........... Paraguay
Uruguay: Suarez (82) Paraguay: Benitez (86)

Chile ....(1) 2-0 (0)............ Uruguay
Chile: Paredes (10) Vargas (78)

Venezuela........(0) 0-1 (1)............ Uruguay
Uruguay: Cavani (28)

Peru.................(0) 1-2 (1)............ Uruguay
Peru: Farfan (84) Uruguay: Suarez (pen 43, 67)

Uruguay ....(0) 2-0 (0).......... Colombia
Uruguay: Cavani (77) Stuani (81)

Ecuador...........(1) 1-0 (0)............ Uruguay
Ecuador: Montero (30)

Uruguay ....(2) 3-2 (2)..........Argentina
Uruguay: Rodriguez (6) Suarez (pen 34) Cavani (49) Argentina: Rodriguez (15, 41)

Intercontinental play-off

Jordan ....(0) 0-5 (2)............ Uruguay
Uruguay: Pereira (22) Stuani (42) Lodeiro (70) Rodriguez (75) Cavani (90)

Uruguay ....(0) 0-0 (0)...............Jordan

Full qualifying results and tables on pages 234-256

URUGUAY

Players used in qualifying		Career			Qualifying		
Pos	**Club**	**Age**	**P**	**G**	**P**	**G**	**Y/R**
G Fernando Muslera	Galatasaray	27	60	0	16	0	0
G Martin Silva	Vasco da Gama	31	4	0	2	0	0
D Alejandro Silva	Lanus	24	2	0	2	0	1
D Alvaro Pereira	Sao Paulo	28	55	6	12	0	3
D Andres Scotti	Nacional	38	40	1	3	0	0
D Diego Godin	Atl Madrid	28	77	3	16	0	5
D Diego Lugano	West Brom	33	92	9	15	2	7
D Jorge Fucile	Porto	29	41	0	5	0	0
D Jose Gimenez	Atl Madrid	19	4	0	3	0	0
D Martin Caceres	Juventus	26	55	1	10	0	3
D Matias Aguirregaray	Estudiantes	24	4	0	1	0	1
D Mauricio Victorino	Palmeiras	31	21	0	2	0	0
D Maxi Pereira	Benfica	29	88	3	16	2	5
D Sebastian Coates	Liverpool	23	13	0	2	0	0
M Alvaro Fernandez	National	28	12	0	1	0	0
M Alvaro Gonzalez	Lazio	29	41	2	12	0	1
M Cristian Rodriguez	Atl Madrid	28	70	8	17	3	1
M Diego Perez	Bologna	33	88	2	10	0	3
M Egidio Arevalo Rios	Morelia	32	53	0	17	0	3
M Gaston Ramirez	Southampton	23	27	0	12	0	1
M Nicolas Lodeiro	Botafogo	25	25	3	6	1	0
M Sebastian Eguren	Palmeiras	33	54	7	4	1	1
M Walter Gargano	Parma	29	60	1	8	0	1
F Abel Hernandez	Palermo	23	11	7	1	0	0
F Christian Stuani	Espanyol	27	8	2	5	2	1
F Diego Forlan	Cerezo Osaka	34	108	36	15	2	0
F Edinson Cavani	Paris St-G.	27	60	20	18	6	1
F Luis Suarez	Liverpool	27	77	39	16	11	4
F Sebastian Abreu	Rosario Central	37	69	25	2	0	0

What happens if ...

Uruguay score first

Uruguay win	13	45%
Draw	5	17%
Uruguay lose	0	0%

29 games since 2010 World Cup

WIN 45%

Opponents score first

Uruguay win	0	0%
Draw	3	10%
Uruguay lose	7	24%

LOSE 24%

Goal times

For		Against
4	0-9	3
3	10-18	4
5	19-27	4
4	28-36	2
8	37-45	4
5	46-54	4
4	55-63	1
7	64-72	2
6	73-81	4
7	82-90	7

Uruguay		Opponents	
24	45% 1st half	17	49%
29	54% 2nd half	18	51%

29 games since 2010 World Cup

Correct scores

	Friendly	Comp
1-0	2	2
2-0	1	2
2-1	0	2
3-0	1	1
3-1	1	0
3-2	2	1
4-0	1	1
4-1	0	0
4-2	1	2
4-3	0	0
0-0	1	1
1-1	4	7
2-2	0	1
3-3	0	0
4-4	0	0
0-1	0	1
0-2	2	1
1-2	1	2
0-3	0	1
1-3	1	0
2-3	0	0
0-4	0	1
1-4	0	1
2-4	0	0
3-4	0	0
Other	1	2

48 games since 2010 World Cup

Bookings

Yellow cards	42
Red cards	0
Avg make-up	23.3

In 2014 World Cup qualifying

Top scorers

	Total	First	%	Anytime	%
L Suarez	11	5	45	7	44
E Cavani	6	2	33	6	33
C Rodriguez	3	1	33	3	18
D Forlan	2	2	100	2	13
D Lugano	2	0	0	1	7
M Pereira	2	1	50	2	13
C Stuani	2	0	0	2	40

In World Cup 2014 qualification

Diego Forlan was awarded the Golden Ball in South Africa

Unders & overs

1.5 goals		2.5 goals		3.5 goals		4.5 goals	
Under	Over	Under	Over	Under	Over	Under	Over
14%	86%	48%	52%	69%	31%	79%	21%

29 games since 2010 World Cup

Half-time/Full-time

WIN 45%

Win/Win	9	31%
Draw/Win	4	14%
Lose/Win	0	0%
Win/Draw	1	3%
Draw/Draw	6	21%
Lose/Draw	2	7%
Win/Lose	0	0%
Draw/Lose	1	3%
Lose/Lose	6	21%

29 games since 2010 World Cup

Penalty shootouts

Won	5	56%
Lost	4	44%

All-time record

Clean sheets

Uruguay	9	31%
Opponents	5	17%

29 games since 2010 World Cup

COSTA RICA

Even a point looks unlikely for makeweights in one of the toughest sections

T hey were never going to win the World Cup and were always going to struggle to qualify so Costa Rica have embraced their difficult draw which sees them tackle three former world champions. The minnows are obviously going to find life tough against Italy, England and Uruguay and while Los Ticos' first aim is to avoid a repeat of the pointless 2006 World Cup campaign, even that looks unlikely in such elite company.

GROUP D

How they qualified
Even the higher seeds still have to play 16 Concacaf matches to reach the World Cup and Costa Rica initially finished second to Mexico to make it through to the Hex.

Costa Rica again finished second, this time to USA and there was a huge contrast in their home and away results. They won all five games in front of their own fans but gained only three points (all draws) on the road with a 1-0 defeat in Denver coming in controversial circumstances when the game was played in horrendous wintery conditions.

The manager
Colombian Jorge Luis Pinto is a much-travelled boss having worked in a number of South American countries. He has previously managed Costa Rica in 2004-05 and was also in charge of Colombia for their failed bid to qualify for the 2010 World Cup.

Pinto bossed Costa Rica in last year's Gold Cup when they were knocked out by Honduras in the last eight but he decided to take a squad lacking many of their star men and it will be a stronger pool of players this time around.

Match winners
Alvaro Saborio missed a penalty in a shootout defeat for Real Salt Lake in the 2013 MLS

Country factfile

FA founded 1921
www fedefutbolcr.com
Head coach Jorge Luis Pinto
National league Primera Division
System of government Democratic republic
Population 5 million
Capital city San Jose
Currency Colon
Official language Spanish

Strengths
☑ Striking department looks healthy

Weaknesses
☒ Lack of players being used at the highest level
☒ Oviedo will be a massive loss if he fails to regain fitness in time
☒ Tough group against three strong sides

Base Santos

Fixtures
1 Uruguay, June 14, Fortaleza
2 Italy, June 20, Recife
3 England, June 24, Belo Horizonte

Alvaro Saborio tries his luck against Belize in the Concacaf Gold Cup

final but he had earlier scored in the match and has been a regular source of goals in America, hitting double figures in each of his four full campaigns.

Arsenal's Joel Campbell (currently on loan at Olympiakos) has potential and Bryan Ruiz, despite an unhappy spell at Fulham, remains influential for Costa Rica in attacking positions. However, whether all three will play remains to be seen, with Pinto often keen to pack the defence.

That tactic certainly worked in qualifying as Costa Rica conceded only four goals in their last eight matches, with Los Ticos commended for their tight rearguard unit.

Question marks

Bryan Oviedo's recovery from a broken leg sustained in an FA Cup tie against Stevenage is ahead of schedule and, as we go to press, it seems that he might be fit for Costa Rica's opener against England. However, missing half the season with a serious injury is not ideal preparation for one of Costa Rica's most important players. The fact they relied so heavily on their home form is a concern and for this level of competition there is a general lack of quality all over the pitch except for the forward department.

How to back them

Bookmakers are certain Costa Rica will claim the Group D wooden spoon. Their most likely chance of points comes in the final match against England but even then they are a 13-2 shot to land a stunning victory.

England, Italy and Uruguay could be involved in a tight battle for the two qualifying spots which means all three will target Costa Rica as the must-win encounter.

Los Ticos could be on the end of some heavy beatings so taking the minnows to return home pointless, just as they did in 2006, is the obvious call.

COSTA RICA

GROUP D

World Cup record

Uruguay 1930	Did not enter
Italy 1934	Did not enter
France 1938	Did not enter
Brazil 1950	Did not enter
Switzerland 1954	Did not enter
Sweden 1958	Did not qualify
Chile 1962	Did not qualify
England 1966	Did not qualify
Mexico 1970	Did not qualify
Germany 1974	Did not qualify
Argentina 1978	Did not qualify
Spain 1982	Did not qualify
Mexico 1986	Did not qualify
Italy 1990	Round of 16
USA 1994	Did not qualify
France 1998	Did not qualify
Korea/Japan 2002	Group stage
Germany 2006	Group stage
South Africa 2010	Did not qualify

Continental titles

CONCACAF Championship (1963, 1969)

Legendary player

Juan Cayasso only scored once at Italia 90, but his cool finish after a fine passing move earned a 1-0 win over Scotland in Costa Rica's first ever game at the finals and paved the way for the Ticos' qualification for the last 16.

Did you know?

Top scorer in qualifying, Alvaro Saborio, scored two goals in English football while on loan at Bristol City in 2009-10

How they qualified

Round 3

Costa Rica ....(2) 2-2 (1)........ El Salvador
Costa Rica: Saborio (10) Campbell (16) El Salvador: Gutierrez (24) Romero (54)

Guyana............(0) 0-4 (2)........ Costa Rica
Costa Rica: Saborio (19, 26, 52) Campbell (78)

Costa Rica ....(0) 0-2 (1).............. Mexico
Mexico: Salcido (43) Zavala (52)

Mexico ....(0) 1-0 (0)......... Costa Rica
Mexico: Hernandez (61)

El Salvador ......(0) 0-1 (1)......... Costa Rica
Costa Rica: Cubero (31)

Costa Rica ....(2) 7-0 (0)............. Guyana
Costa Rica: Brenes (10, 48) Gamboa (14) Saborio (pen 51, 77) Bolanos (61) Borges (70)

Final group	P	W	D	L	F	A	GD	Pts
USA	10	7	1	2	15	8	7	22
Costa Rica	**10**	**5**	**3**	**2**	**13**	**7**	**6**	**18**
Honduras	10	4	3	3	13	12	1	15
Mexico	10	2	5	3	7	9	-2	11
Panama	10	1	5	4	10	14	-4	8
Jamaica	10	0	5	5	5	13	-8	5

Panama ....(2) 2-2 (1)......... Costa Rica
Panama: Henriquez (15) Torres (26) Costa Rica: Saborio (39) Ruiz (84)

USA.................(1) 1-0 (0)......... Costa Rica
USA: Dempsey (16)

Costa Rica ....(1) 2-0 (0).............Jamaica
Costa Rica: Umana (22) Calvo (82)

Costa Rica ....(1) 1-0 (0).......... Honduras
Costa Rica: Miller (25)

Mexico ....(0) 0-0 (0)......... Costa Rica
Costa Rica ....(0) 2-0 (0).............Panama

Costa Rica: Ruiz (49) Borges (52)

Costa Rica ....(2) 3-1 (1)...................USA
Costa Rica: Acosta (3) Borges (10) Campbell (76) USA: Dempsey (pen 43)

Jamaica ....(0) 1-1 (0)......... Costa Rica
Jamaica: Anderson (90) Costa Rica: Brenes (74)

Honduras ....(0) 1-0 (0)......... Costa Rica
Honduras: Bengtson (65)

Costa Rica ....(1) 2-1 (1).............. Mexico
Costa Rica: Ruiz (25) Saborio (64) Mexico: Peralta (29)

Full qualifying results and tables on pages 234-256

Unders & overs

<1.5	>1.5	<2.5	>2.5	<3.5	>3.5	<4.5	>4.5
36%	64%	69%	31%	81%	19%	92%	8%

36 competitive games since 2010 World Cup

Half-time/Full-time

W/W	9	25%	W/D	3	8%	W/L	0	0%
D/W	8	22%	D/D	4	11%	D/L	4	11%
L/W	0	0%	L/D	2	6%	L/L	6	17%

36 competitive games since 2010 World Cup

Bookings

Yellow cards	33
Red cards	0
Avg make-up	20.6

In 2014 World Cup qualifying

Penalty shootouts

Won	0	0%
Lost	2	100%

All-time record

What happens if ...

Costa Rica score first			Their opponents score first		
Costa Rica win	17	47%	Costa Rica win	0	0%
Draw	5	14%	Draw	3	8%
Costa Rica lose	0	0%	Costa Rica lose	10	28%

36 competitive games since 2010 World Cup

Top scorers

	Total	First	%	Anytime	%
A Saborio	8	2	25	5	33
R Brenes	3	2	66	2	25
C Borges	3	0	0	3	23
B Ruiz	3	2	66	3	27
J Campbell	3	0	0	3	20

In World Cup 2014 qualification

Goal times

For			Against
3		0-9	1
6		10-18	3
5		19-27	4
1		28-36	1
4		37-45	6
10		46-54	6
4		55-63	1
7		64-72	2
7		73-81	1
5		82-90	4

Costa Rica		Opponents
19 36%	1st half	15 51%
33 63%	2nd half	14 48%

36 games since 2010 World Cup

Correct scores

	Friendly	Comp
1-0	3	6
2-0	1	5
2-1	2	1
3-0	0	1
3-1	0	1
3-2	1	0
4-0	1	1
4-1	0	0
4-2	0	0
4-3	0	0
0-0	3	1
1-1	3	6
2-2	4	2
3-3	0	0
4-4	0	0
0-1	6	6
0-2	4	1
1-2	0	1
0-3	0	1
1-3	0	0
2-3	0	0
0-4	2	0
1-4	0	1
2-4	0	0
3-4	0	0
Other	0	2

66 games since
2010 World Cup

Clean sheets

Costa Rica 16	44%
Opp	9	25%

36 competitive games
since 2010 World Cup

Players used in qualifying

Pos		Club	Age	Career		Qualifying		
				P	G	P	G	Y/R
G	Keylor Navas	Levante	27	51	0	14	0	3
G	Patrick Pemberton	Alajuelense	31	20	0	2	0	0
D	Bismark Acosta	IK Start	27	5	0	2	0	0
D	Carlos Johnson	Cartagines	29	14	0	1	0	0
D	Christopher Meneses	Norrkoping	23	15	0	2	0	0
D	Cristian Gamboa	Rosenborg	24	24	1	12	1	0
D	Gabriel Badilla	Saprissa	29	25	1	1	0	1
D	Michael Umana	Saprissa	31	80	1	12	1	5
D	Giancarlo Gonzalez	Columbus Crew	26	33	2	14	0	3
D	Heiner Mora	Saprissa	29	21	1	1	0	0
D	Jhonny Acosta	Alajuelense	30	26	1	7	1	2
D	Jose Salvatierra	Alajuelense	24	25	0	5	0	1
D	Juan Madrigal	Cartagines	26	7	0	1	0	0
D	Kendall Waston	Saprissa	26	2	0	1	0	0
D	Pedro Leal	Carmelita	25	11	0	1	0	0
D	Porfirio Lopez	Alajuelense	28	6	0	1	0	0
D	Junior Diaz	Mainz	30	59	1	4	0	0
D	Roy Miller	NY Red Bulls	29	46	1	7	1	2
M	Allen Guevara	Alajuelense	24	14	0	1	0	0
M	Ariel Rodriguez	Alajuelense	27	15	0	5	0	3
M	Celso Borges	AIK Solna	25	61	14	13	3	1
M	Rodney Wallace	Portland Timbers	25	16	3	3	0	0
M	Bryan Oviedo	Everton	24	26	1	9	0	2
M	Christian Bolanos	FC Copenhagen	29	53	2	12	1	2
M	Diego Calvo	Valerenga	21	9	1	6	1	0
M	Jose Cubero	Herediano	27	33	2	9	1	1
M	Mauricio Castillo	Saprissa	26	8	1	2	0	0
M	Michael Barrantes	Aalesund	30	51	4	10	0	1
M	Oscar Rojas	Altamira	34	28	1	3	0	1
M	Osvaldo Rodriguez	Alajuelense	23	11	0	1	0	0
M	Randall Azofeifa	Erciyesspor	29	35	1	1	0	0
M	Yeltsin Tejeda	Saprissa	21	21	0	7	0	0
F	Alvaro Saborio	Real Salt Lake	32	94	32	15	8	1
F	Joel Campbell	Olympiakos	21	31	9	15	3	1
F	Bryan Ruiz	PSV Eindhoven	28	61	12	11	3	1
F	Jairo Arrieta	Columbus Crew	30	16	4	1	0	0
F	Kenny Cunningham	Wellington	28	13	1	2	0	0
F	Olman Vargas	Herediano	28	2	1	1	0	0
F	Randall Brenes	Cartagines	30	38	8	8	3	0
F	Victor Nunez	Herediano	33	27	6	1	0	0

ENGLAND

Improving Sturridge gives Three Lions hope but the draw has not been kind

G one are the days when patriotic punters used to pile on England and in these times of disdain bookmakers are having to push the boat out to attract business on the Three Lions, who have never been a bigger price to win the World Cup. The pessimism seems well placed – with only one semi-final appearance since lifting the Jules Rimet Trophy in 1966, they face a difficult task just to get out of a tough group.

How they qualified

The final statistics don't highlight how tricky things became for England, who finished in top spot, unbeaten and with only four goals conceded. However, it was one of the softer sections in the Uefa region and Roy Hodgson's side drew twice with Ukraine and also against Poland and Montenegro.

In fairness, England were hit by injuries throughout the qualification process and seven-goal top goalscorer Wayne Rooney missed both matches against Ukraine. When the pressure was on, Hodgson's men responded well with convincing home performances against Poland and Montenegro to seal a direct path to Brazil.

However, the euphoria was short lived and November friendly defeats at Wembley against a weakened Chile team and a German B side showed England's limitations.

The manager

Unlike most English managers, Hodgson was happy to go abroad and as well as a whole host of club jobs, he has also coached Switzerland, UAE and Finland. He worked wonders with Fulham, taking them to the Europa League final, and stabilised West Brom but Hodgson also oversaw horrible spells at Blackburn and Liverpool.

Hodgson is a safety-first manager and will make sure England are difficult to beat. That

Country factfile

FA founded 1863
www thefa.com
Head coach Roy Hodgson
National league Premier League
System of government Constitutional monarchy
Population 56 million
Capital city London
Currency Pound
Official language English

Strengths

☑ Sturridge and Rooney give England hope in the attacking third
☑ Last first-stage exit was in 1958

Weaknesses

☒ Hot and humid conditions won't suit direct style of play
☒ Ageing midfield lacks defensive balance
☒ Have lost six of their seven penalty shootouts

Base Rio
Fixtures
1 Italy, June 14, Manaus
2 Uruguay, June 19, Sao Paulo
3 Costa Rica, June 24, Belo Horizonte

was the story of Euro 2012, when the Three Lions finished unbeaten but went out on penalties to Italy at the quarter-final stage.

Match winners

Rooney is the obvious one but the emergence of Daniel Sturridge at Liverpool could take England's attacking play up a notch. Sturridge has always been blessed with tremendous ability but he has found a new level of consistency on Merseyside this campaign.

Question marks

England have always had trouble keeping possession in major tournaments. Midfielders Steven Gerrard and Frank Lampard will have a combined age of 70 come the World Cup final, while young pretender Jack Wilshere has had his career hit by persistent injury problems – he sustained a hairline fracture in his left foot during Engand's March friendly against Denmark.

Rooney has never scored a goal at a World Cup finals, John Terry, arguably their best defender, has retired from international football and speedster Theo Walcott misses out with an anterior cruciate ligament injury.

How to back them

All the early money has been for England to bite the dust and those who took the 6-4 about them missing out on the knockout rounds are on to a good bet.

However, Hodgson's side will be hopeful of competing against Italy and Uruguay as well as beating minnows Costa Rica. The opening contest in the Amazon jungle against Italy will be pivotal. Both nations are unlikely to enjoy the conditions and that match could well end in a draw, just like at Euro 2012. Another stalemate with Uruguay would not be a massive surprise although, like the Italy game, it is a match England are more likely to lose than win before the so-called easy one with Costa Rica. Splitting stakes on the Three Lions collecting four and five points could prove profitable.

Given Rooney's World Cup record he looks one to avoid in the top England goalscorer betting with preference for the improving Sturridge.

ENGLAND

GROUP D

World Cup record

Uruguay 1930	Did not enter
Italy 1934	Did not enter
France 1938	Did not enter
Brazil 1950	Group stage
Switzerland 1954	Quarter-finals
Sweden 1958	Group stage
Chile 1962	Quarter-finals
England 1966	**Winners**
Mexico 1970	Quarter-finals
Germany 1974	Did not qualify
Argentina 1978	Did not qualify
Spain 1982	Second round
Mexico 1986	Quarter-finals
Italy 1990	Fourth place
USA 1994	Did not qualify
France 1998	Round of 16
Korea/Japan 2002	Quarter-finals
Germany 2006	Quarter-finals
South Africa 2010	Round of 16

Continental titles

None

Legendary player

With a World Cup winners' medal and a record 49 goals in 106 internationals, Bobby Charlton is a strong contender but both Pele and Franz Beckenbauer described **Bobby Moore**, England's captain in 1966, as the greatest defender they had ever faced. He finished his playing career with 108 caps.

Did you know?

Wayne Rooney has only scored one goal at a tournament finals since his four at Euro 2004

ENGLAND

How they qualified

Final group	P	W	D	L	F	A	GD	Pts
England	**10**	**6**	**4**	**0**	**31**	**4**	**27**	**22**
Ukraine	10	6	3	1	28	4	24	21
Montenegro	10	4	3	3	18	17	1	15
Poland	10	3	4	3	18	12	6	13
Moldova	10	3	2	5	12	17	-5	11
San Marino	10	0	0	10	1	54	-53	0

Moldova ....(0) 0-5 (3)............ England
England: Lampard (pen 3, 29) Defoe (32) Milner (74) Baines (83)

England............(0) 1-1 (1)............. Ukraine
England: Lampard (pen 87) Ukraine: Konoplyanka (38)

England ....(2) 5-0 (0)....... San Marino
England: Rooney (pen 35, 70) Welbeck (37, 72) Oxlade-Chamberla (77)

Poland ....(0) 1-1 (1)............ England
Poland: Glik (70) England: Rooney (31)

San Marino......(0) 0-8 (5)............ England
England: Della Valle (12 og) Oxlade-Chamberla (29) Defoe (35, 77) Young (39) Lampard (42) Rooney (54) Sturridge (70)

Montenegro ....(0) 1-1 (1)............ England
Montenegro: Damjanovic (76) England: Rooney (6)

England ....(3) 4-0 (0)............Moldova
England: Gerrard (12) Lambert (26) Welbeck (45, 50)

Ukraine............(0) 0-0 (0)............ England

England ....(0) 4-1 (0)......Montenegro
England: Rooney (48) Boskovic (62 og) Townsend (78) Sturridge (pen 90) Montenegro: Damjanovic (71)

England ....(1) 2-0 (0)...............Poland
England: Rooney (41) Gerrard (88)

Full qualifying results and tables on pages 234-256

ENGLAND

Top scorers

	Total	First	%	Anytime	%
W Rooney	7	5	71	6	100
F Lampard	4	1	25	3	42
D Welbeck	4	0	0	2	25
J Defoe	3	0	0	2	50
S Gerrard	2	1	50	2	25
D Sturridge	2	0	0	2	50
A O-Chamberlain	2	0	0	2	40

In World Cup 2014 qualification

Players used in qualifying

Pos		Club	Age	Career P	G	Qualifying P	G	Y/R
G	Joe Hart	Man City	26	39	0	10	0	0
D	Ashley Cole	Chelsea	33	107	0	4	0	1
D	Chris Smalling	Man Utd	24	10	0	3	0	0
D	Gary Cahill	Chelsea	28	22	2	5	0	0
D	Glen Johnson	Liverpool	29	50	1	4	0	3
D	John Terry	Chelsea	33	78	6	1	0	0
D	Joleon Lescott	Man City	31	26	1	5	0	1
D	Kyle Walker	Tottenham	23	10	0	5	0	2
D	Leighton Baines	Everton	29	22	1	7	1	0
D	Phil Jagielka	Everton	31	24	1	7	0	0
D	Ryan Bertrand	Chelsea	24	2	0	1	0	0
M	Aaron Lennon	Tottenham	26	21	0	1	0	0
M	Alex O-Chamberlain	Arsenal	20	14	3	5	2	0
M	Andros Townsend	Tottenham	22	5	1	2	1	0
M	Ashley Young	Man Utd	28	30	7	3	1	0
M	Frank Lampard	Chelsea	35	103	29	7	4	1
M	Jack Wilshere	Arsenal	22	15	0	4	0	0
M	James Milner	Man City	28	45	1	8	1	1
M	Jonjo Shelvey	Swansea	21	1	0	1	0	0
M	Leon Osman	Everton	32	2	0	1	0	0
M	Michael Carrick	Man Utd	32	31	0	6	0	0
M	Ross Barkley	Everton	20	3	0	1	0	0
M	Scott Parker	Fulham	33	18	0	1	0	0
M	Steven Gerrard	Liverpool	33	109	21	8	2	1/1
M	Theo Walcott	Arsenal	25	36	5	4	0	0
M	Tom Cleverley	Man Utd	24	13	0	7	0	0
F	Andy Carroll	West Ham	25	9	2	1	0	0
F	Daniel Sturridge	Liverpool	24	10	3	4	2	0
F	Danny Welbeck	Man Utd	23	21	8	8	4	2
F	Jermain Defoe	Toronto FC	31	55	19	4	3	1
F	Rickie Lambert	Southampton	32	4	2	2	1	0
F	Wayne Rooney	Man Utd	28	89	38	6	7	1

What happens if ...

England score first

England win	13	59%
Draw	4	18%
England lose	0	0%

22 games since 2010 World Cup

Opponents score first

England win	0	0%
Draw	2	9%
England lose	0	0%

GROUP D

Goal times

For			Against
4		0-9	0
6		10-18	0
3		19-27	0
9		28-36	2
7		37-45	3
5		46-54	1
2		55-63	1
5		64-72	3
5		73-81	1
7		82-90	1

England			Opponents	
29	55%	1st half	5	42%
24	45%	2nd half	7	58%

22 games since 2010 World Cup

Correct scores

	Friendly	Comp
1-0	5	2
2-0	0	2
2-1	4	0
3-0	0	1
3-1	0	1
3-2	1	1
4-0	0	2
4-1	0	1
4-2	0	0
4-3	0	0
0-0	0	3
1-1	2	4
2-2	1	2
3-3	0	0
4-4	0	0
0-1	1	0
0-2	1	0
1-2	1	0
0-3	0	0
1-3	0	0
2-3	1	0
0-4	0	0
1-4	0	0
2-4	1	0
3-4	0	0
Other	0	3

40 games since 2010 World Cup

Bookings

Yellow cards	14
Red cards	1
Avg make-up	16.5

In 2014 World Cup qualifying

Get the hankies ready, we all know how this is going to end

Unders & overs

1.5 goals		2.5 goals		3.5 goals		4.5 goals	
Under	Over	Under	Over	Under	Over	Under	Over
23%	77%	50%	50%	55%	45%	77%	23%

22 games since 2010 World Cup

Half-time/Full-time

Win/Win	11	50%
Draw/Win	2	9%
Lose/Win	0	0%
Win/Draw	3	14%
Draw/Draw	4	18%
Lose/Draw	2	9%
Win/Lose	0	0%
Draw/Lose	0	0%
Lose/Lose	0	0%

WIN 59%

22 games since 2010 World Cup

Penalty shootouts

Won	1	14%
Lost	6	86%

All-time record

Clean sheets

England	13	59%
Opponents	3	14%

22 games since 2010 World Cup

ITALY

If Balotelli hits the heights then the Azzurri can be contenders for the trophy

Tournament teams don't come much better than Italy, who have won a World Cup and reached two European Championship finals since the turn of the century. But Fifa's complicated ranking system somehow meant they were not among the top seeds in Brazil and the Azzurri paid the price with a tough assignment that sees them tackle England and Uruguay for a spot in the knockout phase.

GROUP D

How they qualified
Traditionally Italy are slow out of the traps but they qualified with the minimum of fuss this time, finishing unbeaten, six points clear of Denmark. The Azzurri also scored in every match bar one, a goalless stalemate away to Czech Republic when Mario Balotelli was sent off on 72 minutes.

The Confederations Cup came halfway through the qualifying process and Italy made the semi-finals before suffering elimination at the hands of Spain on penalties. They dominated the match but had to settle for third place, with four of their five matches seeing both teams scoring.

The manager
Cesare Prandelli is a gentleman and a total class act. He's an admirer of possession-based football which has taken the Azzurri a long way from the tired catenaccio stereotype, and few men have done more to restore the reputation of Italian football following match-fixing scandals.

The former Lecce, Verona, Venezia, Parma, Roma and Fiorentina boss has agreed a deal to stay on for a further two years and has an excellent relationship with his players, even difficult characters such as Balotelli.

Prandelli said of Italy's chances: "I would say the favourites are Brazil, Argentina, Spain and Germany. Then after that it's

Country factfile

FA founded 1898
www figc.it
Head coach Cesare Prandelli
National league Serie A
System of government Republic
Population 62 million
Capital city Rome
Currency Euro
Official language Italian

Strengths
☑ Tremendous tournament pedigree
☑ Huge experience all over the squad
☑ Plenty of match winners with Balotelli the pick of the bunch

Weaknesses
☒ Tough group and early starts in Recife and Natal as well as trip to Manaus
☒ Could Pirlo and Buffon be a year or two too old?

Base Mangaratiba

Fixtures
1 England, June 14, Manaus
2 Costa Rica, June 20, Recife
3 Uruguay, June 24, Natal

Cesare Prandelli knows how to get the best out of his players

us, Uruguay, England, Holland, Belgium, Colombia and Japan."

Match winners

Balotelli came alive at Euro 2012, scoring both goals in the devastating semi-final success over Germany, and he also notched in two Confederations Cup matches last summer before injury ruled him out of the semi-finals.

Playmaker Andrea Pirlo makes the team tick despite the fact he will turn 35 in May and his Juventus team-mate Gigi Buffon is still capable of pulling off miracle saves at the age of 36.

The defence is based around Juve's excellent trio of Leonardo Bonucci, Andrea Barzagli and Giorgio Chiellini and it will be interesting to see whether Prandelli is brave enough to trust precocious young talents such as Marco Verratti, Lorenzo Insigne and Ciro Immobile.

Question marks

Giuseppe Rossi was flying for Fiorentina and looked nailed on to be Balotelli's partner but another serious injury has left him in a race to be fit. Meanwhile, Balotelli's form has been up and down for Milan, who have struggled in Serie A this season.

Pirlo and Buffon could be considered on the downgrade and the defence conceded ten goals in five Confederations Cup matches.

How to back them

Italy have long been on my radar as a team for the shortlist and they could go well at a nice price despite a group that means a first-round exit, just like in 2010, is a possiblity.

The Azzurri will need Balotelli to hit a hot streak like the one he found at the last European Championship and, if 2006 World Cup winners Pirlo, Buffon, Daniele De Rossi and Barzagli roll back the years, then a repeat of that triumph is possible.

ITALY

GROUP D

World Cup record

Uruguay 1930	Did not enter
Italy 1934	**Winners**
France 1938	**Winners**
Brazil 1950	Group stage
Switzerland 1954	Group stage
Sweden 1958	Did not qualify
Chile 1962	Group stage
England 1966	Group stage
Mexico 1970	Runners-up
Germany 1974	Group stage
Argentina 1978	Fourth place
Spain 1982	**Winners**
Mexico 1986	Round of 16
Italy 1990	Third place
USA 1994	Runners-up
France 1998	Quarter-finals
Korea/Japan 2002	Round of 16
Germany 2006	**Winners**
South Africa 2010	Group stage

Continental titles

European Championships (1968)

Legendary player

There are many candidates – Giuseppe Meazza, Paolo Maldini, Roberto Baggio, to name but three – but **Paolo Rossi** dominated the 1982 World Cup and fired the Azzurri to a first success since 1938. His six goals all came at the business end of the competition, and included a hat-trick against a great Brazil side, both goals in Italy's semi-final victory over Poland and another in the final itself.

Did you know?

Italy have drawn more games at the World Cup finals (21) than any nation since their first appearance in 1934, including four of their last five matches in 90 minutes

Andrea Pirlo in action against Denmark

How they qualified

Final group	P	W	D	L	F	A	GD	Pts
Italy	**10**	**6**	**4**	**0**	**19**	**9**	**10**	**22**
Denmark	10	4	4	2	17	12	5	16
Czech Rep	10	4	3	3	13	9	4	15
Bulgaria	10	3	4	3	14	9	5	13
Armenia	10	4	1	5	12	13	-1	13
Malta	10	1	0	9	5	28	-23	3

Bulgaria...........(1) 2-2 (2)...................Italy
Bulgaria: Manolev (30) Milanov (66) Italy: Osvaldo (36, 40)

Italy ....(1) 2-0 (0)................ Malta
Italy: Destro (5) Peluso (90)

Armenia ....(1) 1-3 (1)...................Italy
Armenia: Mkhitaryan (27) Italy: Pirlo (pen 11) De Rossi (64) Osvaldo (82)

Italy ....(2) 3-1 (1)........... Denmark
Italy: Montolivo (33) De Rossi (37) Balotelli (54) Denmark: Kvist (45)

Malta...............(0) 0-2 (2)...................Italy
Italy: Balotelli (pen 8, 45)

Czech Rep ....(0) 0-0 (0)...................Italy

Italy ....(1) 1-0 (0).............Bulgaria
Italy: Gilardino (38)

Italy ....(0) 2-1 (1)........ Czech Rep
Italy: Chiellini (51) Balotelli (pen 54) Czech Rep: Kozak (19)

Denmark ....(1) 2-2 (1)...................Italy
Denmark: Bendtner (45, 79) Italy: Osvaldo (28) Aquilani (90)

Italy ....(1) 2-2 (1)........... Armenia
Italy: Florenzi (24) Balotelli (76) Armenia: Movsisyan (5) Mkhitaryan (70)

Full qualifying results and tables on pages 234-256

ITALY

Top scorers

	Total	First	%	Anytime	%
M Balotelli	5	1	20	4	80
P Osvaldo	4	1	25	3	43
D De Rossi	2	0	0	2	33

In World Cup 2014 qualification. Plus 8 others on 1 goal

Mario Balotelli

Players used in qualifying — Career / Qualifying

Pos		Club	Age	P	G	P	G	Y/R
G	Federico Marchetti	Lazio	31	11	0	1	0	0
G	Gianluigi Buffon	Juventus	36	139	0	8	0	1
G	Morgan De Sanctis	Roma	36	6	0	1	0	1
D	Andrea Barzagli	Juventus	32	47	0	6	0	0
D	Andrea Ranocchia	Inter	26	12	0	1	0	0
D	Angelo Ogbonna	Juventus	25	9	0	2	0	1
D	Christian Maggio	Napoli	32	34	0	4	0	0
D	Davide Astori	Cagliari	27	7	1	2	0	0
D	Domenico Criscito	Zenit	27	22	0	1	0	0
D	Federico Balzaretti	Roma	32	16	0	2	0	0
D	Federico Peluso	Juventus	29	3	1	2	1	0
D	Giorgio Chiellini	Juventus	29	67	4	5	1	0
D	Ignazio Abate	Milan	27	18	1	5	0	0
D	Leonardo Bonucci	Juventus	26	35	2	8	0	1
D	Lorenzo De Silvestri	Sampdoria	25	2	0	1	0	0
D	Mattia Cassani	Parma	30	11	0	1	0	0
D	Mattia De Sciglio	Milan	21	9	0	1	0	0
D	Luca Antonelli	Genoa	27	6	0	1	0	0
D	Manuel Pasqual	Fiorentina	32	5	0	2	0	1
M	Alberto Aquilani	Fiorentina	29	33	5	3	1	0
M	Alessandro Diamanti	Guangzhou	30	17	1	3	0	1
M	Alessandro Florenzi	Roma	23	4	1	1	1	0
M	Alessio Cerci	Torino	26	10	0	2	0	0
M	Andrea Pirlo	Juventus	34	108	13	9	1	0
M	Antonio Candreva	Lazio	27	19	0	7	0	0
M	Antonio Nocerino	West Ham	28	15	0	1	0	0
M	Claudio Marchisio	Juventus	28	42	2	7	0	0
M	Daniele De Rossi	Roma	30	93	15	6	2	2
M	Riccardo Montolivo	Milan	29	57	2	7	1	1
M	Thiago Motta	Paris St-Germain	31	19	1	3	0	0
M	Emanuele Giaccherini	Sunderland	28	19	3	6	0	1
F	Alberto Gilardino	Genoa	31	57	19	3	1	0
F	Giampaolo Pazzini	Milan	29	25	4	1	0	0
F	Giuseppe Rossi	Fiorentina	27	29	7	1	0	0
F	Lorenzo Insigne	Napoli	22	4	1	3	0	0
F	Mario Balotelli	Milan	23	29	12	5	5	2/1
F	Mattia Destro	Roma	23	5	1	3	1	0
F	Pablo Osvaldo	Southampton	28	14	4	7	4	1
F	Sebastian Giovinco	Juventus	27	17	1	4	0	1
F	Stephan El Shaarawy	Milan	21	10	1	3	0	0

What happens if ...

Italy score first
Italy win	14	45%
Draw	5	16%
Italy lose	0	0%

31 games since 2010 World Cup

Opponents score first
Italy win	3	10%
Draw	2	6%
Italy lose	2	6%

Goal times

For			Against
3	■	0-9	1
3	■	10-18	1
8	■■	19-27	4
5	■	28-36	4
7	■■	37-45	4
7	■■	46-54	0
3	■	55-63	2
3	■	64-72	6
6	■■	73-81	2
7	■■	82-90	4

Italy			Opponents	
26	50%	1st half	14	50%
26	50%	2nd half	14	50%

31 games since 2010 World Cup

Correct scores

	Friendly	Comp
1-0	0	4
2-0	2	3
2-1	1	4
3-0	0	3
3-1	0	2
3-2	0	0
4-0	1	0
4-1	0	0
4-2	0	0
4-3	0	1
0-0	0	4
1-1	4	3
2-2	3	4
3-3	0	0
4-4	0	0
0-1	4	0
0-2	1	0
1-2	3	0
0-3	1	0
1-3	0	0
2-3	0	0
0-4	0	1
1-4	0	0
2-4	0	1
3-4	0	0
Other	0	1

51 games since 2010 World Cup

Bookings

Yellow cards	13
Red cards	2
Avg make-up	18.0

In 2014 World Cup qualifying

Gianluigi Buffon saves a penalty at the Confederations Cup

Unders & overs

1.5 goals		2.5 goals		3.5 goals		4.5 goals	
Under	Over	Under	Over	Under	Over	Under	Over
26%	74%	45%	55%	68%	32%	90%	10%

31 games since 2010 World Cup

Half-time/Full-time

Win/Win	10	32%
Draw/Win	5	16%
Lose/Win	3	10%
Win/Draw	3	10%
Draw/Draw	8	26%
Lose/Draw	0	0%
Win/Lose	0	0%
Draw/Lose	0	0%
Lose/Lose	2	6%

WIN 58%

31 games since 2010 World Cup

Penalty shootouts

Won	3	38%
Lost	5	62%

All-time record

Clean sheets

Italy	15	48%
Opponents	5	16%

31 games since 2010 World Cup

European neighbours can go through to the knockout rounds together

If the schedule had worked out easier then Switzerland would have been maximum bet material to make it out of Group E, **writes Mark Langdon**. But even though the draw means Ottmar Hitzfeld's side are being packed off to Brasilia, Salvador and Manaus, they can come through alongside France.

There's no getting away from the idea that Switzerland feel hard done by in terms of the location of their matches but in terms of the opposition things could have been far worse.

Fifa's controversial ranking system put Switzerland among the top seven teams (along with hosts Brazil) and they are not without hope of living up to that billing with a quarter-final spot, although first they and neighbours France must see off Ecuador and Honduras.

Hitzfeld, a manager who has won Champions League titles with two different clubs, can formulate a plan to overcome the conditions and the players can definitely put on a show.

Bayern Munich's Xherdan Shaqiri and Napoli trio Gokhan Inler, Blerim Dzemaili and Valon Behrami are midfielders used to performing at the highest level, while Juventus wing-back Stephan Lichtsteiner offers defensive solidity to go with his threat in attacking areas.

The first match, an early kick-off in Brasilia against Ecuador, is

It was 0-0 when France and Switzerland met in 2006

the key game. The South Americans were hopeless away from home in qualifying, collecting 22 of their 25 points at their high-altitude Quito base which is 2,850 metres above sea level.

Ecuador are a team lacking in big-name players to match Switzerland and Antonio Valencia, one of the few to shine previously in Europe, has mainly been poor when called upon for deposed Premier League champions Manchester United.

Honduras are set to enjoy the trip to Manaus more than Switzerland for the final group game, but again a manager of Hitzfeld's quality and experience has long enough to formulate a plan to make sure the better team can overcome the conditions.

"We couldn't have asked for better," tweeted former French coach Raymond Domenech after the draw, and that is a fair shout.

Les Bleus have had problems in the past with disharmony in the squad and it's anyone's guess as to whether they will reappear in Brazil but, even when things blew up at Euro 2012, France still had enough individual brilliance to reach the quarter-finals.

This is a better team for the emergence of Paul Pogba and increased responsibility for Franck Ribery and it should be a European one-two.

Recommendation
France-Switzerland dual forecast

	bet365	Coral	Lads	Power	W Hill
France	4-6	8-11	8-11	**4-5**	**4-5**
Switzerland	**11-4**	9-4	5-2	13-5	9-4
Ecuador	4	**9-2**	**9-2**	4	**9-2**
Honduras	33	25	18	20	16

	Lads	Power	W Hill	Power	W Hill
France	**1-5**	1-6	**1-5**	**14**	12
Switzerland	**4-7**	**4-7**	**4-7**	6	**7**
Ecuador	**21-20**	Evs	10-11	**5**	**5**
Honduras	5	6	**7**	**3-10**	2-7

All group betting markets are win only

	Power
France/Switzerland	5-2
France/Ecuador	**10-3**
Switzerland/France	**4**
Ecuador/France	**13-2**
Switzerland/Ecuador	8
Ecuador/Switzerland	9
France/Honduras	13
Switzerland/Honduras	30
Honduras/France	50
Ecuador/Honduras	50
Honduras/Switzerland	75
Honduras/Ecuador	90

Switzerland v Ecuador
Sunday June 15, 5pm, Brasilia

No previous World Cup meetings

No previous meetings

France v Honduras
Sunday June 15, 8pm, Porto Alegre

No previous World Cup meetings

No previous meetings

Switzerland v France
Friday June 20, 8pm, Salvador

They played out a goalless draw in the group stage of Germany 2006

15 French victories, 12 for the Swiss, nine draws

That stalemate in Stuttgart – there were eight bookings in total

Honduras v Ecuador
Friday June 20, 11pm, Curitiba

No previous World Cup meetings

Two Honduras wins, three for Ecuador, a massive eight draws

A draw of course – 2-2 in Houston shortly before the World Cup draw

Honduras v Switzerland
Wednesday June 25, 9pm, Manaus

They drew in the group stage of the last World Cup

One game, one draw

South Africa 2010 – Switzerland had 23 shots at goal but it ended 0-0

Ecuador v France
Wednesday June 25, 9pm, Rio De Janeiro

No previous World Cup meetings

One previous meeting, a 2-0 friendly win for France

Bafetimbi Gomis, one of six French subs, scored twice in May 2008

Group winners

Round of 16 June 30 Brasilia
2F Argentina, Bosnia-Herzegovina, Iran, Nigeria

Quarter-finals July 4 Rio de Janeiro
1G Germany, Portugal, Ghana, USA
2H Belgium, Algeria, Russia, South Korea

Semi-finals July 8 Belo Horizonte
1A Brazil, Croatia, Mexico, Cameroon
2B Spain, Holland, Chile, Australia
1C Colombia, Greece, Ivory Coast, Japan
2D Uruguay, Costa Rica, England, Italy

Final July 13 Rio

Group runners-up

Round of 16 July 1 Sao Paulo
1F Argentina, Bosnia-Herzegovina, Iran, Nigeria

Quarter-finals July 5 Brasilia
1H Belgium, Algeria, Russia, South Korea
2G Germany, Portugal, Ghana, USA

Semi-finals July 9 Sao Paulo
1B Spain, Holland, Chile, Australia
2A Brazil, Croatia, Mexico, Cameroon
1D Uruguay, Costa Rica, England, Italy
2C Colombia, Greece, Ivory Coast, Japan

SWITZERLAND

Best of the longshots but a lack of goals could cap Swiss ambitions in Brazil

T here is always a certain amount of controversy when the seedings are announced for a major tournament – and never more so than when Switzerland saw off Holland and Italy to be housed in pot one of the draw. To most people it made no sense but the Swiss have poured money in their youth system and are beginning to reap the benefits at senior level too.

How they qualified

It was a soft section – Iceland eventually finished second – but Switzerland still hit the summit in fine style.

They finished unbeaten with seven clean sheets in ten matches and, apart from a crazy 4-4 home draw with Iceland when the Swiss uncharacteristically chucked away a three-goal advantage with only 35 minutes remaining, the group winners were defensively outstanding.

The manager

You get what you pay for and Ottmar Hitzfeld has not come cheap. But the 65-year-old oozes class and experience and has come a long way since lifting the Swiss Cup with Aarau in 1985.

Hitzfeld, who will retire at the end of the tournament to be replaced by Vladimir Petkovic, has won the Champions League with Borussia Dortmund and Bayern Munich and will go down as one of Germany's greatest ever managers.

However, Hitzfeld is far from happy with the schedule and told SWR Radio: "I find it almost irresponsible that one has to play football in Manaus, in the middle of the jungle.

"Brazil is a big country and you have to fly for five hours from Salvador to Manaus and that is also a big strain."

Country factfile

FA founded 1895
www football.ch
Head coach Ottmar Hitzfeld
National league Super League
System of government Confederation
Population 8 million
Capital city Bern
Currency Swiss Franc
Official language German, French, Italian, Romansch

Strengths
☑ Successful youth team are making their mark at senior level
☑ Midfield is packed with talent
☑ Lichsteiner is perhaps the world's most consistent right-sided defender

Weaknesses
☒ No regular goalscorer
☒ Horrible schedule, including a trip to Manaus

Base Porto Seguro
Fixtures
1 Ecuador, June 15, Brasilia
2 France, June 20, Salvador
3 Honduras, June 25, Manaus

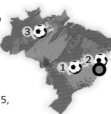

Ottmar Hitzfeld is vastly experienced

Match winners

These are exciting times for Swiss supporters. The youngsters who won the U17 World Cup in 2009 are beginning to break through and a number of the players are at major European clubs.

Valentin Stocker still plays in Switzerland for Basle but it won't be long before the excellent winger joins players such as Xherdan Shaqiri (Bayern Munich), Napoli trio Gokhan Inler, Blerim Dzemaili and Valon Behrami, and Juventus's Stephan Lichsteiner in a major championship.

Marauding left-back Ricardo Rodriguez is a set-piece master, his Wolfsburg team-mate Diego Benaglio is a fine goalkeeper, and Granit Xhaka is what the hipsters would now call a 'baller'. The Gladbach playmaker is inconsistent but can certainly make a team tick.

Question marks

Centre-back Fabian Schar top-scored in qualifying with three goals and the forward position is the missing piece of the jigsaw.

Eren Derdiyok and Haris Seferovic are not regulars at Leverkusen and Sociedad respectively while Freiburg's Admir Mehmedi isn't good enough at this level.

How to back them

In one-off games Switzerland are dangerous opponents. They triumphed against Spain at the 2010 World Cup and beat Brazil in August. Hitzfeld can get them out of a group containing France, Ecuador and Honduras despite being handicapped by a horrible schedule.

If there is to be a huge outsider who wins the competition then the Swiss look best placed of the longshots but a buy on the outright spreads could be more rewarding, with plenty of profit to be made if they can get to the quarter-finals.

Given Switzerland's problems up front it may pay to take a chance on Josip Drmic to be their leading scorer. The speedy striker has been tearing it up for an otherwise struggling Nuremberg in the Bundesliga and he scored twice in a 2-2 friendly with Croatia in March.

SWITZERLAND

World Cup record

Uruguay 1930	Did not enter
Italy 1934	Quarter-finals
France 1938	Quarter-finals
Brazil 1950	Group stage
Switzerland 1954	Quarter-finals
Sweden 1958	Did not qualify
Chile 1962	Group stage
England 1966	Group stage
Mexico 1970	Did not qualify
Germany 1974	Did not qualify
Argentina 1978	Did not qualify
Spain 1982	Did not qualify
Mexico 1986	Did not qualify
Italy 1990	Did not qualify
USA 1994	Round of 16
France 1998	Did not qualify
Korea/Japan 2002	Did not qualify
Germany 2006	Round of 16
South Africa 2010	Group stage

Continental titles

None

Legendary player

Stephane Chapuisat followed in the footsteps of his father, Pierre-Albert, and eclipsed the former Swiss international, winning 103 caps and scoring 21 international goals. He went to the 1994 World Cup and also took part in Euro 96 and Euro 2004. At club level, Chapuisat won the Champions League in 1997 with Borussia Dortmund. The coach? Ottmar Hitzfeld.

Did you know?

Although Switzerland took part in the highest scoring World Cup game ever – a 7-5 quarter-final defeat to Austria in 1954 – their seven matches at the last two World Cups have averaged a total of just 0.86 goals

Xherdan Shaqiri is one of Switzerland's young rising stars

How they qualified

Final group	P	W	D	L	F	A	GD	Pts
Switzerland	**10**	**7**	**3**	**0**	**17**	**6**	**11**	**24**
Iceland	10	5	2	3	17	15	2	17
Slovenia	10	5	0	5	14	11	3	15
Norway	10	3	3	4	10	13	-3	12
Albania	10	3	2	5	9	11	-2	11
Cyprus	10	1	2	7	4	15	-11	5

Slovenia...........(0) 0-2 (1)....... Switzerland
Switzerland: Xhaka (20) Inler (51)

Switzerland .....(1) 2-0 (0)............. Albania
Switzerland: Shaqiri (23) Inler (pen 68)

Switzerland .....(0) 1-1 (0)............. Norway
Switzerland: Gavranovic (79) Norway: Hangeland (81)

Iceland ....(0) 0-2 (0)....... Switzerland
Switzerland: Barnetta (65) Gavranovic (79)

Cyprus ....(0) 0-0 (0)....... Switzerland

Switzerland .....(0) 1-0 (0)...............Cyprus
Switzerland: Seferovic (90)

Switzerland .....(3) 4-4 (1).............. Iceland
Switzerland: Lichtsteiner (15, 30) Schar (27) Dzemaili (pen 54)
Iceland: Gudmundsson (3, 68, 90) Sigthorsson (56)

Norway ....(0) 0-2 (1)....... Switzerland
Switzerland: Schar (12, 51)

Albania............(0) 1-2 (0)....... Switzerland
Albania: Salihi (pen 89) Switzerland: Shaqiri (47) Lang (78)

Switzerland .....(0) 1-0 (0)............ Slovenia
Switzerland: Xhaka (74)

Full qualifying results and tables on pages 234-256

Players used in qualifying

Pos		Club	Age	Career P	G	Qualifying P	G	Y/R
G	Diego Benaglio	Wolfsburg	30	55	0	8	0	3
G	Yann Sommer	Basle	25	5	0	2	0	0
D	Fabian Schar	Basle	22	5	3	3	3	1
D	Johan Djourou	Hamburg	27	43	1	7	0	1
D	Michael Lang	Grasshoppers	23	5	1	2	1	0
D	Philippe Senderos	Valencia	29	52	5	3	0	1
D	Ricardo Rodriguez	Wolfsburg	21	19	0	9	0	1
D	Steve von Bergen	Young Boys	30	39	0	9	0	2
D	Timm Klose	Wolfsburg	25	8	0	2	0	0
D	Reto Ziegler	Sassuolo	28	35	1	1	0	0
D	Stephan Lichtsteiner	Juventus	30	61	4	8	2	1
M	Blerim Dzemaili	Napoli	27	32	1	9	1	1
M	Gelson Fernandes	Freiburg	27	46	2	4	0	0
M	Goekhan Inler	Napoli	29	71	6	9	2	2
M	Granit Xhaka	M'gladbach	21	24	4	9	2	1
M	Pajtim Kasami	Fulham	21	2	1	1	0	0
M	Tranquillo Barnetta	E. Frankfurt	28	73	10	6	1	1/1
M	Valentin Stocker	Basle	24	22	3	6	0	1
M	Valon Behrami	Napoli	28	46	2	9	0	1
M	Xherdan Shaqiri	Bayern Munich	22	31	8	9	2	0
F	Admir Mehmedi	Freiburg	23	19	1	4	0	0
F	Eren Derdiyok	Bayer Leverkusen	25	46	8	5	0	2
F	Haris Seferovic	Sociedad	22	9	1	6	1	1
F	Innocent Emeghara	Livorno	24	9	0	1	0	0
F	Josip Drmic	Nuremberg	21	5	2	3	0	1
F	Mario Gavranovic	FC Zurich	24	10	4	3	2	0

What happens if ...

Switzerland score first

Switzerland win	9	50%
Draw	2	11%
Switzerland lose	0	0%

18 games since 2010 World Cup

Opponents score first

Switzerland win	1	6%
Draw	1	6%
Switzerland lose	3	17%

GROUP E

Goal times

For			Against
1	0-9		2
2	10-18		2
4	19-27		0
3	28-36		0
1	37-45		1
5	46-54		1
1	55-63		2
4	64-72		4
4	73-81		1
4	82-90		3

Switzerland		Opponents	
11	38% 1st half	5	31%
18	62% 2nd half	11	69 %

18 games since 2010 World Cup

Correct scores

	Friendly	Comp
1-0	3	2
2-0	0	5
2-1	2	1
3-0	0	0
3-1	0	1
3-2	0	0
4-0	0	0
4-1	0	1
4-2	1	0
4-3	0	0
0-0	4	2
1-1	0	1
2-2	2	1
3-3	0	0
4-4	0	1
0-1	1	1
0-2	0	1
1-2	1	0
0-3	0	0
1-3	1	1
2-3	0	0
0-4	0	0
1-4	0	0
2-4	0	0
3-4	0	0
Other	1	0

34 games since 2010 World Cup

Bookings

Yellow cards	21
Red cards	1
Avg make-up	23.5

In 2014 World Cup qualifying

Top scorers

	Total	First	%	Anytime	%
F Schar	3	1	33	2	67
S Lichtsteiner	2	0	0	1	13
G Inler	2	0	0	2	22
X Shaqiri	2	2	100	2	22
M Gavranovic	2	1	50	2	67
G Xhaka	2	2	100	2	22

In World Cup 2014 qualification

Fabian Schar

Unders & overs

1.5 goals		2.5 goals		3.5 goals		4.5 goals	
Under	Over	Under	Over	Under	Over	Under	Over
28%	72%	67%	33%	72%	28%	89%	11%

18 games since 2010 World Cup

Half-time/Full-time

Win/Win	4	22%
Draw/Win	6	33%
Lose/Win	0	0%
Win/Draw	2	11%
Draw/Draw	3	17%
Lose/Draw	0	0%
Win/Lose	0	0%
Draw/Lose	2	11%
Lose/Lose	1	6%

WIN 55%

18 games since 2010 World Cup

Penalty shootouts

Won	0	0%
Lost	1	100%

All-time record

Clean sheets

Switzerland	9	50%
Opponents	4	22%

18 games since 2010 World Cup

CHRIST

ECUADOR

Away from Quito, Ecuador lack the quality to make an impression at the finals

The South American challenge is expected to be strong in Brazil but of the sextet competing for the title, Ecuador are seen as the weakest team from the continent to have qualified for the finals – anything better than reaching the last 16 would be a memorable achievement. Home is where the heart is for Ecuador and they could be back in Quito long before the title is decided.

GROUP E

How they qualified

Ecuador sneaked through in the fourth and final automatic qualification position thanks to a goal difference of plus four compared to Uruguay's zero.

Altitude plays a massive part for Ecuador in qualifying and explains why bookmakers see them as the weakest of the South American nations – it is a fair assessment.

Incredibly, 22 of Ecuador's 25 points came at home with section winners Argentina the only team to leave Quito without tasting defeat. On the road they lost to each of the three teams who finished above them in the Conmebol region.

Felipe Caicedo scored seven goals in qualifying. Four of those were scored at home and four came from the penalty spot. Tragically, four-goal former Birmingham forward Christian Benitez died of heart failure last year.

The manager

Reinaldo Rueda worked miracles with the Colombian youth teams and can take a great amount of credit for what is happening with them now at senior level.

He also guided Honduras to the 2010 World Cup finals, and although the Central Americans failed to score a goal, they picked up a point in a stalemate with Switzerland in their final group match.

Country factfile

FA founded 1925
www ecuafutbol.org
Head coach Reinaldo Rueda
National league Primera A
System of government Republic
Population 15 million
Capital city Quito
Currency US dollar
Official language Spanish

Strengths
☑ Caicedo usually delivers for Ecuador

Weaknesses
☒ Rarely show their best outside of Quito and might have preferred to play in more extreme conditions
☒ Valencia has not shown his best for Manchester United
☒ Benitez's sudden death rocked the squad

Base Viamao
Fixtures
1 Switzerland, June 15, Brasilia
2 Honduras, June 20, Curitiba
3 France, June 25, Rio

Felipe Caicedo

Match winners

Antonio Valencia is the man who needs to perform if Ecuador are to make the last 16 and Caicedo must carry his qualifying form into Brazil.

Attacking left-back Walter Ayovi, who can also play on the wing, has a booming shot and is capable of landing the odd spectacular goal.

Question marks

"An irreparable loss to the Ecuadorian team" was how Rueda described the death of Benitez and on both a human and sporting level, he will be missed by everyone in the squad.

Attacking midfielder Christian Noboa, who plays in Russia for Dinamo Moscow, has a better goalscoring record for his club than he does for Ecuador and Rueda could do with him scoring more at international level. His fellow engine-room schemer Segundo Castillo will be 32 in May and plies his trade in Saudi Arabia, which is not ideal.

Valencia's form has deserted him at Manchester United and Ecuador desperately need him to return to his best in time for the big kick-off in Brazil.

How to back them

A straight bet on Ecuador not to qualify is one option because their form outside of Quito is rarely good enough. They were knocked out at the first hurdle of the last Copa America, and France and Switzerland set a decent standard of opposition.

Caicedo should oblige for favourite backers in Ecuador's top goalscorer betting heat but two to consider at whopping prices are Noboa and Walter Ayovi – the latter is not to be confused with forward Jaime Ayovi, who is much shorter in the betting.

Noboa has a disappointing record for his country but has been a regular source of goals in Russian football, first for Rubin Kazan and more recently Dinamo Moscow. Ayovi is somebody who can take penalties and once notched nine goals in one season for Ecuadorian club side Barcelona.

ECUADOR

World Cup record

Uruguay 1930	Did not enter
Italy 1934	Did not enter
France 1938	Did not enter
Brazil 1950	Withdrew
Switzerland 1954	Did not enter
Sweden 1958	Did not enter
Chile 1962	Did not qualify
England 1966	Did not qualify
Mexico 1970	Did not qualify
Germany 1974	Did not qualify
Argentina 1978	Did not qualify
Spain 1982	Did not qualify
Mexico 1986	Did not qualify
Italy 1990	Did not qualify
USA 1994	Did not qualify
France 1998	Did not qualify
Korea/Japan 2002	Group stage
Germany 2006	Round of 16
South Africa 2010	Did not qualify

Continental titles

None

Legendary player

It would be Alberto Spencer had he ever played in a World Cup but **Agustin Delgado**, whose club career was far less remarkable, got Ecuador's first ever World Cup goal in 2002 then scored twice as they reached the last 16 in 2006.

Did you know?

Ecuador have never drawn a match at the World Cup finals

How they qualified

Final group	P	W	D	L	F	A	GD	Pts
Argentina	16	9	5	2	35	15	20	32
Colombia	16	9	3	4	27	13	14	30
Chile	16	9	1	6	29	25	4	28
Ecuador	**16**	**7**	**4**	**5**	**20**	**16**	**4**	**25**
Uruguay	16	7	4	5	25	25	0	25
Venezuela	16	5	5	6	14	20	-6	20
Peru	16	4	3	9	17	26	-9	15
Bolivia	16	2	6	8	17	30	-13	12
Paraguay	16	3	3	10	17	31	-14	12

Ecuador...........(2) 2-0 (0)......... Venezuela
Ecuador: Ayovi (15) Benitez (28)

Paraguay ....(0) 2-1 (0).............Ecuador
Paraguay: Riveros (47) Veron (58) Ecuador: Rojas (90)

Ecuador...........(0) 2-0 (0).................. Peru
Ecuador: Mendez (70) Benitez (89)

Argentina........(3) 4-0 (0).............Ecuador
Argentina: Aguero (20) Higuain (30) Messi (32) Di Maria (76)

Ecuador...........(0) 1-0 (0).......... Colombia
Ecuador: Benitez (54)

Ecuador...........(0) 1-0 (0).............. Bolivia
Ecuador: Caicedo (pen 74)

Uruguay ....(0) 1-1 (1).............Ecuador
Uruguay: Cavani (67) Ecuador: Caicedo (pen 8)

Ecuador...........(1) 3-1 (1).................Chile
Ecuador: Caicedo (33, 56 pen) Castillo (90) Chile: Paredes (25 og)

Venezuela........(1) 1-1 (1).............Ecuador
Venezuela: Arango (6) Ecuador: Castillo (24)

Ecuador...........(1) 4-1 (1)...........Paraguay
Ecuador: Caicedo (37) Montero (49, 75) Benitez (53)
Paraguay: Caballero (14)

Peru.................(1) 1-0 (0).............Ecuador
Peru: Pizarro (11)

Ecuador...........(1) 1-1 (1)..........Argentina
Ecuador: Castillo (17) Argentina: Aguero (4)

Colombia.........(1) 1-0 (0).............Ecuador
Colombia: Rodriguez (30)

Bolivia ....(0) 1-1 (0).............Ecuador
Bolivia: Arrascaita (47) Ecuador: Caicedo (pen 58)

Ecuador...........(1) 1-0 (0)............ Uruguay
Ecuador: Montero (30)

Chile.................(2) 2-1 (0).............Ecuador
Chile: Sanchez (35) Medel (38) Ecuador: Caicedo (66)

Full qualifying results and tables on pages 234-256

Unders & overs

<1.5	>1.5	<2.5	>2.5	<3.5	>3.5	<4.5	>4.5
37%	63%	68%	32%	79%	21%	89%	11%

19 competitive games since 2010 World Cup

Half-time/Full-time

W/W	2	11%	W/D	1	5%	W/L	0	0%
D/W	5	26%	D/D	4	21%	D/L	3	16%
L/W	0	0%	L/D	0	0%	L/L	4	21%

19 competitive games since 2010 World Cup

Bookings

Yellow cards	35
Red cards	3
Avg make-up	26.6

In 2014 World Cup qualifying

Penalty shootouts

Won	1	100%
Lost	0	0%

All-time record

GROUP E

What happens if ...

Ecuador score first			Their opponents score first		
Ecuador win	5	26%	Ecuador win	2	11%
Draw	1	5%	Draw	3	16%
Ecuador lose	0	0%	Ecuador lose	7	37%

19 competitive games since 2010 World Cup

Top scorers

	Total	First	%	Anytime	%
F Caicedo	7	2	28	6	67
C Benitez	4	1	25	4	44
S Castillo	3	0	0	3	25
J Montero	3	1	33	2	15

In World Cup 2014 qualification

Goal times

For			Against
1	0-9		2
2	10-18		2
1	19-27		2
3	28-36		5
2	37-45		1
3	46-54		3
3	55-63		3
2	64-72		2
2	73-81		1
3	82-90		0

Ecuador		Opponents	
9	41%	1st half	12	57%
13	59%	2nd half	9	43%

19 games since 2010 World Cup

Correct scores

	Friendly	Comp
1-0	1	3
2-0	2	2
2-1	1	0
3-0	1	0
3-1	0	1
3-2	1	0
4-0	1	0
4-1	1	1
4-2	0	0
4-3	4	0
0-0	2	1
1-1	3	4
2-2	4	0
3-3	0	0
4-4	0	0
0-1	2	3
0-2	2	0
1-2	0	2
0-3	0	0
1-3	0	0
2-3	0	0
0-4	0	1
1-4	0	0
2-4	1	1
3-4	0	0
Other	2	0

45 games since 2010 World Cup

Clean sheets

Ecuador	6	32%
Opp	5	26%

19 competitive games since 2010 World Cup

Players used in qualifying

Pos		Club	Age	Career P	G	Qualifying P	G	Y/R
G	Alexander Dominguez	LDU Quito	26	18	0	12	0	2
G	Maximo Banguera	Barcelona (Ecu)	28	22	0	4	0	0
D	Frickson Erazo	Flamengo	25	34	1	15	0	2
D	Gabriel Achilier	Emelec	28	19	0	7	0	1/1
D	Jairo Campos	Barcelona (Ecu)	29	20	0	6	0	1
D	Jorge Guagua	Emelec	32	56	2	7	0	1
D	Eduardo Morante	Deportivo Cuenca	26	5	0	2	0	1
D	Juan Paredes	Barcelona (Ecu)	26	35	0	14	1	0
M	Alex Bolanos	Barcelona (Ecu)	28	8	0	0	0	0
M	Christian Noboa	Din. Moscow	28	40	2	13	0	3/1
M	Dennys Quinonez	Deportivo Quito	21	3	0	1	0	0
M	Edison Mendez	Santa Fe	34	108	18	5	1	0
M	Enner Valencia	Pachuca	24	8	2	3	0	0
M	Fidel Martinez	Tijuana	24	7	3	1	0	0
M	Jefferson Montero	Morelia	24	37	7	13	3	0
M	Joao Rojas	Cruz Azul	24	27	2	10	1	2
M	Joffre Guerron	Beijing Guoan	28	18	0	1	0	0
M	Luis Antonio Valencia	Man Utd	28	68	9	15	0	3/1
M	Luis Saritama	Barcelona (Ecu)	30	48	0	11	0	3
M	Michael Arroyo	Atlante	26	19	2	3	0	2
M	Oswaldo Minda	Chivas	30	18	0	4	0	1
M	Pedro Quinonez	Emelec	27	10	0	2	0	0
M	Alex Ibarra	Vitesse Arn.	23	17	0	10	0	0
M	Segundo Castillo	Al-Hilal	31	78	9	12	3	2
M	Walter Ayovi	Pachuca	34	89	6	16	0	0
F	Christian Benitez	-	27	59	24	9	4	4
F	Cristian Suarez	Barcelona (Ecu)	28	10	3	3	0	0
F	Felipe Caicedo	Al-Jazira	25	46	15	9	7	4
F	Felix Borja	LDU Quito	30	21	2	1	0	0
F	Jaime Ayovi	Tijuana	26	28	11	10	1	3
F	Juan Anangono	Chicago Fire	24	2	0	0	0	0
F	Marlon de Jesus	Monterrey	22	5	0	1	0	0
F	Narciso Mina	Atlante	31	10	1	1	0	0

FRANCE

French made hard work of qualifying but ability is not the issue for Les Bleus

I f you believe in teams having their name on the cup then France could be the side. They were nearly out of the competition only to make a storming play-off comeback against Ukraine, then Les Bleus were given one of the softest draws in the competition and none of their three group-stage matches will take place in Brazil's hotter climates. Now all France need to do is take advantage…

How they qualified

Consistency wasn't Les Bleus' strong point – they were good enough to hold Spain to a draw away and yet failed to beat Georgia on the road. The French were also bad enough to lose 2-0 in Ukraine but then showed the world their qualities in the return leg of the play-off, qualifying with a 3-0 victory.

There were the usual rows along the way and Karim Benzema went 1,222 minutes without scoring at international level but, when it mattered most, France were perfect in Paris, outclassing Ukraine with 21 shots and 68 per cent possession.

The manager

Didier Deschamps won the lot with France, captaining them to win the 1998 World Cup on home soil and Euro 2000, while at club level the man cruelly nicknamed the 'water carrier' by Eric Cantona was a double Champions League winner and serial domestic champion.

As a manager Deschamps took Monaco to the Champions League final, gained promotion with Juventus from Serie B and won three League Cups and a Ligue 1 title with Marseille in France.

Match winners

Franck Ribery was the standout performer in qualifying with five goals and six assists

Country factfile

FA founded 1919
www fff.fr
Head coach Didier Deschamps
National league Ligue 1
System of government Republic
Population 66 million
Capital city Paris
Currency Euro
Official language French

Strengths
☑ Outstanding talent throughout the spine of the side
☑ Draw could hardly have worked out better

Weaknesses
☒ Evra is a liability at left-back
☒ Team harmony needs to be taken on trust

Base Ribeirao Preto

Fixtures
1 Honduras, June 15, Porto Alegre
2 Switzerland, June 20, Salvador
3 Ecuador, June 25, Rio

Relief for France after the play-off victory over Ukraine

and the Bayern Munich winger is the man who needs to become the leader of the pack, much like Zinedine Zidane did during the golden period of 1998-2000.

Ribery has many qualities and finished third in the Fifa Ballon d'Or, behind only Cristiano Ronaldo and Lionel Messi. He also walked away with Uefa's Best Player in Europe award, to effectively be crowned European footballer of the year.

France celebrated success in the U20 World Cup last year. Paul Pogba was by far and away the best player in that tournament and the Juventus midfielder is going from strength to strength this season. He is a midfield beast with no weaknesses and the same goes for another youngster, Real Madrid centre-back Raphael Varane.

Madrid team-mate Benzema has had his problems but is a capable performer on his day and Tottenham's athletic goalkeeper Hugo Lloris is also a player who can turn a match with world-class saves.

Question marks

Talent is not the issue here and everything will depend on whether the squad self-destructs once they get in Brazil. There have been problems in each of the last three tournaments for a variety of off-field issues and the challenge for Deschamps is to get everyone singing from the same hymn sheet.

How to back them

France usually go a very long way or go home very early, but they have reached the semi-finals in four of their last six World Cup appearances and have the potential to go all the way if it's a united camp.

At generous prices it may be worth having a speculative few quid on Pogba being named as the player of the tournament, and if France click they are a value bet. However, the required spirit needs to be taken on trust.

FRANCE

World Cup record

Uruguay 1930	Group stage
Italy 1934	First round
France 1938	Quarter-finals
Brazil 1950	Withdrew
Switzerland 1954	Group stage
Sweden 1958	Third place
Chile 1962	Did not qualify
England 1966	Group stage
Mexico 1970	Did not qualify
Germany 1974	Did not qualify
Argentina 1978	Group stage
Spain 1982	Fourth place
Mexico 1986	Third place
Italy 1990	Did not qualify
USA 1994	Did not qualify
France 1998	**Winners**
Korea/Japan 2002	Group stage
Germany 2006	Runners-up
South Africa 2010	Group stage

Continental titles

European Championships (1984, 2000)

Legendary player

There have been some great French players – Zidane, Platini, Henry – but **Just Fontaine**'s 13 goals at the 1958 World Cup is a record that will be very hard to beat. It took him six games and included four goals against West Germany in the third-place match. It took Gerd Muller two World Cups to surpass Fontaine's total and Ronaldo three.

Did you know?

France won the first game at the first World Cup, beating Mexico 4-1 in Montevideo on July 13 1930

Franck Ribery fires through the crowd to score against Finland

GROUP E

How they qualified

Final group	P	W	D	L	F	A	GD	Pts
Spain	8	6	2	0	14	3	11	20
France	**8**	**5**	**2**	**1**	**15**	**6**	**9**	**17**
Finland	8	2	3	3	5	9	-4	9
Georgia	8	1	2	5	3	10	-7	5
Belarus	8	1	1	6	7	16	-9	4

Finland ....(0) 0-1 (1).............. France
France: Diaby (20)

France ....(0) 3-1 (0)............. Belarus
France: Capoue (49) Jallet (68) Ribery (80) Belarus: Putsilo (72)

Spain...............(1) 1-1 (0)............... France
Spain: Ramos (25) France: Giroud (90)

France ....(1) 3-1 (0)............Georgia
France: Giroud (45) Valbuena (47) Ribery (61) Georgia: Kobakhidze (70)

France ....(0) 0-1 (0)................Spain
Spain: Pedro (58)

Georgia ....(0) 0-0 (0)............... France

Belarus ....(1) 2-4 (0)............... France
Belarus: Filipenko (32) Kalachev (57) France: Ribery (pen 47, 64) Nasri (70) Pogba (73)

France ....(1) 3-0 (0).............Finland
France: Ribery (8) Toivio (76 og) Benzema (87)

Play-off

Ukraine............(0) 2-0 (0).............. France
Ukraine: Zozulya (61) Yarmolenko (pen 82)

France ....(2) 3-0 (0)............. Ukraine
France: Sakho (22, 72) Benzema (34)

Full qualifying results and tables on pages 234-256

1998 World Cup winner Didier Deschamps

FRANCE

Players used in qualifying

Pos		Club	Age	P	G	P	G	Y/R
				Career		**Qualifying**		
G	Hugo Lloris	Tottenham	27	55	0	10	0	0
D	Antoine Reveillere	Napoli	34	20	1	1	0	0
D	Bacary Sagna	Arsenal	31	39	0	3	0	0
D	Christophe Jallet	Paris St-Germain	30	5	1	3	1	0
D	Eric Abidal	Monaco	34	67	0	4	0	0
D	Gael Clichy	Man City	28	20	0	2	0	1
D	Laurent Koscielny	Arsenal	28	15	0	6	0	1/1
D	Mamadou Sakho	Liverpool	24	16	2	5	2	1
D	Mapou Yanga	Newcastle	24	3	0	2	0	2
D	Mathieu Debuchy	Newcastle	28	19	2	4	0	2
D	Patrice Evra	Man Utd	32	55	0	8	0	2
D	Raphael Varane	Real Madrid	20	4	0	3	0	0
M	Abou Diaby	Arsenal	27	16	1	1	1	0
M	Rio Mavuba	Lille	30	9	0	2	0	0
M	Blaise Matuidi	Paris St-Germain	26	20	1	9	0	2
M	Dimitri Payet	Marseille	26	7	0	1	0	0
M	Etienne Capoue	Tottenham	25	7	1	1	1	0
M	Franck Ribery	Bayern Munich	30	81	16	10	5	0
M	Jeremy Menez	Paris St-Germain	26	24	2	5	0	0
M	Josua Guilavogui	Atl Madrid	23	5	0	2	0	0
M	Mathieu Valbuena	Marseille	29	31	5	10	1	0
M	Maxime Gonalons	Lyon	25	6	0	1	0	1
M	Moussa Sissoko	Newcastle	24	14	0	6	0	1
M	Paul Pogba	Juventus	21	8	1	6	1	1/1
M	Samir Nasri	Man City	26	41	5	4	1	0
M	Yohan Cabaye	Paris St-Germain	28	27	2	6	0	2
F	Andre-Pierre Gignac	Marseille	28	17	4	1	0	0
F	Bafetimbi Gomis	Lyon	28	12	3	1	0	0
F	Karim Benzema	Real Madrid	26	65	19	9	2	0
F	Loic Remy	Newcastle	27	22	4	3	0	0
F	Olivier Giroud	Arsenal	27	27	5	9	2	1

What happens if ...

France score first

France win	12	50%
Draw	0	0%
France lose	0	0%

24 games since 2010 World Cup

WIN 50%

Opponents score first

France win	1	4%
Draw	4	16%
France lose	5	21%

LOSE 21%

DEDICATED TEAM PAGES

FULL SQUADS AS SOON AS THEY'RE
ANNOUNCED AND PLAYER STATS
AVAILABLE FOR EVERY TEAM AT THE
2014 WORLD CUP IN BRAZIL

SOCCERBASE.COM

Goal times

For			Against
1	0-9		0
3	10-18		0
4	19-27		3
2	28-36		2
3	37-45		1
4	46-54		2
2	55-63		3
7	64-72		2
6	73-81		0
4	82-90		4

France			Opponents	
13	36%	1st half	6	35%
23	64%	2nd half	11	65%

24 games since 2010 World Cup

Top scorers

	Total	First	%	Anytime	%
F Ribery	5	1	20	4	40
K Benzema	2	0	0	2	22
M Sakho	2	1	50	1	20
O Giroud	2	1	50	2	22

In World Cup 2014 qualification

Karim Benzema

Correct scores

	Friendly	Comp
1-0	3	1
2-0	2	5
2-1	3	1
3-0	0	3
3-1	0	2
3-2	1	0
4-0	1	0
4-1	1	0
4-2	0	1
4-3	0	0
0-0	4	2
1-1	1	4
2-2	0	0
3-3	0	0
4-4	0	0
0-1	2	2
0-2	0	3
1-2	2	0
0-3	1	0
1-3	0	0
2-3	0	0
0-4	0	0
1-4	0	0
2-4	0	0
3-4	0	0
Other	1	0

46 games since 2010 World Cup

Unders & overs

1.5 goals		2.5 goals		3.5 goals		4.5 goals	
Under	Over	Under	Over	Under	Over	Under	Over
21%	79%	71%	29%	88%	13%	96%	4%

24 games since 2010 World Cup

Half-time/Full-time

Win/Win	8	33%
Draw/Win	4	17%
Lose/Win	1	4%
Win/Draw	0	0%
Draw/Draw	4	17%
Lose/Draw	2	8%
Win/Lose	0	0%
Draw/Lose	4	17%
Lose/Lose	1	4%

24 games since 2010 World Cup

Bookings

Yellow cards	17
Red cards	2
Avg make-up	22.0

In 2014 World Cup qualifying

Penalty shootouts

Won	3	50%
Lost	3	50%

All-time record

Clean sheets

France	11	46%
Opponents	7	29%

24 games since 2010 World Cup

HONDURAS

They are improving but Luis Suarez's crew look unlikely to find the net

Honduras failed to score in three matches at the last World Cup so target number one will be to at least find the net in Brazil. However, they have over-performed in their last two international tournaments and will be aiming to land shocks – just like the London 2012 quarter-finalists did in the Olympics and the Concacaf Gold Cup semi-finalists did in the USA last year.

GROUP E

How they qualified

Their bid to make Brazil was almost over before it really started and they went into the last round of the first stage of qualifying needing three points against Canada to move into the next phase. Honduras responded with a resounding 8-1 humiliation of their opponents to go through in some style.

Things were easier after that initial scare and Honduras comfortably avoided going through the intercontinental play-offs, finishing third of the six teams and four points superior to Mexico, who they beat 2-1 in a famous success at the Azteca.

That was Honduras' only road triumph in the Hex and away defeats without scoring against Costa Rica, Panama and USA suggest Los Catrachos will struggle at the World Cup.

The manager

Luis Suarez – no, not that one! – has focused heavily on the youth programme and it worked well at the Olympics when Honduras's run at gold was only ended in a 3-2 defeat by Brazil after leading twice.

They had earlier stunned a Spanish side which contained the likes of David de Gea, Javi Martinez, Jordi Alba, Juan Mata, Koke and Isco, and their improvement was shown again last summer when Suarez led the side to the last four of the Gold Cup.

Colombian Suarez guided Ecuador to

Country factfile

FA founded 1951
www fenafuth.org
Head coach Luis Suarez
National league Liga Nacional
System of government
Democratic constitutional republic
Population 9 million
Capital city Tegucigalpa
Currency Lempira
Official language Spanish

Strengths

☑ Used to landing giantkilling results
☑ Playing Switzerland in Manaus should be an advantage

Weaknesses

☒ Sheer lack of ability in most positions
☒ Rely on Costly and Bengtson for goals
☒ Key men sitting on the bench at club level

Base Porto Feliz
Fixtures
1 France, June 15, Porto Alegre
2 Ecuador, June 20, Curitiba
3 Switzerland, June 25, Manaus

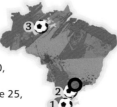

Carlo Costly reacts after scoring his second goal in four minutes in the 2-2 friendly draw with Ecuador

the last 16 of the World Cup in 2006 and that clash in Curitiba on June 20 will be emotional for all concerned as opposition boss Reinaldo Rueda, also a Colombian, used to manage Honduras.

Match winners

British football fans will be familiar with Maynor Figueroa, Emilio Izaguirre, Arnold Peralta, Juan Carlos Garcia, Wilson Palacios and Roger Espinoza but if Honduras are to score at the World Cup then it is likely to be through Carlo Costly or Jerry Bengtson.

Costly is the definition of a well-travelled footballer, having played in Poland, England, Romania, Mexico, the USA, Greece and China before heading back to his homeland and he has tended to be more prolific at international level than for his club outfits, particularly when upped in grade.

Bengtson notched three times at the Olympics – the same as Neymar – and while Izaguirre can provide goalscoring opportunities from the left. Veteran keeper Noel Valladares will need all of his experience to make sure Honduras are not embarrassed.

Question marks

Some of those who have moved to Britain are not playing regularly and nobody outside of Bengtson (nine) and Costly (seven) scored more than twice in qualifying.

Both of those tallies were boosted by hat-tricks in the demolition of Canada and Bengtson scored just three goals in 29 appearances for New England Revolution across two seasons in the MLS in 2012 and 2013.

How to back them

Honduras are likely to be on their way home after three matches even though fixtures against France, Switzerland and Ecuador could have been tougher. No tournament goals – like four years ago – looks the most obvious shout.

HONDURAS

World Cup record

Uruguay 1930	Did not enter
Italy 1934	Did not enter
France 1938	Did not enter
Brazil 1950	Did not enter
Switzerland 1954	Did not enter
Sweden 1958	Did not enter
Chile 1962	Did not qualify
England 1966	Did not qualify
Mexico 1970	Did not qualify
Germany 1974	Did not qualify
Argentina 1978	Withdrew
Spain 1982	Group stage
Mexico 1986	Did not qualify
Italy 1990	Did not qualify
USA 1994	Did not qualify
France 1998	Did not qualify
Korea/Japan 2002	Did not qualify
Germany 2006	Did not qualify
South Africa 2010	Group stage

Continental titles

None

Legendary player

Carlos Pavon didn't find the net in South Africa – he was carrying an injury and only played in their opening game – but it was Honduras's all-time highest scorer who grabbed the goal against El Salvador that got them to the finals.

How they qualified

Round 3

Honduras ....(0) 0-2 (0)............. Panama
Panama: Perez (65, 81)

Canada............(0) 0-0 (0).......... Honduras

Cuba ....(0) 0-3 (1).......... Honduras
Honduras: Bengtson (33) Bernardez (62) Chavez (90)

Honduras ....(1) 1-0 (0)................. Cuba
Honduras: Bengtson (33)

Panama ....(0) 0-0 (0).......... Honduras

Honduras ....(4) 8-1 (0)..............Canada
Honduras: Bengtson (7, 17, 83) Costly (29, 48, 89) Martinez (62, 62) Canada: Hume (77)

Final group	P	W	D	L	F	A	GD	Pts
USA	10	7	1	2	15	8	7	22
Costa Rica	10	5	3	2	13	7	6	18
Honduras	**10**	**4**	**3**	**3**	**13**	**12**	**1**	**15**
Mexico	10	2	5	3	7	9	-2	11
Panama	10	1	5	4	10	14	-4	8
Jamaica	10	0	5	5	13	-8	5	

Honduras ....(1) 2-1 (1)...................USA
Honduras: Garcia (40) Bengtson (79) USA: Dempsey (36)

Honduras ....(0) 2-2 (1).............. Mexico
Honduras: Costly (77) Bengtson (80) Mexico: Hernandez (28, 54)

Panama ....(1) 2-0 (0).......... Honduras
Panama: Tejada (1) Perez (75)

Costa Rica ....(1) 1-0 (0).......... Honduras
Costa Rica: Miller (25)

Honduras ....(1) 2-0 (0).............Jamaica
Honduras: Garcia (10) Rojas (88)

USA ....(0) 1-0 (0).......... Honduras
USA: Altidore (73)

Mexico ....(1) 1-2 (0).......... Honduras
Mexico: Peralta (5) Honduras: Bengtson (63) Costly (66)

Honduras ....(1) 2-2 (0)............. Panama
Honduras: Costly (28) Palacios (61) Panama: Torres (2) Chen (90)

Honduras ....(0) 1-0 (0)......... Costa Rica
Honduras: Bengtson (65)

Jamaica ....(1) 2-2 (2).......... Honduras
Jamaica: Claros (3 og) Austin (pen 59) Honduras: Costly (2) Figueroa (33)

Full qualifying results and tables on pages 234-256

Unders & overs

<1.5	>1.5	<2.5	>2.5	<3.5	>3.5	<4.5	>4.5
35%	65%	68%	32%	79%	21%	94%	6%

34 competitive games since 2010 World Cup

Half-time/Full-time

W/W	8	24%	W/D	2	6%	W/L	0	0%
D/W	6	18%	D/D	7	21%	D/L	3	9%
L/W	1	3%	L/D	2	6%	L/L	5	15%

34 competitive games since 2010 World Cup

Bookings

Yellow cards	22
Red cards	0
Avg make-up	13.8

In 2014 World Cup qualifying

Penalty shootouts

Won	2	67%
Lost	1	33%

All-time record

What happens if ...

Honduras score first			Their opponents score first		
Honduras win	12	35%	Honduras win	3	9%
Draw	3	9%	Draw	4	12%
Honduras lose	0	0%	Honduras lose	9	26%

34 competitive games since 2010 World Cup

Did you know?

Honduras have yet to win a game at the World Cup finals

Top scorers

	Total	First	%	Anytime	%
J Bengtson	9	4	44	7	58
C Costly	7	1	14	5	38
M Martinez	2	0	0	1	11

In World Cup 2014 qualification

Goal times

For			Against
4	▪	0-9	▪ 4
3	▪	10-18	▪ 2
1	▎	19-27	▪ 4
7	▬	28-36	▪ 3
3	▪	37-45	▪ 2
5	▪	46-54	▪ 3
5	▪	55-63	▪ 2
5	▪	64-72	▪ 2
6	▬	73-81	▬ 6
10	▬	82-90	▪ 3

Honduras		Opponents	
18	37% 1st half	15	44%
31	63% 2nd half	16	56%

34 games since 2010 World Cup

Correct scores

	Friendly	Comp
1-0	0	5
2-0	3	3
2-1	3	3
3-0	1	1
3-1	0	1
3-2	0	0
4-0	0	0
4-1	0	0
4-2	0	0
4-3	0	0
0-0	1	4
1-1	3	4
2-2	3	3
3-3	0	0
4-4	0	0
0-1	2	4
0-2	4	3
1-2	1	0
0-3	2	0
1-3	0	1
2-3	0	0
0-4	1	0
1-4	0	0
2-4	0	0
3-4	0	0
Other	1	2

59 games since 2010 World Cup

Clean sheets

Honduras	13	38%
Opp	11	32%

34 competitive games since 2010 World Cup

Players used in qualifying

Pos		Club	Career			Qualifying		
			Age	P	G	P	G	Y/R
G	Donis Escober	Deportivo Olim	34	25	0	2	0	0
G	Jose Mendoza	Xelaju	24	1	0	1	0	0
G	Noel Valladares	Deportivo Olim	36	119	0	14	0	1
D	Brayan Beckeles	Deportivo Olim	28	20	1	3	0	1
D	Jose Velasquez	Victoria	24	6	0	1	0	1
D	Emilio Izaguirre	Celtic	27	64	1	14	0	1
D	Johnny Leveron	Vancouver W.	24	21	3	1	0	0
D	Juan Garcia	Wigan	25	32	1	8	1	0
D	Juan Montes	Motagua	28	9	1	2	0	0
D	Mauricio Sabillon	Marathon	35	49	0	3	0	1
D	Maynor Figueroa	Hull	30	101	3	13	1	1
D	Orlin Peralta	Motagua	24	5	0	1	0	0
D	Osman Chavez	Wisla Krakow	29	52	0	1	0	0
D	Victor Bernardez	San Jose Earth.	31	72	3	15	1	3
D	Wilmer Crisanto	Motagua	24	7	0	1	0	0
M	Alfredo Mejia	Marathon	23	15	1	1	0	0
M	Andy Najar	Anderlecht	20	16	1	5	0	0
M	Oscar Garcia	Houston Dyn.	29	89	2	16	1	1
M	Arnold Peralta	Rangers	24	21	0	12	0	2
M	Carlos Discua	Motagua	29	5	0	1	0	0
M	Edder Delgado	Real Espana	27	25	0	2	0	0
M	Edgar Alvarez	Platense	34	53	3	2	0	0
M	Jorge Claros	Motagua	28	45	4	8	1	0
M	Luis Garrido	Olimpia	23	18	0	11	0	3
M	Mario Martinez	Real Espana	24	34	3	9	2	0
M	Roger Espinoza	Wigan	27	40	3	12	0	1
M	Wilson Palacios	Stoke	29	88	5	11	1	1
F	Marvin Chavez	Colorado Rapids	30	40	4	6	1	1
F	Anthony Lozano	Olimpia	20	4	0	2	0	0
F	Carlo Costly	Real Espana	31	68	30	13	7	3
F	David Suazo	Retired	34	57	17	1	0	0
F	Georgie Welcome	Tero Sasana	28	32	3	4	0	0
F	Jerry Bengtson	New England R.	26	41	19	12	9	1
F	Jerry Palacios	Alajuelense	31	19	5	3	0	0
F	Kervin Johnson	Deportes Savio	26	3	0	1	0	0
F	Roger Rojas	Deportivo Olim	23	23	3	3	1	0

Their fearsome front line makes Argentina bankers for group-stage success

How short is too short? That's the question punters need to ask themselves when weighing up Group F, with Argentina going off at skinny prices to take top spot in a section which also includes Nigeria, Bosnia and Iran, **writes Mark Langdon**.

Alejandro Sabella could not have hand-picked better opponents and Argentina have been given a brilliant opportunity to boost confidence in the group stage with the front three of Lionel Messi, Sergio Aguero and Gonzalo Higuain capable of causing carnage in every match.

It's the most devastating threesome in the competition by some distance and if Argentina are to fall short in their quest for glory then it will almost certainly come in the latter stages when the weaker defence will be more seriously examined.

For now, Argentina appear to be group bankers and sticking them in with South American rivals Brazil to top Group A is the most rock-solid of multiple bets.

The battle for second is more interesting, but the bookmakers' odds which have Bosnia just ahead of Nigeria are difficult to quibble with.

Bosnia are determined to play positively and use two strikers – Edin Dzeko and Vedad Ibisevic – in all their group games, which could produce disastrous consequences against Argentina in their opener but might work to their advantage in the potentially pivotal clash with Nigeria.

The Super Eagles come into this as African champions but they struggled when upped in class at last summer's Confederations Cup and were barely given a test in the qualification play-offs against Ethiopia.

They also struggled initially before being successful at the Africa Cup of Nations, when they nearly went out of the group stage following draws with Burkina Faso and Zambia (neither of whom qualified for the World Cup) and needed two late Victor Moses penalties to see off Ethiopia.

Without wishing to be harsh, it is entirely plausible that Nigeria just got lucky in winning that 2013 tournament and good fortune will also need to be on Iran's side if they are to make any impact.

Iran are a strong defensive unit and will take some breaking down which is why Bosnia, with Dzeko and Ibisevic, hold the edge over an often wasteful Nigeria in the race for a last-16 berth.

Recommendation
Argentina and Brazil to win their groups (double)

	bet365	Coral	Lads	Power	W Hill
Argentina	2-9	2-7	1-6	2-9	1-4
Bosnia-Hz	6	5	15-2	7	13-2
Nigeria	9	7	10	9	11-2
Iran	33	28	28	33	50

To qualify odds

	Lads	Power	W Hill	Power	W Hill
Argentina	1-50	1-25	1-14	66	40
Bosnia-Hz	19-20	10-11	4-6	4	9-2
Nigeria	7-5	13-10	5-4	16-5	11-4
Iran	4	5	5	1-2	4-9

All group betting markets are win only

Straight forecast

	Power
Argentina/Bosnia	7-5
Argentina/Nigeria	15-8
Argentina/Iran	11-2
Bosnia/Argentina	9
Nigeria/Argentina	12
Nigeria/Bosnia	40
Bosnia/Nigeria	40
Iran/Argentina	45
Bosnia/Iran	90
Nigeria/Iran	100
Iran/Bosnia	150
Iran/Nigeria	175

Group matches | World Cup history | Head-to-head record | Last meeting

Group matches	World Cup history	Head-to-head record	Last meeting
Argentina v Bosnia-Hz Sunday June 15, 11pm, Rio De Janeiro	No previous World Cup meetings	Two Argentina wins since 1998 by an aggregate score of 7-0	Sergio Aguero scored two in a 2-0 win for Argentina last November
Iran v Nigeria Monday June 16, 8pm, Curitiba	No previous World Cup meetings	One meeting which finished in a 1-0 win for Nigeria	Hong Kong, January 1998
Argentina v Iran Saturday June 21, 5pm, Belo Horizonte	No previous World Cup meetings	One previous meeting in 1977 which finished as a 1-1 draw	The Bernabeu at a tournament for Real Madrid's 75th anniversary
Nigeria v Bosnia-Hz Saturday June 21, 11pm, Cuiaba	No previous World Cup meetings	No previous meetings	
Nigeria v Argentina Wednesday June 25, 5pm, Porto Alegre	Group-stage wins for Argentina in 1994, 2002 and 2010	Four wins for Argentina, one win for Nigeria and a draw since 1994	Higuain and Di Maria scored in Argentina's 3-1 win in 2011
Bosnia-Hz v Iran Wednesday June 25, 5pm, Salvador	No previous World Cup meetings	Four friendly wins for Iran since a 2-2 draw in 2001	Edin Dzeko scored two but Iran came back to win 3-2 in Sarajevo in 2009

Route to the final

Group winners

Round of 16 July 1 Sao Paulo
2E Switzerland, Ecuador, France, Honduras

Quarter-finals July 5 Brasilia
1H Belgium, Algeria, Russia, South Korea
2G Germany, Portugal, Ghana, USA

Semi-finals July 9 Sao Paulo
1B Spain, Holland, Chile, Australia
2A Brazil, Croatia, Mexico, Cameroon
1D Uruguay, Costa Rica, England, Italy
2C Colombia, Greece, Ivory Coast, Japan

Final July 13 Rio

Group runners-up

Round of 16 June 30 Brasilia
1E Switzerland, Ecuador, France, Honduras

Quarter-finals July 4 Rio de Janeiro
1G Germany, Portugal, Ghana, USA
2H Belgium, Algeria, Russia, South Korea

Semi-finals July 8 Belo Horizonte
1A Brazil, Croatia, Mexico, Cameroon
2B Spain, Holland, Chile, Australia
1C Colombia, Greece, Ivory Coast, Japan
2D Uruguay, Costa Rica, England, Italy

ARGENTINA

Underachievers can step up but defending is a worry against the very best

I t's the same story at every tournament – Argentina bring a stellar cast of superstars but when the major honours are dished out it's usually someone else with their name on the trophy. They have become the biggest underachievers in the game with no World Cup semi-final appearances since 1990 and their last Copa America triumph back in 1993, but hopes are high that things could be different this time.

How they qualified

Argentina were mighty impressive once they recovered from a sticky start which saw them lose 1-0 in Venezuela and draw 1-1 at home to Bolivia. Alejandro Sabella soon sorted out the problems as Argentina finished the marathon Conmebol campaign as top dogs. Their sensational 'goals for' tally of 35 was comfortably the best in South America.

The manager

Sabella won the Copa Libertadores with Estudiantes de la Plata in 2009 and was appointed Argentina's boss after they crashed out of their home Copa America at the quarter-final stage in 2011.

The former Sheffield United and Leeds midfielder replaced Javier Mascherano as captain with Lionel Messi and, following a barren spell at international level, the four-time Ballon d'Or winner responded with ten goals in qualifying.

Match winners

Where do you start? Messi is one of the greatest goalscorers in the history of the game and is finally doing the business for Argentina but the Barcelona superstar is not alone in being a world-class talent in the attacking department.

Gonzalo Higuain grabbed nine goals in qualifying, while Sergio Aguero can be

Country factfile

FA founded 1893
www afa.org.ar
Head coach Alejandro Sabella
National league Primera Division
System of government Republic
Population 42 million
Capital city Buenos Aires
Currency Peso
Official language Spanish

Strengths
- ☑ Messi, Higuain and Aguero form the best attack in Brazil by a long way
- ☑ Cosy draw, which is highlighted by short odds to reach quarters

Weaknesses
- ☒ First-choice keeper Romero does not play regularly at club level
- ☒ Relative lack of depth defensively
- ☒ May struggle with huge expectations

Base Vespasiano
Fixtures
1 Bosnia, June 15, Rio
2 Iran, June 21, Belo Horizonte
3 Nigeria, June 25, Porto Alegre

GROUP F

*Go for Argentina
goals in this easy
looking group*

devastating. His special relationship with Messi started when the pair roomed together as Argentina won the World Youth Cup in 2005. La Albiceleste retained that youth title in 2007 and that successful crop of players, who have come through the ranks together, will be aiming to shed Argentina's tag as nearly men.

Question marks

The attacking talent is so strong that Carlos Tevez is unlikely to be included in the squad but there isn't the same kind of quality in the defensive third with unheralded Marcos Rojo set to fill the problematic left-back position.

First-choice goalie Sergio Romero does not get much playing time at Monaco, regular centre-back Federico Fernandez has been dodgy for Napoli at times this season and Sabella will be praying nothing happens to Ezequiel Garay and Pablo Zabaleta.

How to back them

History would say to back Argentina for a quarter-final exit – after all it has happened in three of the last four World Cups – but Sabella's side won't get a better opportunity to rid themselves of the underachievers tag and must be on any shortlist of potential winners.

That the World Cup is being held in South America should be advantageous and they have been handed a perfect draw, not only in terms of the opposition but also the group-stage locations, where Argentina won't suffer the same travel chaos as some nations.

Whether the defence holds firm at the very highest level remains to be seen but since the last World Cup they have beaten all four of the Euro 2012 semi-finalists (Spain, Portugal, Italy and Germany) and the forwards should get their eye in against group rivals Bosnia, Iran and Nigeria.

Argentina have scored at least seven goals in three of their last four World Cup group stages and backing over 6.5 group-stage goals looks the best bet for those who don't trust them when the going gets tough.

ARGENTINA

World Cup record

Uruguay 1930	Runners-up
Italy 1934	First round
France 1938	Withdrew
Brazil 1950	Withdrew
Switzerland 1954	Did not enter
Sweden 1958	Group stage
Chile 1962	Group stage
England 1966	Quarter-finals
Mexico 1970	Did not qualify
Germany 1974	Second round
Argentina 1978	**Winners**
Spain 1982	Second round
Mexico 1986	**Winners**
Italy 1990	Runners-up
USA 1994	Round of 16
France 1998	Quarter-finals
Korea/Japan 2002	Group stage
Germany 2006	Quarter-finals
South Africa 2010	Quarter-finals

Continental titles

Copa America (1921, 1925, 1927, 1929, 1936, 1941, 1945, 1946, 1947, 1955, 1957, 1959, 1991, 1993)

Legendary player

Argentina have had some true greats and in Lionel Messi they still do, but for his country, **Diego Maradona** is still the greatest. He won the World Cup in 1986, scoring five goals along the way, and although his career after that was dogged by injuries, he led his team to the final four years later. Bad behaviour both on and off the pitch drew plenty of criticism but when he was playing, he had everything – strength, speed, vision and unbelievable skill.

Did you know?

Argentina haven't gone further than the quarter-finals at a World Cup since 1990

How they qualified

Final group	P	W	D	L	F	A	GD	Pts
Argentina	**16**	**9**	**5**	**2**	**35**	**15**	**20**	**32**
Colombia	16	9	3	4	27	13	14	30
Chile	16	9	1	6	29	25	4	28
Ecuador	16	7	4	5	20	16	4	25
Uruguay	16	7	4	5	25	25	0	25
Venezuela	16	5	5	6	14	20	-6	20
Peru	16	4	3	9	17	26	-9	15
Bolivia	16	2	6	8	17	30	-13	12
Paraguay	16	3	3	10	17	31	-14	12

Coach Alejandro Sabella working his magic

Argentina ....(2) 4-1 (0).................Chile
Argentina: Higuain (8, 52, 63) Messi (26) Chile: Fernandez (60)

Venezuela........(0) 1-0 (0)..........Argentina
Venezuela: Amorebieta (61)

Argentina ....(0) 1-1 (0)............... Bolivia
Argentina: Lavezzi (60) Bolivia: Martins (56)

Colombia.........(1) 1-2 (0)...........Argentina
Colombia: Pabon (45) Argentina: Messi (61) Aguero (85)

Argentina ....(3) 4-0 (0).............Ecuador
Argentina: Aguero (20) Higuain (30) Messi (32) Di Maria (76)

Argentina ....(0) 3-1 (0)........... Paraguay
Argentina: Di Maria (3) Higuain (30) Messi (64) Paraguay: Fabbro (pen 17)

Peru.................(1) 1-1 (1)..........Argentina
Peru: Zambrano (22) Argentina: Higuain (38)

Argentina ....(0) 3-0 (0)............. Uruguay
Argentina: Messi (66, 80) Aguero (75)

Chile................(0) 1-2 (2).........Argentina
Chile: Gutierrez (90) Argentina: Messi (28) Higuain (31)

Argentina ....(2) 3-0 (0)......... Venezuela
Argentina: Higuain (29, 59) Messi (pen 45)

Bolivia ....(1) 1-1 (1).................Argentina
Bolivia: Moreno (24) Argentina: Banega (44)

Argentina ....(0) 0-0 (0).......... Colombia

Ecuador...........(1) 1-1 (1).........Argentina
Ecuador: Castillo (17) Argentina: Aguero (4)

Paraguay ....(1) 2-5 (2)..........Argentina
Paraguay: Nunez (17) Santa Cruz (86) Argentina: Messi (pen 12, pen 53) Aguero (32) Di Maria (50) Rodriguez (90)

Argentina ....(2) 3-1 (1)................. Peru
Argentina: Lavezzi (23, 35) Palacio (47) Peru: Pizarro (21)

Uruguay ....(2) 3-2 (2)..........Argentina
Uruguay: Rodriguez (6) Suarez (pen 34) Cavani (49) Argentina: Rodriguez (15, 41)

Full qualifying results and tables on pages 234-256

Clockwise from main: the pressure is on Lionel Messi to deliver the World Cup on his home continent, Sergio Aguero is devastating, but Federico Fernandez is a potential weak link at the back

ARGENTINA

Pos		Club	Career			Qualifying		
			Age	P	G	P	G	Y/R
G	Mariano Andujar	Catania	30	10	0	2	0	0
G	Sergio Romero	Monaco	27	45	0	14	0	0
D	Clemente Rodriguez	Sao Paulo	32	20	0	4	0	1
D	Ezequiel Garay	Benfica	27	18	0	9	0	2
D	Fabricio Coloccini	Newcastle	32	39	1	1	0	0
D	Federico Fernandez	Napoli	25	24	2	11	0	2
D	Gino Peruzzi	Catania	21	4	0	2	0	0
D	Hugo Campagnaro	Inter	33	13	0	7	0	1
D	Jose Maria Basanta	Monterrey	29	8	0	4	0	1
D	Leandro Desabato	Estudiantes	35	5	0	1	0	0
D	Marcos Rojo	Sporting Lisbon	24	21	0	10	0	2
D	Martin Demichelis	Man City	33	37	2	2	0	0
D	Nicolas Burdisso	Genoa	32	49	2	4	0	1
D	Nicolas Otamendi	Porto	26	16	1	2	0	0
D	Pablo Zabaleta	Man City	29	36	0	11	0	3
D	Sebastian Dominguez	Velez	33	8	0	2	0	0
M	Angel Di Maria	Real Madrid	26	45	9	12	3	3
M	Augusto Fernandez	Celta Vigo	27	7	1	1	0	0
M	Eduardo Salvio	Benfica	23	5	0	1	0	0
M	Enzo Perez	Benfica	28	6	1	1	0	0
M	Erik Lamela	Tottenham	22	6	0	2	0	1
M	Ever Banega	Newell's OB	25	24	2	8	1	2
M	Fabian Rinaudo	Catania	26	4	0	1	0	0
M	Fernando Gago	Boca Juniors	27	47	0	9	0	0
M	Javier Mascherano	Barcelona	29	95	2	11	0	3/1
M	Javier Pastore	Paris St-G.	24	13	0	2	0	0
M	Jonas Gutierrez	Norwich	30	22	1	1	0	0
M	Jose Sosa	Atl Madrid	28	18	1	6	0	0
M	Leandro Somoza	Lanus	33	5	0	2	0	0
M	Leonardo Ponzio	River Plate	32	8	0	1	0	0
M	Lucas Biglia	Lazio	28	18	0	6	0	1
M	Maxi Rodriguez	Newell's OB	33	53	15	6	3	0
M	Pablo Guinazu	Vasco de Gama	35	16	0	6	0	0
M	Ricardo Alvarez	Inter	25	5	0	1	0	0
M	Rodrigo Brana	Quilmes	35	9	0	4	0	2
M	Walter Montillo	Shandong Lun.	29	6	0	2	0	0
F	Ezequiel Lavezzi	Paris St-G.	28	29	4	8	3	0
F	Franco Di Santo	Werder Bremen	24	3	0	1	0	0
F	Gonzalo Higuain	Napoli	26	36	22	11	9	2/1
F	Hernan Barcos	Gremio	29	4	0	2	0	0
F	Lionel Messi	Barcelona	26	84	37	14	10	0
F	Mauro Icardi	Inter	21	1	0	1	0	0
F	Rodrigo Palacio	Inter	32	21	2	8	1	1
F	Sergio Aguero	Man City	25	50	21	8	5	3

What happens if ...

Argentina score first

Argentina win	8	40%
Draw	1	5%
Argentina lose	0	0%

20 games since 2010 World Cup

Opponents score first

Argentina win	2	10%
Draw	5	25%
Argentina lose	2	10%

Goal times

For			Against
3		0-9	2
3		10-18	3
3		19-27	3
8		28-36	1
5		37-45	1
5		46-54	2
4		55-63	3
3		64-72	0
4		73-81	0
2		82-90	2

Argentina			Opponents	
22	55%	1st half	10	59%
18	45%	2nd half	7	41%

20 games since 2010 World Cup

Correct scores

	Friendly	Comp
1-0	3	0
2-0	1	0
2-1	3	2
3-0	0	3
3-1	3	2
3-2	1	0
4-0	2	1
4-1	2	1
4-2	1	0
4-3	1	0
0-0	5	2
1-1	1	6
2-2	1	0
3-3	0	0
4-4	0	0
0-1	1	1
0-2	1	0
1-2	2	0
0-3	0	0
1-3	0	0
2-3	0	1
0-4	0	0
1-4	1	0
2-4	0	0
3-4	0	0
Other	0	1

49 games since 2010 World Cup

Bookings

Yellow cards	31
Red cards	2
Avg make-up	22.5

In 2014 World Cup qualifying

Top scorers

	Total	First	%	Anytime	%
L Messi	10	3	30	8	57
G Higuain	9	2	22	6	55
S Aguero	5	2	40	5	63
M Rodriguez	3	0	0	2	33
A Di Maria	3	1	33	3	25
E Lavezzi	3	0	0	2	25

In World Cup 2014 qualification

Gonzalo Higuain

Unders & overs

1.5 goals		2.5 goals		3.5 goals		4.5 goals	
Under	Over	Under	Over	Under	Over	Under	Over
15%	85%	45%	55%	70%	30%	85%	15%

20 games since 2010 World Cup

Half-time/Full-time

Win/Win	7	35%
Draw/Win	2	10%
Lose/Win	1	5%
Win/Draw	0	0%
Draw/Draw	8	40%
Lose/Draw	0	0%
Win/Lose	0	0%
Draw/Lose	2	10%
Lose/Lose	0	0%

20 games since 2010 World Cup

Penalty shootouts

Won	3	33%
Lost	6	67%

All-time record

Clean sheets

Argentina	6	30%
Opponents	3	15%

20 games since 2010 World Cup

BOSNIA-HZ

Bosnians possess the firepower to make it into the knockout rounds

F ew countries deserve a shot on the big stage more than Bosnia, who finally made it through to a major tournament for the first time after suffering a couple of near misses with play-off defeats at the hands of Portugal in qualifying for both the 2010 World Cup and Euro 2012. Winning the World Cup is almost certainly beyond them but Bosnia could become a neutrals' favourite in Brazil.

How they qualified

A 1-0 home defeat by Slovakia when the nerves kicked in was the only blemish for Bosnia. They won eight of their ten matches and eventually qualified ahead of Greece on goal difference (plus 24 to plus eight).

The Bosnians scored 30 goals in qualifying, with Edin Dzeko bagging ten of those from 900 minutes played and Vedad Ibisevic weighing in with eight. But they showed they can also defend when they have to, with a goalless draw away to Greece ultimately proving pivotal in taking a direct route to Brazil.

The manager

Safet Susic was a genius as a footballer and he is committed to playing attacking football in Brazil. His style is best summed up by an interview with Fifa.com when he said: "I like my team to attack, hold onto the ball and try to out-score the opposition.

"Sometimes we do neglect the defensive side of the game a little and concede goals, but we don't have the resources to play any other way. I really don't know what coaches do if they prefer defensive football. Personally, I don't like it and I don't believe in that style of play."

Match winners

As you can gather this is a team built to

Country factfile

FA founded 1992
www nfsbih.ba
Head coach Safet Susic
National league Premijer Liga
System of government Federal democratic republic
Population 4 million
Capital city Sarajevo
Currency Convertible Marka
Official languages Bosnian, Croatian, Serbian

Strengths
- ☑ Dzeko and Ibisevic can win any game
- ☑ Pjanic and Misimovic are technically gifted playmakers of ace ability

Weaknesses
- ☒ Little depth in any position
- ☒ Nobody to anchor midfield
- ☒ Poor centre-back options outside of Spahic

Base Guaruja
Fixtures
1 Argentina, June 15, Rio
2 Nigeria, June 21, Cuiaba
3 Iran, June 25, Salvador

GROUP F

*Edin Dzeko and Vedad Ibisevic scored
18 goals between them in qualification*

attack so Bosnia will play with two central forwards, even against Argentina, with Dzeko partnering Stuttgart's Ibisevic and Roma's beautifully gifted player Miralem Pjanic the man charged with making the team tick.

Much-travelled Zvjezdan Misimovic can still cause problems – sometimes for the opposition and sometimes for his own managers – while Lazio's Senad Lulic and emerging Schalke full-back Sead Kolasinac provide a nice balance to the left side.

Question marks
There is not much talent beyond the starting XI and few teams will be as reliant on one defender as Bosnia, who are pinning their hopes on the shoulders of skipper Emir Spahic.

The draw gives Bosnia a fair chance of following Argentina through but an early start in Salvador to take on Iran could be tricky given the hot climate on the north-east coast.

How to back them
Opening group matches can often be tight affairs but taking over 2.5 goals when Bosnia face Argentina in Rio on June 15 could be a nice way to profit from two attacking teams in what has the potential to be a shootout for top spot in the section.

Bosnia possess the firepower to make sure they come through against Nigeria and Iran even if they lose the Argentina match, with the last 16 looking the most likely stopping point unless Dzeko goes on a scoring spree to get the limited defence out of trouble.

The Manchester City hotshot is a worthy favourite to be Bosnia's top scorer. He gels well with Misimovic, who provided Dzeko with plenty of goalscoring opportunities when the pair linked up to help Wolfsburg win the Bundesliga in 2008-09.

BOSNIA-HZ

World Cup record

Uruguay 1930	Fourth place*
Italy 1934	Did not qualify*
France 1938	Did not qualify*
Brazil 1950	Group stage*
Switzerland 1954	Quarter-finals*
Sweden 1958	Quarter-finals*
Chile 1962	Fourth place*
England 1966	Did not qualify*
Mexico 1970	Did not qualify*
Germany 1974	Second round*
Argentina 1978	Did not qualify*
Spain 1982	Group stage*
Mexico 1986	Did not qualify*
Italy 1990	Quarter-finals*
USA 1994	Did not enter
France 1998	Did not qualify
Korea/Japan 2002	Did not qualify
Germany 2006	Did not qualify
South Africa 2010	Did not qualify

*Part of Yugoslavia until 1992, recognised by Fifa 1996

Continental titles

None

Legendary player

Bosnia's attacking players are highly regarded but they will have to go some to eclipse the coach, **Safet Susic**. His 21 goals in 54 games for Yugoslavia included hat-tricks against Italy and Argentina in 1979 and he's followed it up by leading Bosnia to their first ever World Cup.

Did you know?

Three of Bosnia-Herzegovina's four all-time top scorers are in contention to make the squad – Dzeko, Misimovic and Ibisevic

Edin Dzeko scored a third of Bosnia-Herzegovina's goals in qualifying

How they qualified

Final group	P	W	D	L	F	A	GD	Pts
Bosnia-Hz	10	8	1	1	30	6	24	25
Greece	10	8	1	1	12	4	8	25
Slovakia	10	3	4	3	11	10	1	13
Lithuania	10	3	2	5	9	11	-2	11
Latvia	10	2	2	6	10	20	-10	8
Liechtenstein	10	0	2	8	4	25	-21	2

These days you'll find Safet Susic in the dugout

Liechtenstein ...(0) 1-8 (4)......... Bosnia-Hz.
Liechtenstein: Christen (61) Bosnia-Hz.: Misimovic (26, 31)
Ibisevic (34, 40, 83) Dzeko (46, 64, 81)

Bosnia-Hz. ....(2) 4-1 (1)................ Latvia
Bosnia-Hz.: Misimovic (pen 12, 54) Pjanic (44) Dzeko (90)
Latvia: Gorkss (5)

Greece.............(0) 0-0 (0)......... Bosnia-Hz.

Bosnia-Hz. ....(3) 3-0 (0)........... Lithuania
Bosnia-Hz.: Ibisevic (29) Dzeko (35) Pjanic (41)

Bosnia-Hz. ....(2) 3-1 (0)............... Greece
Bosnia-Hz.: Dzeko (29, 53) Ibisevic (36) Greece: Gekas (90)

Latvia ....(0) 0-5 (0)......... Bosnia-Hz.
Bosnia-Hz.: Lulic (48) Ibisevic (53) Medunjanin (63) Pjanic
(80) Dzeko (82)

Bosnia-Hz. ....(0) 0-1 (0)............. Slovakia
Slovakia: Pecovsky (77)

Slovakia...........(1) 1-2 (0)......... Bosnia-Hz.
Slovakia: Hamsik (42) Bosnia-Hz.: Bicakcic (69) Hajrovic (78)

Bosnia-Hz. ....(4) 4-1 (0)..... Liechtenstein
Bosnia-Hz.: Dzeko (27, 39) Misimovic (34) Ibisevic (38)
Liechtenstein: Hasler (61)

Lithuania ....(0) 0-1 (0)......... Bosnia-Hz.
Bosnia-Hz.: Ibisevic (68)

Full qualifying results and tables on pages 234-256

BOSNIA-HZ

Players used in qualifying		Career			Qualifying		
Pos		Club	Age	P	G	P	G	Y/R
G	Asmir Begovic	Stoke	26	28	0	10	0	1
D	Avdija Vrsajevic	Hajduk Split	27	12	0	7	0	0
D	Emir Spahic	B Leverkusen	33	71	3	10	0	0
D	Ermin Bicakcic	Braunschweig	24	7	1	4	1	0
D	Ervin Zukanovic	Gent	27	6	0	3	0	0
D	Mensur Mujdza	Freiburg	29	22	0	6	0	0
D	Ognjen Vranjes	Elazigspor	24	12	0	5	0	1
D	Toni Sunjic	Zorya	25	5	0	2	0	0
D	Zoran Kvrzic	Rijeka	25	3	0	1	0	0
M	Adnan Zahirovic	Bochum	23	20	0	7	0	0
M	Edin Visca	Istanbul Buyuk.	23	8	0	3	0	0
M	Elvir Rahimic	CSKA Moscow	37	40	0	2	0	0
M	Haris Medunjanin	Gaziantepspor	29	34	5	8	1	1
M	Izet Hajrovic	Galatasaray	22	5	1	3	1	0
M	Miralem Pjanic	Roma	23	46	8	8	3	1
M	Miroslav Stevanovic	Alaves	23	10	1	5	0	1
M	Muama Svraka	Zeljeznicar	25	6	2	1	0	0
M	Sejad Salihovic	Hoffenheim	29	40	4	9	0	0
M	Senad Lulic	Lazio	28	32	1	9	1	1
M	Senidad Ibricic	Erciyesspor	28	43	4	4	0	1
M	Zviezdan Misimovic	Guizhou Rende	31	79	25	9	5	0
F	Damir Vrancic	Braunschweig	28	4	0	1	0	0
F	Edin Dzeko	Man City	28	60	33	10	10	1
F	Vedad Ibisevic	Stuttgart	29	53	20	10	8	1

What happens if ...

Bosnia-Hz score first

Bosnia-Hz win	11	50%
Draw	2	9%
Bosnia-Hz lose	0	0%

22 games since 2010 World Cup

Opponents score first

Bosnia-Hz win	3	14%
Draw	0	0%
Bosnia-Hz lose	4	18%

GROUP F

Goal times

For		Against
1	0-9	2
5	10-18	0
6	19-27	1
8	28-36	2
7	37-45	3
6	46-54	1
2	55-63	3
5	64-72	2
3	73-81	4
6	82-90	2

Bosnia-Hz		Opponents	
27	55%	1st half	8	40%
22	45%	2nd half	12	60%

22 games since 2010 World Cup

Correct scores

	Friendly	Comp
1-0	1	2
2-0	1	2
2-1	0	2
3-0	1	2
3-1	0	1
3-2	1	0
4-0	0	0
4-1	0	2
4-2	0	0
4-3	0	0
0-0	1	2
1-1	1	2
2-2	0	0
3-3	0	0
4-4	0	0
0-1	2	1
0-2	3	1
1-2	2	0
0-3	0	1
1-3	0	0
2-3	1	0
0-4	0	0
1-4	0	0
2-4	0	0
3-4	1	0
Other	0	4

37 games since 2010 World Cup

Bookings

Yellow cards	9
Red cards	0
Avg make-up	0.9

In 2014 World Cup qualifying

Top scorers

	Total	First	%	Anytime	%
E Dzeko	10	2	20	6	60
V Ibisevic	8	2	25	6	60
Z Misimovic	5	1	20	3	33
M Pjanic	3	0	0	3	38

In World Cup 2014 qualification

Miralem Pjanic makes Bosnia tick

Unders & overs

1.5 goals		2.5 goals		3.5 goals		4.5 goals	
Under	Over	Under	Over	Under	Over	Under	Over
23%	77%	45%	55%	68%	32%	73%	27%

22 games since 2010 World Cup

Half-time/Full-time

Win/Win	8	36%
Draw/Win	4	18%
Lose/Win	2	9%
Win/Draw	1	5%
Draw/Draw	3	14%
Lose/Draw	0	0%
Win/Lose	0	0%
Draw/Lose	2	9%
Lose/Lose	2	9%

WIN 63%

22 games since 2010 World Cup

Penalty shootouts

Won	-	-
Lost	-	-

All-time record

Clean sheets

Bosnia-Hz	10	45%
Opponents	5	23%

22 games since 2010 World Cup

Iranian goals will be at a premium as Quieroz's men are no entertainers

Stade Gerland in Lyon will always hold happy memories for Iranian football supporters. It was the venue for their one and only World Cup win in three tournament attempts and the result could not have been any sweeter, with goalscorers Hamid Estili and Mehdi Mahdavikia becoming national heroes for beating old enemies USA. However, few of the current crop look ready to join the class of 98 in Iranian folklore.

How they qualified

The scenes that followed the final matchday win in South Korea stunned the watching world.

The subsequent war of words between the nations lasted several months, and culminated with Heung-Min Son threatening to leave Iran captain Javad Nekounam "crying tears of blood."

It all started with South Korea complaining about off-field skulduggery before the reverse fixture and the spat ended in quite farcical scenes.

Iran coach Carlos Queiroz made an "obscene gesture" towards the South Korean bench, one of his players was punched in the face after celebrating near the home dugout and the visiting players were pelted with objects after going on an ill-advised 'lap of honour.'

Korean paper Sports Chosun commented at the time: "Iran stuck their tongues out to the audience and made fun of them. Those who are only good at playing games but have no respect for sportsmanship do not deserve to go to the World Cup."

In terms of results, Iran cruised through a play-off with Maldives and went through the easy first section unbeaten before topping the second qualifying group two points clear of South Korea.

They conceded only two goals in eight

Country factfile

FA founded 1920

www ffiri.ir

Head coach Carlos Queiroz

National league Persian Gulf League

System of government Theocratic republic

Population 80 million

Capital city Tehran

Currency Rial

Official language Persian

Strengths

☑ Don't concede many goals

☑ Will stick to the gameplan

☑ Skipper Nekounam has over 130 caps

Weaknesses

☒ Goals a problem in qualifying

☒ Queiroz has complained about poor preparation

☒ Political interference never far away

Base Guarulhos

Fixtures

1 Nigeria, June 16, Curitiba

2 Argentina, June 21, Belo Horizonte

3 Bosnia, June 25, Salvador

GROUP F

matches during that second phase, keeping six clean sheets. Seven of those fixtures featured no more than one goal so forget about watching the highlights on YouTube and head straight to the fight scenes.

The manager

Queiroz is held in high regard for his coaching capabilities and was twice assistant to Sir Alex Ferguson at Manchester United. He has been the number one on numerous occasions too with Portugal, South Africa and Real Madrid, but the coach probably did his best work in bringing through Portugal's golden generation from the youth ranks in the early 1990s.

Match winners

Charlton new boy Reza Ghoochannejhad was the goalscoring hero in South Korea but skipper Nekounam is the heartbeat of the team. The former Osasuna man dictates play expertly from midfield and is also strong at set pieces but Iran's World Cup will be mainly about parking the bus defensively while hoping for something on the break or from a dead-ball situation.

Question marks

Very few of the players are involved at the highest level and those who are registered in bigger leagues, such as Fulham's Ashkan Dejagah, struggle to consistently hold down a place in the starting XI. Iran find goals difficult to come by and Queiroz has complained about poor preparation.

How to back them

Two bets stand out – backing Iran to score under 2.5 tournament goals and for them to secure no more than one point from a hard group containing Argentina, Bosnia and Nigeria.

Iran have never scored more than two goals in a World Cup finals and qualification showed they focus mainly on nullifying the opposition. That could work in terms of saving face but is unlikely to see Queiroz's unadventurous side grab points and goals.

Javad Nekounam

IRAN

World Cup record

Uruguay 1930	Did not enter
Italy 1934	Did not enter
France 1938	Did not enter
Brazil 1950	Did not enter
Switzerland 1954	Did not enter
Sweden 1958	Did not enter
Chile 1962	Did not enter
England 1966	Did not enter
Mexico 1970	Did not enter
Germany 1974	Did not qualify
Argentina 1978	Group stage
Spain 1982	Withdrew
Mexico 1986	Disqualified
Italy 1990	Did not qualify
USA 1994	Did not qualify
France 1998	Group stage
Korea/Japan 2002	Did not qualify
Germany 2006	Group stage
South Africa 2010	Did not qualify

Continental titles

Asian Cup 1968, 1972, 1976

Legendary player

Ali Daei is a goalscoring legend but it was **Mehdi Mahdavikia** who delivered Iran's greatest moment on the world stage, scoring their winner in the 2-1 victory over the USA at France 98 for their first ever World Cup victory.

Did you know?

Iran have taken at least a point in each of their three World Cup appearances

How they qualified

Round 2

Iran ....(1) 4-0 (0)...........Maldives
Iran: Ansari (4) Karimi (61, 69) Daghighi (88)

Maldives..........(0) 0-1 (1)..................Iran
Iran: Khalatbari (45)

Round 3

Iran ....(0) 3-0 (0)..........Indonesia
Iran: Nekounam (53, 74) Teymourian (87)

Qatar...............(0) 1-1 (0)..................Iran
Qatar: Mohammed Jeedo (56) Iran: Aghili (46)

Iran ....(3) 6-0 (0).............Bahrain
Iran: Hosseini (22) Jabari (34) Aghili (42) Teymourian (62) Karimi (76) Rezaei (84)

Bahrain............(0) 1-1 (0)..................Iran
Bahrain: Mahmood Al Ajmi (46) Iran: Jabari (90)

Indonesia ....(1) 1-4 (3)..................Iran
Indonesia: Pamungkas (44) Iran: Meydavoodi (7) Jabari (21) Rezaei (25) Nekounam (pen 73)

Iran ....(1) 2-2 (1)................Qatar
Iran: Dejagah (5, 50) Qatar: Khalfan Ibrahim (pen 9) Kasola (86)

Final group	P	W	D	L	F	A	GD	Pts
Iran	8	5	1	2	8	2	6	16
S Korea	8	4	2	2	13	7	6	14
Uzbekistan	8	4	2	2	11	6	5	14
Qatar	8	2	1	5	5	13	-8	7
Lebanon	8	1	2	5	3	12	-9	5

Uzbekistan ......(0) 0-1 (0).................Iran
Iran: Khalatbari (90)

Iran ....(0) 0-0 (0)................Qatar

Lebanon ....(1) 1-0 (0)..................Iran
Lebanon: Roda Antar (28)

Iran ....(0) 1-0 (0)...... South Korea

Iran: Nekounam (75)

Iran ....(0) 0-1 (0)........ Uzbekistan
Uzbekistan: Bakaev (71)

Qatar...............(0) 0-1 (0)..................Iran
Iran: Ghoochanneijhad (66)

Iran ....(2) 4-0 (0)...........Lebanon
Iran: Khalatbari (39) Nekounam (45, 86) Ghoochanneijhad (46)

South Korea ....(0) 0-1 (0)..................Iran
Iran: Ghoochanneijhad (60)

Full qualifying results and tables on pages 234-256

Unders & overs

<1.5	>1.5	<2.5	>2.5	<3.5	>3.5	<4.5	>4.5
40%	60%	52%	48%	72%	28%	84%	16%

25 competitive games since 2010 World Cup

Half-time/Full-time

W/W	8	32%		W/D	1	4%		W/L	0	0%
D/W	9	36%		D/D	5	20%		D/L	1	4%
L/W	0	0%		L/D	0	0%		L/L	1	4%

25 competitive games since 2010 World Cup

Bookings

Yellow cards	27
Red cards	1
Avg make-up	18.4

In 2014 World Cup qualifying

Penalty shootouts

Won	2	29%
Lost	5	71%

All-time record

What happens if ...

Iran score first			Their opponents score first		
Iran win	15	60%	Iran win	1	4%
Draw	2	8%	Draw	1	4%
Iran lose	0	0%	Iran lose	3	12%

25 competitive games since 2010 World Cup

Goal times

For			Against
3	▪	0-9	1
0		10-18	1
3	▪	19-27	0
2	▪	28-36	1
7	▬	37-45	1
5	▬	46-54	1
5	▬	55-63	1
6	▬	64-72	1
4	▪	73-81	2
10	▬▬	82-90	2

Iran			Opponents	
15	33%	1st half	4	36%
30	67%	2nd half	7	63%

25 games since 2010 World Cup

Top scorers

	Total	First	%	Anytime	%
J Nekounam	6	2	33	4	29
A Karimi	3	0	0	2	25
M Khalatbari	3	3	100	3	20
M Jabari	3	0	0	3	38
R Ghoochanneijhad	3	2	67	3	60

In World Cup 2014 qualification

Correct scores

	Friendly	Comp
1-0	4	6
2-0	1	0
2-1	1	2
3-0	1	3
3-1	1	0
3-2	0	0
4-0	0	2
4-1	0	2
4-2	0	0
4-3	0	0
0-0	4	2
1-1	0	3
2-2	2	1
3-3	0	0
4-4	0	0
0-1	1	2
0-2	0	0
1-2	1	0
0-3	1	0
1-3	0	0
2-3	0	0
0-4	0	0
1-4	0	0
2-4	0	0
3-4	0	0
Other	2	2

45 games since 2010 World Cup

Clean sheets

Iran	15	60%
Opp	4	16%

25 competitive games since 2010 World Cup

Players used in qualifying

Pos		Club	Career			Qualifying		
			Age	P	G	P	G	Y/R
G	Rahman Ahmadi	Sepahan	33	10	0	3	0	0
G	Seyed M Rahmati	Esteghlal	30	72	0	13	0	0
D	Amir Sadeqi	Esteghlal	32	13	1	2	0	0
D	Ehsan Haji Safi	Sepahan	23	56	2	8	0	0
D	Hadi Aghili	Sepahan	33	67	10	10	2	1
D	Hashem Beikzadeh	Esteghlal	30	15	1	3	0	0
D	Hossein Mahini	Persepolis	27	20	0	9	0	1
D	Khosro Heydari	Esteghlal	30	43	0	13	0	1
D	Mohammad Nosrati	Teraktor Sazi	33	82	5	1	0	0
D	Pejman Montazeri	Umm-Salal	30	19	1	7	0	0
D	Seyed J Hosseini	Perspolis	32	81	6	15	1	1
M	Mehrdad Pooladi	Persepolis	26	18	0	10	0	1
M	Ali Karimi	Teraktor Sazi	35	127	38	8	3	2
M	Andranik Timotian	Esteghlal	30	75	8	12	2	3
M	Ashkan Dejagah	Fulham	27	11	4	4	2	1
M	Farhad Majidi	Esteghlal	37	47	11	2	0	0
M	Ghasem Hadadifar	Zob Ahan	30	13	0	3	0	0
M	Gholam Rezaei	Foolad	29	48	11	8	2	1
M	Milad Zanidpour	Malavan	27	15	1	1	0	0
M	Javad Nekonam	SC Kuwait	33	139	37	14	6	0
M	Masoud Shojaei	Las Palmas	29	48	5	5	2	2/1
M	Mazyar Zare	Malavan	29	23	3	6	0	3
M	Mohammad Ebrahimi	Teraktor Sazi	29	4	0	1	0	0
M	Mohammad Khalatbari	Perspolis	30	52	5	15	3	0
M	Mohammad Nori	Persepolis	31	25	3	4	0	2
M	Mohsen Mosalman	Persepolis	22	3	1	1	0	0
M	Mojtaba Jabari	Al-Ahli	30	28	3	8	3	1
M	Omid Ebrahimi	Sepahan	26	5	0	1	0	0
M	Pezhman Nouri	Esteghlal	33	44	4	5	0	2
F	Alireza Abbasfard	Sorinet	32	3	1	1	0	0
F	Javad Kazemian	Teraktor Sazi	32	44	4	2	0	1
F	Karim Ansari	Tractor Sazi	23	37	8	10	1	2
F	Mohammad Gholami	Sepahan	31	14	3	1	0	0
F	R Ghoochanneijhad	Charlton	26	9	7	5	3	1
F	Saeed Daghighi	Teraktor Sazi	28	2	1	1	1	0
F	Mohammad Ghazi	Esteghlal	29	12	3	6	0	0
F	Hadi Norozipori	Persepolis	28	9	0	2	0	0
F	Milad Midavoodi	Esteghlal	29	29	6	3	1	1

Goal-shy champions could be facing a frustrating tournament in Brazil

N igeria proved themselves the best team on their own continent when they won the 2013 Africa Cup of Nations but the Super Eagles were then downed fairly comfortably in the Confederations Cup, leaving more questions than answers regarding their position in the world pecking order. Despite some wonderful individual talent over the years, Nigeria have never been past the last 16 of a World Cup and that looks the limit again.

How they qualified

Unbeaten Nigeria strolled through the process but it was rarely pretty stuff. All six of their group matches went under 2.5 goals with only ten in total. That was in arguably the weakest section in Africa which also included Malawi, Kenya and Namibia.

The Super Eagles also had a nice play-off draw and they took advantage by beating Ethiopia 2-1 away and 2-0 at home. Emmanuel Emenike's brace in the away leg meant he took top goalscoring honours in Nigeria's qualifying campaign with a grand total of three.

The manager

The no-nonsense Stephen Keshi was exactly what Nigeria needed and he won the 2013 Africa Cup of Nations with a squad that included local players who may well have been overlooked by foreign bosses.

Keshi, who has resisted calls from certain sections of the Nigerian FA to bring in a foreign assistant to work alongside him in Brazil, qualified Togo for the 2006 World Cup – although he was sacked before the finals – and has also managed Mali.

Match winners

Emenike won the Golden Boot at the Africa Cup of Nations and has been regularly on target for Fenerbahce after joining the

Country factfile

FA founded 1945
Head coach Stephen Keshi
National league Nigeria Premier League
System of government
Federal republic
Population 175 million
Capital city Abuja
Currency Naira
Official language English
Strengths
☑ Enyeama is a one-man wall in goal
☑ Interesting forward options
☑ Keshi won't stand for outside interference
Weaknesses
☒ A lack of coolness in front of goal
☒ Limited options in central midfield
☒ Quality of domestic players

Base Campinas
Fixtures
1 Iran, June 16, Curitiba
2 Bosnia, June 21, Cuiaba
3 Argentina, June 25, Porto Alegre

*Ahmed Musa
in full flight*

Turkish side from Spartak Moscow. John Obi Mikel plays a more progressive role at international level than he does for Chelsea and erratic wide players Ahmed Musa and Victor Moses are both capable of moments of brilliance.

Joseph Yobo was recalled for the March friendly against Mexico but the future of Nigerian defenders is Kenneth Omeruo. Chelsea snapped him up a couple of years ago and have since parked him at Den Haag and Middlesbrough, while goalkeeper Vincent Enyeama has been in inspired form for Lille this season.

Question marks
There has to be a chance that Nigeria's Africa Cup of Nations success in South Africa last year was a fluke.

They lost to Spain (3-0) and Uruguay (2-1) and even managed to concede to Tahiti at last summer's Confederations Cup, which does not bode well for the main event.

Moses has not had many opportunities at Liverpool, recalling Yobo is a backward step and Sunday Mba, scorer of the winner in the Africa Cup of Nations quarter-final over Ivory Coast and the solitary goal in the final against Burkina Faso, has found himself playing for CA Bastia in the lower reaches of the French second division following a contract dispute with two Nigerian clubs.

How to back them
Facing Argentina last could be in Nigeria's favour because the South Americans are likely to have already qualified by then but even their second team should be too strong for the African champions.

Iran are the type of defensively shrewd side who have the potential to frustrate Nigeria and Bosnia are at least the equals of the Super Eagles, so it could pay to take Keshi's side to collect under 3.5 group points.

Musa is an interesting alternative to Emenike in the goalscorer markets with the CSKA Moscow utility man often popping up in dangerous positions.

World Cup record

Uruguay 1930	Did not enter
Italy 1934	Did not enter
France 1938	Did not enter
Brazil 1950	Did not enter
Switzerland 1954	Did not enter
Sweden 1958	Did not enter
Chile 1962	Did not qualify
England 1966	Withdrew
Mexico 1970	Did not qualify
Germany 1974	Did not qualify
Argentina 1978	Did not qualify
Spain 1982	Did not qualify
Mexico 1986	Did not qualify
Italy 1990	Did not qualify
USA 1994	Round of 16
France 1998	Round of 16
Korea/Japan 2002	Group stage
Germany 2006	Did not qualify
South Africa 2010	Group stage

Continental titles

Africa Cup of Nations (1980, 1994, 2013)

Legendary player

Daniel Amokachi got a winners' medal at the 1994 Africa Cup of Nations and his two goals in the USA later that year included a real beauty against Greece. It took an inspired performance by Italy's Roberto Baggio to stop the Super Eagles in the last 16.

How they qualified

Final group	P	W	D	L	F	A	GD	Pts
Nigeria	6	3	3	0	7	3	4	12
Malawi	6	1	4	1	4	5	-1	7
Kenya	6	1	3	2	4	5	-1	6
Namibia	6	1	2	3	2	4	-2	5

Nigeria ....(0) 1-0 (0)........... Namibia
Nigeria: Uche (80)

Malawi ....(0) 1-1 (0)............. Nigeria
Malawi: Banda (90) Nigeria: Egwuekwe (89)

Nigeria ....(0) 1-1 (1)............... Kenya
Nigeria: Oduamadi (88) Kenya: Kahata (35)

Kenya ....(0) 0-1 (0)............. Nigeria
Nigeria: Musa (81)

Namibia...........(0) 1-1 (0)............. Nigeria
Namibia: Hotto (77) Nigeria: Oboabona (82)

Nigeria ....(1) 2-0 (0)............ Malawi
Nigeria: Emenike (45) Moses (pen 51)

Round 3

Ethiopia...........(0) 1-2 (0)........... Nigeria
Ethiopia: Assefa (56) Nigeria: Emenike (67, pen 90)

Nigeria ....(0) 2-0 (0)........... Ethiopia
Nigeria: Moses (pen 20) Obinna (82)

Full qualifying results and tables on pages 234-256

Unders & overs

<1.5	>1.5	<2.5	>2.5	<3.5	>3.5	<4.5	>4.5
20%	80%	54%	46%	69%	31%	83%	17%

35 competitive games since 2010 World Cup

Half-time/Full-time

W/W	11	31%	W/D	2	6%	W/L	0	0%
D/W	8	23%	D/D	7	20%	D/L	1	3%
L/W	0	0%	L/D	2	6%	L/L	4	11%

35 competitive games since 2010 World Cup

Bookings

Yellow cards	9
Red cards	0
Avg make-up	11.3

In 2014 World Cup qualifying

Penalty shootouts

Won	6	60%
Lost	4	40%

All-time record

What happens if ...

Nigeria score first			Their opponents score first		
Nigeria win	17	49%	Nigeria win	3	9%
Draw	4	11%	Draw	4	11%
Nigeria lose	0	0%	Nigeria lose	5	14%

35 competitive games since 2010 World Cup

Did you know?

In their four World Cup appearances, Nigeria have either won their group or finished bottom

Top scorers

	Total	First	%	Anytime	%
E Emenike	3	1	33	2	67
V Moses	2	1	50	2	33

In World Cup 2014 qualification

Goal times

For		Against
4	0-9	4
4	10-18	2
9	19-27	3
3	28-36	2
7	37-45	4
7	46-54	5
5	55-63	3
7	64-72	1
8	73-81	4
14	82-90	5

Nigeria			Opponents	
27	40%	1st half	15	45%
41	60%	2nd half	18	55%

35 games since 2010 World Cup

Correct scores

	Friendly	Comp
1-0	0	4
2-0	3	6
2-1	1	2
3-0	1	0
3-1	1	1
3-2	0	0
4-0	0	1
4-1	2	2
4-2	0	1
4-3	0	1
0-0	6	2
1-1	0	5
2-2	2	3
3-3	0	0
4-4	0	0
0-1	2	1
0-2	0	1
1-2	1	2
0-3	0	1
1-3	1	0
2-3	1	0
0-4	0	0
1-4	0	0
2-4	0	0
3-4	0	0
Other	0	2

56 games since 2010 World Cup

Clean sheets

Nigeria	13	37%
Opp	5	14%

35 competitive games since 2010 World Cup

Players used in qualifying

Pos		Club	Career Age	P	G	Qualifying P	G	Y/R
G	Vincent Enyeama	Lille	31	89	0	8	0	0
D	Azubuike Egwuekwe	Warri Wolves	24	29	0	5	1	0
D	Efe Ambrose	Celtic	25	34	1	7	0	2
D	Uwa Echiejile	Monaco	26	38	2	6	0	1
D	Godfrey Oboabona	Rizespor	23	31	1	8	1	2
D	James Okwuosa	Chippa Utd	23	3	0	1	0	0
D	Juwon Oshaniwa	MS Ashdod	23	10	0	2	0	0
D	Kenneth Omeruo	Middlesbrough	20	16	0	4	0	1
D	Solomon Kwambe	Sunshine Stars	20	12	0	1	0	0
M	Ejike Uzoenyi	Enugu Rangers	26	20	3	2	0	0
M	Fegor Ogude	Valerenga	26	16	0	2	0	0
M	Obiora Nwankwo	Cordoba	22	8	0	2	0	0
M	John Obi Mikel	Chelsea	26	56	4	6	0	0
M	John Oguchukwu	Acad. Coimbra	25	7	1	3	0	0
M	Iffanyi Henry	Enyimba	23	5	0	1	0	0
M	John Utaka	Sivasspor	32	43	6	2	0	0
M	Nosa Igiebor	Real Betis	23	11	2	2	0	0
M	Ogenyi Onazi	Lazio	21	19	1	6	0	1
M	Raheem Lawal	Eskisehirspor	23	4	0	1	0	0
M	Reuben Gabriel	W Beveren	23	10	1	2	0	0
M	Sunday Mba	Ath Bastiais	25	21	5	4	0	0
M	Victor Moses	Liverpool	23	18	6	6	2	1
M	Ahmed Musa	CSKA Moscow	21	37	5	8	1	0
F	Anthony Ujah	Cologne	23	4	0	2	0	0
F	Emmanuel Emenike	Fenerbahce	26	21	9	3	3	1
F	Ideye Brown	Dynamo Kiev	25	24	5	4	0	0
F	Ikenchukwu Uche	Villarreal	30	45	18	2	1	0
F	Kalu Uche	El Jaish	31	34	5	2	0	0
F	Nnamdi Oduamadi	Brescia	23	12	4	5	1	0
F	Obafemi Martins	Seattle	29	39	18	1	0	0
F	Shola Ameobi	Newcastle	32	5	2	1	0	0
F	Victor Obinna	Chievo	27	48	12	1	1	0
F	Uche Nwofor	Heerenveen	25	4	2	1	0	0

Ballon d'Or Ronaldo can fire Portugal to top spot in Brazil's group of death

Judging the strength of a group by its weakest member suggests that Group G is the real group of death at this World Cup – every point is going to be a tremendous battle in matches between Germany, Portugal, USA and Ghana, **writes Mark Langdon**.

The market predicts both European nations will eventually come through but it may pay to debate the order, with Portugal having the potential to cause an upset by pipping the Germans to the post.

The countries were in the same group at Euro 2012 when Germany came out on top thanks to a second-half Mario Gomez goal in Ukraine. However, it was as close as the 1-0 scoreline suggests – Portugal had seven shots on target to Germany's four and dominated the corner count 11-2.

Those who can cast their minds back two years will remember Pepe and Nani both hit the woodwork for Portugal, who were also denied late on by a fantastic Manuel Neuer save from substitute Silvestre Varela.

It could easily have been a draw at the very least for Portugal and virtually the same starting XI will take to the Salvador field in the opening match of this group. Paulo Bento's boys will rightly fancy their chances with Cristiano Ronaldo in their ranks.

For all of Germany's unquestionable quality, Ronaldo will still be the best player on the pitch and in recent tournaments they have managed to stay competitive in their matches before allowing the Real Madrid superstar to create something special.

Germany have a favourites' chance of franking the form but they are little value at the prices with that win over Portugal the only time Neuer kept a clean sheet at Euro 2012. A draw on June 16 may be seen as a decent result for both teams, although USA and Ghana will also have a say in the group finishing order.

USA are rated as the slight favourites to finish bottom and there is not much between the two nations, who also met in the first knockout stage of the 2010 World Cup.

Asamoah Gyan's extra-time goal saw Ghana through in South Africa but the fact the game finished level after normal time illustrates how competitive it is likely to be.

Recommendation
Portugal

Group winner odds

	bet365	Coral	Lads	Power	W Hill
Germany	1-2	1-2	8-15	8-15	4-7
Portugal	11-4	11-4	5-2	11-4	5-2
USA	12	11	12	11	10
Ghana	11	10	12	12	10

To qualify odds

	Lads	Power	W Hill
Germany	1-10	1-8	1-7
Portugal	4-9	1-2	4-11
USA	3	13-5	3
Ghana	16-5	11-4	11-4

All group betting markets are win only

Finish bottom

	Power	W Hill
Germany	20	20
Portugal	11-2	13-2
USA	Evs	10-11
Ghana	13-10	13-10

Straight forecast

	Power
Germany/Portugal	8-5
Portugal/Germany	7-2
Germany/USA	5
Germany/Ghana	5
Portugal/Ghana	17
USA/Germany	18
Portugal/USA	18
Ghana/Germany	18
Ghana/Portugal	30
USA/Portugal	30
Ghana/USA	75
USA/Ghana	75

Group matches | World Cup history | Head-to-head record | Last meeting

Group matches	World Cup history	Head-to-head record	Last meeting
Germany v Portugal Monday June 16, 5pm, Salvador	Germany won 3-1 in the third-place match in 2006	Three wins for Portugal, nine for Germany, five draws since 1936	Mario Gomez got Germany's goal in a 1-0 group-stage win at Euro 2012
Ghana v USA Monday June 16, 11pm, Natal	Wins for Ghana at Germany 2006 and South Africa 2010	A win for Ghana and a 90-minutes draw	The last 16 in 2010 – Ghana won 2-1, but the match went to extra-time
Germany v Ghana Saturday June 21, 8pm, Fortaleza	A group-stage win for Germany in South Africa	Two meetings since 1993 and two wins for Germany	Mesut Ozil got the only goal in the Group D decider in 2010
USA v Portugal Sunday June 22, 11pm, Manaus	USA beat Portugal 3-2 in the group stage of the 2002 World Cup	Two wins each and one draw since 1978	Suwon, 2002: USA were 3-1 up at half-time of their opening game
USA v Germany Thursday June 26, 5pm, Recife	Group stage 1998, quarters 2002 – Germany won both games to nil	Six wins for the Germans, three wins for the States since 1993	Jurgen Klinsmann's side won a friendly 4-3 in Washington last June
Portugal v Ghana Thursday June 26, 5pm, Brasilia	No previous World Cup meetings	No previous meetings	

Route to the final

Group winners

Round of 16 June 30 Porto Alegre
2H Belgium, Algeria, Russia, South Korea

Quarter-finals July 4 Rio de Janeiro
1E Switzerland, Ecuador, France, Honduras
2F Argentina, Bosnia-Herzegovina, Iran, Nigeria

Semi-finals July 8 Belo Horizonte
1A Brazil, Croatia, Mexico, Cameroon
2B Spain, Holland, Chile, Australia
1C Colombia, Greece, Ivory Coast, Japan
2D Uruguay, Costa Rica, England, Italy

Final July 13 Rio

Group runners-up

Round of 16 July 1 Salvador
1H Belgium, Algeria, Russia, South Korea

Quarter-finals July 5 Brasilia
1F Argentina, Bosnia-Herzegovina, Iran, Nigeria
2E Switzerland, Ecuador, France, Honduras

Semi-finals July 9 Sao Paulo
1B Spain, Holland, Chile, Australia
2A Brazil, Croatia, Mexico, Cameroon
1D Uruguay, Costa Rica, England, Italy
2C Colombia, Greece, Ivory Coast, Japan

GERMANY

Pressure is on Low's nearly men to draw a veil over a string of recent near misses

Always the bridesmaid and never the bride. That has been the story of Germany's recent attempts after a run of near misses, with the Nationalmannschaft finalists in 2002, semi-finalists in 2006 and 2010 and also beaten in the final of Euro 2008 and the semi-finals of Euro 2012. It would be good enough for most nations but for three-time world champions Germany, first is first and second is nowhere.

How they qualified

No European country scored more goals than Germany in qualifying, with Joachim Low's side hitting the target a mind-boggling 36 times in ten matches and the frightening prospect was the relentlessness in every match. A 2-1 win away to Austria was the only time Germany failed to score at least three times, with Mesut Ozil the star man with eight goals.

Tricky road games such as Ireland (6-1) and Sweden (5-3) were dealt with confidently, although from a defensive point of view there were problems. Low's men kept clean sheets in only half of their qualifiers, and two of those shutouts were against the Faroe Islands.

Perhaps the most remarkable result in the whole of European qualifying came when Germany led 4-0 at home to Sweden with 28 minutes remaining but drew 4-4 – those defensive frailties need to be ironed out in Brazil.

The manager

Low was assistant to Jurgen Klinsmann for Germany's home finals in 2006 and was seen as the brains behind the relationship. He has been the number one since July 2006 and has signed a new contract which will take him up to the summer of 2016, but at some stage Low will have to win a trophy with

Country factfile

FA founded 1900
www dfb.de
Head coach Joachim Low
National league Bundesliga
System of government Federal republic
Population 81 million
Capital city Berlin
Currency Euro
Official language German

Strengths
- ☑ Midfield reads like a who's who of world football
- ☑ Deep squad
- ☑ Neuer and Lahm best in their positions

Weaknesses
- ☒ Consistently struggle as defensive unit
- ☒ Not too many natural striking options
- ☒ Recent near misses may have left mental scars

Base Santa Cruz Cabralia

Fixtures
1 Portugal, June 16, Salvador
2 Ghana, June 21, Fortaleza
3 USA, June 26, Recife

Germany's golden generation or be deemed a nearly man.

Match winners

Germany could use their second-choice midfield and it would still be among the best in Brazil. Low could be tempted to play with a false number nine to get six of them in the team because otherwise so much quality will be wasted on the bench.

It's hard to know exactly who Low will select but it's an embarrassment of riches, with Bayern Munich quartet Bastian Schweinsteiger, Toni Kroos, Thomas Muller and Mario Gotze, Borussia Dortmund's Marco Reus and Sven Bender plus Ozil and Julian Draxler. That's without even mentioning Sami Khedira and Ilkay Gundogan, who have suffered serious injuries this season.

Question marks

"I am convinced it will be difficult to score against us at the World Cup," claimed Schweinsteiger once qualification was completed and you can understand why he said that with Manuel Neuer between the sticks, Philipp Lahm as full-back and Mats Hummels in the back four.

However, Germany kept just one clean sheet in five matches at Euro 2012 and they are also light on striking choices with Miroslav Klose, who will be 36 by the start of the finals, and injury-hit Mario Gomez the only real options. You can see why Low is tempted to go strikerless.

It's also a brutal schedule, with all three group games in the north-east and two of those early starts, too.

How to back them

The old saying goes you should never write them off and Germany deserve to be among the market leaders, but bookmakers are giving little away with their outright price which sees them quoted at shorter odds than Spain, particularly as a group containing Portugal, Ghana and USA is by no means the easiest for a top seed.

With the potential for Low to go with a midfielder as his focal point, it may pay to have dabbles on Muller, Reus and Gotze to top the German goalscoring charts, with all three capable of making their mark from up top or in a deeper attacking midfield position.

GERMANY

World Cup record

Uruguay 1930	Did not enter
Italy 1934	Third place
France 1938	First round
Brazil 1950	Banned
Switzerland 1954	**Winners**
Sweden 1958	Fourth place
Chile 1962	Quarter-finals
England 1966	Runners-up
Mexico 1970	Third place
Germany 1974	**Winners**
Argentina 1978	Second round
Spain 1982	Runners-up
Mexico 1986	Runners-up
Italy 1990	**Winners**
USA 1994	Quarter-finals
France 1998	Quarter-finals
Korea/Japan 2002	Runners-up
Germany 2006	Third place
South Africa 2010	Third place

Continental titles

European Championships (1972, 1980, 1996)

Legendary player

Mexico 1970 was all about Brazil but **Gerd Muller** grabbed ten goals in his six games for West Germany and four years later, his four goals included the winner in the final. In between he finished as top scorer in the 1972 European Championships, with two of his four goals coming in the final. The 1974 final was his last game for Germany – he retired from international football at just 28 – but his 62 internationals saw him score an incredible 68 goals.

Did you know?

Germany's opener against Portugal will be their 100th game at the World Cup finals – it would be their 106th if you counted East Germany's matches in 1974

Germany have reached the semi-finals or final of the last three World Cups without winning – Bastian Schweinsteiger will want to put that right

How they qualified

Final group	P	W	D	L	F	A		Pts
Germany	10	9	1	0	36	10	26	28
Sweden	10	6	2	2	19	14	5	20
Austria	10	5	2	3	20	10	10	17
Rep of Ireland	10	4	2	4	16	17	-1	14
Kazakhstan	10	1	2	7	6	21	-15	5
Faroe Islands	10	0	1	9	4	29	-25	1

Manuel Neuer during the 4-4 draw with Sweden

Germany ....(1) 3-0 (0)..... Faroe Islands
Germany: Gotze (28) Ozil (54, 71)

Austria ....(0) 1-2 (1)........... Germany
Austria: Junuzovic (57) Germany: Reus (44) Ozil (pen 52)

Ireland.............(0) 1-6 (2)........... Germany
Ireland: Keogh (90) Germany: Reus (32, 40) Ozil (pen 55)
Klose (58) Kroos (61, 83)

Germany ....(3) 4-4 (0)............. Sweden
Germany: Klose (8, 15) Mertesacker (39) Ozil (55) Sweden:
Ibrahimovic (62) Lustig (64) Elmander (76) Elm (90)

Kazakhstan......(0) 0-3 (2)........... Germany
Germany: Muller (20, 74) Gotze (22)

Germany ....(3) 4-1 (0)........Kazakhstan
Germany: Reus (23, 89) Gotze (27) Gundogan (31)
Kazakhstan: Schmidtgal (46)

Germany ....(1) 3-0 (0).............. Austria
Germany: Klose (33) Kroos (51) Muller (88)

Faroe Islands ...(0) 0-3 (1)........... Germany
Germany: Mertesacker (22) Ozil (pen 74) Muller (84)

Germany ....(1) 3-0 (0).............. Ireland
Germany: Khedira (12) Schurrle (58) Ozil (90)

Sweden ....(2) 3-5 (1)........... Germany
Sweden: Hysen (6, 69) Kacaniklic (42) Germany: Ozil (44)
Gotze (53) Schurrle (57, 66, 76)

Full qualifying results and tables on pages 234-256

GERMANY

Players used in qualifying

Pos		Club	Age	P	G	P	G	Y/R
				Career			**Qualifying**	
G	Manuel Neuer	Bayern Munich	28	45	0	10	0	0
D	Benedikt Howedes	Schalke	26	18	1	3	0	2
D	Holger Badstuber	Bayern Munich	25	30	1	4	0	1
D	Jerome Boateng	Bayern Munich	25	37	0	7	0	0
D	Marcel Schmelzer	B Dortmund	26	16	0	6	0	0
D	Marcell Jansen	Hamburg	28	45	3	3	0	0
D	Mats Hummels	B Dortmund	25	28	2	3	0	1
D	Per Mertesacker	Arsenal	29	96	4	8	2	0
D	Philipp Lahm	Bayern Munich	30	105	5	9	0	3
M	Andre Schurrle	Chelsea	23	31	11	6	4	1
M	Bastian Schweinsteiger	Bayern Munich	29	101	23	5	0	2
M	Ilkay Gundogan	B Dortmund	23	8	2	2	1	0
M	Jermaine Jones	Besiktas	32	39	2	0	0	0
M	Julian Draxler	Schalke	20	10	1	5	0	0
M	Marco Reus	B Dortmund	24	19	7	6	5	3
M	Mario Gotze	Bayern Munich	21	27	7	7	4	0
M	Max Kruse	Mgladbach	26	6	1	3	0	0
M	Mesut Ozil	Arsenal	25	53	17	10	8	0
M	Sami Khedira	Real Madrid	26	44	4	8	1	2
M	Sidney Sam	B Leverkusen	26	5	0	2	0	0
M	Sven Bender	B Dortmund	24	7	0	1	0	0
M	Thomas Muller	Bayern Munich	24	47	16	10	4	0
M	Toni Kroos	Bayern Munich	24	42	5	7	3	0
F	Lukas Podolski	Arsenal	28	112	46	5	0	0
F	Miroslav Klose	Lazio	35	131	68	6	4	1

What happens if ...

Germany score first

Germany win	22	88%
Draw	1	4%
Germany lose	0	0%

25 games since 2010 World Cup

Opponents score first

Germany win	1	4%
Draw	0	0%
Germany lose	1	4%

GROUP G

Goal times

For		Against
3	0-9	1
2	10-18	0
9	19-27	2
10	28-36	1
12	37-45	2
9	46-54	3
7	55-63	4
5	64-72	2
7	73-81	3
16	82-90	5

Germany			Opponents
36	45%	1st half	6	26%
44	55%	2nd half	17	74%

25 games since 2010 World Cup

Correct scores

	Friendly	Comp
1-0	2	2
2-0	1	0
2-1	2	4
3-0	1	7
3-1	0	3
3-2	1	0
4-0	0	1
4-1	0	1
4-2	1	1
4-3	0	0
0-0	2	0
1-1	2	0
2-2	2	0
3-3	2	0
4-4	0	1
0-1	0	0
0-2	0	0
1-2	2	1
0-3	0	0
1-3	1	0
2-3	0	0
0-4	0	0
1-4	0	0
2-4	0	0
3-4	1	0
Other	1	4

46 games since 2010 World Cup

Bookings

Yellow cards	16
Red cards	0
Ave make-up	16.0

In 2014 World Cup qualifying

Top scorers

	Total	First	%	Anytime	%
M Ozil	8	0	0	7	70
M Reus	5	3	60	3	50
M Klose	4	2	50	3	50
T Muller	4	1	25	3	30
A Schurrle	4	0	0	2	33
M Gotze	4	1	25	4	57
T Kroos	3	0	0	2	29
P Mertesacker	2	1	50	2	25

In World Cup 2014 qualification

Eight-goal Mesut Ozil

Unders & overs

1.5 goals		2.5 goals		3.5 goals		4.5 goals	
Under	Over	Under	Over	Under	Over	Under	Over
8%	92%	8%	92%	56%	44%	72%	28%

25 games since 2010 World Cup

Half-time/Full-time

Win/Win	18	72%
Draw/Win	4	16%
Lose/Win	1	4%
Win/Draw	1	4%
Draw/Draw	0	0%
Lose/Draw	0	0%
Win/Lose	0	0%
Draw/Lose	0	0%
Lose/Lose	1	4%

25 games since 2010 World Cup

Penalty shootouts

Won	5	83%
Lost	1	17%

All-time (includes West Germany)

Clean sheets

Germany	10	40%
Opponents	0	0%

25 games since 2010 World Cup

Portuguese could go a long way but they'll need Ronaldo to be at his best

There is plenty to be said for the old tournament football adage of "it's not how you get there but what you do when you get there" and Portugal will be hoping that rings true this summer. Portugal have developed a habit of leaving qualifying until the last possible moment but they have gone close in recent World Cups and European Championships and they can do so again.

How they qualified

It was a nervous mess, although they still lost only one match and that came in a narrow 1-0 away defeat to Russia. However, Paulo Bento's side failed to beat Israel in two games, were held to a home draw by Northern Ireland and were even trailing away to Luxembourg.

At one stage Portugal looked as if they were going to miss out but a late comeback to draw 3-3 in Israel and a strong finish of 13 points from a possible 15 booked a play-off showdown with Sweden, where Cristiano Ronaldo stole the show in a duel with Zlatan Ibrahimovic.

Ronaldo grabbed the only goal of the first leg and a hat-trick in the away clash, while he also notched all three goals when Portugal were in a desperate state away to Northern Ireland. So much for accusations the Fifa Ballon d'Or winner doesn't turn up in big matches.

The manager

Bento is someone who is extremely loyal to the Portugal squad so the team rarely changes, and his bond with Ronaldo is obviously important from their time together at Sporting Lisbon.

He was a defensive midfielder in his playing days and usually puts substance before style. His approach nearly worked at

Country factfile

FA founded 1914

www fpf.pt

Head coach Paulo Bento

National league Primeira Liga

System of government Republic

Population 11 million

Capital city Lisbon

Currency Euro

Official language Portuguese

Strengths

- ☑ Ronaldo wins matches on his own
- ☑ Settled side with experience at the highest level
- ☑ Should feel at home in Portuguese-speaking Brazil

Weaknesses

- ☒ Tough group and schedule
- ☒ Bruno Alves and Pepe pick up cards
- ☒ No prolific striker puts pressure on Ronaldo

Base Campinas

Fixtures

1 Germany, June 16, Salvador

2 USA, June 22, Manaus

3 Ghana, June 26, Brasilia

Euro 2012, only for Portugal to lose a semi-final penalty shootout against neighbours Spain following a goalless 120 minutes.

Match winners

The way Ronaldo has risen to the challenge of matching Lionel Messi in La Liga is quite sensational and the Real Madrid superstar is capable of winning a World Cup almost on his own.

There are not many midfielders who can pick a pivotal pass quite like Joao Moutinho, Pepe and Fabio Coentrao are strong defensive players also capable of causing carnage in the opposition box, and keeper Rui Patricio was superb at Euro 2012.

Question marks

Ronaldo's record at the World Cup is not good – he has scored only two goals (one each in 2006 and 2010) and even then, they came against Iran and North Korea. There is a reliance on him to be a difference maker, so

he needs to deliver.

The age-old problem of no top class number nine (Helder Postiga usually starts) remains an issue and 32-year-old defensive warrior Bruno Alves has seen better days. Just don't tell him to his face!

How to back them

Portugal are potential winners even though their group, with Germany, USA and Ghana, could have been much easier. In the last five tournaments Portugal have reached two semi-finals and one final, and in 2010 and 2012 it took Spain to eliminate them in close battles.

Backing Bento's boys to make the last eight is another option – Portugal have reached at least the quarter-finals in eight of their 11 appearances at a major tournament – and a last-16 date with a team from the Belgium-Russia-South Korea-Algeria group is nothing to be afraid of should the Iberians progress past the first stage.

PORTUGAL

World Cup record

Uruguay 1930	Did not enter
Italy 1934	Did not qualify
France 1938	Did not qualify
Brazil 1950	Did not qualify
Switzerland 1954	Did not qualify
Sweden 1958	Did not qualify
Chile 1962	Did not qualify
England 1966	Third place
Mexico 1970	Did not qualify
Germany 1974	Did not qualify
Argentina 1978	Did not qualify
Spain 1982	Did not qualify
Mexico 1986	Group stage
Italy 1990	Did not qualify
USA 1994	Did not qualify
France 1998	Did not qualify
Korea/Japan 2002	Group stage
Germany 2006	Fourth place
South Africa 2010	Round of 16

Continental titles

None

Legendary player

Portugal finally made it to a World Cup in 1966 and **Eusebio** lit up the tournament, scoring nine times as the debutants finished third. He never got another chance to perform on the biggest stage but Eusebio won plenty of silverware with Benfica – 11 Portuguese titles and a European Cup.

Did you know?

Cristiano Ronaldo was one of three players to pick up five yellow cards in European qualifying – nobody's name went in the book more times

Cristiano Ronaldo scored all four of Portugal's goals in the qualification play-off against Sweden

How they qualified

Final group	P	W	D	L	F	A	GD	Pts
Russia	10	7	1	2	20	5	15	22
Portugal	**10**	**6**	**3**	**1**	**20**	**9**	**11**	**21**
Israel	10	3	5	2	19	14	5	14
Azerbaijan	10	1	6	3	7	11	-4	9
N Ireland	10	1	4	5	9	17	-8	7
Luxembourg	10	1	3	6	7	26	-19	6

Portugal made hard work of qualification

Luxembourg ....(1) 1-2 (1)............ Portugal
Luxembourg: Da Mota (13) Portugal: Ronaldo (28) Postiga (54)

Portugal ....(0) 3-0 (0).........Azerbaijan
Portugal: Varela (63) Postiga (85) Alves (88)

Russia ....(1) 1-0 (0)............ Portugal
Russia: Kerzhakov (6)

Portugal ....(0) 1-1 (1)........... N Ireland
Portugal: Postiga (79) N Ireland: McGinn (30)

Israel ....(2) 3-3 (1)............ Portugal
Israel: Hemed (24) Ben Basat (40) Gershon (70) Portugal: Alves (2) Postiga (72) Coentrao (90)

Azerbaijan ....(0) 0-2 (0)............ Portugal
Portugal: Alves (63) Almeida (79)

Portugal ....(1) 1-0 (0)................Russia
Portugal: Postiga (9)

N Ireland ....(1) 2-4 (1)............ Portugal
N Ireland: McAuley (36) Ward (52) Portugal: Alves (21) Ronaldo (68, 77, 83)

Portugal ....(1) 1-1 (0)................ Israel
Portugal: Costa (28) Israel: Ben Basat (85)

Portugal ....(2) 3-0 (0)......Luxembourg
Portugal: Varela (30) Nani (36) Postiga (78)

Play-off

Portugal ....(0) 1-0 (0)............. Sweden
Portugal: Ronaldo (82)

Sweden ....(0) 2-3 (0)............ Portugal
Sweden: Ibrahimovic (68, 72) Portugal: Ronaldo (50, 77, 79)

Full qualifying results and tables on pages 234-256

PORTUGAL

Players used in qualifying		Career			Qualifying		
Pos		**Club**	**Age**	**P**	**G**	**P**	**G**	**Y/R**
G	Rui Patricio	Sporting Lisbon	26	29	0	12	0	0
D	Pepe	Real Madrid	31	57	3	10	0	4
D	Bruno Alves	Fenerbahce	32	70	9	10	4	1
D	Fabio Coentrao	Real Madrid	26	43	3	10	1	3
D	Sereno	Kayserispor	28	2	0	1	0	0
D	Joao Pereira	Valencia	30	34	0	10	0	1
D	Luis Neto	Zenit	25	6	0	2	0	1
D	Miguel Lopes	Lyon	27	4	0	2	0	0
D	Ricardo Costa	Valencia	32	17	1	3	1	0
D	Vitorino Antunes	Malaga	26	8	0	3	0	0
M	Custodio	Braga	30	10	0	3	0	0
M	Andre Almeida	Benfica	23	2	0	2	0	0
M	Danny	Zenit	30	26	4	1	0	0
M	Josue	Porto	23	4	0	3	0	1
M	Nani	Man Utd	27	72	14	10	1	1
M	Raul Meireles	Fenerbahce	31	73	10	8	0	0
M	Vieirinha	Wolfsburg	28	6	0	4	0	0
M	Carlos Martins	Benfica	31	17	2	1	0	1
M	Joao Moutinho	Monaco	27	66	2	12	0	0
M	Miguel Veloso	Dynamo Kiev	27	46	2	12	0	1
M	Ruben Amorim	Benfica	29	10	0	4	0	0
M	Ruben Micael	Braga	27	16	2	4	0	0
M	William Carvalho	Sporting Lisbon	21	2	0	1	0	0
F	Nelson Oliveira	Rennes	22	14	1	2	0	0
F	Cristiano Ronaldo	Real Madrid	29	110	49	10	8	5
F	Eder	Braga	26	6	0	4	0	0
F	Helder Postiga	Lazio	31	66	27	10	6	0/1
F	Hugo Almeida	Besiktas	29	53	17	6	1	0
F	Silvestre Varela	Porto	29	21	4	7	2	1

What happens if ...

Portugal score first

Portugal win	15	56%
Draw	2	7%
Portugal lose	0	0%

27 games since 2010 World Cup

WIN 56%

Opponents score first

Portugal win	2	7%
Draw	2	7%
Portugal lose	4	15%

LOSE 15%

Goal times

For		Against
5	0-9	2
1	10-18	5
5	19-27	2
10	28-36	2
1	37-45	3
5	46-54	2
3	55-63	2
4	64-72	6
10	73-81	2
13	82-90	3

Portugal		Opponents
22 39%	1st half	14 48%
35 61%	2nd half	15 52%

27 games since 2010 World Cup

Correct scores

	Friendly	Comp
1-0	1	4
2-0	2	1
2-1	0	2
3-0	0	2
3-1	0	2
3-2	0	2
4-0	1	1
4-1	0	0
4-2	0	1
4-3	0	0
0-0	2	2
1-1	2	2
2-2	1	0
3-3	0	1
4-4	0	1
0-1	0	3
0-2	0	0
1-2	1	1
0-3	0	0
1-3	2	0
2-3	1	0
0-4	0	0
1-4	0	0
2-4	0	0
3-4	0	0
Other	2	2

42 games since 2010 World Cup

Bookings

Yellow cards	20
Red cards	1
Avg make-up	18.8

In 2014 World Cup qualifying

Top scorers

	Total	First	%	Anytime	%
C Ronaldo	8	2	25	4	40
H Postiga	6	1	17	6	60
B Alves	4	3	75	4	40
S Varela	2	2	100	2	28

In World Cup 2014 qualification

Helder Postiga

Unders & overs

1.5 goals		2.5 goals		3.5 goals		4.5 goals	
Under	Over	Under	Over	Under	Over	Under	Over
33%	67%	44%	56%	63%	37%	74%	26%

27 games since 2010 World Cup

Half-time/Full-time

Win/Win	8	30%
Draw/Win	9	33%
Lose/Win	0	0%
Win/Draw	1	4%
Draw/Draw	3	11%
Lose/Draw	2	7%
Win/Lose	0	0%
Draw/Lose	1	4%
Lose/Lose	3	11%

WIN 63%

27 games since 2010 World Cup

Penalty shootouts

Won	2	67%
Lost	1	33%

All-time record

Clean sheets

Portugal	10	37%
Opponents	5	19%

27 games since 2010 World Cup

GHANA

They qualified in style but an early flight home looks to be written in the stars

A missed Asamoah Gyan penalty away from the World Cup semi-finals in 2010, Ghana are back for another crack and the play-off thrashing of Egypt saw confidence rise again with coach Kwesi Appiah claiming his side can "surprise the world." However, underdogs rarely get a second bite of the cherry and the Black Stars may be left to rue missing their golden opportunity in South Africa four years ago.

How they qualified

Ghana scored the most goals in African qualifying with Asamoah Gyan contributing six of their total of 25. The stunning 7-3 demolition of Egypt in what was supposed to be a close play-off tie was the standout result by some distance.

It was all over after Ghana triumphed 6-1 in the first leg and there was only one moment of concern in the entire process, a 1-0 defeat to then African champions Zambia in June 2012. However, the Black Stars won all of their other five group matches.

The manager

Appiah is unusual in that he is a Ghanaian coach, with the country having been led by foreigners in each of the last two World Cups. He previously coached the Ghana U23 side but this is his first job at senior level with the players giving him the nickname the "silent killer" because he is quiet.

He publicly lavishes praise on his players and in return is given a huge amount of respect in the dressing room but these will be his first competitive fixtures against non-African sides at senior level.

Match winners

Appiah says he already knows 20 members of his 23-man squad and Ghana's World Cup bid will be in familiar hands.

Country factfile

FA founded 1957
www ghanafa.org
Head coach Kwesi Appiah
National league Premier League
System of government Constitutional democracy
Population 25 million
Capital city Accra
Currency Ghana cedi
Official language English

Strengths
- ☑ Strong midfield with excellent depth
- ☑ Gyan is a consistent threat at this level

Weaknesses
- ☒ Soft mentality when pressure is on
- ☒ Inexperienced coach
- ☒ Defence may be exposed by Germany and Cristiano Ronaldo

Base Maceio

Fixtures

1 USA, June 16, Natal
2 Germany, June 21, Fortaleza
3 Portugal, June 26, Brasilia

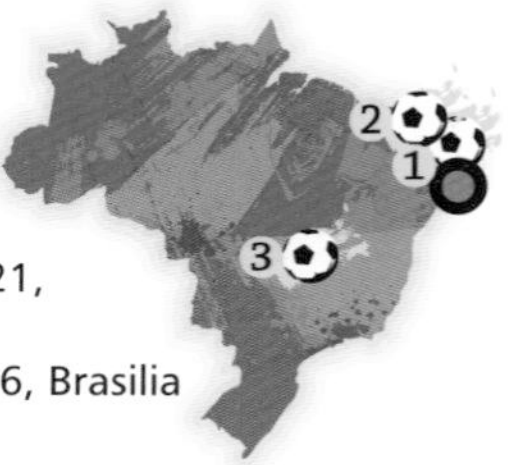

Kevin-Prince Boateng celebrates scoring against the States in the last 16 in 2010

Al Ain's Gyan leads the line and could still be playing at a higher level if he hadn't chosen money over a better domestic competition, while Andre Ayew has long been seen as the shining light of the Black Stars and Michael Essien is a legend in his homeland.

However, Ghana's best player by some distance is Kevin-Prince Boateng, who has thrived in a deeper playmaking role for Schalke since the Bundesliga's winter break, and youngsters Christian Atsu, Emmanuel Agyemang-Badu and Wakaso Mubarak are all capable of enhancing their growing reputations.

Milan's Sulley Muntari is inconsistent but is another who can make things happen when on song.

Question marks

All of those listed in the match winners section are forward-thinking players, except for Essien. However, his legs look to have gone, with injuries taking their toll.

Defensively Ghana could struggle in a group containing class European acts in Germany and Portugal, while this is a big test of Appiah's credentials given his relative lack of experience.

The Black Stars have also become a squad of chokers. Ghana have not won the Africa Cup of Nations since 1982 even though they have reached the semi-finals in each of the last four competitions. The heartbreak of losing to Uruguay in such dramatic circumstances in the 2010 World Cup (on penalties after Gyan missed a spot-kick to win the match with the last action of extra-time) remains painful four years on.

How to back them

Quite reasonably, bookmakers are expecting Ghana to suffer a first-round exit, although it is also right that they are considered slight favourites to overcome USA in their opening match. Back the Black Stars to take exactly three points from this tough section.

GHANA

World Cup record

Uruguay 1930	Did not enter
Italy 1934	Did not enter
France 1938	Did not enter
Brazil 1950	Did not enter
Switzerland 1954	Did not enter
Sweden 1958	Did not enter
Chile 1962	Did not qualify
England 1966	Withdrew
Mexico 1970	Did not qualify
Germany 1974	Did not qualify
Argentina 1978	Did not qualify
Spain 1982	Withdrew
Mexico 1986	Did not qualify
Italy 1990	Did not qualify
USA 1994	Did not qualify
France 1998	Did not qualify
Korea/Japan 2002	Did not qualify
Germany 2006	Round of 16
South Africa 2010	Quarter-finals

How they qualified

Final group	P	W	D	L	F	A	Pts
Ghana	**6**	**5**	**0**	**1**	**18**	**3**	**15**
Zambia	6	3	2	1	11	4	11
Lesotho	6	1	2	3	4	15	5
Sudan	6	0	2	4	3	14	2

Ghana ....(3) 7-0 (0)............ Lesotho
Ghana: Muntari (15) Adiyiah (24, 49) Ayew (45, 89) Atsu (86) Akaminko (90)

Zambia ....(1) 1-0 (0)............... Ghana
Zambia: Katongo (18)

Ghana ....(2) 4-0 (0)............... Sudan
Ghana: Gyan (19) Mubarak (38) Waris (80) Agyemang-Badu (83)

Sudan.............(1) 1-3 (1)............... Ghana
Sudan: El-Tahir (pen 26) Ghana: Gyan (20, 57) Muntari (83)

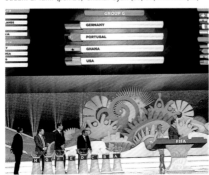

Ghana's fate is sealed at December's draw

Continental titles

None

Legendary player

He never got the chance to play at a World Cup but **Abedi Pele**'s outrageous blend of pace, power and, above all, skill, made him a key member of Marseille's 1993 Champions League winning side.

Did you know?

Ghana haven't beaten a team from outside of Africa since the last World Cup (four defeats, five draws)

Lesotho ....(0) 0-2 (1)............... Ghana
Ghana: Boye (45) Gyan (82)

Ghana ....(1) 2-1 (0)..............Zambia
Ghana: Waris (18) Asamoah (61) Zambia: Sinkala (74)

Round 3

Ghana ....(3) 6-1 (1)............... Egypt
Ghana: Gyan (4, 54) Gomaa (22 og) Waris (44) Muntari (pen 73) Atsu (89) Egypt: Aboutraika (pen 41)

Egypt...............(0) 2-1 (0)............... Ghana
Egypt: Zaki (25) Gedo (84) Ghana: Boateng (89)

Full qualifying results and tables on pages 234-256

Unders & overs

<1.5	>1.5	<2.5	>2.5	<3.5	>3.5	<4.5	>4.5
21%	79%	54%	46%	75%	25%	93%	7%

28 competitive games since 2010 World Cup

Half-time/Full-time

W/W	14	50%	W/D	2	7%	W/L	0	0%
D/W	4	14%	D/D	3	11%	D/L	2	7%
L/W	0	0%	L/D	0	0%	L/L	3	11%

28 competitive games since 2010 World Cup

Bookings

Yellow cards	14
Red cards	1
Avg make-up	20.6

In 2014 World Cup qualifying

Penalty shootouts

Won	5	50%
Lost	5	50%

All-time record

What happens if ...

Ghana score first			Their opponents score first		
Ghana win	19	68%	Ghana win	0	0%
Draw	3	10%	Draw	0	0%
Ghana lose	0	0%	Ghana lose	5	18%

28 competitive games since 2010 World Cup

Top scorers

	Total	First	%	Anytime	%
A Gyan	6	3	50	4	67
S Muntari	3	1	33	3	43
M Waris	3	1	33	3	75
D Adiyiah	2	0	0	1	33
J Ayew	2	0	0	1	50
C Atsu	2	0	0	2	40

In World Cup 2014 qualification

Goal times

For			Against
6		0-9	0
6		10-18	1
8		19-27	4
1		28-36	0
6		37-45	3
6		46-54	2
4		55-63	1
3		64-72	1
6		73-81	4
11		82-90	2

Ghana			Opponents
27 47%	1st half	8	44%
30 53%	2nd half	10	56%

28 games since 2010 World Cup

Correct scores

	Friendly	Comp
1-0	2	3
2-0	0	6
2-1	3	2
3-0	1	3
3-1	0	2
3-2	0	0
4-0	0	1
4-1	1	0
4-2	1	0
4-3	0	0
0-0	2	1
1-1	3	2
2-2	1	1
3-3	0	0
4-4	0	0
0-1	4	2
0-2	1	1
1-2	1	1
0-3	0	0
1-3	1	1
2-3	0	0
0-4	0	0
1-4	0	0
2-4	0	0
3-4	0	0
Other	0	2

49 games since 2010 World Cup

Clean sheets

Ghana	15	54%
Opp	4	14%

28 competitive games since 2010 World Cup

Players used in qualifying

Pos		Club	Career			Qualifying		
			Age	P	G	P	G	Y/R
G	Adam Larsen	Stromsgodset	26	21	0	2	0	0
G	Fatau Dauda	Orlando Pirates	28	15	0	6	0	1
D	Daniel Opare	Standard Liege	23	17	0	4	0	2
D	Harrison Afful	Esperance	27	38	0	7	0	2
D	Isaac Vorsah	RB Salzburg	25	42	1	2	0	0
D	Jerry Akaminko	Eskisehirspor	25	8	1	3	1	1
D	John Boye	Rennes	26	30	2	6	1	0
D	Jonathan Mensah	Evian	23	23	1	3	0	0
D	Rashid Sumaila	Sundowns	21	7	0	4	0	1
D	Richard Boateng	TP Mazembe	25	6	0	2	0	1
D	Samuel Inkoom	Platanias	24	45	1	5	0	0
M	Albert Adomah	Middlesbrough	26	13	1	1	0	0
M	Andre Ayew	Marseille	24	45	3	3	0	0
M	Anthony Annan	Schalke	27	67	2	2	0	0
M	Derek Boateng	Fulham	30	46	3	2	0	0
M	Emmanuel Badu	Udinese	23	48	8	8	1	0
M	Emmanuel Frimpong	Barnsley	22	1	0	1	0	0
M	Kevin Boateng	Schalke	26	11	2	1	1	0
M	Kwadwo Asamoah	Juventus	25	59	4	7	1	0
M	Michael Essien	Milan	31	56	9	3	0	0
M	Mohammed Rabiu	Kuban K	24	15	0	4	0	0
M	Solomon Asante	TP Mazembe	23	12	0	1	0	0
M	Sulley Ali Muntari	Milan	29	80	22	7	3	1
M	Wakaso Mubarak	Rubin	23	16	7	5	1	2
F	Asamoah Gyan	Al-Ain	28	78	39	6	6	1
F	Christian Atsu	Vitesse Arn.	22	21	4	5	2	1
F	Dominic Adiyiah	Arsenal Kiev	24	19	4	3	2	0
F	Jordan Ayew	Marseille	22	13	2	2	2	1
F	A Majeed Waris	Valenciennes	22	11	3	4	3	1
F	Richard Mpong	Medeama	23	6	1	1	0	0
F	Richmond Boakye	Elche	21	7	2	2	0	0

Positive thinking won't be enough to compensate for the worst possible draw

I f World Cups were handed out for positive thinking the USA would already have the tournament sewn up. "We are expecting to go to the knockout stage which means Germany, Portugal and Ghana will have to fight it out for the other spot," said optimistic manager Jurgen Klinsmann, who is clearly up for the challenge of a difficult group with horrendous travelling thrown in for good measure.

How they qualified

USA claimed the most wins in the Concacaf region with 11 victories in 16 matches and improved as the campaign went on. As expected, they finished top of their first group before claiming first place in the much more difficult Hex. That's where they played their best stuff, compiling a perfect home record of five straight wins and no goals conceded.

The manager

In Klinsmann they trust. The US Soccer Federation surprised many by giving Klinsmann a new contract without waiting to see how the World Cup panned out and the German has been given the keys to the kingdom with total control of all levels of the international set-up.

Klinsmann took Germany to the World Cup semi-finals on home soil in 2006 but Joachim Low was said to be the brains behind the partnership, something which was rammed home during an unsuccessful period as Bayern Munich boss when the players allegedly spent more time doing yoga than talking tactics.

Ze Roberto claimed Klinsmann's half-time team-talk in his final game was just "you have to score a goal" and the Bayern fans were calling for the head of someone who had previously graced the German giants as a player.

Country factfile

FA founded 1913

www ussoccer.com

Head coach Jurgen Klinsmann

National league MLS

System of government Federal republic

Population 316 million

Capital city Washington DC

Currency US dollar

Official language English

Strengths

☑ No team will work harder this summer

☑ USA scored in 15 of their 16 qualifiers

Weaknesses

☒ Terrible draw and horrendous travelling schedule

☒ Altidore and Dempsey have struggled this season

☒ Lack of technical ability on the roster

Base Sao Paulo

Fixtures

1 Ghana, June 16, Natal

2 Portugal, June 22, Manaus

3 Germany, June 26, Recife

GROUP G

Klinsmann's main strength is supposed to be as a motivator and the USA have taken some notable scalps in friendlies with wins over Italy and Germany as well as victory in the 2013 Gold Cup.

Match winners
The US have always produced good goalkeepers and Tim Howard is the latest steady stopper who will have to be at his best for the States to get out of the group.

Klinsmann places a large emphasis on grit so the grafters will stand out – Jermaine Jones and Michael Bradley get through an enormous amount of hard work in central midfield.

The front two of Clint Dempsey and Jozy Altidore combined for seven goals between them in the Hex. Landon Donovan, so often USA's main man, is no longer certain of a place in the team but he should be in the squad having returned from a footballing sabbatical.

Question marks
USA don't have the players to keep possession and there has to be a doubt as to whether they can rely on energy alone for 90 minutes against high quality opponents in hot conditions.

No team has a worse travelling schedule and Klinsmann's comments – "For a team to travel long distances is not that difficult because you are well taken care of with charter flights and road escorts" – is a positive spin on what is widely perceived as the worst possible draw.

How to back them
The MLS-based players had a January training camp in Brazil so USA have prepared perfectly but as Klinsmann says the first match against Ghana is "basically a World Cup final."

However, even if USA start with a win, Portugal and Germany can make sure it's three and out.

USA

World Cup record

Uruguay 1930	Third place
Italy 1934	First round
France 1938	Withdrew
Brazil 1950	Group stage
Switzerland 1954	Did not qualify
Sweden 1958	Did not qualify
Chile 1962	Did not qualify
England 1966	Did not qualify
Mexico 1970	Did not qualify
Germany 1974	Did not qualify
Argentina 1978	Did not qualify
Spain 1982	Did not qualify
Mexico 1986	Did not qualify
Italy 1990	Group stage
USA 1994	Round of 16
France 1998	Group stage
Korea/Japan 2002	Quarter-finals
Germany 2006	Group stage
South Africa 2010	Round of 16

Continental titles

CONCACAF Gold Cup (1991, 2002, 2005, 2007, 2013)

Legendary player

Joe Gaetjens only scored once for the USA national team but the fact that it was the only goal of the game against England in the 1950 World Cup in Brazil made him a legend. However, **Landon Donovan** holds the record for goals and assists for his country and has played in the last three World Cups. While he has spent most of his club career in the MLS, he has also played in the Bundesliga for Bayer Leverkusen and Bayern Munich as well as for Everton in the Premier League.

Did you know?

The States scored in 15 of their 16 qualifiers

The States' top scorer during qualification, Clint Dempsey

Round 3

USA ....(2) 3-1 (0) Antigua & Barb
USA: Bocanegra (8) Dempsey (pen 44) Gomez (72) Antigua & Barb: Byers (65)

Guatemala ......(0) 1-1 (1)..................USA
Guatemala: Pappa (83) USA: Dempsey (40)

Jamaica ....(1) 2-1 (1)..................USA
Jamaica: Austin (22) Shelton (62) USA: Dempsey (1)

USA ....(0) 1-0 (0).............Jamaica
USA: Gomez (55)

Antigua & Barb(1) 1-2 (1)..................USA
Antigua & Barb: Blackstock (25) USA: Johnson (20, 90)

USA ....(3) 3-1 (1)........ Guatemala
USA: Bocanegra (10) Dempsey (18, 36) Guatemala: Ruiz (5)

The States beat Antigua home and away

Final group	P	W	D	L	F	A	GD	Pts
USA	**10**	**7**	**1**	**2**	**15**	**8**	**7**	**22**
Costa Rica	10	5	3	2	13	7	6	18
Honduras	10	4	3	3	13	12	1	15
Mexico	10	2	5	3	7	9	-2	11
Panama	10	1	5	4	10	14	-4	8
Jamaica	10	0	5	5	5	13	-8	5

Honduras ....(1) 2-1 (1)..................USA
Honduras: Garcia (40) Bengtson (79) USA: Dempsey (36)

USA ....(1) 1-0 (0)......... Costa Rica
USA: Dempsey (16)

Mexico ....(0) 0-0 (0)..................USA

Jamaica ....(0) 1-2 (1)..................USA
Jamaica: Beckford (89) USA: Altidore (30) Evans (90)

USA ....(1) 2-0 (0)............. Panama
USA: Altidore (36) Johnson (53)

USA ....(0) 1-0 (0).......... Honduras
USA: Altidore (73)

Costa Rica ....(2) 3-1 (1)..................USA
Costa Rica: Acosta (3) Borges (10) Campbell (76) USA: Dempsey (pen 43)

USA ....(0) 2-0 (0).............. Mexico
USA: Johnson (49) Donovan (78)

USA ....(0) 2-0 (0).............Jamaica
USA: Zusi (77) Altidore (80)

Panama ....(1) 2-3 (0)..................USA
Panama: Torres (18) Tejada (83) USA: Orozco (64) Johannsson (90) Zusi (90)

Full qualifying results and tables on pages 234-256

USA

Pos	Players used in qualifying	Club	Age	Career P	G	Qualifying P	G	Y/R
G	Brad Guzan	Aston Villa	29	24	0	3	0	0
G	Tim Howard	Everton	34	97	0	13	0	1
D	Carlos Bocanegra	Chivas	34	110	14	5	2	0
D	Clarence Goodson	San Jose	31	45	5	7	0	2
D	Edgar Castillo	Tijuana	27	16	0	4	0	0
D	Fabian Johnson	Hoffenheim	26	19	0	9	0	1
D	Geoff Cameron	Stoke	28	24	1	13	0	2
D	Matt Besler	Kansas City	27	13	0	6	0	2
D	Michael Orozco	Puebla	28	11	3	2	1	0
D	Michael Parkhurst	Columbus Crew	30	24	0	3	0	0
D	Oguchi Onyewu	Sheff Wed	31	69	6	1	0	0
D	Omar Gonzalez	LA Galaxy	25	17	0	8	0	0
D	Timothy Chandler	Nuremberg	23	10	0	1	0	0
D	Steve Cherundolo	Hannover	35	87	2	5	0	0
D	Daniel Williams	Reading	24	13	0	5	0	0
M	Alejandro Bedoya	Nantes	26	26	1	3	0	1
M	Brad Davis	Houston Dyn.	32	13	0	4	0	1
M	Brad Evans	Seattle	28	17	1	5	1	1
M	Brek Shea	Barnsley	23	26	2	3	0	0
M	Clint Dempsey	Seattle	30	102	36	14	8	1
M	DaMarcus Beasley	Puebla	31	114	17	7	0	2
M	Graham Zusi	Kansas City	27	19	3	12	2	2
M	Jermaine Jones	Besiktas	32	39	2	12	0	3
M	Joe Corona	Tijiana	23	11	2	2	0	0
M	Francisco Jose Torres	Tigres	26	26	0	2	0	0
M	Kyle Beckerman	Real Salt Lake	31	34	1	5	0	0
M	Maurice Edu	Philadelphia U.	27	45	1	8	0	1
M	Michael Bradley	Toronto FC	26	82	11	10	0	1
M	Mikkel Diskerud	Rosenborg	23	17	2	3	0	0
M	Sacha Kljestan	Anderlecht	28	46	4	5	0	1
F	Alan Gordon	San Jose	32	1	0	1	0	0
F	Landon Donovan	Los Angeles	31	155	57	5	1	1
F	Aron Johannsson	AZ Alkmaar	23	7	1	3	1	0
F	Eddie Johnson	DC United	29	62	19	10	4	0
F	Herculez Gomez	Tijiana	31	24	6	8	2	0
F	Jozy Altidore	Sunderland	24	67	21	13	4	2
F	Terrence Boyd	Rapid Vienna	23	12	0	3	0	0

What happens if ...

USA score first

USA win	18	64%
Draw	1	4%
USA lose	3	11%

28 games since 2010 World Cup

Opponents score first

USA win	3	11%
Draw	0	0%
USA lose	2	7%

DEDICATED TEAM PAGES

FULL SQUADS AS SOON AS THEY'RE ANNOUNCED AND PLAYER STATS AVAILABLE FOR EVERY TEAM AT THE 2014 WORLD CUP IN BRAZIL **SOCCERBASE.COM**

GROUP G

Goal times

For		Against
4	0-9	2
6	10-18	2
4	19-27	3
5	28-36	4
6	37-45	3
4	46-54	2
5	55-63	1
6	64-72	1
8	73-81	3
7	82-90	3

USA			Opponents	
25	45%	1st half	14	58%
30	55%	2nd half	10	42%

28 games since 2010 World Cup

Top scorers

	Total	First	%	Anytime	%
C Dempsey	8	4	50	7	50
E Johnson	4	2	50	3	30
J Altidore	4	3	75	4	31
H Gomez	2	1	50	2	25
G Zusi	2	1	50	2	17
C Bocanegra	2	1	50	2	40

In World Cup 2014 qualification

Eddie Johnson

Correct scores

	Friendly	Comp
1-0	6	7
2-0	1	5
2-1	0	2
3-0	0	0
3-1	0	3
3-2	1	1
4-0	0	0
4-1	0	1
4-2	0	0
4-3	2	0
0-0	4	1
1-1	3	1
2-2	2	0
3-3	0	0
4-4	0	0
0-1	6	0
0-2	2	0
1-2	0	3
0-3	0	0
1-3	0	1
2-3	0	0
0-4	1	0
1-4	1	0
2-4	1	1
3-4	0	0
Other	2	2

60 games since 2010 World Cup

Unders & overs

1.5 goals		2.5 goals		3.5 goals		4.5 goals	
Under	Over	Under	Over	Under	Over	Under	Over
29%	71%	50%	50%	68%	32%	82%	18%

28 games since 2010 World Cup

Half-time/Full-time

Win/Win	10	36%
Draw/Win	10	36%
Lose/Win	1	4%
Win/Draw	1	4%
Draw/Draw	1	4%
Lose/Draw	0	0%
Win/Lose	0	0%
Draw/Lose	3	11%
Lose/Lose	2	7%

WIN 76%

28 games since 2010 World Cup

Bookings

Yellow cards	25
Red cards	0
Av make-up	15.6

In 2014 World Cup qualifying

Penalty shootouts

Won	4	80%
Lost	1	20%

All-time record

Clean sheets

USA	13	46%
Opponents	1	4%

28 games since 2010 World Cup

Russia's vulnerability on the counter could mean an early exit for the next hosts

Punters should not ignore the obvious in most of the groups because there is a clear gulf between the best and the rest, but that is far from the case in Group H where Russia are being completely overrated, **writes Mark Langdon**.

Russia topped a qualifying group which included Portugal, although past competitions have shown us it's usually best to tread extremely carefully when judging tournament thoughts on an outcome where the process started in September 2012.

One look at the Russian squad does not scream out good things to qualify, even if coach Fabio Capello would have struggled to pick out an easier set of group opponents had the Italian veteran been given licence to select his own fixtures.

Belgium, despite being hyped up to the hills and therefore little value themselves, should still have the necessary depth of talent to take a spot in the top two.

Eden Hazard, Kevin De Bruyne, Jan Vertonghen, Vincent Kompany, Thibaut Courtois and the rest of the Red Devils squad should make sure of that which would leave Russia with one qualifying spot to play for against South Korea and Algeria.

And Russia showed at the last European Championships how easy it was for them to fold under pressure when they managed to exit at the first hurdle despite being given what looked a gimme of a group against Poland, Czech Republic and Greece.

There isn't a huge amount of young potential to get excited about, either. Capello's side lack firepower in the attacking third, are stodgy in midfield and cumbersome enough at the back to be vulnerable to the counter attack in all three matches.

First up is a clash with South Korea, who had trouble in qualifying, but again that should not be considered as a complete problem. A new manager who guided the young players to third spot at the 2012 Olympics now makes the Asian outfit a different proposition.

The majority of the South Korean midfield plays in England and there's also a heavy Bundesliga influence to suggest they will be quick and direct which could unsettle the robust Russians.

If Russia flop, as the odds suggest, against Belgium it could mean everything is on the line for the final match with Algeria and, with a mainly young squad which is being boosted as the North Africans raid France's reject bin, they are potentially tricky opponents.

Recommendation
Russia not to qualify

	bet365	Coral	Lads	Power	W Hill
Belgium	**4-6**	8-13	8-15	**4-6**	4-7
Russia	7-4	9-4	**5-2**	11-5	2
South Korea	9	6	17-2	8	9
Algeria	33	25	18	22	25

	Power
Belgium/Russia	2
Russia/Belgium	10-3
Belgium/S Korea	4
Russia/S Korea	9
S Korea/Belgium	10
Belgium/Algeria	10
S Korea/Russia	14
Russia/Algeria	20
Algeria/Belgium	35
Algeria/Russia	50
S Korea/Algeria	55
Algeria/S Korea	90

	Lads	Power	W Hill	Power	W Hill
Belgium	1-9	**1-5**	1-6	**25**	16
Russia	**1-2**	2-5	2-5	**15-2**	7
South Korea	2	7-4	15-8	**15-8**	7-4
Algeria	4	**9-2**	4	4-7	**4-6**

All group betting markets are win only

Group matches	World Cup history	Head-to-head record	Last meeting
Belgium v Algeria Tuesday June 17, 5pm, Belo Horizonte	No previous World Cup meetings	Two friendlies since 2002, a draw and a Belgian win	Belgium won 3-1 in Annaba in February 2003
Russia v South Korea Tuesday June 17, 11pm, Cuiaba	No previous World Cup meetings	They've played once, last November, and Russia won 2-1	Russia were behind after six minutes but came back to win
Belgium v Russia Sunday June 22, 5pm, Rio De Janeiro	USSR beat Belgium in 1970 and 1982, Belgium won in 86 (aet) and 2002	Four wins for Russia, three for Belgium and a draw since 1970	Lukaku scored twice in Belgium's 2-0 win over Dick Advocaat's side
South Korea v Algeria Sunday June 22, 8pm, Porto Alegre	No previous World Cup meetings	The only game finished 2-0 to South Korea	Nezahualcoyotl, Mexico, 1985
South Korea v Belgium Thursday June 26, 9pm, Sao Paulo	Two group-stage meetings, Belgium won in 1990, they drew in 1998	Two wins for Belgium and a draw since 1990	Belgium beat South Korea 2-1 in a friendly in Seoul in 1999
Algeria v Russia Thursday June 26, 9pm, Curitiba	No previous World Cup meetings	They've only played once, and it ended as a 2-2 draw	Algeria and USSR drew 2-2 in Algiers in November 1964

Group winners

Round of 16 July 1 Salvador
2G Germany, Portugal, Ghana, USA

Quarter-finals July 5 Brasilia
1F Argentina, Bosnia-Herzegovina, Iran, Nigeria
2E Switzerland, Ecuador, France, Honduras

Semi-finals July 9 Sao Paulo
1B Spain, Holland, Chile, Australia
2A Brazil, Croatia, Mexico, Cameroon
1D Uruguay, Costa Rica, England, Italy
2C Colombia, Greece, Ivory Coast, Japan

Final July 13 Rio

Group runners-up

Round of 16 June 30 Porto Alegre
1G Germany, Portugal, Ghana, USA

Quarter-finals July 4 Rio de Janeiro
1E Switzerland, Ecuador, France, Honduras
2F Argentina, Bosnia-Herzegovina, Iran, Nigeria

Semi-finals July 8 Belo Horizonte
1A Brazil, Croatia, Mexico, Cameroon
2B Spain, Holland, Chile, Australia
1C Colombia, Greece, Ivory Coast, Japan
2D Uruguay, Costa Rica, England, Italy

BELGIUM

It's their best team in years but the last 16 is the limit for the Red Devils

I t's hard to believe but not even four years ago Belgium were available to back at 500-1 to win the 2014 World Cup and now they find themselves fifth favourites to win the competition. Back then, in July 2010, Belgium were ranked 48th by Fifa – to put that into context Scotland were 41st – but their golden generation has come together nicely and by the end of qualifying, the Red Devils were in their highest ever position of fifth.

How they qualified

There was not much strength to the group with most of their rivals encountering problems, but Belgium still made smooth progress, winning eight and drawing two of their ten matches, and one of those stalemates came against Wales with their qualification already secured.

Belgium conceded only four goals in ten matches and never leaked more than once in any game. The pick of the performances was a Romelu Lukaku-inspired 2-1 win in Croatia to nail down a berth in Brazil.

The manager

A Uefa Cup winner as a player, Marc Wilmots does not have a vast amount of managerial experience at club level with a couple of short periods, first at Schalke before leaving that post to pursue a career in politics, and then at Sint-Truiden.

However, Wilmots knew the Belgium set-up, having been number two to Dick Advocaat and Georges Leekens, and was the obvious choice to take over the role when the job became vacant in May 2012.

Match winners

Belgium have stars throughout their team with Eden Hazard carrying the main hopes of matching the 1986 vintage who reached the semi-finals in Mexico. Hazard was starting to

GROUP H

look the part towards the end of last season at Chelsea and has gone up several notches this term, with the Blues winger producing some scintillating displays.

Kevin De Bruyne, harshly treated by Jose Mourinho at Stamford Bridge, was directly involved in 44 per cent of Belgium's goals in qualifying, Manchester City skipper Vincent Kompany is a defensive rock for club and country, and clean sheet machine Thibaut Courtois is unquestionably the best young goalkeeper in world football.

Question marks

Wilmots must be pulling his hair out at with so many of his go-to men out of favour at club level – De Bruyne was forced to leave Chelsea for more minutes at Wolfsburg while defenders Toby Alderweireld and Thomas Vermaelen are reserves at Atletico and Arsenal respectively.

Marouane Fellaini, Christian Benteke, Nacer Chadli and Lukaku are among others who have struggled with either fitness or form this season and a home loss to Colombia perhaps highlights their limitations.

There is also a weird imbalance in the full-back positions, where centre-backs Alderweireld and Jan Vertonghen are usually asked to fill in. That could become a problem in the latter stages.

How to back them

They have the players to go well and could do some damage but the current price offers terrible value. It could be argued the Red Devils are a whopping price to go out in the group stage even if Russia, South Korea and Algeria can't be considered strong opposition.

A safer punt comes in backing Belgium for a last-16 exit – they are likely to take on Germany or Portugal in the first knockout stage and there is no way Wilmots' men can be considered good things to overcome that proper test.

BELGIUM

World Cup record

Uruguay 1930	Group stage
Italy 1934	First round
France 1938	First round
Brazil 1950	Withdrew
Switzerland 1954	Group stage
Sweden 1958	Did not qualify
Chile 1962	Did not qualify
England 1966	Did not qualify
Mexico 1970	Group stage
Germany 1974	Did not qualify
Argentina 1978	Did not qualify
Spain 1982	Second round
Mexico 1986	Fourth place
Italy 1990	Round of 16
USA 1994	Round of 16
France 1998	Group stage
Korea/Japan 2002	Round of 16
Germany 2006	Did not qualify
South Africa 2010	Did not qualify

Continental titles

None

Legendary player

A toss up between Belgium's record goalscorer Paul van Himst and **Enzo Scifo**, and while Van Himst's appearance in Escape To Victory is a huge point in his favour, Scifo's presence at four World Cups, including the Red Devils' run to the semi-finals in 1986, swings it. Blessed with great vision for a pass and the skill to deliver it, Scifo was a superb No.10.

Did you know?

Both of Eden Hazard's parents were footballers – his mother played until she was three months pregnant with him

Eden Hazard will be the creative focus for Belgium as they attempt to hit the heights of Mexico 86

How they qualified

Final group	P	W	D	L	F	A		Pts
Belgium	10	8	2	0	18	4	14	26
Croatia	10	5	2	3	12	9	3	17
Serbia	10	4	2	4	18	11	7	14
Scotland	10	3	2	5	8	12	-4	11
Wales	10	3	1	6	9	20	-11	10
Macedonia	10	2	1	7	7	16	-9	7

Belgium coach
Marc Wilmots

Wales ....(0) 0-2 (1).............Belgium
Belgium: Kompany (41) Vertonghen (83)

Belgium...........(1) 1-1 (1)..............Croatia
Belgium: Gillet (45) Croatia: Perisic (6)

Serbia...............(0) 0-3 (1).............Belgium
Belgium: Benteke (34) De Bruyne (68) Mirallas (90)

Belgium...........(0) 2-0 (0)............Scotland
Belgium: Benteke (69) Kompany (71)

Macedonia ......(0) 0-2 (1).............Belgium
Belgium: De Bruyne (26) Hazard (pen 62)

Belgium...........(0) 1-0 (0)........Macedonia
Belgium: Hazard (63)

Belgium...........(1) 2-1 (0)...............Serbia
Belgium: De Bruyne (13) Fellaini (60) Serbia: Kolarov (87)

Scotland ....(0) 0-2 (1).............Belgium
Belgium: Defour (38) Mirallas (89)

Croatia ....(0) 1-2 (2).............Belgium
Croatia: Kranjcar (83) Belgium: Lukaku (15, 38)

Belgium...........(0) 1-1 (0)................Wales
Belgium: De Bruyne (64) Wales: Ramsey (88)

Full qualifying results and tables on pages 234-256

BELGIUM

Romelu Lukaku enjoys the moment as Belgium book their place in Brazil

Players used in qualifying			Career			Qualifying		
Pos		**Club**	**Age**	**P**	**G**	**P**	**G**	**Y/R**
G	Thibaut Courtois	Atl Madrid	21	15	0	10	0	0
D	Daniel van Buyten	Bayern Munich	36	77	10	5	0	0
D	Jan Vertonghen	Tottenham	26	55	4	10	1	1
D	Nicolas Lombaerts	Zenit	29	25	2	2	0	1
D	Sebastien Pocognoli	Hannover	26	12	0	2	0	0
D	Thomas Vermaelen	Arsenal	28	46	1	7	0	1
D	Toby Alderweireld	Atl Madrid	25	32	1	8	0	0
D	Vincent Kompany	Man City	27	57	4	6	2	0
M	Axel Witsel	Zenit	25	46	5	10	0	1
M	Dries Mertens	Napoli	26	23	2	5	0	0
M	Eden Hazard	Chelsea	23	43	5	9	2	0
M	Guillaume Gillet	Anderlecht	30	20	1	2	1	2
M	Kevin De Bruyne	Wolfsburg	22	19	4	10	4	0
M	Marouane Fellaini	Man Utd	26	48	8	7	1	2
M	Mousa Dembele	Tottenham	26	55	5	10	0	1
M	Nacer Chadli	Tottenham	24	18	2	8	0	1
M	Steven Defour	Porto	25	42	2	3	1	0
F	Zakaria Bakkali	PSV Eindhoven	17	1	0	1	0	0
F	Christian Benteke	Aston Villa	23	18	6	7	2	1
F	Ilombe M'Boyo	Genk	26	2	0	1	0	0
F	Kevin Mirallas	Everton	26	43	9	9	2	1
F	Romelu Lukaku	Everton	20	27	5	4	2	0

What happens if ...

Belgium score first

Belgium win	12	60%
Draw	4	20%
Belgium lose	1	5%

20 games since 2010 World Cup

Opponents score first

Belgium win	0	0%
Draw	1	5%
Belgium lose	2	10%

Goal times

For		Against
2	0-9	1
4	10-18	2
1	19-27	1
3	28-36	3
7	37-45	0
4	46-54	3
4	55-63	1
6	64-72	1
1	73-81	1
7	82-90	6

Belgium			Opponents	
17	44%	1st half	7	37%
22	56%	2nd half	12	63%

20 games since 2010 World Cup

Correct scores

	Friendly	Comp
1-0	1	1
2-0	1	6
2-1	2	2
3-0	0	1
3-1	0	0
3-2	0	0
4-0	0	0
4-1	0	2
4-2	2	0
4-3	0	0
0-0	3	0
1-1	2	4
2-2	2	0
3-3	0	0
4-4	0	1
0-1	2	1
0-2	1	0
1-2	1	0
0-3	0	0
1-3	0	1
2-3	1	1
0-4	0	0
1-4	0	0
2-4	0	0
3-4	0	0
Other	0	0

38 games since 2010 World Cup

Bookings

Yellow cards	12
Red cards	0
Avg make-up	12.0

In 2014 World Cup qualifying

Top scorers

	Total	First	%	Anytime	%
K De Bruyne	4	3	75	4	40
V Kompany	2	1	50	2	33
K Mirallas	2	0	0	2	22
E Hazard	2	1	50	2	22
C Benteke	2	2	100	2	28
R Lukaku	2	1	50	1	25

In World Cup 2014 qualification

Kevin De Bruyne was involved in almost half of Belgium's goals

Unders & overs

1.5 goals		2.5 goals		3.5 goals		4.5 goals	
Under	Over	Under	Over	Under	Over	Under	Over
10%	90%	60%	40%	75%	25%	80%	20%

20 games since 2010 World Cup

Half-time/Full-time

Win/Win	9	45%
Draw/Win	3	15%
Lose/Win	0	0%
Win/Draw	0	0%
Draw/Draw	4	20%
Lose/Draw	1	5%
Win/Lose	1	5%
Draw/Lose	1	5%
Lose/Lose	1	5%

WIN 60%

20 games since 2010 World Cup

Penalty shootouts

Won	1	100%
Lost	0	0%

All-time record

Clean sheets

Belgium	8	40%
Opponents	1	5%

20 games since 2010 World Cup

ALGERIA

Valencia star Feghouli can help the Desert Foxes get on the scoresheet this time

A lgeria have failed to win a match in their last two World Cup appearances in 1986 and 2010 and North Africa's sole representative look set to struggle this summer despite being housed in one of the weaker groups in the tournament. Bookmakers rate them Africa's weakest qualifier and among the rank outsiders in the whole competition but wily boss Vahid Halilhodzic insists "we're not going to Brazil as tourists."

How they qualified
The Desert Foxes lost away to principal rivals Mali early on but still finished seven points clear in their group, before qualifying on away goals in a play-off against Burkina Faso. A partisan crowd – the stadium in Blida was full six hours before kick-off – helped Algeria to a crucial 1-0 win to overturn a 3-2 first-leg deficit.

The manager
Halilhodzic is both proud and passionate. The much-travelled former Yugoslavia forward was in tears after overcoming Burkina Faso and this shot at the finals is well deserved after he was cruelly sacked by Ivory Coast just a few months before the start of the 2010 World Cup.

He is best remembered for his work in France, where he took Lille from Ligue 2 to the upper echelons of Ligue 1 and won the French Cup with Paris Saint-Germain long before the Qatari money rolled into town.

Match winners
Five-goal Islam Slimani was the top scorer in qualifying and also found some form in the latter stages of the Portuguese SuperLiga with Sporting Lisbon. But Sofiane Feghouli is the star attraction of a nation who are raiding the French system for young players deemed not good enough for Les Bleus.

Country factfile
FA founded 1962
www faf.dz
Head coach Vahid Halilhodzic
National league Ligue 1
System of government Republic
Population 38 million
Capital city Algiers
Currency Dinar
Official language Arabic
Strengths
☑ Left-back Ghoulam delivers excellent crosses
☑ Midfield should keep Algeria competitive
Weaknesses
☒ Big emphasis on captain Madjid Bougherra to hold defence together
☒ Lack of international experience could be a problem for the youngsters

Base Sorocaba
Fixtures
1 Belgium, June 17, Belo Horizonte
2 S Korea, June 22, Porto Alegre
3 Russia, June 26, Curitiba

الجزائر

Sofiane Feghouli on Champions League duty for Valencia

Feghouli has impressed for Valencia, while Napoli's Faouzi Ghoulam, and Inter pair Saphir Taider and Ishak Belfodil are all on the books of a Serie A giant. Algeria also pushed hard to persuade Tottenham's Nabil Bentaleb to turn down France to play for them and he made his debut in March.

Question marks

Algeria scored in every qualifier which is testament to Halilhodzic instilling his footballing beliefs in the team, but there are defensive concerns.

They conceded three times in Burkina Faso – a performance which saw keeper Rais M'Bolhi dropped – and in both matches against Benin so it's fairly safe to assume the Desert Foxes could struggle for clean sheets.

How to back them

The Desert Foxes failed to score a goal in South Africa and it's only natural to look at them notching under 2.5 tournament goals this time around, but Halilhodzic was a lethal finisher in his playing days and the 2014 crop should be more attacking than the vintage of four years ago.

That said, taking them to collect under 1.5 points isn't the worst bet despite the soft group with Belgium, Russia and South Korea. However, a better way to profit could be to take Feghouli to be Algeria's leading scorer in the tournament.

Feghouli, a former French Under-21 international before switching to Algeria, is not the only youngster to fail to live up to the billing as the 'new Zinedine Zidane' but this technically gifted attacking midfielder showed in Valencia's La Liga win away to Barcelona in February that he deserves to strut his stuff in the highest company.

Halilhodzic used a 4-2-3-1 formation throughout qualifying and Feghouli, either from a position advanced on the right or just behind lone forward Slimani, can do some damage even if Algeria are eliminated early.

World Cup record

Uruguay 1930	Did not enter
Italy 1934	Did not enter
France 1938	Did not enter
Brazil 1950	Did not enter
Switzerland 1954	Did not enter
Sweden 1958	Did not enter
Chile 1962	Did not enter
England 1966	Withdrew
Mexico 1970	Did not qualify
Germany 1974	Did not qualify
Argentina 1978	Did not qualify
Spain 1982	Group stage
Mexico 1986	Group stage
Italy 1990	Did not qualify
USA 1994	Did not qualify
France 1998	Did not qualify
Korea/Japan 2002	Did not qualify
Germany 2006	Did not qualify
South Africa 2010	Group stage

Continental titles

Africa Cup of Nations (1990)

Legendary player

Rabah Madjer was there for Algeria's two World Cup appearances in the 1980s and their Africa Cup of Nations win, but his crowning glory was an audacious backheeled goal for Porto in the 1987 European Cup final.

Did you know?

Algeria beat West Germany 2-1 in their first ever World Cup match

How they qualified

Final group	P	W	D	L	F	A	GD	Pts
Algeria	6	5	0	1	13	4	9	15
Mali	6	2	2	2	7	7	0	8
Benin	6	2	2	2	8	9	-1	8
Rwanda	6	0	2	4	3	11	-8	2

Algeria.............(2) 4-0 (0).............Rwanda
Algeria: Feghouli (26) Soudani (32, 83) Slimani (80)

Mali.................(1) 2-1 (1)............. Algeria
Mali: N'Diaye (30) Maiga (81) Algeria: Slimani (6)

Algeria.............(1) 3-1 (1).................Benin
Algeria: Feghouli (10) Sliti Taider (59) Slimani (90) Benin: Gestede (26)

Benin...............(1) 1-3 (2)............. Algeria
Benin: Gestede (31) Algeria: Slimani (38, 42) Ghilas (78)

Rwanda...........(0) 0-1 (0)............. Algeria
Algeria: Sliti Taider (51)

Algeria.............(0) 1-0 (0)...................Mali
Algeria: Soudani (51)

Round 3

Burkina Faso....(1) 3-2 (0).............. Algeria
Burkina Faso: Pitroipa (45) Kone (65) Bance (86) Algeria: Feghouli (50) Medjani (69)

Algeria.............(0) 1-0 (0)......Burkina Faso
Algeria: Bougherra (49)

Full qualifying results and tables on pages 234-256

Unders & overs

<1.5	>1.5	<2.5	>2.5	<3.5	>3.5	<4.5	>4.5
29%	71%	57%	43%	67%	33%	90%	10%

21 competitive games since 2010 World Cup

Half-time/Full-time

W/W	6	29%	W/D	0	0%	W/L	0	0%
D/W	5	24%	D/D	2	10%	D/L	3	14%
L/W	1	5%	L/D	1	5%	L/L	3	14%

21 competitive games since 2010 World Cup

Algeria coach Vahid Halilhodzic

Bookings

Yellow cards	12
Red cards	0
Ave make-up	15.0

In 2014 World Cup qualifying

Penalty shootouts

Won	2	40%
Lost	3	60%

All-time record

الجزائر

What happens if ...

Algeria score first			Their opponents score first		
Algeria win	10	48%	Algeria win	2	10%
Draw	1	5%	Draw	2	10%
Algeria lose	1	5%	Algeria lose	5	24%

21 competitive games since 2010 World Cup

Top scorers

	Total	First	%	Anytime	%
I Slimani	5	1	20	4	57
S Feghouli	3	2	67	3	43
E Soudani	3	1	33	2	29
S Sliti Taider	2	1	50	2	33

In World Cup 2014 qualification

Goal times

For			Against
7	0-9		0
1	10-18		1
1	19-27		4
2	28-36		4
3	37-45		2
6	46-54		0
3	55-63		1
4	64-72		2
2	73-81		4
3	82-90		4

Algeria		Opponents	
14 43%	1st half	11	50%
18 56%	2nd half	11	50%

21 games since 2010 World Cup

Correct scores

	Friendly	Comp
1-0	2	5
2-0	2	2
2-1	0	1
3-0	1	0
3-1	0	2
3-2	0	0
4-0	0	1
4-1	0	1
4-2	0	0
4-3	0	0
0-0	2	0
1-1	0	2
2-2	1	1
3-3	0	0
4-4	0	0
0-1	1	1
0-2	0	2
1-2	1	1
0-3	0	0
1-3	0	0
2-3	0	1
0-4	0	1
1-4	0	0
2-4	0	0
3-4	0	0
Other	0	0

31 games since 2010 World Cup

Clean sheets

Algeria	8	38%
Opp	4	19%

21 competitive games since 2010 World Cup

Players used in qualifying

Pos		Club	Age	Career P	G	Qualifying P	G	Y/R
G	M Zemmamouche	USM Alger	29	6	0	1	0	0
G	Adi M'Bolhi	CSKA Moscow	27	27	0	7	0	0
D	A Hachoud	MC Algiers	25	3	0	1	0	0
D	Carl Medjani	Valenciennes	28	24	1	8	1	0
D	Djamel Mesbah	Livorno	29	25	0	6	0	1
D	Essaid Belkalem	Watford	25	12	0	4	0	2
D	Faouzi Ghoulam	Napoli	23	5	0	3	0	0
D	Ismael Bouzid	Kilmarnock	30	13	0	2	0	1
D	Madjid Bougherra	Lekhwiya	31	61	4	6	1	2
D	N Khoualed	USM Alger	27	3	0	2	0	0
M	Adlene Guedioura	Crystal Palace	28	27	2	6	0	2
M	Amir Karaoui	ES Setif	26	1	0	1	0	0
M	Hamza Koudri	USM Alger	26	1	0	1	0	0
M	Hassan Yebda	Udinese	29	24	2	3	0	1
M	Hocine El Orfi	USM Alger	27	1	0	1	0	1
M	Khaled Lemmouchia	Club Africain	32	27	0	1	0	0
M	Mehdi Lacen	Getafe	29	28	0	5	0	0
M	Mehdi Mostefa	Ajaccio	30	22	0	6	0	0
M	Ryad Boudebouz	Bastia	23	16	1	2	0	0
M	Saphir Sliti Taider	Inter	21	9	3	6	2	0
M	Sofiane Feghouli	Valencia	24	17	5	7	3	1
M	Yacine Brahimi	Granada	24	4	0	3	0	0
M	Foued Kadir	Rennes	30	23	2	5	0	0
F	El Arbi Soudani	Dynamo Zagreb	26	20	10	7	3	0
F	Nabil Ghilas	Porto	23	4	1	2	1	0
F	Ishak Belfodil	Livorno	22	2	0	1	0	0
F	Islam Slimani	Sporting Lisbon	25	18	9	7	5	1
F	Rafik Djebbour	Nottm Forest	30	33	5	4	0	0
F	A Djabou	Club Africain	27	6	1	2	0	0
F	Hameur Bouazza	ES Setif	28	22	3	1	0	0

Capello's grafters lack the flair to make even the 'easy' games a formality

Fabio Capello could only watch on as his England side nearly made a complete mess of a supposedly easy World Cup group in South Africa four years ago and the Italian will be hoping to take greater advantage of another lucky draw when his Russia side head to Brazil this summer. A section containing Algeria, Belgium and South Korea could have been much worse and Capello was right when he said: "Our group is perhaps not as hard as others."

How they qualified

Russia did not concede more than a goal in any of their ten matches and they were helped by some poor Portuguese performances in the early part of the process.

Capello's side were always in control of proceedings. Not even a couple of defeats in the middle section away to Portugal and Northern Ireland could dampen spirits, and a point in Azerbaijan on the final matchday sealed a direct passage to the World Cup.

The manager

Despite being linked with a stack of clubs, Capello has signed a new contract which runs until the end of the 2018 World Cup. That tournament is being hosted by Russia and the veteran boss is getting an increased level of power at younger age groups. On signing he said: "We have big plans."

There is an equally big pay packet which has scared off Premier League suitors.

Capello is seen as a disciplinarian, old-school coach who takes a hands-off approach when it comes to being friendly with the players. He finally quit his role as England manager after John Terry was removed as England captain by the Football Association over his head.

A five-time Scudetto-winning boss in Serie A (four titles with Milan and one with Roma), Capello also claimed two Primera

Country factfile

FA founded 1912
www rfs.ru
Head coach Fabio Capello
National league Premier League
System of government Federation
Population 143 million
Capital city Moscow
Currency Ruble
Official language Russian

Strengths
☑ A well-drilled unit
☑ Capello "happy" with the location of Russia's group-stage games
☑ Soft-looking opening set of fixtures

Weaknesses
☒ The squad will contain mainly domestically based players
☒ Poor record at tournaments apart from semi-finals of Euro 2008
☒ Lack pace at centre-back

Base Itu

Fixtures
1 S Korea, June 17, Cuiaba
2 Belgium, June 22, Rio
3 Algeria, June 26, Curitiba

Liga titles with Real Madrid in separate spells at the Bernabeu.

Match winners

It's fair to say Russia won't be the easiest on the eye in the World Cup and they are a team more about organisation than wonderful individuals.

Midfielder Roman Shirokov can chip in with vital goals, although the skipper's shock switch from Zenit to Krasnodar caused some in Russia to question his role within the team and CSKA Moscow goalkeeper Igor Akinfeev is a reliable last form of defence.

Aleksandr Kokorin and Denis Cheryshev are the pick of the younger generation and Aleksandr Kerzhakov top-scored in qualifying with five goals.

Question marks

Cheryshev was the only member of the original squad selected for March's friendly to play his football abroad and most of the entertainment in the domestic Premier League comes from expensive, usually overpaid, foreigners.

Alan Dzagoev, the star of Russia's otherwise miserable Euro 2012, has suffered with form and fitness and Kerzhakov had a shocking tournament two years ago when Opta recorded all 14 of his shots off target.

Towering CSKA centre-backs Sergei Ignashevich and Vasili Berezutski are both in their thirties and were never the quickest even in their younger days.

How to back them

This Russian side does not look particularly strong and under 5.5 group points could be the way to go.

Capello's team don't score enough goals to be considered good things against either South Korea or Algeria and grabbing two wins is far from a formality.

Since the break-up of the former Soviet Union, Russia have played six matches at the World Cup and won only two, while Euro 2012 saw them collect just four points from a similarly soft section alongside Czech Republic, Greece and Poland.

RUSSIA

World Cup record

Uruguay 1930	Did not enter
Italy 1934	Did not enter
France 1938	Did not enter
Brazil 1950	Did not enter
Switzerland 1954	Did not enter
Sweden 1958	Quarter-finals
Chile 1962	Quarter-finals
England 1966	Fourth place
Mexico 1970	Quarter-finals
Germany 1974	Disqualified
Argentina 1978	Did not qualify
Spain 1982	Second round
Mexico 1986	Round of 16
Italy 1990	Group stage
USA 1994	Group stage
France 1998	Did not qualify
Korea/Japan 2002	Group stage
Germany 2006	Did not qualify
South Africa 2010	Did not qualify

Continental titles

European Championships (1960)

Legendary player

Only one goalkeeper has ever won the Ballon d'Or and that honour went to **Lev Yashin**, the Black Spider, in 1963. His career between the Soviet Union's sticks saw him win Olympic Gold, the 1960 European Championships and take part in three World Cups.

Did you know?

Since the break-up of the Soviet Union, Russia's record at the finals reads W2, D0, L4

How they qualified

Final group	P	W	D	L	F	A	GD	Pts
Russia	**10**	**7**	**1**	**2**	**20**	**5**	**15**	**22**
Portugal	10	6	3	1	20	9	11	21
Israel	10	3	5	2	19	14	5	14
Azerbaijan	10	1	6	3	7	11	-4	9
N Ireland	10	1	4	5	9	17	-8	7
Luxembourg	10	1	3	6	7	26	-19	6

Russia ....(1) 2-0 (0)........... N Ireland
Russia: Fayzulin (30) Shirokov (pen 78)

Israel ....(0) 0-4 (2)...............Russia
Russia: Kerzhakov (6, 64) Kokorin (18) Fayzulin (77)

Russia ....(1) 1-0 (0)........... Portugal
Russia: Kerzhakov (6)

Russia ....(0) 1-0 (0).........Azerbaijan
Russia: Shirokov (pen 84)

Portugal ....(1) 1-0 (0)...............Russia
Portugal: Postiga (9)

N Ireland ....(1) 1-0 (0)...............Russia
N Ireland: Paterson (43)

Russia ....(2) 4-1 (0)......Luxembourg
Russia: Kokorin (1, 36) Kerzhakov (59) Samedov (90)
Luxembourg: Joachim (90)

Russia ....(0) 3-1 (0)................ Israel
Russia: Berezutsky (49) Kokorin (52) Glushakov (74) Israel:
Zahavi (90)

Luxembourg ....(0) 0-4 (3)...............Russia
Russia: Samedov (9) Fayzulin (39) Glushakov (45) Kerzhakov
(73)

Azerbaijan ....(0) 1-1 (1)...............Russia
Azerbaijan: Javadov (90) Russia: Shirokov (16)

Full qualifying results and tables on pages 234-256

Aleksandr Kerzhakov (left) fired blanks at Euro 2012 but was Russia's top scorer in World Cup qualifying with five goals

A photo op on Russia's Northern Ireland trip

Aleksandr Kokorin, one of Russia's bright young things

Players used in qualifying

Pos		Club	Age	Career P	G	Qualifying P	G	Y/R
G	Igor Akinfeev	CSKA Moscow	27	66	0	10	0	0
D	Aleksandr Anyukov	Zenit St Petersburg	31	77	1	5	0	1
D	Aleksei Kozlov	Dinamo Moscow	27	8	0	5	0	0
D	Andrey Yeshchenko	Anzhi Makhachkala	29	9	0	3	0	0
D	Georgy Schennikov	CSKA Moscow	22	3	0	1	0	0
D	Sergei Ignashevich	CSKA Moscow	34	94	5	9	0	2
D	Vasili Berezutsky	CSKA Moscow	31	75	3	9	1	2
D	Vladimir Granat	Dinamo Moscow	26	4	0	2	0	0
D	Yuri Zhirkov	Dinamo Moscow	30	60	0	2	0	0
M	Alan Dzagoev	CSKA Moscow	23	30	8	4	0	0
M	Aleksandr Ryazantsev	Zenit St Petersburg	27	4	0	1	0	0
M	Aleksandr Samedov	Lokomotiv Moscow	29	14	3	8	2	1
M	Alexei Ionov	Dinamo Moscow	25	3	0	1	0	0
M	Denis Glushakov	Spartak Moscow	27	25	3	8	2	2
M	Dmitri Kombarov	Spartak Moscow	27	20	1	10	0	1
M	Igor Denisov	Dinamo Moscow	29	41	0	8	0	0
M	Oleg Shatov	Zenit St Petersburg	23	4	1	1	0	0
M	Pavel Mamaev	Krasnodar	25	3	0	1	0	0
M	Roman Shirokov	Krasnodar	32	41	12	10	3	1
M	Viktor Fayzulin	Zenit St Petersburg	27	16	4	10	3	0
M	Vladimir Bystrov	Anzhi Makhachkala	30	47	4	9	0	0
F	Aleksandr Kokorin	Dinamo Moscow	23	19	5	8	4	1
F	Alexander Kerzhakov	Zenit St Petersburg	31	78	24	10	5	0
F	Artem Dzyuba	R. Rostov	25	3	0	1	0	0
F	Denis Cheryshev	Seville	23	2	0	1	0	0
F	Fedor Smolov	Anzhi Makhachkala	24	5	2	1	0	0

What happens if ...

Russia score first

Russia win	14	61%
Draw	2	9%
Russia lose	0	0%

23 games since 2010 World Cup

Opponents score first

Russia win	1	4%
Draw	0	0%
Russia lose	4	17%

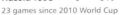

Goal times

For		Against
6	0-9	1
5	10-18	0
3	19-27	2
4	28-36	0
5	37-45	2
3	46-54	1
3	55-63	1
3	64-72	1
7	73-81	1
3	82-90	3

Russia			Opponents	
23	55%	1st half	5	42%
19	45%	2nd half	7	58%

23 games since 2010 World Cup

Correct scores

	Friendly	Comp
1-0	2	5
2-0	3	2
2-1	1	0
3-0	1	0
3-1	0	2
3-2	0	1
4-0	0	2
4-1	0	2
4-2	0	0
4-3	0	0
0-0	2	2
1-1	6	2
2-2	1	0
3-3	0	0
4-4	0	0
0-1	1	4
0-2	1	0
1-2	0	0
0-3	0	0
1-3	0	0
2-3	0	0
0-4	0	0
1-4	0	0
2-4	0	0
3-4	0	0
Other	0	1

41 games since 2010 World Cup

Bookings

Yellow cards	11
Red cards	0
Avg make-up	11.0

In 2014 World Cup qualifying

Top scorers

	Total	First	%	Anytime	%
A Kerzhakov	5	2	40	4	40
A Kokorin	4	1	25	3	37
R Shirokov	3	2	67	3	30
V Fayzulin	3	1	33	3	30
A Samedov	2	1	50	2	25
D Glushakov	2	0	0	2	25

In World Cup 2014 qualification

Unders & overs

1.5 goals		2.5 goals		3.5 goals		4.5 goals	
Under	Over	Under	Over	Under	Over	Under	Over
48%	52%	65%	35%	65%	35%	83%	17%

23 games since 2010 World Cup

Half-time/Full-time

Win/Win	11	48%
Draw/Win	4	17%
Lose/Win	0	0%
Win/Draw	2	9%
Draw/Draw	2	9%
Lose/Draw	0	0%
Win/Lose	0	0%
Draw/Lose	0	0%
Lose/Lose	4	17%

WIN 65%

23 games since 2010 World Cup

Penalty shootouts

Won	-	-
Lost	-	-

All-time record

Clean sheets

Russia	12	52%
Opponents	6	26%

23 games since 2010 World Cup

SOUTH KOREA

The last 16 is a realistic target but then things will get too tough too quickly

A repeat of the 2002 heroics which saw South Korea reach the World Cup semi-finals may never be repeated – at least not until they host the tournament again, anyway – but they have been improving without the aid of home advantage and matching the second-round effort of 2010 was seen as a realistic target even before being drawn in a group of life alongside Belgium, Russia and Algeria.

How they qualified

At times it looked as if the World Cup would be taking place without South Korea for the first time since 1982 but the long process eventually worked in their favour.

A 2-1 defeat in Lebanon saw coach Kwang-Rae Cho sacked but South Korea still topped the first phase before coming second under Kang-Hee Choi in the final group stage. Only goal difference allowed them to qualify automatically, as Uzbekistan were sent to the play-offs.

The final game against Iran was played out in a tense atmosphere (see Iran team profile, page 158) with Choi adding to the bad blood when he said: "I will defeat Iran no matter what. Iran coach Carlos Queiroz will be watching the Brazil World Cup on TV."

However, it will be Choi watching on the box – he was sacked after Iran beat South Korea 1-0 to top the group, leaving them needing results elsewhere to go their way to make it to the finals.

The manager

Myung-Bo Hong is South Korea's most capped player with 136 appearances and made the 2002 World Cup all-star team alongside the likes of Sol Campbell, Fernando Hierro and Roberto Carlos for his performances during that tournament.

As a coach he started off with the South

Ex-Sunderland man Dong-Won Ji is thriving in the Bundesliga

Korean youth teams – he led them to the 2009 U20 World Cup quarter-finals – and in 2012, the Olympic outfit won the bronze medal when their run to the semi-finals in London was eventually ended by Brazil after first-choice goalie Sung-Ryong Jung was injured.

Match winners
The Taeguk Warriors have some interesting forward options where Heung-Min Son of Leverkusen and Dong-Won Ji, who will play for Borussia Dortmund next season, are highly regarded in the Bundesliga, as is classy Mainz midfielder Ja-Cheol Koo.

Sung-Yueng Ki (Sunderland, on loan from Swansea), Chung-Yong Lee (Bolton) and Bo-Kyung Kim (Cardiff) are all technical talents who ply their trade in British football, while Chinese-based defender Young-Gwon Kim won the Asian Champions League with Marcello Lippi's moneybags outfit Guangzhou Evergrande.

Shin-Wook Kim may be the best of the domestic talents after finishing joint-top of the K League scoring charts in 2013.

Question marks
It has the look of a nice, balanced squad with potential to improve and yet the youngsters are far from wet behind the years, and possess the experience to cope at this level.

The biggest concern is the lack of playing time given to Chu-Young Park, who would previously have been seen as South Korea's leading light. Park is by no means a regular despite moving to Watford but Hong decided to recall him for the March friendly against Greece and the Arsenal reject responded with a goal in the 2-0 victory.

How to back them
Back South Korea to go out in the second round, just like four years ago when Uruguay eliminated them.

With a group of players who are being underrated, South Korea can definitely get out of this section but Germany or Portugal could be waiting in the last 16.

SOUTH KOREA

World Cup record

Uruguay 1930	Did not enter
Italy 1934	Did not enter
France 1938	Did not enter
Brazil 1950	Did not enter
Switzerland 1954	Group stage
Sweden 1958	Entry not accepted
Chile 1962	Did not qualify
England 1966	Did not enter
Mexico 1970	Did not qualify
Germany 1974	Did not qualify
Argentina 1978	Did not qualify
Spain 1982	Did not qualify
Mexico 1986	Group stage
Italy 1990	Group stage
USA 1994	Group stage
France 1998	Group stage
Korea/Japan 2002	Fourth place
Germany 2006	Group stage
South Africa 2010	Round of 16

Continental titles

Asian Nations Cup (1956, 1960)

Legendary player

Ji-Sung Park made over 200 appearances for Manchester United and was part of the team that finished fourth at the 2002 World Cup. Goals in 2006 and 2010 meant that he found the net in three consecutive World Cups.

Did you know?

South Korea played at five World Cups before their first win, as co-hosts, in 2002

How they qualified

Round 3

South Korea ....(2) 6-0 (0)............Lebanon
South Korea: Park Chu-Young (8, 45, 67) Ji Dong-Won (66, 85) Kim Jung-Woo (82)

Kuwait.............(0) 1-1 (1)...... South Korea
Kuwait: Fadhel (54) South Korea: Park Chu-Young (9)

South Korea ....(0) 2-1 (0)...................UAE
South Korea: Park Chu-Young (50) Al Kamali (63 og) UAE: Ismaeel Matar Al (90)

UAE ....(0) 0-2 (0)...... South Korea
South Korea: Lee Keun-Ho (88) Park Chu-Young (90)

Lebanon ....(2) 2-1 (1)...... South Korea
Lebanon: Ali Al Saadi (5) Ahmad Atwi (pen 32) South Korea: Ja-Cheol (pen 21)

South Korea ....(0) 2-0 (0)............. Kuwait
South Korea: Lee Dong-Gook (66) Lee Keun-Ho (72)

Final group	P	W	D	L	F	A	Pts
Iran	8	5	1	2	8	2	16
S Korea	**8**	**4**	**2**	**2**	**13**	**7**	**6**	**14**
Uzbekistan	8	4	2	2	11	6	5	14
Qatar	8	2	1	5	5	13	-8	7
Lebanon	8	1	2	5	3	12	-9	5

Qatar..............(1) 1-4 (1)...... South Korea
Qatar: Yusef Ahmed (22) South Korea: Lee Keun-Ho (26, 80) Kwak Tae-Hwi (55) Kim Shin-Wook (63)

South Korea ....(1) 3-0 (0)............Lebanon
South Korea: Bo-Kyung (31, 49) Ja-Cheol (90)

Uzbekistan ......(1) 2-2 (1)...... South Korea
Uzbekistan: Kim Jae-Sung (13 og) Tursunov (59) South Korea: Filiposyan (43 og) Lee Dong-Gook (58)

Iran ....(0) 1-0 (0)...... South Korea
Iran: Nekounam (75)

South Korea ....(0) 2-1 (0)................Qatar
South Korea: Lee Keun-Ho (60) Son Heung-Min (90) Qatar: Khalfan Ibrahim (64)

Lebanon ....(1) 1-1 (0)...... South Korea
Lebanon: Maatouk (12) South Korea: Kim Chi-Woo (90)

South Korea ....(1) 1-0 (0)........ Uzbekistan
South Korea: Shorakhmedov (42 og)

South Korea ....(0) 0-1 (0)...................Iran
Iran: Ghoochanneijhad (60)

Full qualifying results and tables on pages 234-256

Unders & overs

<1.5	>1.5	<2.5	>2.5	<3.5	>3.5	<4.5	>4.5
26%	74%	48%	52%	74%	26%	83%	17%

23 competitive games since 2010 World Cup

Half-time/Full-time

W/W	6	26%	W/D	2	9%	W/L	0	0%
D/W	5	22%	D/D	5	22%	D/L	3	13%
L/W	0	0%	L/D	1	4%	L/L	1	4%

23 competitive games since 2010 World Cup

Bookings

Yellow cards	19
Red cards	0
Avg make-up	13.6

In 2014 World Cup qualifying

Penalty shootouts

Won	4	67%
Lost	2	33%

All-time record

GROUP H

What happens if ...

South Korea score first

South Korea win	11	48%
Draw	3	13%
South Korea lose	0	0%

Their opponents score first

South Korea win	1	4%
Draw	2	9%
South Korea lose	4	17%

23 competitive games since 2010 World Cup

Top scorers

	Total	First	%	Anytime	%
Park Chu-Young	6	3	50	4	57
Lee Keun-Ho	5	2	40	4	33
Lee Dong-Gook	2	1	50	2	22
K Bo-Kyung	2	1	50	1	17
K Ja-Cheol	2	0	0	2	25
Ji Dong-Won	2	0	0	1	9

In World Cup 2014 qualification

Goal times

For		Against
4	0-9	1
1	10-18	3
5	19-27	2
3	28-36	2
5	37-45	1
3	46-54	2
5	55-63	3
4	64-72	1
2	73-81	1
9	82-90	4

South Korea		Opponents
18 44%	1st half	9 45%
23 56%	2nd half	11 55%

23 games since 2010 World Cup

Correct scores

	Friendly	Comp
1-0	2	1
2-0	2	2
2-1	5	3
3-0	0	1
3-1	1	0
3-2	0	1
4-0	1	0
4-1	1	2
4-2	1	0
4-3	0	0
0-0	3	3
1-1	1	3
2-2	1	2
3-3	0	0
4-4	0	0
0-1	1	2
0-2	2	0
1-2	3	2
0-3	1	0
1-3	0	0
2-3	0	0
0-4	2	0
1-4	1	0
2-4	0	0
3-4	0	0
Other	0	1

51 games since 2010 World Cup

Clean sheets

S Korea	8	35%
Opp	5	22%

23 competitive games since 2010 World Cup

Players used in qualifying

Pos		Club	Age	Career P	G	Qualifying P	G	Y/R
G	Sung-Ryong Jung	Suwon B W	29	59	0	14	0	0
D	Beom-Seok Oh	Suwon B W	29	44	2	3	0	1
D	Chang-Soo Kim	Kashiwa Reysol	28	8	0	2	0	0
D	Chul Hong	Suwon B W	23	4	0	3	0	0
D	Du-Ri Cha	FC Seoul	33	65	4	4	0	1
D	Hyo-Jin Choi	FC Seoul	30	19	1	3	0	0
D	Hyun-Soo Jang	Guangzhou	22	4	0	1	0	0
D	In-Hwan Jung	Chonbuk Motors	27	5	0	2	0	0
D	Jeong-Ho Hong	Augsburg	25	23	1	5	0	1
D	Joo-Ho Park	Mainz	27	13	0	3	0	1
D	Jung-Soo Lee	Al-Sadd	34	56	5	9	0	0
D	Ki-Hee Kim	Chonbuk Motors	24	7	0	3	0	0
D	Kwang-Hoon Shin	Pohang Steelers	26	5	0	1	0	0
D	Sang-Sik Kim	No club	37	60	2	1	0	0
D	Suk-Young Yun	QPR	24	2	0	1	0	0
D	Yo-Han Ko	FC Seoul	25	11	0	1	0	0
D	Yong Lee	Ulsan Hyundai	27	10	0	5	0	0
D	Young-Gwon Kim	Guangzhou E.	24	19	1	3	0	0
M	Bit-Garam Yoon	Jeju United	33	15	2	3	0	0
M	Bo-Kyung Kim	Cardiff	24	27	3	6	2	0
M	Chi-Woo Kim	FC Seoul	30	29	5	3	1	0
M	Chung-Yong Lee	Bolton	25	54	6	5	0	1
M	Dae-Sung Ha	Beijing Guoan	29	12	0	2	0	0
M	Do-Heon Kim	Suwon B W	31	61	12	2	0	0
M	Ja-Cheol Koo	Mainz	25	35	12	8	2	2
M	Jae-Park Won	Jeonbuk Motors	29	11	0	2	0	0
M	Jae-Sung Kim	Pohang Steelers	30	17	2	2	1	1
M	Jin-Seo Jung	Suwon B W	24	4	0	3	0	0
M	Jong-Woo Park	Busan I'Park	24	11	0	2	0	2
M	Jung-Woo Kim	Sharjah	31	72	7	3	1	0
M	Kook-Young Han	Kashiwa Reysol	23	8	0	1	0	0
M	Myung-Joo Lee	Pohang Steelers	23	9	0	2	0	0
M	Nam-Il Kim	Incheon Utd	36	98	2	1	0	0
M	Seung-Gi Lee	Chonbuk Motors	25	12	0	2	0	0
M	Sung-Yong Ki	Sunderland	25	58	5	9	0	2
M	Tae-Hee Nam	Lekhwiya	22	12	0	5	0	0
M	Tae-Hwi Kwak	Al-Hilal	32	34	5	10	1	1
F	Chu-Young Park	Watford	28	65	26	7	6	3
F	Dong-Gook Lee	Chonuk Motors	34	101	30	9	2	0
F	Dong-Won Ji	Augsburg	22	27	8	11	2	0
F	Heung-Min Son	B Leverkusen	21	24	6	9	1	0
F	Keun-Ho Lee	Sangju Sangmu	28	64	18	12	5	0
F	Ki-Hun Yeom	Suwon B W	30	49	3	2	0	0
F	Sang-Wun Han	Ulsan Hyundai	27	2	0	1	0	0
F	Shin-Ouk Kim	Ulsan Hyundai	25	26	3	8	1	3

June 12

Group	bet365	Coral	Lads	Power	W Hill	Home	Draw	Away	bet365	Coral	Lads	Power	W Hill	Best %	Best as decimal
Group A	2-7	1-3	1-4	3-10	1-4	Brazil	9-2	Croatia	17-2	8-1	10-1	8-1	10-1	102%	1.33 - 5.5 - 11

June 13

Group	bet365	Coral	Lads	Power	W Hill	Home	Draw	Away	bet365	Coral	Lads	Power	W Hill	Best %	Best as decimal
Group A	23-20	6-5	Evs	Evs	21-20	Mexico	9-4	Cameroon	13-5	11-5	3-1	11-4	13-5	101%	2.2 - 3.25 - 4
Group B	10-11	Evs	Evs	Evs	Evs	Spain	12-5	Holland	3-1	13-5	11-4	13-5	13-5	104%	2 - 3.4 - 4
Group B	1-2	8-15	8-15	8-15	1-2	Chile	3-1	Australia	6-1	5-1	11-2	5-1	11-2	104%	1.53 - 4 - 7

June 14

Group	bet365	Coral	Lads	Power	W Hill	Home	Draw	Away	bet365	Coral	Lads	Power	W Hill	Best %	Best as decimal
Group C	4-6	8-13	4-6	4-6	4-7	Colombia	5-2	Greece	9-2	5-1	9-2	21-5	5-1	105%	1.66 - 3.5 - 6
Group D	1-3	2-5	2-5	2-7	1-3	Uruguay	4-1	Costa Rica	10-1	8-1	13-2	9-1	8-1	100%	1.4 - 5 - 11
Group D	2-1	2-1	11-5	7-4	9-5	England	21-10	Italy	6-4	11-8	7-5	8-5	7-5	102%	3.2 - 3.1 - 2.6

June 15

Group	bet365	Coral	Lads	Power	W Hill	Home	Draw	Away	bet365	Coral	Lads	Power	W Hill	Best %	Best as decimal
Group C	13-8	9-5	29-20	6-4	6-4	Ivory Coast	11-5	Japan	15-8	7-5	9-5	7-4	19-10	101%	2.8 - 3.2 - 2.9
Group E	5-4	6-4	13-10	13-10	23-20	Switzerland	11-5	Ecuador	5-2	7-4	11-5	2-1	12-5	100%	2.5 - 3.2 - 3.5
Group E	1-4	2-7	1-3	3-10	1-4	France	17-4	Honduras	12-1	9-1	9-1	10-1	11-1	102%	1.33 - 5.25 - 13
Group F	2-5	2-5	1-3	4-11	2-5	Argentina	7-2	Bosnia-Hz.	7-1	6-1	8-1	15-2	6-1	105%	1.4 - 4.5 - 9

June 16

Group	bet365	Coral	Lads	Power	W Hill	Home	Draw	Away	bet365	Coral	Lads	Power	W Hill	Best %	Best as decimal
Group G	10-11	8-11	5-6	10-11	10-11	Germany	12-5	Portugal	3-1	4-1	3-1	3-1	14-5	102%	1.9 - 3.4 - 5
Group F	16-5	11-4	11-4	10-3	3-1	Iran	12-5	Nigeria	Evs	Evs	Evs	4-5	Evs	102%	4.33 - 3.4 - 2
Group G	6-4	6-4	13-8	13-8	6-4	Ghana	11-5	USA	15-8	7-4	13-8	13-8	19-10	104%	2.62 - 3.2 - 2.9

June 17

Group	bet365	Coral	Lads	Power	W Hill	Home	Draw	Away	bet365	Coral	Lads	Power	W Hill	Best %	Best as decimal
Group H	4-11	2-5	1-3	2-5	1-3	Belgium	7-2	Algeria	9-1	7-1	17-2	7-1	15-2	104%	1.4 - 4.5 - 10
Group A	1-3			3-10	3-10	Brazil	4-1	Mexico	15-2		17-2	17-2		106%	1.33 - 5 - 9.5
Group H	Evs	10-11	Evs	10-11	10-11	Russia	23-10	South Korea	3-1	3-1	11-4	3-1	3-1	105%	2 - 3.3 - 4

June 18

Group	bet365	Coral	Lads	Power	W Hill	Home	Draw	Away	bet365	Coral	Lads	Power	W Hill	Best %	Best as decimal
Group B	10-1	-	7-1	13-2	-	Australia	4-1	Holland	2-7	-	4-11	4-11	-	102%	11 - 5 - 1.36
Group B	8-11	-	4-6	7-10	-	Spain	13-5	Chile	9-2	-	4-1	7-2	-	104%	1.72 - 3.6 - 5.5
Group A	16-5	-	11-4	3-1	-	Cameroon	23-10	Croatia	10-11	-	21-20	10-11	-	103%	4.2 - 3.3 - 2.05

June 19

Group	bet365	Coral	Lads	Power	W Hill	Home	Draw	Away	bet365	Coral	Lads	Power	W Hill	Best %	Best as decimal
Group C	10-11	-	10-11	10-11	-	Colombia	12-5	Ivory Coast	3-1	-	11-4	3-1	-	107%	1.9 - 3.4 - 4
Group D	11-8	6-4	6-4	8-5	-	Uruguay	9-4	England	2-1	7-4	9-5	8-5	-	102%	2.6 - 3.25 - 3
Group C	6-4	-	6-4	8-5	-	Japan	23-10	Greece	7-4	-	9-5	13-8	-	104%	2.6 - 3.3 - 2.8

June 20

Group	bet365	Coral	Lads	Power	W Hill	Home	Draw	Away	bet365	Coral	Lads	Power	W Hill	Best %	Best as decimal
Group D	1-3	-	1-3	1-4	-	Italy	9-2	Costa Rica	8-1	-	8-1	9-1	-	103%	1.33 - 5.5 - 10
Group E	5-2	-	3-1	5-2	-	Switzerland	23-10	France	11-10	-	10-11	11-10	-	103%	4 - 3.3 - 2.1
Group E	15-4	-	7-2	9-2	-	Honduras	13-5	Ecuador	8-11	-	8-11	8-13	-	104%	5.5 - 3.6 - 1.72

June 21

Group	bet365	Coral	Lads	Power	W Hill	Home	Draw	Away	bet365	Coral	Lads	Power	W Hill	Best %	Best as decimal
Group F	1-6	-	1-7	2-11	-	Argentina	6-1	Iran	14-1	-	16-1	14-1	-	105%	1.18 - 7 - 17
Group G	4-11	-	2-7	4-9	-	Germany	4-1	Ghana	15-2	-	8-1	11-2	-	100%	1.44 - 5 - 9
Group F	2-1	-	9-5	8-5	-	Nigeria	9-4	Bosnia-Hz.	11-8	-	13-10	8-5	-	102%	3 - 3.25 - 2.6

June 22

Group	bet365	Coral	Lads	Power	W Hill	Home	Draw	Away	bet365	Coral	Lads	Power	W Hill	Best %	Best as decimal
Group H	11-10	-	5-6	11-10	-	Belgium	12-5	Russia	5-2	-	11-4	12-5	-	104%	2.1 - 3.4 - 3.75
Group H	11-10	-	6-5	10-11	-	South Korea	23-10	Algeria	5-2	-	2-1	3-1	-	101%	2.2 - 3.3 - 4
Group G	9-2	-	7-2	4-1	-	USA	11-4	Portugal	4-6	-	4-6	8-13	-	105%	5.5 - 3.75 - 1.66

June 23

Group	bet365	Coral	Lads	Power	W Hill	Home	Draw	Away	bet365	Coral	Lads	Power	W Hill	Best %	Best as decimal
Group B	-	-	9-1	11-1	-	Australia	9-2	Spain	-	-	1-4	2-9	-	106%	12 - 5.5 - 1.25
Group B	-	-	23-20	5-4	-	Holland	12-5	Chile	-	-	2-1	2-1	-	107%	2.25 - 3.4 - 3
Group A	-	-	14-1	12-1	-	Cameroon	11-2	Brazil	-	-	1-7	1-5	-	105%	15 - 6.5 - 1.2
Group A	-	-	6-4	6-4	-	Croatia	9-4	Mexico	-	-	13-8	13-8	-	109%	2.5 - 3.25 - 2.62

June 24

Group	bet365	Coral	Lads	Power	W Hill	Home	Draw	Away	bet365	Coral	Lads	Power	W Hill	Best %	Best as decimal
Group D	6-1	13-2	6-1	13-2	-	Costa Rica	10-3	England	4-9	1-2	9-20	2-5	-	103%	7.5 - 4.33 - 1.5
Group D	-	-	7-5	6-4	-	Italy	23-10	Uruguay	-	-	15-8	9-5	-	105%	2.5 - 3.3 - 2.87
Group C	-	-	9-5	15-8	-	Greece	23-10	Ivory Coast	-	-	13-10	13-10	-	108%	2.87 - 3.3 - 2.3
Group C	-	-	3-1	10-3	-	Japan	5-2	Colombia	-	-	4-5	5-6	-	106%	4.33 - 3.5 - 1.83

June 25

Group	bet365	Coral	Lads	Power	W Hill	Home	Draw	Away	bet365	Coral	Lads	Power	W Hill	Best %	Best as decimal
Group F	-	-	4-7	4-6	-	Bosnia-Hz.	13-5	Iran	-	-	9-2	4-1	-	106%	1.66 - 3.6 - 5.5
Group F	-	-	10-1	15-2	-	Nigeria	9-2	Argentina	-	-	2-9	4-11	-	100%	11 - 5.5 - 1.36
Group E	-	-	10-3	11-4	-	Ecuador	5-2	France	-	-	3-4	10-11	-	104%	4.33 - 3.5 - 1.9
Group E	-	-	9-2	13-2	-	Honduras	3-1	Switzerland	-	-	4-7	4-9	-	102%	7.5 - 4 - 1.57

June 26

Group	bet365	Coral	Lads	Power	W Hill	Home	Draw	Away	bet365	Coral	Lads	Power	W Hill	Best %	Best as decimal
Group G	-	-	8-15	3-4	-	Portugal	11-4	Ghana	-	-	9-2	16-5	-	102%	1.75 - 3.75 - 5.5
Group G	-	-	13-2	11-2	-	USA	11-4	Germany	-	-	4-11	4-9	-	106%	6.5 - 4.33 - 1.44
Group H	-	-	10-3	11-2	-	Algeria	11-4	Russia	-	-	8-11	8-15	-	100%	6.5 - 3.75 - 1.72
Group H	-	-	9-2	4-1	-	South Korea	3-1	Belgium	-	-	1-2	8-11	-	101%	5.5 - 4 - 1.72

Underlined prices indicate firms that are best-priced about the draw. Prices shown available to online/telephone customers and correct on March 28 2014. Some firms' shop prices may differ.

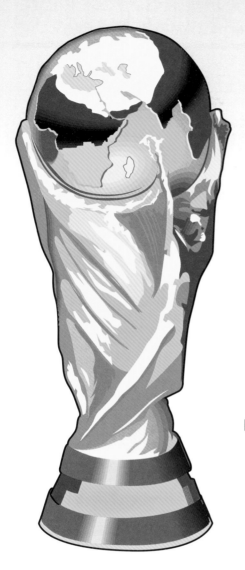

PAST WORLD CUPS

History tells us that World Cup hosts rarely let the home supporters down

Brazil 2014 will be the 20th World Cup and there is a wealth of history for punters to draw upon, **writes Paul Charlton**. Sometimes history repeats itself – either Germany or Brazil have reached at least the semi-finals of every World Cup since 1934, for example – but sometimes there will be a bolt from the blue, like Croatia's third place as debutants in 1998. Here is some context to some of the factors you might be thinking about.

Host nation
South Africa are the only host nation to go out at the group stage but even that early exit equalled their best ever performance at a World Cup. So far, six of the 19 hosts have won the trophy, two more have been beaten in the final and three more have finished third. In the 18 World Cups since Uruguay won as hosts in 1930, ten of the hosts have produced their best performance up to that point, as did both co-hosts in 2002. A further four nations, including South Africa, equalled their previous best performance.

The only hosts to fall short of their previous best were Spain in 1982, Italy in 1990 and Germany in 2006. The latter pair, both multiple former winners, went as far as the semi-finals.

Famously, Brazil were the only nation to have won the cup outside their own continent until Spain won in South Africa four years ago.

Performance of seeds in group stage
Of the 32 top seeds in the draw for the four 32-team tournaments since USA 94, 23 have finished as group winners – seven in 1998, five in 2002 and 2010, and six in 2006 – while a further four have finished as runners-up.

South Africa are the only hosts not to qualify and, while the four hosts include very strong sides in France and Germany, the list also includes Japan and South Korea.

The only seeds, other than the two World Cup holders, France in 2002 and Italy in 2010, to have gone through qualifying and failed to get out of the group stage were Argentina in 2002 – who were beaten by a David Beckham penalty and drew with Sweden – and Spain, who never recovered from a surprise loss to Nigeria in their opening match of France 98.

The seeded teams this time are Brazil, Spain, Germany, Argentina, Colombia, Belgium, Uruguay and Switzerland.

Home-based players in winning squad
At the last six World Cups, three of the winners and two of the beaten finalists have had predominantly home-based squads (three-quarters or more). All of Italy's players were at Serie A clubs when they won it in 2006 and finished runners-up in 1994. However, seven of the 12 teams in those finals had 13 players or fewer playing in their domestic leagues.

Total goals since 1950
The trend for goals, expressed as average goals per game, has been downwards since Brazil 1950. Switzerland 1954 saw an average of 5.38 goals a game, the highest at any World Cup, and while 11 of the 14 subsequent tournaments have seen the average come in at over 2.5 goals, Germany

2006 and South Africa 2010 were well below, at 2.3 and 2.27 respectively. Five of the last six finals have finished with under 2.5 goals but the last time the third-place match was an unders game was in 1974.

Fifa Ranking

Brazil have been the top-ranked team going into four of the five World Cups since the Fifa Rankings were launched in August 1993. They won it as the top-ranked side in 1994, reached the final in 1998 and won it rated as the second-best team in 2002. France were ranked 18th for their victory in 1998 and top in 2002, when they went out at the group stage. At the last two World Cups, top-ranked Brazil have been knocked out in the quarter-finals, while the winners, Italy and Spain, were ranked 13th and second respectively in the final set of rankings released ahead of the tournament.

Performance at previous World Cup

Four years is a long time in football and a good performance one World Cup does not necessarily predict a good performance at the next.

Italy in 1938 and Brazil in 1962 are the only nations to have defended the trophy. Uruguay and Germany, the first two post-war winners, did not take part in the previous World Cups and of the 14 winners since, Brazil in 1962, West Germany in 1990 and Brazil again in 2002 were the only teams to have appeared in the final four years earlier. Italy in 1982 and West Germany in 1974 had reached the semi-finals at the previous World Cup. Three of the last five winners had been knocked out in the last 16 at the previous tournament while France, who won as hosts in 1998, failed to qualify for USA 94.

Continental champions

For the first time since the World Cup was expanded to its current 32-team format, the champions of all the regions represented at the finals have qualified for the tournament.

Egypt missed out in 1998, 2006 and 2010, Colombia failed to qualify for 2002,

Greece were absent in 2006 and Iraq didn't get to South Africa last time, but European champions Spain, Africa Cup of Nations winners Nigeria, Asian Cup kings Japan, Concacaf Gold Cup holders USA and Copa America winners Uruguay will all be in Brazil. The only absentees are OFC Nations Cup winners Tahiti but Oceania are not represented at the finals this time.

Spain are the only regional champions to win the tournament in the last four editions, although Brazil reached the final in 1998. France went to South Korea/Japan as world and European champions in 2002 but crashed out in the group stage.

Only four of the 14 continental champions who appeared at the last four World Cups were the best from their region (Brazil and Mexico in 1998, USA in 2002 and Spain in 2010) but Saudi Arabia (1998), Japan and Brazil (2006), and Mexico (2010) equalled the best performance of their continent in terms of their point of exit from the competition.

In each case, it was a disappointing end to the tournament with only Brazil getting as far as the quarter-finals, Mexico reaching the last 16 and the two Asian sides going home after the group stage.

Confederations Cup

The Confederations Cup was first contested under its current name in the year before the World Cup in 1997, although it was not until 2001 that the tournament was used as a dress rehearsal for the main event with the matches being played in the host country.

None of the winners have gone on to the win the World Cup the following summer, although Brazil won in Saudi Arabia in December 1997 and were runners-up at France 98 the following July. Australia, the beaten finalists in Riyadh, did not qualify for the World Cup and France, winners of the dress rehearsal in 2001, failed to get out of the group stage in South Korea and Japan. But otherwise, the last four finals have produced one World Cup runner-up, two last-16 exits and two beaten quarter-finalists.

Four European nations offered to host the first World Cup but Olympic champions Uruguay got the nod after offering to build a new stadium (ready five days into the tournament) and pay the expenses of all the participants.

Every member of Fifa was invited to enter. Nine teams from the Americas took part but the European nations were less enthusiastic about the long trip.

Eventually, France, Belgium, Yugoslavia and Romania agreed to compete and once everyone had arrived in Montevideo, where the matches were to be played, the draw took place. The winners of the four groups would qualify for the semi-finals.

France's Lucien Laurent scored the first World Cup goal but it was Argentina who won that section, and they reached the final with a 6-1 win over the USA. They would face the hosts, who beat Yugoslavia, also 6-1.

Uruguay opened the scoring in the final, but were 2-1 down at half-time. Pedro Cea equalised on 57 minutes, Santos Iriarte gave Uruguay the lead 11 minutes later and, with a minute left on the clock, one-armed striker Hector Castro put the result beyond doubt.

Group 1

	P	W	D	L	F	A	GD	Pts
Argentina	3	3	0	0	10	4	+6	6
Chile	3	2	0	1	5	3	+2	4
France	3	1	0	2	4	3	+1	2
Mexico	3	0	0	3	4	13	−9	0

France...........(3) 4-1 (0).........Mexico
Argentina .....(0) 1-0 (0).........France
Chile.............(1) 3-0 (0).........Mexico
Chile.............(0) 1-0 (0).........France
Argentina .....(3) 6-3 (1).........Mexico
Argentina .....(2) 3-1 (1)............ Chile

Group 2

	P	W	D	L	F	A	GD	Pts
Yugoslavia	2	2	0	0	6	1	+5	4
Brazil	2	1	0	1	5	2	+3	2
Bolivia	2	0	0	2	0	8	−8	0

Yugoslavia ....(2) 2-1 (0)............Brazil
Yugoslavia ....(0) 4-0 (0)..........Bolivia
Brazil ....(1) 4-0 (0)..........Bolivia

Group 3

	P	W	D	L	F	A	GD	Pts
Uruguay	2	2	0	0	5	0	+5	4
Romania	2	1	0	1	3	5	−2	2
Peru	2	0	0	2	1	4	−3	0

Romania ....(1) 3-1 (0).............. Peru
Uruguay ....(0) 1-0 (0).............. Peru
Uruguay ....(4) 4-0 (0).......Romania

Group 4

	P	W	D	L	F	A	GD	Pts
USA	2	2	0	0	6	0	+6	4
Paraguay	2	1	0	1	1	3	−2	2
Belgium	2	0	0	2	0	4	−4	0

USA ....(2) 3-0 (0)........Belgium
USA ....(2) 3-0 (0).....Paraguay
Paraguay ......(1) 1-0 (0)........Belgium

Semi-finals
Argentina .....(1) 6-1 (0)..............USA
Uruguay ....(3) 6-1 (1)....Yugoslavia

Final
Uruguay ....(1) 4-2 (2).....Argentina

Captains Manuel Ferreira (Argentina) and Jose Nasazzi (Uruguay) lead out the teams for the 1930 World Cup final

This was the first World Cup with a qualifying round and there was no group stage. Uruguay, smarting at the lack of European teams in 1930, did not take part and all three sides to cross the Atlantic – Argentina, Brazil and the USA – went home after one game.

Italy kicked off with a 7-1 win over the USA but needed a replay to beat Spain in their quarter-final. That meant the semi-final against Austria was the Azzurri's third game in four days. Stamina told again in the final with extra time required to beat Czechoslovakia, Angelo Schiavio grabbing the winner.

Italy had followed World Cup triumph with Gold at the Berlin Olympics and Vittorio Pozzo's side were triumphant again in France.

They beat Norway, France and Brazil en route to the final, although the Brazilian coach had rested Leonidas, the tournament's top scorer with seven goals, for the semi.

In the final, Italy took on a Hungary team who had notched 13 goals in their three matches. It took the Magyars less than two minutes to match Gino Colaussi's sixth-minute opener, but they were 3-1 down by half time, and the Italians ran out 4-2 victors.

Italy 1934

First round
Sweden ....(1) 3-2 (1)..... Argentina
Austria..........(1) 3-2 (1).......... France
AET 1-1 90 mins
Germany.......(1) 5-2 (2)........Belgium
Spain ....(3) 3-1 (0)............Brazil
Hungary ....(2) 4-2 (2).......... Egypt
Switzerland...(2) 3-2 (1)........ Holland
Italy ....(3) 7-1 (0)..............USA
Czechoslovakia(0)2-1 (1).......Romania

Quarter-finals
Czechoslovakia (1) 3-2 (1).. Switzerland
Germany.......(0) 2-1 (0)........ Sweden
Italy ....(1) 1-1 (1)............Spain
AET 1-1 90 mins
Austria..........(1) 2-1 (0)....... Hungary
Italy ....(1) 1-0 (0)............Spain

Semi-finals
Italy ....(1) 1-0 (0)......... Austria
Czechoslovakia (1) 3-1 (0)...... Germany

3rd/4th place play-off
Germany.......(3) 3-2 (1)........ Austria

Final
Italy ....(0) 2-1 (0) Czechoslovakia
AET 1-1 90 mins

France 1938

First round
Switzerland...(1) 1-1 (1)...... Germany
AET 1-1 90 mins
Hungary ....(4) 6-0 (0)Dutch Antilles
France...........(2) 3-1 (1)........Belgium
Cuba.............(1) 3-3 (1).......Romania
AET 2-2 90 mins
Italy ....(1) 2-1 (0)........ Norway
AET 1-1 90 mins
Brazil ....(3) 6-5 (1)..........Poland
AET 4-4 90 mins
Czechoslovakia (0) 3-0 (0)........ Holland
AET 0-0 90 mins
Sweden .... W/O .... Austria
Sweden walkover – Austria withdrew
Cuba.............(0) 2-1 (1).......Romania
Switzerland...(1) 4-2 (2)..... Germany

Quarter-finals
Brazil ....(1) 1-1 (0) Czechoslovakia
AET 1-1 90 mins

Brazil 1950

A four-team group decided the winner but the final game was the crucial one. Before that, though, came several withdrawals – unthinkable today – and England's greatest humiliation, defeat by the USA's amateurs.

Brazil went into the final match only needing a draw against a Uruguay side who had needed to come from behind against Sweden and Spain, a pair of sides Brazil had thrashed 7-1 and 6-1. Friaca scored for the hosts just after half-time, but Uruguay rallied again, goals from Juan Schiaffino and Alcides Ghiggia breaking Brazilian hearts.

Switzerland 1954

Hungary went to Switzerland unbeaten in four years and considered the team to beat.

West German coach Sepp Herberger rotated heavily for an 8-3 group stage loss to the Mighty Magyars, in which Sandor Kocsis scored four and Ferenc Puskas was injured.

Puskas was back for the final, this time against Germany's best XI, and Hungary were 2-0 up after eight minutes.

But the Germans were soon level and Helmut Rahn's second of the game with six minutes left proved to be Germany's winner, a comeback dubbed the Miracle of Berne.

Hungary ....(1) 2-0 (0).. Switzerland
Sweden ....(4) 8-0 (0)............ Cuba
France...........(1) 1-3 (1).............Italy
Brazil ....(0) 2-1 (1) Czechoslovakia

Semi-finals
Hungary ....(3) 5-1 (1).......Sweden
Italy ....(0) 2-1 (0)...........Brazil

3rd/4th place play-off
Brazil ....(1) 4-2 (2)........Sweden

Final
Italy ....(3) 4-2 (1)......Hungary

Brazil 1950

Group 1

	P	W	D	L	F	A	GD	Pts
Brazil	3	2	1	0	8	2	6	5
Yugoslavia	3	2	0	1	7	3	4	4
Switzerland	3	1	1	1	4	6	-2	3
Mexico	3	0	0	3	2	10	-8	0

Brazil ....(1) 4-0 (0)......... Mexico
Yugoslavia ....(0) 3-0 (0).. Switzerland
Brazil ....(2) 2-2 (1).. Switzerland
Yugoslavia ....(2) 4-1 (0)......... Mexico
Brazil ....(1) 2-0 (0)....Yugoslavia
Switzerland...(2) 2-1 (0)......... Mexico

Group 2

	P	W	D	L	F	A	GD	Pts
Spain	3	3	0	0	6	1	5	6
England	3	1	0	2	2	2	0	2
Chile	3	1	0	2	5	6	-1	2
USA	3	1	0	2	4	8	-4	2

England........(1) 2-0 (0)........... Chile
Spain ....(0) 3-1 (1).............USA
Spain ....(2) 2-0 (0)........... Chile
USA ....(1) 1-0 (0).......England
Spain ....(0) 1-0 (0).......England
Chile..............(2) 5-2 (0).............USA

Group 3

	P	W	D	L	F	A	GD	Pts
Sweden	2	1	1	0	5	4	1	3
Italy	2	1	0	1	4	3	1	2
Paraguay	2	0	1	1	2	4	-2	1

Sweden ....(2) 3-2 (1)..............Italy
Sweden ....(2) 2-2 (1)......Paraguay
Italy ....(1) 2-0 (0)......Paraguay

Group 4

	P	W	D	L	F	A	GD	Pts
Uruguay	1	1	0	0	8	0	8	2
Bolivia	1	0	0	1	0	8	-8	0

Uruguay ....(4) 8-0 (0).........Bolivia

Final round

	P	W	D	L	F	A	GD	Pts
Uruguay	3	2	1	0	7	5	2	5
Brazil	3	2	0	1	14	4	10	4
Sweden	3	1	0	2	6	11	-5	2
Spain	3	0	1	2	4	11	-7	1

Uruguay ....(1) 2-2 (2)............Spain
Brazil ....(3) 7-1 (0)........Sweden
Brazil ....(3) 6-1 (0)..........Spain
Uruguay ....(1) 3-2 (2)........Sweden
Sweden ....(2) 3-1 (1)..........Spain
Brazil ....(0) 1-2 (0)....... Uruguay

Switzerland 1954

Group 1

	P	W	D	L	F	A	GD	Pts
Brazil	2	1	1	0	6	1	5	3
Yugoslavia	2	1	1	0	2	1	1	3
France	2	1	0	1	3	3	0	2
Mexico	2	0	0	2	2	8	-6	0

Yugoslavia ....(1) 1-0 (0)......... France
Brazil ....(4) 5-0 (0)......... Mexico
Brazil ....(0) 1-1 (0)....Yugoslavia
AET 1-1 90 mins
France...........(1) 3-2 (0)......... Mexico

Group 2

	P	W	D	L	F	A	GD	Pts
Hungary	2	2	0	0	17	3	14	4
W Germany	2	1	0	1	7	9	-2	2
Turkey	2	1	0	1	8	4	4	2
South Korea	2	0	0	2	0	16	-16	0

W Germany ..(1) 4-1 (1).......... Turkey
Hungary ....(4) 9-0 (0).........S Korea
Hungary ....(3) 8-3 (1)..W Germany
Turkey...........(4) 7-0 (0)........S Korea

Play-off
W Germany ..(3) 7-2 (1).......... Turkey

Group 3

	P	W	D	L	F	A	GD	Pts
Uruguay	2	2	0	0	9	0	9	4
Austria	2	2	0	0	6	0	6	4
Czechoslovakia	2	0	0	2	0	7	-7	0
Scotland	2	0	0	2	0	8	-8	0

Austria..........(1) 1-0 (0).......Scotland
Uruguay ....(0) 2-0 (0) Czechoslovakia
Uruguay ....(2) 7-0 (0).......Scotland
Austria..........(4) 5-0 (0) Czechoslovakia

Group 4

	P	W	D	L	F	A	GD	Pts
England	2	1	1	0	6	4	2	3
Switzerland	2	1	0	1	2	3	-1	2
Italy	2	1	0	1	5	3	2	2
Belgium	2	0	1	1	5	8	-3	1

Switzerland...(1) 2-1 (1)..............Italy

England's Stanley Mortenson and Billy Wright meet one of the air hostesses before flying off to Brazil for the 1950 World Cup

Sweden saw the first goalless draw at a World Cup finals – Brazil v England – but the tournament is remembered for the first Brazilian win and the emergence of Pele, then 17, on the world stage.

There were a couple of other footnotes. The four home nations all qualified for the only time and Just Fontaine scored 13 goals, a record that still stands.

Pele's six goals included two in the 5-2 win over the hosts in the final, the first of which – a bit like Gazza's against Scotland at Euro 96 – was a beauty.

Pele scored in Brazil's opener but his World Cup was over when he pulled up in their second game, a 0-0 with Czechoslovakia.

The group stage also saw the 'Battle of Santiago', Chile's notorious 2-0 win over Italy. Amidst ugly scenes, two Italians were sent off – the first, Giorgio Ferrini, had to be removed by police after refusing to walk.

Garrincha scored twice against England in the quarters and although he was then sent off in Brazil's 4-2 semi-final win over the hosts, he was still available for the final, where the Czechs were beaten 3-1.

England ....(2) 4-4 (1) ....Belgium
AET 3-3 90 mins
Italy ....(1) 4-1 (0) ....Belgium
Switzerland...(0) 0-2 (1) ....England
Play-off
Switzerland...(1) 4-1 (0) ....Italy
Quarter-finals
Switzerland...(4) 5-7 (5) .... Austria
Uruguay ....(2) 4-2 (1) ....England
Hungary ....(2) 4-2 (1) ....Brazil
W Germany ..(1) 2-0 (0) ....Yugoslavia
Semi-finals
Hungary ......(1) 4-2 (0) .... Uruguay
AET 2-2 90 mins
W Germany ..(1) 6-1 (0) .... Austria
3rd/4th place play-off
Austria..........(1) 3-1 (1) .... Uruguay
Final
W Germany ..(2) 3-2 (2) .... Hungary

Group 1

	P	W	D	L	F	A	GD	Pts
W Germany	3	1	2	0	7	5	2	4
N Ireland	3	1	1	1	4	5	-1	3
Czechoslovakia	3	1	1	1	8	4	4	3
Argentina	3	1	0	2	5	10	-5	2

Argentina .....(1) 1-3 (2)..W Germany
N Ireland ......(1) 1-0 (0) Czechoslovakia
W Germany ..(0) 2-2 (2) Czechoslovakia
Argentina .....(1) 3-1 (1)...... N Ireland
W Germany ..(2) 2-2 (1)...... N Ireland
Czechoslovakia (3) 6-1 (0) ..... Argentina
Play-off
N Ireland ......(1) 2-1 (1) Czechoslovakia
AET 1-1 90 mins

Group 2

	P	W	D	L	F	A	GD	Pts
France	3	2	0	1	11	7	4	4
Yugoslavia	3	1	2	0	7	6	1	4
Paraguay	3	1	1	1	9	12	-3	3
Scotland	3	0	1	2	4	6	-2	1

France...........(2) 7-3 (2) ..... Paraguay
Yugoslavia ....(1) 1-1 (0) ...... Scotland
Paraguay ......(2) 3-2 (1) ...... Scotland
Yugoslavia ....(1) 3-2 (1) .... France
Paraguay ......(3) 3-3 (2) ....Yugoslavia
France...........(2) 2-1 (0) ...... Scotland

Group 3

	P	W	D	L	F	A	GD	Pts
Sweden	3	2	1	0	5	1	4	5
Wales	3	0	3	0	2	2	0	3
Hungary	3	1	1	1	6	3	3	3
Mexico	3	0	1	2	1	8	-7	1

Sweden ....(1) 3-0 (0) .... Mexico
Hungary ......(1) 1-1 (1) .... Wales
Mexico..........(0) 1-1 (1) .... Wales
Sweden ....(1) 2-1 (0) ...... Hungary
Sweden ....(0) 0-0 (0) .... Wales
Hungary ......(1) 4-0 (0) .... Mexico
Play-off
Wales ....(0) 2-1 (1) .... Hungary

Group 4

	P	W	D	L	F	A	GD	Pts
Brazil	3	2	1	0	5	0	5	5
USSR	3	1	1	1	4	4	0	3
England	3	0	3	0	4	4	0	3
Austria	3	0	1	2	2	7	-5	1

USSR.............(1) 2-2 (0) ....England
Brazil ....(1) 3-0 (0) .... Austria
Brazil ....(0) 0-0 (0) ....England
USSR.............(1) 2-0 (0) .... Austria
Brazil ....(1) 2-0 (0) .... USSR
England ....(0) 2-2 (1) .... Austria
Play-off
USSR.............(0) 1-0 (0) ....England
Quarter-finals
Sweden ....(0) 2-0 (0) .... USSR
France...........(1) 4-0 (0)...N Ireland
Brazil ....(1) 1-0 (0) .... Wales
W Germany ..(1) 1-0 (0) ....Yugoslavia
Semi-finals
Brazil ....(2) 5-2 (1) .... France
Sweden ....(1) 3-1 (1)..W Germany
3rd/4th place play-off
France...........(3) 6-3 (1)..W Germany
Final
Sweden ....(1) 2-5 (2) ....Brazil

Group 1

	P	W	D	L	F	A	GD	Pts
USSR	3	2	1	0	8	5	3	5
Yugoslavia	3	2	0	1	8	3	5	4
Uruguay	3	1	0	2	4	6	-2	2
Colombia	3	0	1	2	5	11	-6	1

Uruguay ....(0) 2-1 (1) ......Colombia
USSR.............(0) 2-0 (0) ....Yugoslavia
Yugoslavia ....(2) 3-1 (1) .... Uruguay
USSR.............(3) 4-4 (1) ......Colombia
USSR.............(1) 2-1 (0) ...... Uruguay
Yugoslavia ....(2) 5-0 (0) ......Colombia

Group 2

	P	W	D	L	F	A	GD	Pts
W Germany	3	2	1	0	4	1	3	5
Chile	3	2	0	1	5	3	2	4
Italy	3	1	1	1	3	2	1	3
Switzerland	3	0	0	3	2	8	-6	0

Chile ....(1) 3-1 (1).. Switzerland
W Germany ..(0) 0-0 (0) ....Italy
Chile ....(0) 2-0 (0) ....Italy
W Germany ..(1) 2-1 (0).. Switzerland
Chile ....(0) 0-2 (1)..W Germany
Italy ....(1) 3-0 (0).. Switzerland

Group 3

	P	W	D	L	F	A	GD	Pts
Brazil	3	2	1	0	4	1	3	5
Czechoslovakia	3	1	1	2	3	-1	3
Mexico	3	1	0	2	3	4	-1	2
Spain	3	1	0	2	2	3	-1	2

Brazil ....(0) 2-0 (0) .... Mexico
Czechoslovakia (0) 1-0 (0) .... Spain
Brazil ....(0) 0-0 (0) Czechoslovakia
Spain ....(0) 1-0 (0) .... Mexico
Brazil ....(0) 2-1 (1) .... Spain
Mexico..........(2) 3-1 (1) Czechoslovakia

Group 4

	P	W	D	L	F	A	GD	Pts
Hungary	3	2	1	0	8	2	6	5
England	3	1	1	1	4	3	1	3
Argentina	3	1	1	1	2	3	-1	3
Bulgaria	3	0	1	2	1	7	-6	1

Argentina .....(1) 1-0 (0) .... Bulgaria
Hungary ....(1) 2-1 (0) ....England
England ....(2) 3-1 (0) ..... Argentina
Hungary ....(4) 6-1 (0) .... Bulgaria
England ....(0) 0-0 (0) ..... Argentina
England ....(0) 0-0 (0) .... Bulgaria
Quarter-finals
Chile ....(2) 2-1 (1) .... USSR
Yugoslavia ....(1) 1-0 (0)..W Germany
Brazil ....(1) 3-1 (1).......England
Czechoslovakia (1) 1-0 (0) .... Hungary
Semi-finals
Chile ....(1) 2-4 (2) ....Brazil
Czechoslovakia (0) 3-1 (0) ....Yugoslavia
3rd/4th place play-off
Chile ....(0) 1-0 (0) ....Yugoslavia
Final
Brazil ....(1) 3-1 (1) Czechoslovakia

Still the high watermark for English football, the 1966 World Cup served up any number of heroes, from Eusebio, to the spirited North Koreans, to Bobbys Moore and Charlton and Geoff Hurst, and Pickles the dog, who discovered the Jules Rimet trophy, which had been stolen, wrapped in newspaper under a hedge in Norwood, south London.

Champions Brazil went out in the group stage, but not before Pele and Garrincha had become the first men to score at three consecutive World Cups. The major upsets were provided by North Korea, who beat Italy en route to qualifying from the group stage and led Portugal 3-0 in their quarter-final until Eusebio turned the match around with four of the nine goals that won him the Golden Boot.

Meanwhile West Germany, featuring a young Franz Beckenbauer, were making steady progress, finishing top of their group ahead of Argentina, and beating Uruguay and the USSR – both of whom had players sent off – in the knockout rounds, with Beckenbauer and Helmut Haller, who finished the tournament with six goals, scoring in both games.

But in the end, it was all about England. Alf Ramsey's wingless wonders beat Argentina and Portugal in the knockout rounds to set up a Wembley final famous for England's third goal that may or may not have crossed the line, Hurst's hat-trick, Kenneth Wolstenholme's "they think it's all over…" and that picture of Moore lifting the trophy.

Group 1

	P	W	D	L	F	A	GD	Pts
England	3	2	1	0	4	0	4	5
Uruguay	3	1	2	0	2	1	1	4
Mexico	3	0	2	1	1	3	-2	2
France	3	0	1	2	2	5	-3	1

England ....(0) 0-0 (0) .... Uruguay
France............(0) 1-1 (0) .... Mexico
Uruguay ......(2) 2-1 (1) .... France
England ....(1) 2-0 (0) .... Mexico
Uruguay ......(0) 0-0 (0) .... Mexico
England ....(1) 2-0 (0) .... France

Group 2

	P	W	D	L	F	A	GD	Pts
W Germany	3	2	1	0	7	1	6	5
Argentina	3	2	1	0	4	1	3	5
Spain	3	1	0	2	4	5	-1	2
Switzerland	3	0	0	3	1	9	-8	0

W Germany ..(3) 5-0 (0) .. Switzerland
Argentina .....(0) 2-1 (0) ....Spain
Spain ....(0) 2-1 (1) .. Switzerland
W Germany ..(0) 0-0 (0) ..... Argentina
Argentina .....(0) 2-0 (0) .. Switzerland
W Germany ..(1) 2-1 (1) ....Spain

Group 3

	P	W	D	L	F	A	GD	Pts
Portugal	3	3	0	0	9	2	7	6
Hungary	3	2	0	1	7	5	2	4
Brazil	3	1	0	2	4	6	-2	2
Bulgaria	3	0	0	3	1	8	-7	0

Brazil ....(1) 2-0 (0) .... Bulgaria
Portugal........(1) 3-1 (0) .... Hungary
Hungary ......(1) 3-1 (1) ....Brazil
Portugal........(2) 3-0 (0) .... Bulgaria
Portugal........(2) 3-1 (0) ....Brazil
Hungary ......(2) 3-1 (1) .... Bulgaria

Group 4

	P	W	D	L	F	A	GD	Pts
USSR	3	3	1	1	2	4	-2	3
Italy	3	1	0	2	2	2	0	2
Chile	3	0	1	2	2	5	-3	1

USSR..............(2) 3-0 (0) .....N Korea
Italy ....(1) 2-0 (0) ....Chile
N Korea ....(0) 1-1 (1) ....Chile
USSR..............(0) 1-0 (0) ....Italy
N Korea ....(1) 1-0 (0) ....Italy
USSR..............(1) 2-1 (1) ....Chile

Quarter-finals

England ....(0) 1-0 (0) ..... Argentina
W Germany ..(1) 4-0 (0) .... Uruguay
USSR..............(1) 2-1 (0) .... Hungary
Portugal........(2) 5-3 (3) .....N Korea

Semi-finals

W Germany ..(1) 2-1 (0) .... USSR
England ....(1) 2-1 (0) .... Portugal

3rd/4th place play-off

Portugal........(1) 2-1 (1) .... USSR

Final

England ....(1) 4-2 (1) .. W Germany
AET 2-2 90 mins

Clockwise from main: Bobby Moore lifts the trophy; the Queen makes the presentation; "It is now"; Pickles watches the final; Nobby Stiles; Eusebio congratulates Bobby Charlton after England's semi-final victory

If 1966 set the benchmark for English football, 1970 is widely regarded as having set the benchmark for football – and the fact that it was the first World Cup broadcast in colour makes Carlos Alberto's stunning fourth goal in the final at the Azteca Stadium look even better.

England's defence of the World Cup ended against West Germany in the quarter-finals, Geoff Hurst having a goal disallowed before Gerd Muller's winner, but the highlight for the Three Lions was a gutsy group-stage defeat against a Brazilian side that included Jairzinho, Pele, Tostao and Rivelino. The match became famous for Bobby Moore's performance against Pele and Gordon Banks's 'save of the century', but England had chances too, Jeff Astle missing a sitter just after coming on as a substitute.

Brazil faced Italy in the final, with Pele, Gerson, Jairzinho and, finally, Carlos Alberto scoring in the 4-1 win that meant the Selecao got to keep the Jules Rimet trophy.

Group 1

	P	W	D	L	F	A	GD	Pts
USSR	3	2	1	0	6	1	5	5
Mexico	3	2	1	0	5	0	5	5
Belgium	3	1	0	2	4	5	-1	2
El Salvador	3	0	0	3	0	9	-9	0

Mexico..........(0) 0-0 (0)............ USSR
Belgium ....(1) 3-0 (0)... El Salvador
USSR.............(1) 4-1 (0)..........Belgium
Mexico..........(1) 4-0 (0)... El Salvador
USSR.............(0) 2-0 (0)... El Salvador
Mexico..........(1) 1-0 (0)..........Belgium

Group 2

	P	W	D	L	F	A	GD	Pts
Italy	3	1	2	0	1	0	1	4
Uruguay	3	1	1	1	2	1	1	3
Sweden	3	1	1	1	2	2	0	3
Israel	3	0	2	1	1	3	-2	2

Uruguay ....(1) 2-0 (0)...........Israel
Italy ....(1) 1-0 (0)........Sweden
Uruguay ....(0) 0-0 (0)..............Italy
Sweden ....(0) 1-1 (0)...........Israel
Sweden ....(0) 1-0 (0)...... Uruguay
Italy ....(0) 0-0 (0)...........Israel

Group 3

	P	W	D	L	F	A	GD	Pts
Brazil	3	3	0	0	8	3	5	6
England	3	2	0	1	2	1	1	4
Romania	3	1	0	2	4	5	-1	2
Czechoslovakia	3	0	0	3	2	7	-5	0

England ....(0) 1-0 (0).......Romania
Brazil ....(1) 4-1 (1) Czechoslovakia
Romania ....(0) 2-1 (1) Czechoslovakia
Brazil ....(0) 1-0 (0).......England
Brazil ....(2) 3-2 (1).......Romania
England ....(0) 1-0 (0) Czechoslovakia

Group 3

	P	W	D	L	F	A	GD	Pts
W Germany	3	3	0	0	10	4	6	6
Peru	3	2	0	1	7	5	2	4
Bulgaria	3	0	1	2	5	9	-4	1
Morocco	3	0	1	2	2	6	-4	1

Peru..............(0) 3-2 (1)....... Bulgaria
W Germany ..(0) 2-1 (1)....... Morocco
Peru..............(0) 3-0 (0)....... Morocco
W Germany ..(2) 5-2 (1)....... Bulgaria
W Germany ..(3) 3-1 (1)............. Peru
Bulgaria ....(1) 1-1 (0)....... Morocco

Quarter-finals
Brazil ....(2) 4-2 (1)............. Peru
W Germany ..(0) 3-2 (1)........England
AET 2-2 90 mins

Mexico..........(1) 1-4 (1)..............Italy
Uruguay ....(0) 1-0 (0)............ USSR
AET 0-0 90 mins

Semi-finals
Brazil ....(1) 3-1 (1)....... Uruguay
Italy ....(1) 4-3 (0).. W Germany
AET 1-1 90 mins

3rd/4th place play-off
W Germany ..(1) 1-0 (0)....... Uruguay

Final
Brazil ....(1) 4-1 (1)..............Italy

Group 1

	P	W	D	L	F	A	GD	Pts
E Germany	3	2	1	0	4	1	3	5
W Germany	3	2	0	1	4	1	3	4
Chile	3	0	2	1	1	2	-1	2
Australia	3	0	1	2	0	5	-5	1

W Germany ..(1) 1-0 (0) .... Chile
E Germany ....(0) 2-0 (0) .... Australia
W Germany ..(2) 3-0 (0) .... Australia
Chile ....(0) 1-1 (0)... E Germany
Australia ....(0) 0-0 (0) .... Chile
W Germany ..(0) 0-1 (0)... E Germany

Group 2

	P	W	D	L	F	A	GD	Pts
Yugoslavia	3	1	2	0	10	1	9	4
Brazil	3	1	2	0	3	0	3	4
Scotland	3	1	2	0	3	1	3	4
Zaire	3	0	0	3	0	14	-14	0

Brazil ....(0) 0-0 (0) ....Yugoslavia
Zaire ....(0) 0-2 (2) .... Scotland
Scotland ....(0) 0-0 (0) .... Brazil
Yugoslavia ....(6) 9-0 (0) ....Zaire
Scotland ....(0) 1-1 (0) ....Yugoslavia
Zaire ....(0) 0-3 (1) .... Brazil

Group 3

	P	W	D	L	F	A	GD	Pts
Holland	3	2	1	0	6	1	5	5
Sweden	3	1	2	0	3	0	3	4
Bulgaria	3	0	2	1	2	5	-3	2
Uruguay	3	0	1	2	1	6	-5	1

Sweden ....(0) 0-0 (0) ...... Bulgaria
Uruguay ....(0) 0-2 (1) .... Holland
Holland.........(0) 0-0 (0) .... Sweden
Bulgaria ....(0) 1-1 (0) .... Uruguay
Bulgaria ....(0) 1-4 (2) .... Holland
Sweden ....(0) 3-0 (0) .... Uruguay

Group 4

	P	W	D	L	F	A	GD	Pts
Poland	3	3	0	0	12	3	9	6
Argentina	3	1	1	1	7	5	2	3
Italy	3	1	1	1	5	4	1	3
Haiti	3	0	0	3	2	14	-12	0

Italy ....(0) 3-1 (0) .... Haiti
Poland ....(2) 3-2 (0) ..... Argentina
Argentina .....(1) 1-1 (1) ....Italy
Haiti ....(0) 0-7 (5) ....Poland
Poland ....(2) 2-1 (0) ....Italy
Argentina .....(2) 4-1 (0) .... Haiti

Second round Group A

	P	W	D	L	F	A	GD	Pts
Holland	3	3	0	0	8	0	8	6
Brazil	3	2	0	1	3	3	0	4
E Germany	3	0	1	2	1	4	-3	1
Argentina	3	0	1	2	2	7	-5	1

Holland.........(2) 4-0 (0) ..... Argentina
Brazil ....(0) 1-0 (0)... E Germany
Argentina .....(1) 1-2 (1) ....Brazil
E Germany ....(0) 0-2 (1) .... Holland
Argentina .....(1) 1-1 (1)... E Germany
Holland.........(0) 2-0 (0) ....Brazil

East Germany upset the hosts early on, winning 1-0 in Hamburg in the final group game to top Group 1 but West Germany had the last laugh. In the second group stage, East Germany had to face Holland, Brazil and Argentina, and their tournament was over.

The hosts won their section and faced the Dutch side of Rinus Michels and Johan Cruyff in the final. Within the first minute, Holland's number 14 had carried the ball from the centre circle to the German penalty box to win the first spot kick in a World Cup final, duly converted by Johan Neeskens.

But a little over 20 minutes later, Paul Breitner scored from the spot to equalise for Germany and Gerd Muller's goal just before the break meant that Franz Beckenbauer had the honour of becoming the first man to lift the new World Cup trophy.

Second round Group B

	P	W	D	L	F	A	GD	Pts
W Germany	3	3	0	0	7	2	5	6
Poland	3	2	0	1	3	2	1	4
Sweden	3	1	0	2	4	6	-2	2
Yugoslavia	3	0	0	3	2	6	-4	0

W Germany ..(1) 2-0 (0) ....Yugoslavia
Sweden ....(0) 0-1 (1) ....Poland
Poland ....(1) 2-1 (1) ....Yugoslavia
W Germany ..(0) 4-2 (1) .... Sweden
W Germany ..(0) 1-0 (0) ....Poland
Sweden ....(1) 2-1 (1) ....Yugoslavia

3rd/4th place play-off
Brazil ....(0) 0-1 (0) ....Poland

Final
W Germany ..(2) 2-1 (1) .... Holland

As in 1974, the finalists had to negotiate two group stages and, again, it ended with the Dutch beaten in the final by the hosts.

Both finalists were runners-up in the first group stage, with Holland's second place the result of a 3-2 loss to Scotland that featured a superb goal by Archie Gemmill.

The Dutch finished ahead of Italy in the second round to reach the final, but Argentina earned their place in controversial circumstances, breezing past Peru 6-0 in their final match of the second phase, a game that kicked off 45 minutes after Brazil's last match in the group had concluded.

Mario Kempes opened the scoring in the final, Dick Nanninga equalised with a bullet header and the Dutch nearly won it when Rob Rensenbrink hit the post in injury time. But the hosts scored in either half of extra time to leave the Oranje disappointed again.

Daniel Bertoni fires home Argentina's third goal to wrap up their World Cup win with five minutes of extra time remaining

Group 1

	P	W	D	L	F	A	GD	Pts
Italy	3	3	0	0	6	2	4	6
Argentina	3	2	0	1	4	3	1	4
France	3	1	0	2	5	5	0	2
Hungary	3	0	0	3	3	8	-5	0

Argentina .....(1) 2-1 (1) ...... Hungary
Italy ....(1) 2-1 (1) .... France
Argentina .....(1) 2-1 (0) .... France
Italy ....(2) 3-1 (0) ...... Hungary
Argentina .....(0) 0-1 (0) .... Italy
France..........(3) 3-1 (1) ...... Hungary

Group 2

	P	W	D	L	F	A	GD	Pts
Poland	3	2	1	0	4	1	3	5
W Germany	3	1	2	0	6	0	6	4
Tunisia	3	1	1	1	3	2	1	3
Mexico	3	0	0	3	2	12	-10	0

W Germany ..(0) 0-0 (0) ....Poland
Tunisia..........(0) 3-1 (1) .... Mexico
Poland ....(1) 1-0 (0) ....Tunisia
W Germany ..(4) 6-0 (0) .... Mexico
Poland ....(1) 3-1 (0) .... Mexico
W Germany ..(0) 0-0 (0) ....Tunisia

Group 3

	P	W	D	L	F	A	GD	Pts
Austria	3	2	0	1	3	2	1	4
Brazil	3	1	2	0	2	1	1	4
Spain	3	1	1	1	2	2	0	3
Sweden	3	0	1	2	1	3	-2	1

Austria..........(1) 2-1 (1) ....Spain
Sweden ....(1) 1-1 (1) ....Brazil
Austria..........(1) 1-0 (0) .... Sweden
Brazil ....(0) 0-0 (0) ....Spain
Spain ....(0) 1-0 (0) .... Sweden
Brazil ....(1) 1-0 (0) .... Austria

Group 4

	P	W	D	L	F	A	GD	Pts
Peru	3	2	1	0	7	2	5	5
Holland	3	1	1	1	5	3	2	3
Scotland	3	1	1	1	5	6	-1	3
Iran	3	0	1	2	2	8	-6	1

Peru.............(1) 3-1 (1) .... Scotland
Holland.........(1) 3-0 (0) .... Iran
Scotland ......(1) 1-1 (1) .... Iran
Holland.........(0) 0-0 (0) .... Peru
Peru..............(3) 4-1 (1) .... Iran
Scotland ......(1) 3-2 (1) .... Holland

Second round Group A

	P	W	D	L	F	A	GD	Pts
Holland	3	2	1	0	9	4	5	5
Italy	3	1	1	1	2	2	0	3
W Germany	3	0	2	1	4	5	-1	2
Austria	3	1	0	2	4	8	-4	2

W Germany ..(0) 0-0 (0) ....Italy
Holland.........(3) 5-1 (0) .... Austria
Italy ....(1) 1-0 (0) .... Austria
W Germany ..(1) 2-2 (1) .... Holland
Holland.........(0) 2-1 (1) ....Italy
Austria..........(0) 3-2 (1) .. W Germany

Second round Group B

	P	W	D	L	F	A	GD	Pts
Argentina	3	2	1	0	8	0	8	5
Brazil	3	2	1	0	6	1	5	5
Poland	3	1	0	2	2	5	-3	2
Peru	3	0	0	3	0	10	-10	0

Argentina .....(1) 2-0 (0) ....Poland
Brazil ....(2) 3-0 (0) .... Peru
Argentina .....(0) 0-0 (0) ....Brazil
Poland ....(0) 1-0 (0) .... Peru
Argentina .....(2) 6-0 (0) .... Peru
Brazil ....(1) 3-1 (1) ....Poland

3rd/4th place play-off
Brazil ....(0) 2-1 (1) ....Italy

Final
Argentina .....(1) 3-1 (0) .... Holland
AET 1-1 90 mins

Expanded to 24 teams, Spain 1982 featured two group stages ahead of the semi-finals and produced plenty of memorable moments: Norman Whiteside becoming the youngest ever scorer, Bryan Robson's goal against France 27 seconds into England's opener, Diego Maradona's red card for a kick on Brazil's Batista and Harald Schumacher's disgraceful foul on French substitute Patrick Battiston in the semi-finals, which the West German keeper followed by saving two French penalties in the subsequent shootout.

They met Paolo Rossi's Italy in the final. He had scored a hat-trick in the second group stage to see off the Brazil of Zico, Socrates and Falcao, and got two more against Poland in the semis before opening the scoring in the final.

Marco Tardelli and Alessandro Altobelli's second-half goals meant Paul Breitner's late reply for the Germans was a mere consolation.

Group 1

	P	W	D	L	F	A	GD	Pts
Poland	3	1	2	0	5	1	4	4
Italy	3	0	3	0	2	2	0	3
Cameroon	3	0	3	0	1	1	0	3
Peru	3	0	2	1	2	6	-4	2

Italy..............(0) 0-0 (0).........Poland
Peru..............(0) 0-0 (0)....Cameroon
Italy..............(1) 1-1 (0)............Peru
Poland.........(0) 0-0 (0).....Cameroon
Poland.........(0) 5-1 (0).............Peru
Italy..............(0) 1-1 (0)....Cameroon

Group 2

	P	W	D	L	F	A	GD	Pts
W Germany	3	2	0	1	6	3	3	4
Austria	3	2	0	1	3	1	2	4
Algeria	3	2	0	1	5	5	0	4
Chile	3	0	0	3	3	8	-5	0

W Germany ..(0) 1-2 (0)......... Algeria
Chile.............(0) 0-1 (1)......... Austria
W Germany ..(1) 4-1 (0)............ Chile
Algeria..........(0) 0-2 (0)........ Austria
Algeria..........(3) 3-2 (0)............ Chile
W Germany ..(1) 1-0 (0)........ Austria

Group 3

	P	W	D	L	F	A	GD	Pts
Belgium	3	2	1	0	3	1	2	5
Argentina	3	2	0	1	6	2	4	4
Hungary	3	1	1	1	12	6	6	3
El Salvador	3	0	0	3	1	13	-12	0

Argentina .....(0) 0-1 (1)......Belgium
Hungary ....(3)10-1(0)... El Salvador
Argentina .....(2) 4-1 (0) ....Hungary
Belgium........(1) 1-0 (0)... El Salvador
Belgium........(0) 1-1 (1) ......Hungary
Argentina .....(1) 2-0 (0)... El Salvador

Group 4

	P	W	D	L	F	A		Pts
England	3	3	0	0	6	1		6
France	3	1	1	1	6	5		3
Czechoslovakia	3	0	2	1	2	4		2
Kuwait	3	0	1	2	2	6		1

England........(1) 3-1 (1) .... France
Czechoslovakia (1) 1-1 (0) .... Kuwait
England ....(0) 2-0 (0) Czechoslovakia
France...........(2) 4-1 (0) .... Kuwait
France...........(0) 1-1 (0) Czechoslovakia
England ....(1) 1-0 (0) .... Kuwait

Group 5

	P	W	D	L	F	A	GD	Pts
N Ireland	3	1	2	0	2	1	1	4
Spain	3	1	1	1	3	3	0	3
Yugoslavia	3	1	1	1	2	2	0	3
Honduras	3	0	2	1	2	3	-1	2

Spain ....(0) 1-1 (1)..... Honduras
Yugoslavia ....(0) 0-0 (0)..... N Ireland
Spain ....(1) 2-1 (1)....Yugoslavia
Honduras......(0) 1-1 (1)......N Ireland
Honduras......(0) 0-1 (0).....Yugoslavia
Spain ....(0) 0-1 (0).....N Ireland

Group 6

	P	W	D	L	F	A	GD	Pts
Brazil	3	3	0	0	10	2	8	6
USSR	3	1	1	1	6	4	2	3
Scotland	3	1	1	1	8	8	0	3
New Zealand	3	0	0	3	2	12	-10	0

Brazil ....(0) 2-1 (1)........... USSR
Scotland ....(3) 5-2 (0) New Zealand
Brazil ....(1) 4-1 (1).......Scotland
USSR.............(1) 3-0 (0) New Zealand
USSR.............(0) 2-2 (1).......Scotland
Brazil ....(2) 4-0 (0) New Zealand

Second round Group 1

	P	W	D	L	F	A	GD	Pts
Poland	2	1	1	0	3	0	3	3
USSR	2	1	1	0	1	0	1	3
Belgium	2	0	0	2	0	4	-4	0

Poland..........(2) 3-0 (0).......Belgium
Belgium ....(0) 0-1 (0) .... USSR
Poland..........(0) 0-0 (0) .... USSR

Second round Group 2

	P	W	D	L	F	A	GD	Pts
W Germany	2	1	1	0	2	1	1	3
England	2	0	2	0	0	0	0	2
Spain	2	0	1	1	1	2	-1	1

W Germany ..(0) 0-0 (0)........England
Spain ....(0) 1-2 (0)..W Germany
Spain ....(0) 0-0 (0)........England

Second round Group 3

	P	W	D	L	F	A	GD	Pts
Italy	2	2	0	0	5	3	2	4
Brazil	2	1	0	1	5	4	1	2
Argentina	2	0	0	2	2	5	-3	0

Italy..............(0) 2-1 (0).....Argentina
Argentina .....(0) 1-3 (1)...........Brazil
Italy..............(2) 3-2 (1)...........Brazil

Second round Group 4

	P	W	D	L	F	A	GD	Pts
France	2	2	0	0	5	1	4	4
Austria	2	0	1	1	2	3	-1	1
N Ireland	2	0	1	1	3	6	-3	1

Austria..........(0) 0-1 (1) .... France
Austria..........(0) 2-2 (1)......N Ireland
France...........(1) 4-1 (0)......N Ireland

Semi-finals

Poland ....(0) 0-2 (1)..............Italy
W Germany ..(1) 3-3 (1)......... France
AET 1-1 90 mins. W Germany 5-4 pens

3rd/4th place play-off

Poland ....(2) 3-2 (1).......... France

Final

Italy..............(0) 3-1 (0)..W Germany

Alessandro Altobelli puts the result of the final beyond doubt

Mexico hosted again after Colombia pulled out over the costs and 1986 was all about Diego Maradona, whose five goals included the 'hand of God' and the 'goal of the century' in Argentina's quarter-finals win over England.

Argentina met West Germany in the final and Lothar Matthaus stuck to Maradona like glue. Even so, Argentina took charge, taking a 2-0 lead within the hour through Jose Brown and Jorge Valdano before Karl-Heinz Rummenigge and Rudi Voller got the Germans back into it. Inevitably, Maradona played the telling pass for Jorge Burruchaga's winner.

Group A

	P	W	D	L	F	A	GD	Pts
Argentina	3	2	1	0	6	2	4	5
Italy	3	1	2	0	5	4	1	4
Bulgaria	3	0	2	1	2	4	-2	2
S Korea	3	0	1	2	4	7	-3	1

Bulgaria.........(0) 1-1 (1).................Italy
Argentina .....(2) 3-1 (0).........S Korea
Italy...............(1) 1-1 (1).... Argentina
S Korea.........(0) 1-1 (1)...... Bulgaria
S Korea.........(0) 2-3 (1)..............Italy
Argentina .....(1) 2-0 (0)...... Bulgaria

Group B

	P	W	D	L	F	A	GD	Pts
Mexico	3	2	1	0	4	2	2	5
Paraguay	3	1	2	0	4	3	1	4
Belgium	3	1	1	1	5	5	0	3
Iraq	3	0	0	3	1	4	-4	0

Mexico..........(2) 2-1 (1).........Belgium
Paraguay ......(1) 1-0 (0)..............Iraq
Mexico..........(1) 1-1 (0)......Paraguay
Iraq.................(0) 1-2 (2).........Belgium
Mexico..........(0) 1-0 (0)..............Iraq
Paraguay ......(0) 2-2 (1).........Belgium

Group C

	P	W	D	L	F	A	GD	Pts
USSR	3	2	1	0	9	1	8	5
France	3	2	1	0	5	1	4	5
Hungary	3	1	0	2	2	9	-7	2
Canada	3	0	0	3	0	5	-5	0

Canada.........(0) 0-1 (0)....... France
USSR.............(3) 6-0 (0)...... Hungary
France...........(0) 1-1 (0).......... USSR
Hungary ....(1) 2-0 (0)........Canada
Hungary ....(0) 0-3 (1)....... France
USSR.............(0) 2-0 (0)........Canada

Group D

	P	W	D	L	F	A	GD	Pts
Brazil	3	3	0	0	5	0	5	6
Spain	3	2	0	1	5	2	3	4
N Ireland	3	0	1	2	2	6	-4	1
Algeria	3	0	1	2	1	5	-4	1

Spain.............(0) 0-1 (0)...........Brazil
Algeria..........(0) 1-1 (1)......N Ireland
Brazil ....(1) 1-0 (0).........Algeria
N Ireland ......(0) 1-2 (2)...........Spain
N Ireland ......(0) 0-3 (2)...........Brazil
Algeria..........(0) 0-3 (1)...........Spain

Group E

	P	W	D	L	F	A	GD	Pts
Denmark	3	3	0	0	9	1	8	6
W Germany	3	1	1	1	3	4	-1	3
Uruguay	3	0	2	1	2	7	-5	2
Scotland	3	0	1	2	1	3	-2	1

Uruguay ....(1) 1-1 (0).. W Germany
Scotland ....(0) 0-1 (0)...... Denmark
W Germany ..(1) 2-1 (1)...... Scotland
Denmark.......(2) 6-1 (1)...... Uruguay
Denmark.......(1) 2-0 (0).. W Germany
Scotland ....(0) 0-0 (0)...... Uruguay

Group F

	P	W	D	L	F	A	GD	Pts
Morocco	3	1	2	0	3	1	2	4
England	3	1	1	1	3	1	2	3
Poland	3	1	1	1	1	3	-2	3
Portugal	3	1	0	2	2	4	-2	2

Morocco........(0) 0-0 (0)..........Poland
Portugal........(0) 1-0 (0).........England
England ....(0) 0-0 (0)......Morocco
Poland ....(0) 1-0 (0)...... Portugal
Portugal........(0) 1-3 (2)......Morocco
England ....(3) 3-0 (0)..........Poland

Round of 16

Mexico..........(1) 2-0 (0)...... Bulgaria
USSR..............(1) 3-4 (0).........Belgium
AET 2-2 90 mins
Argentina .....(1) 1-0 (0)...... Uruguay
Brazil ....(1) 4-0 (0)..........Poland
Italy...............(0) 0-2 (1)........ France
Morocco........(0) 0-1 (0).. W Germany
England ....(1) 3-0 (0)...... Paraguay
Denmark.......(1) 1-5 (1)............Spain

Quarter-finals

Brazil ....(1) 1-1 (1).......... France
AET 1-1 90 mins. France 4-3 pens
Mexico..........(0) 0-0 (0).. W Germany
AET 0-0 90 mins. W Germany 4-1 pens
Spain.............(0) 1-1 (1)....... Belgium
AET 1-1 90 mins. Belgium 5-4 pens
Argentina .....(0) 2-1 (0).........England

Semi-finals

Argentina .....(0) 2-0 (0).........Belgium
France............(0) 0-2 (1).. W Germany

3rd/4th place play-off

France............(2) 4-2 (1).........Belgium
AET 2-2 90 mins

Final

Argentina .....(1) 3-2 (0).. W Germany

Group A

	P	W	D	L	F	A	GD	Pts
Italy	3	3	0	0	4	0	4	6
Czechoslovakia	3	2	0	1	6	3	3	4
Austria	3	1	0	2	2	3	-1	2
USA	3	0	0	3	2	8	-6	0

Italy...............(0) 1-0 (0)........ Austria
USA ....(0) 1-5 (2) Czechoslovakia
Italy...............(1) 1-0 (0)..............USA
Austria...........(0) 0-1 (1) Czechoslovakia
Italy...............(1) 2-0 (0) Czechoslovakia
Austria...........(0) 2-1 (0)..............USA

Group B

	P	W	D	L	F	A	GD	Pts
Cameroon	3	2	0	1	3	5	-2	4
Romania	3	1	1	1	4	3	1	3
Argentina	3	1	1	1	3	2	1	3
USSR	3	1	0	2	4	4	0	2

Argentina .....(0) 0-1 (0).... Cameroon
USSR..............(0) 0-2 (1)......Romania
Argentina .....(1) 2-0 (0)..........USSR
Cameroon.....(0) 2-1 (0)......Romania
Argentina .....(0) 1-1 (0)......Romania
Cameroon.....(0) 0-4 (2)............USSR

Group C

	P	W	D	L	F	A	GD	Pts
Brazil	3	3	0	0	4	1	3	6
Costa Rica	3	2	0	1	3	2	1	4
Scotland	3	1	0	2	2	3	-1	2
Sweden	3	0	0	3	3	6	-3	0

Brazil ....(1) 2-1 (0)........ Sweden
Costa Rica.....(0) 1-0 (0)....... Scotland
Brazil ....(1) 1-0 (0).... Costa Rica
Sweden ....(0) 1-2 (1)....... Scotland
Brazil ....(0) 1-0 (0)....... Scotland
Sweden ....(1) 1-2 (1).... Costa Rica

Group D

	P	W	D	L	F	A	GD	Pts
W Germany	3	2	1	0	10	3	7	5
Yugoslavia	3	2	0	1	6	5	1	4
Colombia	3	1	1	1	3	2	1	3
UAE	3	0	0	3	2	11	-9	0

UAE ....(0) 0-2 (0)......Colombia
W Germany ..(2) 4-1 (0)...Yugoslavia
Yugoslavia ....(0) 1-0 (0)......Colombia
W Germany ..(2) 5-1 (0)..............UAE
W Germany ..(0) 1-1 (0)......Colombia
Yugoslavia ....(2) 4-1 (1)..............UAE

Group E

	P	W	D	L	F	A	GD	Pts
Spain	3	2	1	0	5	2	3	5
Belgium	3	2	0	1	6	3	3	4
Uruguay	3	1	1	1	2	3	-1	3
S Korea	3	0	0	3	1	6	-5	0

Belgium.........(0) 2-0 (0).........S Korea
Uruguay ....(0) 0-0 (0)...........Spain
Belgium.........(2) 3-1 (0)...... Uruguay
S Korea.........(1) 1-3 (1)...........Spain
Belgium.........(1) 1-2 (2)...........Spain
S Korea.........(0) 0-1 (0)...... Uruguay

It was lowest scoring World Cup so far but there was no shortage of drama, particularly for England fans.

Even the opening game provided a shock, as Cameroon, 500-1 outsiders to lift the trophy, beat defending world champions Argentina. They went on to win their group, and a last-16 victory over Colombia, sealed by two extra-time goals from Roger Milla, set up a quarter-final clash with England.

Bobby Robson's side had finished ahead of Jack Charlton's Republic of Ireland (who reached the quarter-finals on their World Cup debut) and Holland to reach the last 16, where David Platt volleyed the only goal of the game against Belgium with a minute of extra-time remaining. Cameroon were next and it took two Gary Lineker penalties for the Three Lions to fight back from 2-1 down and reach the last four.

Germany lay in wait in England's semi-final in Turin and the match is remembered as much for Paul Gascoigne's tears after picking up the yellow card that would rule him out of the final as for Stuart Pearce and Chris Waddle missing the penalties in the shootout that meant England failed to get there.

Argentina also penalties to get past Italy in their semi (as they had against Yugoslavia in the quarters) and it was a spot kick in the final that won the cup for Germany. The penalty award, on 85 minutes, was controversial, but Andreas Brehme didn't let that concern him.

By then, Argentina had already spent 20 minutes playing with ten men after Pedro Monzon's red card for a high studs-up tackle on Jurgen Klinsmann, who evaded the challenge but made sure everyone knew he had been fouled with a theatrical reaction. And they finished the final with nine after Gustavo Dezotti manhandled Jurgen Kohler to the ground with three minutes to go.

Group F

	P	W	D	L	F	A	GD	Pts
England	3	1	2	0	2	1	1	4
Rep of Ireland	3	0	3	0	2	2	0	3
Holland	3	0	3	0	2	2	0	3
Egypt	3	0	2	1	1	2	-1	2

England ....(1) 1-1 (0) Rep of Ireland
Holland..........(0) 1-1 (0)........... Egypt
England ....(0) 0-0 (0)........ Holland
Rep of Ireland (0) 0-0 (0).......... Egypt
England ....(0) 1-0 (0).......... Egypt
Rep of Ireland (0) 1-1 (1) .... Holland

Round of 16
Cameroon .....(0) 2-1 (0) ......Colombia
    AET 0-0 90 mins
Czechoslovakia (1) 4-1 (0) .... Costa Rica
Brazil ....(0) 0-1 (0) ..... Argentina
W Germany ..(0) 2-1 (0) .... Holland
Rep of Ireland (0) 0-0 (0) ....Romania
    AET 0-0 90 mins. Rep of Ire 5-4 pens
Italy ....(0) 2-0 (Uruguay) ....
Spain ....(0) 1-2 (0) ....Yugoslavia
    AET 1-1 90 mins
England ....(0) 1-0 (0) ....Belgium
    AET 0-0 90 mins

Quarter-finals
Yugoslavia ....(0) 0-0 (0) ..... Argentina

    AET 0-0 90 mins. Argentina 3-2 pens
Italy ....(1) 1-0 (0) Rep of Ireland
W Germany ..(1) 1-0 (0) Czechoslovakia
England ....(1) 3-2 (0) .... Cameroon
    AET 2-2 90 mins

Semi-finals
Italy ....(1) 1-1 (0) ..... Argentina
    AET 1-1 90 mins. Argentina 4-3 pens
W Germany ..(0) 1-1 (0) ....England
    AET 1-1 90 mins. W Germany 4-3 pens

3rd/4th place play-off
Italy ....(0) 2-1 (0) ....England

Final
W Germany ..(0) 1-0 (0) ..... Argentina

USA 94 started with Diana Ross missing a penalty in the opening ceremony and ended with Roberto Baggio missing one in the final. In between there was plenty of drama.

Maradona, now 33, looked back to his best but left in disgrace after failing a drug test. There was also the murder of Colombian defender Andres Escobar after his own goal against the USA ended their World Cup.

There was also lots to like – Ireland's famous victory over Italy, Saeed Owairan's superb goal for Saudi Arabia against Belgium, Russia's Oleg Salenko scoring five goals in a game, Hristo Stoichkov leading Bulgaria to the semi-finals, the superb form of Baggio and a first Brazilian victory since 1970.

The final was a disappointment, finishing goalless and going to penalties.

Group A

	P	W	D	L	F	A	GD	Pts
Romania	3	2	0	1	5	5	0	6
Switzerland	3	1	1	1	5	4	1	4
USA	3	1	1	1	3	3	0	4
Colombia	3	1	0	2	4	5	-1	3

USA ....(1) 1-1 (1) .. Switzerland
Colombia .....(1) 1-3 (2) ....Romania
Romania ......(1) 1-4 (1) .. Switzerland
USA ....(1) 2-1 (0) ......Colombia
USA ....(0) 0-1 (1) ....Romania
Switzerland...(0) 0-2 (1) ......Colombia

Group B

	P	W	D	L	F	A	GD	Pts
Brazil	3	2	1	0	6	1	5	7
Sweden	3	1	2	0	6	4	2	5
Russia	3	1	0	2	7	6	-1	3
Cameroon	3	0	1	2	3	11	-8	1

Cameroon.....(1) 2-2 (1) ....Sweden
Brazil ....(1) 2-0 (0) .... Russia
Brazil ....(1) 3-0 (0) .... Cameroon
Sweden ....(1) 3-1 (1) .... Russia
Russia...........(3) 6-1 (0) .... Cameroon
Brazil ....(0) 1-1 (1) ....Sweden

Group C

	P	W	D	L	F	A	GD	Pts
Germany	3	2	1	0	5	3	2	7
Spain	3	1	2	0	6	4	2	5
S Korea	3	0	2	1	4	5	-1	2
Bolivia	3	0	1	2	1	4	-3	1

Germany.......(0) 1-0 (0) ....Bolivia
Spain ....(0) 2-2 (0) ....S Korea
Germany.......(0) 1-1 (1) ....Spain
S Korea ....(0) 0-0 (0) ....Bolivia
Bolivia ....(0) 1-3 (1) ....Spain
Germany.......(3) 3-2 (0) ....S Korea

Group D

	P	W	D	L	F	A	GD	Pts
Nigeria	3	2	0	1	6	2	4	6
Bulgaria	3	2	0	1	6	3	3	6
Argentina	3	2	0	1	6	3	3	6
Greece	3	0	0	3	0	10	-10	0

Argentina .....(2) 4-0 (0) ....Greece
Nigeria ....(2) 3-0 (0) ...... Bulgaria
Argentina .....(2) 2-1 (0) .... Nigeria
Bulgaria........(1) 4-0 (0) ....Greece
Greece ....(0) 0-2 (1) .... Nigeria
Argentina .....(0) 0-2 (0) .... Bulgaria

Group E

	P	W	D	L	F	A	GD	Pts
Mexico	3	1	1	1	3	3	0	4
Rep of Ireland	3	1	1	1	2	2	0	4
Italy	3	1	1	1	2	2	0	4
Norway	3	1	1	1	1	1	0	4

Italy ....(0) 0-1 (1) Rep of Ireland
Norway ....(0) 1-0 (0) ....Mexico
Italy ....(0) 1-0 (0) ....Norway
Mexico..........(1) 2-1 (0) Rep of Ireland
Rep of Ireland (0) 0-0 (0) ....Norway
Italy ....(0) 1-1 (0) ....Mexico

Group F

	P	W	D	L	F	A	GD	Pts
Holland	3	2	0	1	4	3	1	6
Saudi Arabia	3	2	0	1	4	3	1	6
Belgium	3	2	0	1	2	1	1	6
Morocco	3	0	0	3	2	5	-3	0

Belgium ....(1) 1-0 (0) ......Morocco
Holland..........(0) 2-1 (1) .Saudi Arabia
Belgium ....(0) 1-0 (0) ....Holland
Saudi Arabia .(2) 2-1 (1) ......Morocco
Morocco........(0) 1-2 (1) ....Holland
Belgium ....(0) 0-1 (1) .Saudi Arabia

Round of 16

Germany.......(3) 3-2 (1) ....Belgium
Spain ....(1) 3-0 (0)... Switzerland
Saudi Arabia .(0) 1-3 (1) ....Sweden
Romania ....(2) 3-2 (1) .....Argentina
Holland.........(2) 2-0 (0) Rep of Ireland
USA ....(0) 0-1 (0) ....Brazil
Nigeria ....(1) 1-2 (0) ....Italy
AET 1-1 90 mins
Mexico..........(1) 1-1 (1) .... Bulgaria
AET 1-1 90 mins. Bulgaria 3-1 pens

Quarter-finals

Italy ....(1) 2-1 (0) ....Spain
Holland.........(0) 2-3 (0) ....Brazil
Bulgaria........(0) 2-1 (0) ..... Germany
Romania ....(0) 2-2 (0) ....Sweden
AET 1-1 90 mins. Sweden 5-4 pens

Semi-finals

Bulgaria........(1) 1-2 (2) ....Italy
Sweden ....(0) 0-1 (0) ....Brazil

3rd/4th place play-off

Sweden ....(4) 4-0 (0) .... Bulgaria

Final

Brazil ....(0) 0-0 (0) ....Italy
AET 0-0 90 mins. Brazil 3-2 pens

Heartbreak for Baggio, disgrace for Maradona, joy for Brazil

Group A

	P	W	D	L	F	A	GD	Pts
Brazil	3	2	0	1	6	3	3	6
Norway	3	1	2	0	5	4	1	5
Morocco	3	1	1	1	5	5	0	4
Scotland	3	0	1	2	2	6	-4	1

Brazil ....(1) 2-1 (1) .... Scotland
Morocco ....(1) 2-2 (1) .... Norway
Scotland ....(0) 1-1 (0) .... Norway
Brazil ....(2) 3-0 (0) ...... Morocco
Scotland ....(0) 0-3 (1) ...... Morocco
Brazil ....(0) 1-2 (0) .... Norway

Group B

	P	W	D	L	F	A	GD	Pts
Italy	3	2	1	0	7	3	4	7
Chile	3	0	3	0	4	4	0	3
Austria	3	0	2	1	3	4	-1	2
Cameroon	3	0	2	1	2	5	-3	2

Cameroon.....(0) 1-1 (0) .... Austria
Italy ....(1) 2-2 (1) .... Chile
Chile ....(0) 1-1 (0) .... Austria
Italy ....(1) 3-0 (0) .... Cameroon
Italy ....(0) 2-1 (0) .... Austria
Chile ....(1) 1-1 (0) .... Cameroon

Group C

	P	W	D	L	F	A	GD	Pts
France	3	3	0	0	9	1	8	9
Denmark	3	1	1	1	3	3	0	4
South Africa	3	0	2	1	3	6	-3	2
Saudi Arabia	3	0	1	2	2	7	-5	1

Saudi Arabia .(0) 0-1 (0) ..... Denmark
France...........(1) 3-0 (0) ....S Africa
France...........(1) 4-0 (0) .Saudi Arabia
S Africa ....(0) 1-1 (1) ..... Denmark
France...........(1) 2-1 (1) ..... Denmark
S Africa ....(1) 2-2 (1) .Saudi Arabia

Group D

	P	W	D	L	F	A	GD	Pts
Nigeria	3	2	0	1	5	5	0	6
Paraguay	3	1	2	0	3	1	2	5
Spain	3	1	1	1	8	4	4	4
Bulgaria	3	0	1	2	1	7	-6	1

Paraguay ......(0) 0-0 (0) ...... Bulgaria
Spain ....(1) 2-3 (1) .... Nigeria
Nigeria ....(1) 1-0 (0) ...... Bulgaria
Spain ....(0) 0-0 (0) ......Paraguay
Spain ....(2) 6-1 (0) ...... Bulgaria
Nigeria ....(1) 1-3 (0) .....Paraguay

Group E

	P	W	D	L	F	A	GD	Pts
Holland	3	1	2	0	7	2	5	5
Mexico	3	1	2	0	7	5	2	5
Belgium	3	0	3	0	3	3	0	3
South Korea	3	0	1	2	2	9	-7	1

Holland.........(0) 0-0 (0) ....Belgium
S Korea ....(1) 1-3 (0) .... Mexico
Holland.........(2) 5-0 (0) ....S Korea
Belgium ....(1) 2-2 (0) .... Mexico
Belgium ....(1) 1-1 (0) ....S Korea
Holland.........(2) 2-2 (0) .... Mexico

Group F

	P	W	D	L	F	A	GD	Pts
Germany	3	2	1	0	6	2	4	7
Yugoslavia	3	2	1	0	4	2	2	7
Iran	3	1	0	2	2	4	-2	3
USA	3	0	0	3	1	5	-4	0

Yugoslavia ....(0) 1-0 (0) .... Iran
Germany.......(1) 2-0 (0) .... USA
Germany.......(0) 2-2 (1) ....Yugoslavia
USA ....(0) 1-2 (1) .... Iran
Germany.......(0) 2-0 (0) .... Iran
USA ....(0) 0-1 (1) ....Yugoslavia

Group G

	P	W	D	L	F	A	GD	Pts
Romania	3	2	1	0	4	2	2	7
England	3	2	0	1	5	2	3	6
Colombia	3	1	0	2	1	3	-2	3
Tunisia	3	0	1	2	1	4	-3	1

Romania.......(1) 1-0 (0) ......Colombia
England ....(1) 2-0 (0) ....Tunisia
Colombia......(0) 1-0 (0) ....Tunisia
Romania.......(0) 2-1 (0) ....England
Romania.......(0) 1-1 (1) ....Tunisia
Colombia......(0) 0-2 (2) ....England

Group H

	P	W	D	L	F	A	GD	Pts
Argentina	3	3	0	0	7	0	7	9
Croatia	3	2	0	1	4	2	2	6
Jamaica	3	1	0	2	3	9	-6	3
Japan	3	0	0	3	1	4	-3	0

Zinedine Zidane heads home the opening goal of the 1998 final

The tournament was expanded to 32 teams but Croatia were the only debutants to get through the group stage – they made it all the way to the semi-finals and finished third.

England lost out on penalties to Argentina in the last 16 after a classic that saw Michael Owen score a superb goal, David Beckham get sent off and Sol Campbell have his 'winner' ruled out. Paul Ince and David Batty missed their spot kicks.

The final was between the hosts and Brazil but Ronaldo suffered a seizure before the game and was anonymous throughout. It was Zinedine Zidane who stole the show, heading two first-half corners into the net before Emmanuel Petit scored France's third in injury time.

Jamaica ....(1) 1-3 (1) .... Croatia
Argentina .....(1) 1-0 (0) .... Japan
Japan............(0) 0-1 (0) .... Croatia
Argentina .....(1) 5-0 (0) ....Jamaica
Japan............(0) 1-2 (1) ....Jamaica
Argentina .....(1) 1-0 (0) .... Croatia

Round of 16

Brazil ....(3) 4-1 (0) .... Chile
Italy ....(1) 1-0 (0) .... Norway
Nigeria ....(0) 1-4 (2) ..... Denmark
France...........(0) 1-0 (0) ..... Paraguay
AET 0-0 90 mins
Germany.......(0) 2-1 (0) .... Mexico
Holland.........(1) 2-1 (0) ....Yugoslavia
Argentina .....(2) 2-2 (2) ....England
AET 2-2 90 mins. Argentina 4-3 pens
Romania ....(0) 0-1 (1) .... Croatia

Quarter-finals

France...........(0) 0-0 (0) ....Italy
AET 0-0 90 mins. France 4-3 pens
Brazil ....(2) 3-2 (1) ..... Denmark
Germany.......(0) 0-3 (1) .... Croatia
Holland.........(1) 2-1 (1) ..... Argentina

Semi-finals

Brazil ....(0) 1-1 (0) .... Holland
AET 1-1 90 mins. Brazil 4-2 pens
France...........(0) 2-1 (0) .... Croatia

3rd/4th place play-off

Holland.........(1) 1-2 (2) .... Croatia

Final

France............(2) 3-0 (0) ....Brazil

In Thierry Henry, David Trezeguet and Djibril Cisse, the French set out to defend the World Cup with the top scorers in England, Italy and France, but they failed to score a single goal and didn't get out of the group stage.

That wasn't the only upset. The USA beat Portugal, co-hosts South Korea knocked out Spain and Italy en route to the semi-finals and Argentina were also group-stage casualties. Ireland's Roy Keane went home early too, after launching his infamous rant at Mick McCarthy.

In the end, Brazil won their fifth World Cup, knocking out England along the way, with Ronaldo, who had spent much of the four years since the 1998 final injured, grabbing eight goals.

Group A

	P	W	D	L	F	A	GD	Pts
Denmark	3	2	1	0	5	2	3	7
Senegal	3	1	2	0	5	4	1	5
Uruguay	3	0	2	1	4	5	-1	2
France	3	0	1	2	0	3	-3	1

France...........(0) 0-1 (1)........ Senegal
Uruguay ....(0) 1-2 (1)...... Denmark
France...........(0) 0-0 (0)....... Uruguay
Denmark.......(1) 1-1 (0)........ Senegal
Denmark.......(1) 2-0 (0).......... France
Senegal ....(3) 3-3 (0)....... Uruguay

Group B

	P	W	D	L	F	A	GD	Pts
Spain	3	3	0	0	9	4	5	9
Paraguay	3	1	1	1	6	6	0	4
South Africa	3	1	1	1	5	5	0	4
Slovenia	3	0	0	3	2	7	-5	0

Paraguay ......(1) 2-2 (0).........S Africa
Spain ....(1) 3-1 (0)...... Slovenia
Spain ....(0) 3-1 (1)...... Paraguay
S Africa ....(1) 1-0 (0)...... Slovenia
S Africa ....(1) 2-3 (2)............Spain
Slovenia........(1) 1-3 (0)...... Paraguay

Group C

	P	W	D	L	F	A	GD	Pts
Brazil	3	3	0	0	11	3	8	9
Turkey	3	1	1	1	5	3	2	4
Costa Rica	3	1	1	1	5	6	-1	4
China	3	0	0	3	0	9	-9	0

Brazil ....(0) 2-1 (1).......... Turkey
China PR.......(0) 0-2 (0).... Costa Rica
Brazil ....(3) 4-0 (0)...... China PR
Costa Rica.....(0) 1-1 (0).......... Turkey
Costa Rica.....(1) 2-5 (3)............Brazil
Turkey............(2) 3-0 (0).... China PR

Group D

	P	W	D	L	F	A	GD	Pts
S Korea	3	2	1	0	4	1	3	7
USA	3	1	1	1	5	6	-1	4
Portugal	3	1	0	2	6	4	2	3
Poland	3	1	0	2	3	7	-4	3

S Korea.........(1) 2-0 (0)..........Poland
USA ....(3) 3-2 (1)....... Portugal
S Korea.........(1) 1-1 (1)..............USA
Portugal........(1) 4-0 (0)..........Poland
S Korea.........(0) 1-0 (0)....... Portugal
Poland ....(2) 3-1 (0)..............USA

Group E

	P	W	D	L	F	A	GD	Pts
Germany	3	2	1	0	11	1	10	7
Rep of Ireland	3	1	2	0	5	2	3	5
Cameroon	3	1	1	1	2	3	-1	4
Saudi Arabia	3	0	0	3	0	12	-12	0

Rep of Ireland(0) 1-1 (1).... Cameroon
Germany.......(4) 8-0 (0).Saudi Arabia
Germany.......(1) 1-1 (0)Rep of Ireland
Cameroon.....(0) 1-0 (0).Saudi Arabia
Cameroon.....(0) 0-2 (0)...... Germany
Saudi Arabia .(0) 0-3 (1) Rep of Ireland

Ronaldo scores the first of his two goals in the final

Group F

	P	W	D	L	F	A	GD	Pts
Sweden	3	1	2	0	4	3	1	5
England	3	1	2	0	2	1	1	5
Argentina	3	1	1	1	2	2	0	4
Nigeria	3	0	1	2	1	3	-2	1

England ....(1) 1-1 (0) ....Sweden
Argentina .....(0) 1-0 (0) ....Nigeria
Sweden ....(1) 2-1 (1) ....Nigeria
Argentina .....(0) 0-1 (1) ....England
Sweden ....(0) 1-1 (0) ....Argentina
Nigeria ....(0) 0-0 (0) ....England

Group G

	P	W	D	L	F	A	GD	Pts
Mexico	3	2	1	0	4	2	2	7
Italy	3	1	1	1	4	3	1	4
Croatia	3	1	0	2	2	3	-1	3
Ecuador	3	1	0	2	2	4	-2	3

Croatia..........(0) 0-1 (0) ....Mexico
Italy ....(2) 2-0 (0) ....Ecuador
Italy ....(0) 1-2 (0) ....Croatia
Mexico..........(1) 2-1 (1) ....Ecuador
Mexico..........(1) 1-1 (0) ....Italy
Ecuador ....(0) 1-0 (0) ....Croatia

Group H

	P	W	D	L	F	A	GD	Pts
Japan	3	2	1	0	5	2	3	7
Belgium	3	1	2	0	6	5	1	5
Russia	3	1	0	2	4	4	0	3
Tunisia	3	0	1	2	1	5	-4	1

Japan............(0) 2-2 (0) ....Belgium
Russia...........(0) 2-0 (0) ....Tunisia
Japan............(0) 1-0 (0) .... Russia
Tunisia ....(1) 1-1 (1) ....Belgium
Japan............(0) 2-0 (0) ....Tunisia
Belgium ....(1) 3-2 (0) .... Russia

Round of 16

Germany.......(0) 1-0 (0) .... Paraguay
Denmark.......(0) 0-3 (3) ....England
Sweden ....(1) 1-2 (1) .... Senegal
   AET 1-1 90 mins
Spain ....(1) 1-1 (0) Rep of Ireland
   AET 1-1 90 mins. Spain 3-2 pens
Mexico...........(0) 0-2 (1) ....USA
Brazil ....(0) 2-0 (0) ....Belgium
Japan............(0) 0-1 (1) .... Turkey
S Korea ....(0) 2-1 (1) ....Italy
   AET 1-1 90 mins

Quarter-finals

England ....(1) 1-2 (1) ....Brazil
Germany.......(1) 1-0 (0) ....USA
S Korea ....(0) 0-0 (0) ....Spain
   AET 0-0 90 mins. S Korea 5-3 pens
Senegal ....(0) 0-1 (0) .... Turkey
   AET 0-0 90 mins

Semi-finals

S Korea ....(0) 0-1 (0) ..... Germany
Brazil ....(0) 1-0 (0) .... Turkey

3rd/4th place play-off

S Korea ....(1) 2-3 (3) .... Turkey

Final

Germany.......(0) 0-2 (0) ....Brazil

Italy coach Marcello Lippi loves it when a plan comes together

Germany 2006

One moment above all stands out from Germany 2006 – Zinedine Zidane receiving a red card for headbutting Marco Materazzi with ten minutes of extra time remaining.

Zidane had started the tournament slowly but huge performances against Spain and Brazil in the knockout rounds, plus the winner against Portugal in the semi-final and the opening goal in the final itself – an audacious panenka penalty – saw him voted player of the tournament.

The poll took place at half time, just over an hour before Zizou's moment of infamy, leaving punters who had backed Fabio Cannavaro at odds-on after the red card to count the cost.

The final finished 1-1 and, in a fitting tribute to a fine team performance that had seen Marcello Lippi use 21 members of Italy's 23-man squad during the tournament, all five of Italy's penalty takers scored in the shootout.

Group A

	P	W	D	L	F	A	GD	Pts
Germany	3	3	0	0	8	2	6	9
Ecuador	3	2	0	1	5	3	2	6
Poland	3	1	0	2	2	4	-2	3
Costa Rica	3	0	0	3	3	9	-6	0

Germany.......(2) 4-2 (1).... Costa Rica
Poland ....(0) 0-2 (1)........Ecuador
Germany.......(0) 1-0 (0)..........Poland
Ecuador ....(1) 3-0 (0).... Costa Rica
Germany.......(2) 3-0 (0).........Ecuador
Costa Rica.....(1) 1-2 (1).........Poland

Group B

	P	W	D	L	F	A	GD	Pts
England	3	2	1	0	5	2	3	7
Sweden	3	1	2	0	3	2	1	5
Paraguay	3	1	0	2	2	2	0	3
Trinidad & T	3	0	1	2	0	4	-4	1

England........(1) 1-0 (0)...... Paraguay
Trinidad & T ..(0) 0-0 (0)..........Sweden
England........(0) 2-0 (0).. Trinidad & T
Sweden ....(0) 1-0 (0)...... Paraguay
Sweden ....(0) 2-2 (1)........England
Paraguay ......(1) 2-0 (0).. Trinidad & T

Group C

	P	W	D	L	F	A	GD	Pts
Argentina	3	2	1	0	8	1	7	7
Holland	3	2	1	0	3	1	2	7
Ivory Coast	3	1	0	2	5	6	-1	3
Serbia & M	3	0	0	3	2	10	-8	0

Argentina & M....(2) 2-1 (0)...Ivory Coast
Serbia & M....(0) 0-1 (1)........ Holland
Argentina .....(3) 6-0 (0)... Serbia & M
Holland.........(2) 2-1 (1)...Ivory Coast
Holland.........(0) 0-0 (0).....Argentina
Ivory Coast ...(1) 3-2 (2)... Serbia & M

Group D

	P	W	D	L	F	A	GD	Pts
Portugal	3	3	0	0	5	1	4	9
Mexico	3	1	1	1	4	3	1	4
Angola	3	0	2	1	1	2	-1	2
Iran	3	0	1	2	2	6	-4	1

Mexico..........(1) 3-1 (1).............. Iran
Angola..........(0) 0-1 (1)....... Portugal
Mexico..........(0) 0-0 (0)......... Angola
Portugal........(0) 2-0 (0)............. Iran
Portugal........(2) 2-1 (0)..........Mexico
Iran...............(0) 1-1 (0)......... Angola

Group E

	P	W	D	L	F	A	GD	Pts
Italy	3	2	1	0	5	1	4	7
Ghana	3	2	0	1	4	3	1	6
Czech Rep	3	1	0	2	3	4	-1	3
USA	3	0	1	2	2	6	-4	1

Italy ....(1) 2-0 (0)........... Ghana
USA ....(0) 0-3 (2).... Czech Rep
Italy ....(1) 1-1 (0)...............USA
Czech Rep.....(0) 0-2 (1).......... Ghana
Czech Rep.....(0) 0-2 (1)............Italy
Ghana...........(2) 2-1 (1)..............USA

Group F

	P	W	D	L	F	A	GD	Pts
Brazil	3	3	0	0	7	1	6	9
Australia	3	1	1	1	5	5	0	4
Croatia	3	0	2	1	2	3	-1	2
Japan	3	0	1	2	2	7	-5	1

Brazil ....(1) 1-0 (0) .... Croatia
Australia ....(0) 3-1 (1) .... Japan
Brazil ....(0) 2-0 (0) ......Australia
Japan............(0) 0-0 (0) .... Croatia
Japan............(1) 1-4 (1) ....Brazil
Croatia..........(1) 2-2 (1) ......Australia

Group G

	P	W	D	L	F	A	GD	Pts
Switzerland	3	2	1	0	4	0	4	7
France	3	1	2	0	3	1	2	5
S Korea	3	1	1	1	3	4	-1	4
Togo	3	0	0	3	1	6	-5	0

France...........(0) 0-0 (0) .. Switzerland
S Korea ....(0) 2-1 (1) ....Togo
France...........(1) 1-1 (0) ....S Korea
Togo ....(0) 0-2 (1) .. Switzerland
Togo ....(0) 0-2 (0) .... France
Switzerland...(1) 2-0 (0) ....S Korea

Group H

	P	W	D	L	F	A	GD	Pts
Spain	3	3	0	0	8	1	7	9
Ukraine	3	2	0	1	5	4	1	6
Tunisia	3	0	1	2	3	6	-3	1
Saudi Arabia	3	0	1	2	2	7	-5	1

Spain ....(2) 4-0 (0) .... Ukraine
Tunisia ....(1) 2-2 (0) .Saudi Arabia
Spain ....(0) 3-1 (1) ....Tunisia
Saudi Arabia .(0) 0-4 (2) .... Ukraine
Saudi Arabia .(0) 0-1 (1) ....Spain
Ukraine ....(0) 1-0 (0) ....Tunisia

Round of 16

Germany.......(2) 2-0 (0) .... Sweden
Argentina .....(1) 2-1 (1) .... Mexico
AET 1-1 90 mins
England ....(0) 1-0 (0) ....Ecuador
Portugal........(1) 1-0 (0) .... Holland
Italy ....(1) 1-0 (0) ......Australia
Switzerland...(0) 0-0 (0) .... Ukraine
AET 0-0 90 mins. Ukraine 3-0 pens
Brazil ....(2) 3-0 (0) .... Ghana
Spain ....(1) 1-3 (1) .... France

Quarter-finals

Germany.......(0) 1-1 (0) ..... Argentina
AET 1-1 90 mins. Germany 4-2 pens
Italy ....(1) 3-0 (0) .... Ukraine
England ....(0) 0-0 (0) .... Portugal
AET 0-0 90 mins. Portugal 3-1 pens
Brazil ....(0) 0-1 (0) .... France

Semi-finals

Germany.......(0) 0-2 (0) ....Italy
AET 0-0 90 mins
Portugal........(0) 0-1 (0) .... France

3rd/4th place play-off

Germany.......(0) 3-1 (0) .... Portugal

Final

Italy ....(1) 1-1 (1) .... France
AET 1-1 90 mins. Italy 5-3 pens

All five South American teams qualified from the group stage, which perhaps bodes well for a strong performance from the host continent in Brazil, but Europe dominated the latter stages of the competition, with Spain and Holland contesting the final and Germany beating Uruguay to third place.

Uruguay only got there thanks to a blatant handball late in their quarter-final against Ghana and if Asamoah Gyan had converted the spot kick, the Black Stars would have been Africa's first ever World Cup semi-finalists.

The final was also full of foul play, as the Dutch attempted to unsettle a brilliant Spanish side by any means necessary and the European champions responded in kind. In the end, Howard Webb got his yellow card out 14 times and sent off Johnny Heitinga in the second half of extra time.

Andres Iniesta got the only goal of the game with four minutes to go before penalties would have been required.

Nigel de Jong was one of eight Dutch players booked in the final

Group A

	P	W	D	L	F	A	GD	Pts
Uruguay	3	2	1	0	4	0	4	7
Mexico	3	1	1	1	3	2	1	4
South Africa	3	1	1	1	3	5	-2	4
France	3	0	1	2	1	4	-3	1

S Africa ....(0) 1-1 (0) .... Mexico
Uruguay ....(0) 0-0 (0) .... France
S Africa ....(0) 0-3 (1) .... Uruguay
France...........(0) 0-2 (0) .... Mexico
Mexico..........(0) 0-1 (0) .... Uruguay
S Africa ....(2) 2-1 (0) .... France

Group B

	P	W	D	L	F	A	GD	Pts
Argentina	3	3	0	0	7	1	6	9
S Korea	3	1	1	1	5	6	-1	4
Greece	3	1	0	2	2	5	-3	3
Nigeria	3	0	1	2	3	5	-2	1

Argentina .....(1) 1-0 (0) .... Nigeria
S Korea ....(1) 2-0 (0) .... Greece
Greece ....(1) 2-1 (1) .... Nigeria
Argentina .....(2) 4-1 (1) ....S Korea
Nigeria ....(1) 2-2 (1) ....S Korea
Greece ....(0) 0-2 (0) ..... Argentina

Group C

	P	W	D	L	F	A	GD	Pts
USA	3	1	2	0	4	3	1	5
England	3	1	2	0	2	1	1	5
Slovenia	3	1	1	1	3	3	0	4
Algeria	3	0	1	2	0	2	-2	1

England ....(1) 1-1 (1) ....USA
Algeria..........(0) 0-1 (0) .... Slovenia
Slovenia........(2) 2-2 (0) ....USA
England ....(0) 0-0 (0) .... Algeria
Slovenia........(0) 0-1 (1) ....England
USA ....(0) 1-0 (0) .... Algeria

Group D

	P	W	D	L	F	A	GD	Pts
Germany	3	2	0	1	5	1	4	6
Ghana	3	1	1	1	2	2	0	4
Australia	3	1	1	1	3	6	-3	4
Serbia	3	1	0	2	2	3	-1	3

Germany.......(2) 4-0 (0) ......Australia
Serbia ....(0) 0-0 (0) .... Ghana
Germany.......(0) 0-1 (0) .... Serbia
Ghana...........(1) 1-1 (0) ......Australia
Ghana...........(0) 0-1 (0) ...... Germany
Australia ....(0) 2-1 (0) ....Serbia

Spain's Andres Iniesta
poses for the cameras

Group E

	P	W	D	L	F	A	GD	Pts
Holland	3	3	0	0	5	1		9
Japan	3	2	0	1	4	2		6
Denmark	3	1	0	2	3	6		3
Cameroon	3	0	0	3	2	5		0

Holland.........(0) 2-0 (0) ..... Denmark
Japan.............(1) 1-0 (0) .... Cameroon
Holland.........(0) 1-0 (0) .... Japan
Cameroon.....(1) 1-2 (1) ...... Denmark
Denmark.......(0) 1-3 (2) .... Japan
Cameroon.....(0) 1-2 (1) .... Holland

Group F

	P	W	D	L	F	A	GD	Pts
Paraguay	3	1	2	0	3	1	2	5
Slovakia	3	1	1	1	4	5	-1	4
New Zealand	3	0	3	0	2	2	0	3
Italy	3	0	2	1	4	5	-1	2

Italy ....(0) 1-1 (1) ..... Paraguay
New Zealand (0) 1-1 (0) .... Slovakia
Slovakia........(0) 0-2 (1) ..... Paraguay
Italy ....(1) 1-1 (1) New Zealand
Slovakia ....(1) 3-2 (1) .... Italy
Paraguay ......(0) 0-0 (0) New Zealand

Group G

	P	W	D	L	F	A	GD	Pts
Brazil	3	2	1	0	5	2	3	7
Portugal	3	1	2	0	7	0	7	5
Ivory Coast	3	1	1	1	4	3	1	4
N Korea	3	0	0	3	1	12	-11	0

Ivory Coast ...(0) 0-0 (0) ...... Portugal
Brazil ....(0) 2-1 (0) .... N Korea
Brazil ....(1) 3-1 (0) ...Ivory Coast
Portugal........(1) 7-0 (0) .... N Korea
Portugal........(0) 0-0 (0) .... Brazil
N Korea ....(0) 0-3 (2) ...Ivory Coast

Group H

	P	W	D	L	F	A	GD	Pts
Spain	3	2	0	1	4	2	2	6
Chile	3	2	0	1	3	2	1	6
Switzerland	3	1	1	1	1	1	0	4
Honduras	3	0	1	2	0	3	-3	1

Honduras.......(0) 0-1 (1) .... Chile
Spain ....(0) 0-1 (0) .. Switzerland
Chile ....(0) 1-0 (0) .. Switzerland
Spain ....(1) 2-0 (0) ..... Honduras
Chile ....(0) 1-2 (2) .... Spain
Switzerland...(0) 0-0 (0) ..... Honduras

Round of 16

Uruguay ....(1) 2-1 (0) ....S Korea
USA ....(0) 1-2 (1) .... Ghana
AET 1-1 90 mins
Germany.......(2) 4-1 (1).......England
Argentina .....(2) 3-1 (0) ...... Mexico
Holland.........(1) 2-1 (0) ...... Slovakia
Brazil ....(2) 3-0 (0) .... Chile
Paraguay ......(0) 0-0 (0) .... Japan
AET 0-0 90 mins. Paraguay 5-3 pens
Spain ....(0) 1-0 (0) .... Portugal

Quarter-finals

Holland.........(0) 2-1 (1) ....Brazil
Uruguay ....(0) 1-1 (1) .... Ghana
AET 1-1 90 mins. Uruguay 4-2 pens
Argentina .....(0) 0-4 (1) ...... Germany
Paraguay ......(0) 0-1 (0) ....Spain

Semi-finals

Uruguay ....(1) 2-3 (1) .... Holland
Germany.......(0) 0-1 (0) ....Spain

3rd/4th place play-off

Uruguay ....(1) 2-3 (1) ...... Germany

Final

Holland.........(0) 0-1 (0) ....Spain
AET 0-0 90 mins

QUALIFICATION

European qualifying

Four of the top seeds failed to win their groups, with two of the underdogs from pot three standing out as the star performers.

Belgium had been fancied to run **Croatia** close but outperformed all expectations to finish nine points clear, dropping just two points in a tricky group that also contained Serbia, Wales, Scotland and Macedonia.

Bosnia-Herzegovina also impressed, taking four points off Group G rivals **Greece** to reach their first ever World Cup finals on goal difference after scoring 30 goals in ten games – 18 more than the runners-up.

The success of another team from pot three, nine-time finalists **Switzerland,** was less of a surprise given that Norway were top seeds in their group and Slovenia, Iceland, Albania and Cyprus made up the numbers. Ottmar Hitzfeld's side put in a couple of unconvincing performances against Cyprus and also survived home draws with Iceland and Norway, but still finished seven points clear of the chasing pack.

Seeded **Portugal** also failed to top their group and were left to rue the dismal home draws against Northern Ireland and Israel that allowed Russia to sneak into top spot.

Five seeded teams did oblige. **Germany** and **Italy** dominated from the first whistle, and **Holland** bounced back from a poor Euro 2012 to romp home in Group D. But the route to Brazil was rather more fraught for **Spain** and **England**, with the reigning World Cup holders given an extremely tough draw in Group I alongside **France**. The Spanish started in unconvincing style, drawing at home with Finland and France and only just scraping a last-gasp win over Georgia in their first four outings, but Vicente del Bosque's men showed their class at the Stade de France to grind out a crucial 1-0 win.

England swatted the minnows aside in Group H but suffered frustrating draws in each of their first four meetings with serious opponents, leaving them needing Wembley wins over both Montenegro and Poland in their final two group games. In the end

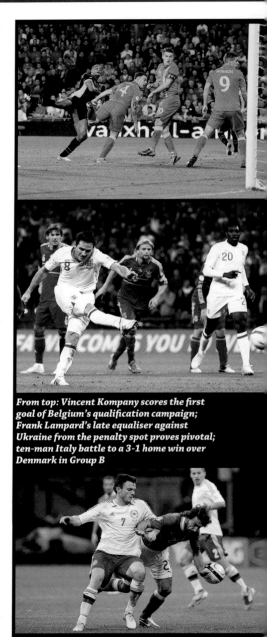

From top: Vincent Kompany scores the first goal of Belgium's qualification campaign; Frank Lampard's late equaliser against Ukraine from the penalty spot proves pivotal; ten-man Italy battle to a 3-1 home win over Denmark in Group B

Hodgson's men did just that, but it wasn't quite as comfortable as the 4-1 and 2-0 scorelines might suggest.

The play-offs saw Croatia ease past Iceland and Greece beat Romania, but France's meeting with Ukraine was a thriller. Didier Deschamps' side were beaten 2-0 in Kiev in the first leg but rallied to win 3-0 at Stade de France, booking their place in Brazil amid scenes of jubilation.

Portugal versus Sweden was billed as Cristiano Ronaldo versus Zlatan Ibrahimovic, and so it proved with the two men scoring all six goals over two legs. It was the Real Madrid man who won the battle, scoring a hat-trick in Solna to complete a 4-2 aggregate victory.

The ever humble Zlatan took it well, however, declaring after the match that "one thing is for sure, a World Cup without me is nothing to watch."

Top scorers

	P	Gls
Robin van Persie (Holland)	9	11
Edin Dzeko (Bosnia-Hz)	10	10
Mesut Ozil (Germany)	10	8
Vedad Ibisevic (Bosnia-Hz)	10	8
Cristiano Ronaldo (Portugal)	10	8
Zlatan Ibrahimovic (Sweden)	11	8
Wayne Rooney (England)	6	7
Tomer Hemed (Israel)	4	6
Eden Ben Basat (Israel)	7	6
Robbie Keane (Rep of Ireland)	7	6
David Alaba (Austria)	8	6
Helder Postiga (Portugal)	10	6

Format 53 participating teams, 13 qualify **Round 1** 53 teams, 8 groups of 6, 1 group of 5, round-robin home-and-away format. 9 group winners qualify, 8 best group runners-up advance **Round 2** 8 teams, 4 two-legged knockout ties, winners qualify for World Cup

Group A

	P	W	D	L	F	A	GD	Pts
Belgium	10	8	2	0	18	4	14	26
Croatia	10	5	2	3	12	9	3	17
Serbia	10	4	2	4	18	11	7	14
Scotland	10	3	2	5	8	12	-4	11
Wales	10	3	1	6	9	20	-11	10
Macedonia	10	2	1	7	7	16	-9	7

Friday September 7 2012
Croatia..........(0) 1-0 (0) ... Macedonia
Wales ....(0) 0-2 (1).......Belgium
Saturday September 8 2012
Scotland ....(0) 0-0 (0)...........Serbia
Tuesday September 11 2012
Belgium ....(1) 1-1 (1).........Croatia
Scotland ....(1) 1-1 (1)...Macedonia
Serbia...........(3) 6-1 (1).........Wales
Friday October 12 2012
Macedonia....(1) 1-2 (1).........Croatia
Serbia ....(0) 0-3 (1).......Belgium
Wales ....(0) 2-1 (1).......Scotland
Tuesday October 16 2012
Belgium ....(0) 2-0 (0).......Scotland

Croatia..........(1) 2-0 (0)..........Wales
Macedonia....(0) 1-0 (0)..........Serbia
Friday March 22 2013
Croatia..........(2) 2-0 (0)..........Serbia
Macedonia....(0) 0-2 (1).......Belgium
Scotland ....(1) 1-2 (0)..........Wales
Tuesday March 26 2013
Belgium ....(0) 1-0 (0)... Macedonia
Serbia ....(0) 2-0 (0)...... Scotland
Wales ....(1) 1-2 (0).........Croatia
Friday June 7 2013
Belgium ....(1) 2-1 (0)..........Serbia
Croatia..........(0) 0-1 (1)....... Scotland
Friday September 6 2013
Macedonia....(1) 2-1 (1)..........Wales
Scotland ....(0) 0-2 (1).......Belgium
Serbia ....(0) 1-1 (0).........Croatia
Wednesday October 9 2013
Macedonia....(0) 1-2 (0)...... Scotland
Wales ....(0) 0-3 (2)..........Serbia
Friday October 11 2013
Croatia..........(0) 1-2 (2).......Belgium
Wales ....(0) 1-0 (0)... Macedonia
Tuesday October 15 2013
Belgium ....(0) 1-1 (0)..........Wales
Scotland ....(1) 2-0 (0).........Croatia
Serbia...........(3) 5-1 (0)... Macedonia

Group B

	P	W	D	L	F	A	GD	Pts
Italy	10	6	4	0	19	9	10	22
Denmark	10	4	4	2	17	12	5	16
Czech Rep	10	4	3	3	13	9	4	15
Bulgaria	10	3	4	3	14	9	5	13
Armenia	10	4	1	5	12	13	-1	13
Malta	10	1	0	9	5	28	-23	3

Friday September 7 2012
Bulgaria........(1) 2-2 (2)..........Italy
Malta............(0) 0-1 (1).......Armenia
Saturday September 8 2012
Denmark.......(0) 0-0 (0).... Czech Rep
Tuesday September 11 2012
Bulgaria........(1) 1-0 (0).......Armenia
Italy ....(1) 2-0 (0)..........Malta

Friday October 12 2012
Armenia........(1) 1-3 (1)..............Italy
Bulgaria........(1) 1-1 (1)...... Denmark
Czech Rep.....(1) 3-1 (1)........... Malta
Tuesday October 16 2012
Czech Rep.....(0) 0-0 (0)....... Bulgaria
Italy ....(2) 3-1 (1)...... Denmark
Friday March 22 2013
Bulgaria........(2) 6-0 (0)........... Malta
Czech Rep.....(0) 0-3 (0)...... Denmark
Tuesday March 26 2013
Armenia........(0) 0-3 (0).... Czech Rep
Denmark.......(0) 1-1 (0)....... Bulgaria
Malta.............(0) 0-2 (2)..............Italy
Friday June 7 2013
Armenia........(0) 0-1 (1)........... Malta
Czech Rep.....(0) 0-0 (0)..............Italy
Tuesday June 11 2013
Denmark.......(0) 0-4 (0) .... Armenia
Friday September 6 2013
Czech Rep.....(0) 1-2 (1)....... Armenia
Italy ....(1) 1-0 (0)....... Bulgaria
Malta.............(1) 1-2 (0)...... Denmark
Wednesday October 9 2013
Armenia........(0) 0-1 (0)....... Denmark
Italy ....(0) 2-1 (1).... Czech Rep
Malta.............(0) 1-2 (1).... Bulgaria
Friday October 11 2013
Armenia........(1) 2-1 (0)....... Bulgaria
Denmark.......(1) 2-2 (1)..............Italy
Malta.............(0) 1-4 (2).... Czech Rep
Tuesday October 15 2013
Bulgaria........(0) 0-1 (0).... Czech Rep
Denmark.......(4) 6-0 (0)........... Malta
Italy ....(1) 2-2 (1)....... Armenia

Group C

	P	W	D	L	F	A	GD	Pts
Germany	10	9	1	0	36	10	26	28
Sweden	10	6	2	2	19	14	5	20
Austria	10	5	2	3	20	10	10	17
Rep of Ireland	10	4	2	4	16	17	-1	14
Kazakhstan	10	1	2	7	6	21	-15	5
Faroe Islands	10	0	1	9	4	29	-25	1

Friday September 7 2012
Germany.......(1) 3-0 (0) Faroe Islands

Kazakhstan ...(1) 1-2 (0) Rep of Ireland

Tuesday September 11 2012
Austria..........(0) 1-2 (1)...... Germany
Sweden ....(1) 2-0 (0)...Kazakhstan

Friday October 12 2012
Faroe Islands (0) 1-2 (0)......... Sweden
Kazakhstan ...(0) 0-0 (0)......... Austria
Rep of Ireland (0) 1-6 (2)...... Germany

Tuesday October 16 2012
Austria..........(1) 4-0 (0)...Kazakhstan
Faroe Islands (0) 1-4 (0) Rep of Ireland
Germany.......(3) 4-4 (0)........ Sweden

Friday March 22 2013
Austria..........(3) 6-0 (0) Faroe Islands
Kazakhstan ...(0) 0-3 (2)...... Germany
Sweden ....(0) 0-0 (0) Rep of Ireland

Tuesday March 26 2013
Germany.......(3) 4-1 (0)...Kazakhstan
Rep of Ireland (2) 2-2 (1)......... Austria

Friday June 7 2013
Austria..........(2) 2-1 (0)........ Sweden
Rep of Ireland (1) 3-0 (0) Faroe Islands

Tuesday June 11 2013
Sweden ....(1) 2-0 (0) Faroe Islands

Friday September 6 2013
Germany.......(1) 3-0 (0)......... Austria
Kazakhstan ...(0) 2-1 (1) Faroe Islands
Rep of Ireland (1) 1-2 (1)....... Sweden

Wednesday October 9 2013
Austria..........(0) 1-0 (0) Rep of Ireland
Faroe Islands (0) 0-3 (1)...... Germany
Kazakhstan ...(0) 0-1 (1)...... Sweden

Friday October 11 2013
Faroe Islands (1) 1-1 (0)...Kazakhstan
Germany.......(1) 3-0 (0) Rep of Ireland
Sweden ....(0) 2-1 (1)....... Austria

Tuesday October 15 2013
Faroe Islands (0) 0-3 (1)......... Austria
Rep of Ireland (2) 3-1 (1)...Kazakhstan
Sweden ....(2) 3-5 (1)...... Germany

Group D

	P	W	D	L	F	A	GD	Pts
Holland	10	9	1	0	34	5	29	28
Romania	10	6	1	3	19	12	7	19
Hungary	10	5	2	3	21	20	1	17
Turkey	10	5	1	4	16	9	7	16
Estonia	10	2	1	7	6	20	-14	7
Andorra	10	0	0	10	0	30	-30	0

Friday September 7 2012
Andorra ....(0) 0-5 (2)....... Hungary
Estonia ....(0) 0-2 (0).......Romania
Holland........(1) 2-0 (0)........ Turkey

Tuesday September 11 2012
Hungary ....(1) 1-4 (2)........ Holland
Romania ....(2) 4-0 (0)........Andorra
Turkey...........(1) 3-0 (0)........Estonia

Friday October 12 2012
Estonia ....(0) 0-1 (0)....... Hungary
Holland........(2) 3-0 (0)........Andorra
Turkey...........(0) 0-1 (1)......Romania

Tuesday October 16 2012
Andorra ....(0) 0-1 (0)........Estonia

Hungary ....(1) 3-1 (1).......... Turkey
Romania ....(1) 1-4 (3)........ Holland

Friday March 22 2013
Andorra ....(0) 0-2 (2).......... Turkey
Holland........(0) 3-0 (0)........Estonia
Hungary ....(1) 2-2 (0)......Romania

Tuesday March 26 2013
Estonia ....(1) 2-0 (0)........Andorra
Holland........(1) 4-0 (0)......Romania
Turkey...........(0) 1-1 (0)....... Hungary

Friday September 6 2013
Estonia ....(1) 2-2 (1)....... Holland
Romania ....(2) 3-0 (0)...... Hungary
Turkey...........(2) 5-0 (0)......Andorra

Wednesday October 9 2013
Andorra ....(0) 0-2 (0)....... Holland
Hungary ....(3) 5-1 (0).........Estonia
Romania ....(0) 0-2 (1)........ Turkey

Friday October 11 2013
Andorra ....(0) 0-4 (1)......Romania
Estonia ....(0) 0-2 (1)........ Turkey
Holland........(4) 8-1 (0)....... Hungary

Tuesday October 15 2013
Hungary ....(0) 2-0 (0)........Andorra
Romania ....(1) 2-0 (0)........Estonia
Turkey...........(0) 0-2 (1)........ Holland

Group E

	P	W	D	L	F	A	GD	Pts
Switzerland	10	7	3	0	17	6	11	24
Iceland	10	5	2	3	17	15	2	17
Slovenia	10	5	0	5	14	11	3	15
Norway	10	3	3	4	10	13	-3	12
Albania	10	3	2	5	9	11	-2	11
Cyprus	10	1	2	7	4	15	-11	5

Friday September 7 2012
Albania.........(1) 3-1 (1).........Cyprus
Iceland ....(1) 2-0 (0)........ Norway
Slovenia........(0) 0-2 (1).. Switzerland

Tuesday September 11 2012
Cyprus ....(0) 1-0 (0)........ Iceland
Norway ....(1) 2-1 (1)....... Slovenia
Switzerland...(1) 2-0 (0)........ Albania

Friday October 12 2012
Albania.........(1) 1-2 (1)......... Iceland
Slovenia........(1) 2-1 (0).........Cyprus
Switzerland...(0) 1-1 (0)....... Norway

Tuesday October 16 2012
Albania.........(1) 1-0 (0)....... Slovenia
Cyprus ....(1) 1-3 (1)....... Norway
Iceland ....(0) 0-2 (0).. Switzerland

Friday March 22 2013
Norway ....(0) 0-1 (0)........ Albania
Slovenia........(1) 1-2 (0)......... Iceland

Saturday March 23 2013
Cyprus ....(0) 0-0 (0).. Switzerland

Friday June 7 2013
Albania.........(1) 1-1 (0)........ Norway
Iceland ....(2) 2-4 (1)....... Slovenia

Saturday June 8 2013
Switzerland...(0) 1-0 (0).........Cyprus

Friday September 6 2013
Norway ....(1) 2-0 (0)..........Cyprus

Slovenia........(1) 1-0 (0)........ Albania
Switzerland...(3) 4-4 (1)......... Iceland

Wednesday October 9 2013
Cyprus ....(0) 0-2 (1)........ Slovenia
Iceland ....(1) 2-1 (1)........ Albania
Norway ....(0) 0-2 (1)... Switzerland

Friday October 11 2013
Albania.........(0) 1-2 (0)... Switzerland
Iceland ....(0) 2-0 (0).........Cyprus
Slovenia........(2) 3-0 (0)........ Norway

Tuesday October 15 2013
Cyprus ....(0) 0-0 (0)........ Albania
Norway ....(1) 1-1 (1)......... Iceland
Switzerland...(1) 1-0 (0)...... Slovenia

Group F

	P	W	D	L	F	A	GD	Pts
Russia	10	7	1	2	20	5	15	22
Portugal	10	6	3	1	20	9	11	21
Israel	10	3	5	2	19	14	5	14
Azerbaijan	10	1	6	3	7	11	-4	9
N Ireland	10	1	4	5	9	17	-8	7
Luxembourg	10	1	3	6	7	26	-19	6

Friday September 7 2012
Azerbaijan ....(0) 1-1 (0)............Israel
Luxembourg .(1) 1-2 (1)....... Portugal
Russia...........(1) 2-0 (0)...... N Ireland

Tuesday September 11 2012
Israel ....(0) 0-4 (2).......... Russia
N Ireland ......(1) 1-1 (0).. Luxembourg
Portugal........(0) 3-0 (0)....Azerbaijan

Friday October 12 2012
Luxembourg .(0) 0-6 (3)............Israel
Russia...........(0) 0-1 (0)....... Portugal

Tuesday October 16 2012
Israel ....(2) 3-0 (0). Luxembourg
Portugal........(0) 1-1 (0)...... N Ireland
Russia...........(0) 0-1 (0)....Azerbaijan

Wednesday November 14 2012
N Ireland ......(0) 1-1 (1)....Azerbaijan

Friday March 22 2013
Israel ....(2) 3-3 (1)...... Portugal
Luxembourg .(0) 0-0 (0)....Azerbaijan

Tuesday March 26 2013
Azerbaijan ....(0) 0-2 (0)...... Portugal
N Ireland ......(0) 0-2 (0)............Israel

Friday June 7 2013
Azerbaijan ....(0) 1-1 (0). Luxembourg
Portugal........(1) 1-0 (0).......... Russia

Wednesday August 14 2013
N Ireland ......(1) 1-0 (0).......... Russia

Friday September 6 2013
Israel ....(0) 1-1 (0)....Azerbaijan
N Ireland ......(1) 2-4 (1)...... Portugal
Russia...........(2) 4-1 (0). Luxembourg

Wednesday October 9 2013
Luxembourg .(1) 3-2 (1)... N Ireland
Russia...........(0) 3-1 (0)............Israel

Friday October 11 2013
Azerbaijan ....(0) 2-0 (0)... N Ireland
Luxembourg .(0) 0-4 (3)........... Russia
Portugal........(1) 1-1 (0)............Israel

Tuesday October 15 2013
Azerbaijan ....(0) 1-1 (1).......... Russia
Israel ....(1) 1-1 (0)...... N Ireland
Portugal........(2) 3-0 (0). Luxembourg

Group G

	P	W	D	L	F	A	GD	Pts
Bosnia-Hz	10	8	1	1	30	6	24	25
Greece	10	8	1	1	12	4	8	25
Slovakia	10	3	4	3	11	10	1	13
Lithuania	10	3	2	5	9	11	-2	11
Latvia	10	2	2	6	10	20	-10	8
Liechtenstein	10	0	2	8	4	25	-21	2

Friday September 7 2012
Latvia ....(1) 1-2 (0).........Greece
Liechtenstein (0) 1-8 (4).....Bosnia-Hz
Lithuania ......(1) 1-1 (1)....... Slovakia

Tuesday September 11 2012
Bosnia-Hz .....(2) 4-1 (1)............Latvia
Greece ....(0) 2-0 (0)...... Lithuania
Slovakia........(1) 2-0 (0) Liechtenstein

Friday October 12 2012
Greece ....(0) 0-0 (0).... Bosnia-Hz
Liechtenstein (0) 0-2 (0)...... Lithuania
Slovakia........(2) 2-1 (0)...........Latvia

Tuesday October 16 2012
Bosnia-Hz .....(3) 3-0 (0)...... Lithuania
Latvia ....(1) 2-0 (0) Liechtenstein
Slovakia........(0) 0-1 (0)..........Greece

Friday March 22 2013
Bosnia-Hz .....(2) 3-1 (0)..........Greece
Liechtenstein (1) 1-1 (1)...........Latvia
Slovakia........(1) 1-1 (1)......Lithuania

Friday June 7 2013
Latvia ....(0) 0-5 (0)..... Bosnia-Hz
Liechtenstein (1) 1-1 (0)....... Slovakia
Lithuania ......(0) 0-1 (1)..........Greece

Friday September 6 2013
Bosnia-Hz .....(0) 0-1 (0)....... Slovakia
Latvia ....(2) 2-1 (1)...... Lithuania
Liechtenstein (0) 0-1 (0)..........Greece

Wednesday October 9 2013
Greece ....(0) 1-0 (0)...........Latvia
Lithuania ......(2) 2-0 (0) Liechtenstein
Slovakia........(1) 1-2 (0)..... Bosnia-Hz

Friday October 11 2013
Bosnia-Hz .....(4) 4-1 (0) Liechtenstein
Greece ....(1) 1-0 (0)....... Slovakia
Lithuania ......(1) 2-0 (0)...........Latvia

Tuesday October 15 2013
Greece ....(1) 2-0 (0) Liechtenstein
Latvia ....(0) 2-2 (2)....... Slovakia
Lithuania ......(0) 0-1 (0).....Bosnia-Hz

Group H

	P	W	D	L	F	A	GD	Pts
England	10	6	4	0	31	4	27	22
Ukraine	10	6	3	1	28	4	24	21
Montenegro	10	4	3	3	18	17	1	15
Poland	10	3	4	3	18	12	6	13
Moldova	10	3	2	5	12	17	-5	11
San Marino	10	0	0	10	1	54	-53	0

Friday September 7 2012
Moldova ....(0) 0-5 (3)........England
Montenegro..(2) 2-2 (1)..........Poland

Tuesday September 11 2012
England ....(0) 1-1 (1)........ Ukraine
Poland ....(1) 2-0 (0)......Moldova
San Marino...(0) 0-6 (2). Montenegro

Friday October 12 2012
England ....(2) 5-0 (0)...San Marino
Moldova ....(0) 0-0 (0)........ Ukraine

Tuesday October 16 2012
San Marino...(0) 0-2 (0).......Moldova
Ukraine.........(0) 0-1 (1). Montenegro

Wednesday October 17 2012
Poland ....(0) 1-1 (1)........England

Wednesday November 14 2012
Montenegro..(2) 3-0 (0)...San Marino

Friday March 22 2013
Moldova ....(0) 0-1 (0). Montenegro
Poland ....(1) 1-3 (3)........ Ukraine
San Marino...(0) 0-8 (5)........England

Tuesday March 26 2013
Montenegro..(0) 1-1 (1)........England
Poland ....(2) 5-0 (0)...San Marino
Ukraine.........(0) 2-1 (0)......Moldova

Friday June 7 2013
Moldova ....(1) 1-1 (0)..........Poland
Montenegro..(0) 0-4 (0)........ Ukraine

Friday September 6 2013
England ....(3) 4-0 (0)......Moldova
Poland ....(1) 1-1 (1). Montenegro
Ukraine.........(4) 9-0 (0)...San Marino

Wednesday October 9 2013
Ukraine.........(0) 0-0 (0)........England
San Marino...(1) 1-5 (3)..........Poland

Friday October 11 2013
England ....(0) 4-1 (0). Montenegro
Moldova ....(0) 3-0 (0)...San Marino
Ukraine.........(0) 1-0 (0)..........Poland

Tuesday October 15 2013
England ....(1) 2-0 (0)..........Poland
Montenegro..(0) 2-5 (1).......Moldova
San Marino...(0) 0-8 (3)........ Ukraine

Group I

	P	W	D	L	F	A	GD	Pts
Spain	8	6	2	0	14	3	11	20
France	8	5	2	1	15	6	9	17
Finland	8	2	3	3	5	9	-4	9
Georgia	8	1	2	5	3	10	-7	5
Belarus	8	1	1	6	7	16	-9	4

Friday September 7 2012
Finland ....(0) 0-1 (1).......... France
Georgia ....(0) 1-0 (0)........Belarus

Tuesday September 11 2012
France............(0) 3-1 (0).........Belarus
Georgia ....(0) 0-1 (0)...........Spain

Friday October 12 2012
Belarus ....(0) 0-4 (2)...........Spain
Finland ....(0) 1-1 (0)....... Georgia

Tuesday October 16 2012
Belarus ....(2) 2-0 (0)...... Georgia
Spain ....(1) 1-1 (0)......... France

Friday March 22 2013
France............(1) 3-1 (0)...... Georgia
Spain ....(0) 1-1 (0).........Finland

Tuesday March 26 2013
France............(0) 0-1 (0)...........Spain

Friday June 7 2013
Finland ....(0) 1-0 (0).........Belarus

Tuesday June 11 2013
Belarus ....(0) 1-1 (0).........Finland

Friday September 6 2013
Finland ....(0) 0-2 (0)...........Spain
Georgia ....(0) 0-0 (0)......... France

Wednesday October 9 2013
Belarus ....(1) 2-4 (0)......... France
Georgia ....(0) 0-1 (0).........Finland

Friday October 11 2013
Spain ....(0) 2-1 (0).........Belarus

Tuesday October 15 2013
Spain ....(1) 2-0 (0)...... Georgia
France............(1) 3-0 (0).........Finland

Play-offs
Friday November 15 2013
Ukraine.........(0) 2-0 (0)......... France
Greece ....(2) 3-1 (1).......Romania
Portugal........(1) 1-0 (0).........Sweden
Iceland ....(0) 0-0 (0)........ Croatia

Tuesday November 19 2013
Romania ....(0) 1-1 (1)..........Greece
Agg: 2-4
France............(2) 3-0 (0)........ Ukraine
Agg: 3-2
Sweden ....(0) 2-3 (0)...... Portugal
Agg: 2-4
Croatia..........(1) 2-0 (0)......... Iceland
Agg: 2-0

Iceland hold Croatia to a 0-0 draw in the first leg of their play-off

African qualifying had an unfamiliar feel but there was nothing unfamiliar about the list of teams to make it through.

The final round in the CAF section consisted not of several groups but five two-legged knockout ties contested between the ten winners of the second-round group stage. The format resulted in a qualifying campaign that failed to ignite until October 2013, as seven of the eight top seeds cruised through uncompetitive groups.

A poor South Africa team were the only seeded team to fall, with minnows Ethiopia shocking the rest of Group A, but the success of the big guns did set up a thrilling shootout as the big guns aimed for Brazil.

Senegal eventually succumbed to hot favourites **Ivory Coast** but they gave the Elephants a scare. Fighting back from 3-0 down to 2-3, they pressed for the goal that would send them to Brazil on away goals but Salomon Kalou's injury-time strike confirmed Ivory Coast's third successive World Cup appearance.

Africa Cup of Nations champions **Nigeria** eased past rank outsiders Ethiopia with a comfortable 3-1 aggregate success while **Cameroon** became the first African side to reach seven World Cup finals following a classic two-legged performance, drawing 0-0 in Tunisia before overpowering the north African favourites 4-1 in Yaounde.

Seven-time African champions Egypt extended a poor run of qualifying attempts as they were thrashed 6-1 by **Ghana** in the first leg of their tie. Ghana lost 1-2 in Cairo but still qualified comfortably.

Algeria need to come from behind three times to get past Burkina Faso on away goals and the North Africans' success meant that the exact same five African sides who qualified in 2010 made it to Brazil.

A goalless draw in Tunisia set up Cameroon to reach their seventh World Cup

Top scorers	P	Gls
Asamoah Gyan (Ghana)	6	6
Mohamed Aboutrika (Egypt)	8	6
Mohamed Salah (Egypt)	8	6
Bernard Parker (South Africa)	4	5
Islam Slimani (Algeria)	7	5
Juvenal (Equatorial Guinea)	6	5
Papiss Cisse (Senegal)	7	5
Salomon Kalou (Ivory Coast)	7	5
Getaneh Gibeto (Ethiopia)	6	4
Yaya Toure (Ivory Coast)	6	4
Mabi Mputu (DR Congo)	7	4
Salahdin Ahmed (Ethiopia)	8	4

Format 52 participating teams,
5 qualify. **Round 1** 24 teams, 12
two-legged knockout ties **Round 2**
40 teams, 10 round-robin home-and-
away groups of 4. Group winners
advance **Round 3** 10 teams, 5 two-
legged knockout ties, winners qualify
for World Cup

Round 1

Friday November 11 2011
Chad.............(1) 1-2 (1).......Tanzania
Comoros......(0) 0-1 (0) Mozambique
Djibouti ....(0) 0-4 (1)....... Namibia
Eq Guinea.....(1) 2-0 (0). Madagascar
Eritrea..........(1) 1-1 (0)..........Rwanda
Guinea-Biss...(1) 1-1 (1).............Togo
Lesotho.........(0) 1-0 (0).... Burundi
Sao Tome.....(0) 0-5 (3)...........Congo
Seychelles.....(0) 0-3 (1)...........Kenya
Swaziland.....(0) 1-3 (2)....DR Congo

Saturday November 12 2011
Somalia ....(0) 0-0 (0)........Ethiopia

Tuesday November 15 2011
Burundi.........(1) 2-2 (2)........ Lesotho
Agg: 2-3
Congo............(0) 1-1 (0).... Sao Tome
Agg: 6-1
DR Congo .....(1) 5-1 (0).... Swaziland
Agg: 8-2
Kenya ....(3) 4-0 (0)..... Seychelles
Agg: 7-0
Madagascar..(0) 2-1 (1).... Eq Guinea
Agg: 3-2
Mozambique (2) 4-1 (0).......Comoros
Agg: 5-1
Namibia........(2) 4-0 (0)........ Djibouti
Agg: 8-0
Rwanda........(1) 3-1 (0).......... Eritrea
Agg: 4-2
Tanzania ....(0) 0-1 (0)............ Chad
Agg: 2-2
Togo ....(1) 1-0 (0).. Guinea-Biss
Agg: 2-1

Wednesday November 16 2011
Ethiopia........(1) 5-0 (0)........ Somalia
Agg: 5-0

Round 2

Group A

	P	W	D	L	F	A	GD	Pts
Ethiopia	6	4	1	1	8	6	2	13
South Africa	6	3	2	1	12	5	7	11
Botswana	6	2	1	3	8	10	-2	7
C African Rep	6	1	0	5	5	12	-7	3

Saturday June 2 2012
C African Rep(1) 2-0 (0).....Botswana

Sunday June 3 2012
S Africa ....(0) 1-1 (1)........Ethiopia

Saturday June 9 2012
Botswana .....(1) 1-1 (1).........S Africa

Sunday June 10 2012
Ethiopia........(1) 2-0 (0)C African Rep

Saturday March 23 2013
S Africa ....(1) 2-0 (0)C African Rep

Sunday March 24 2013
Ethiopia........(0) 1-0 (0)..... Botswana

Saturday June 8 2013
Botswana .... 0-3 ....Ethiopia
Match awarded
C African Rep(0) 0-3 (2).........S Africa

Saturday June 15 2013
Botswana .....(1) 3-2 (1)C African Rep

Saturday June 16 2013
Ethiopia........(1) 2-1 (1).........S Africa

Saturday September 7 2013
C African Rep(1) 1-2 (0)........Ethiopia
S Africa ....(2) 4-1 (0).....Botswana

Group B

	P	W	D	L	F	A	GD	Pts
Tunisia	6	4	2	0	13	6	7	14
Cape Verde I	6	3	0	3	9	7	2	9
Sierra Leone	6	2	2	2	10	10	0	8
Eq Guinea	6	0	2	4	6	15	-9	2

Saturday June 2 2012
Sierra Leone..(2) 2-1 (1)...Cape Verde
Tunisia ....(0) 3-1 (1).... Eq Guinea

Saturday June 9 2012
Cape Verde ...(1) 1-2 (1)..........Tunisia
Eq Guinea.....(2) 2-2 (2). Sierra Leone

Saturday March 23 2013
Tunisia ....(0) 2-1 (0). Sierra Leone

Sunday March 24 2013
Eq Guinea....... 0-3 .....Cape Verde
Match awarded

Saturday June 8 2013
Cape Verde ..... 3-0 ...... Eq Guinea
Match awarded
Sierra Leone..(1) 2-2 (0).........Tunisia

Saturday June 15 2013
Cape Verde ...(1) 1-0 (0). Sierra Leone

Saturday June 16 2013
Eq Guinea.....(1) 1-1 (0)..........Tunisia

Saturday September 7 2013
Sierra Leone..(2) 3-2 (0).... Eq Guinea
Tunisia .... 3-0 .....Cape Verde
Match awarded

Group C

	P	W	D	L	F	A	GD	Pts
Ivory Coast	6	4	2	0	15	5	10	14
Morocco	6	2	3	1	9	8	1	9
Tanzania	6	2	0	4	8	12	-4	6
Gambia	6	1	1	4	4	11	-7	4

Saturday June 2 2012
Gambia.........(1) 1-1 (0).......Morocco
Ivory Coast ...(1) 2-0 (0).......Tanzania

Saturday June 9 2012
Morocco ....(1) 2-2 (1)...Ivory Coast

Sunday June 10 2012
Tanzania ......(0) 2-1 (1)........ Gambia

Saturday March 23 2013
Ivory Coast ...(0) 3-0 (0)........ Gambia

Sunday March 24 2013
Tanzania ......(0) 3-1 (0).......Morocco

Saturday June 8 2013
Gambia.........(0) 0-3 (1)...Ivory Coast
Morocco ....(1) 2-1 (0)....Tanzania

Saturday June 15 2013
Morocco ....(1) 2-0 (0)........ Gambia

Saturday June 16 2013
Tanzania ......(2) 2-4 (3)...Ivory Coast

Saturday September 7 2013
Gambia.........(1) 2-0 (0).......Tanzania
Ivory Coast ...(0) 1-1 (0).......Morocco

Group D

	P	W	D	L	F	A	GD	Pts
Ghana	6	5	0	1	18	3	15	15
Zambia	6	3	2	1	14	7	11	11
Lesotho	6	1	2	3	4	15	-11	5
Sudan	6	0	2	4	3	14	-11	2

Friday June 1 2012
Ghana...........(3) 7-0 (0)........ Lesotho

Saturday June 2 2012
Sudan............. 0-3 ....Zambia
Match awarded

Saturday June 9 2012
Zambia ....(1) 1-0 (0)..........Ghana

Sunday June 10 2012
Lesotho.........(0) 0-0 (0)...........Sudan

Sunday March 24 2013
Ghana...........(2) 4-0 (0)...........Sudan
Lesotho.........(0) 1-1 (0)..........Zambia

Friday June 7 2013
Sudan............(1) 1-3 (1)..........Ghana

Saturday June 8 2013
Zambia ....(1) 4-0 (0)........ Lesotho

Saturday June 15 2013
Zambia ....(0) 1-1 (0)...........Sudan

Saturday June 16 2013
Lesotho.........(0) 0-2 (1)..........Ghana

Friday September 6 2013
Ghana...........(1) 2-1 (0)..........Zambia

Sunday September 8 2013
Sudan............(1) 1-3 (1)........ Lesotho

Group E

	P	W	D	L	F	A	GD	Pts
Burkina Faso	6	4	0	2	7	4	3	12
Congo	6	3	2	1	7	3	4	11
Gabon	6	2	1	3	5	6	-1	7
Niger	6	1	1	4	6	12	-6	4

Saturday June 2 2012
Burkina Faso... 0-3 ....Congo
Match awarded

Sunday June 3 2012
Niger .... 3-0 ....Gabon
Match awarded

Saturday June 9 2012
Congo..........(0) 1-0 (0)............Niger
Gabon ....(0) 1-0 (0).Burkina Faso
Saturday March 23 2013
Burkina Faso.(2) 4-0 (0)............Niger
Congo..........(1) 1-0 (0)..........Gabon
Saturday June 8 2013
Gabon ....(0) 0-0 (0)..........Congo
Sunday June 9 2013
Niger ....(0) 0-1 (0).Burkina Faso
Saturday June 15 2013
Congo..........(0) 0-1 (1).Burkina Faso
Gabon ....(1) 4-1 (1)..........Niger
Saturday September 7 2013
Burkina Faso.(0) 1-0 (0)..........Gabon
Niger ....(1) 2-2 (0)..........Congo

Group F

	P	W	D	L	F	A	GD	Pts
Nigeria	6	3	3	0	7	3	4	12
Malawi	6	1	4	1	4	5	-1	7
Kenya	6	1	3	2	4	5	-1	6
Namibia	6	1	2	3	2	4	-2	5

Saturday June 2 2012
Kenya ....(0) 0-0 (0).........Malawi
Sunday June 3 2012
Nigeria ....(0) 1-0 (0).......Namibia
Saturday June 9 2012
Malawi ....(0) 1-1 (0).........Nigeria
Namibia.........(0) 1-0 (0)..........Kenya
Saturday March 23 2013
Namibia........(0) 0-1 (0).........Malawi
Nigeria ....(0) 1-1 (1)..........Kenya
Wednesday June 5 2013
Kenya ....(0) 0-1 (0).........Nigeria
Malawi ....(0) 0-0 (0).......Namibia
Thursday June 12 2013
Malawi ....(0) 2-2 (0).........Kenya
Namibia........(0) 1-1 (0).........Nigeria
Saturday September 7 2013
Nigeria ....(1) 2-0 (0).........Malawi
Sunday September 8 2013
Kenya ....(1) 1-0 (0).......Namibia

Group G

	P	W	D	L	F	A	GD	Pts
Egypt	6	6	0	0	16	7	9	18
Guinea	6	3	1	2	12	8	4	10
Mozambique	6	0	3	3	2	10	-8	3
Zimbabwe	6	0	2	4	4	9	-5	2

Friday June 1 2012
Egypt............(0) 2-0 (0) Mozambique
Sunday June 3 2012
Zimbabwe ....(0) 0-1 (1)........ Guinea
Sunday June 10 2012
Guinea..........(1) 2-3 (0).......... Egypt
Mozambique (0) 0-0 (0)....Zimbabwe
Saturday March 24 2013
Mozambique (0) 0-0 (0)......... Guinea
Tuesday March 26 2013
Egypt............(0) 2-1 (0)....Zimbabwe
Sunday June 9 2013
Guinea..........(3) 6-1 (1) Mozambique
Zimbabwe ....(1) 2-4 (2).......... Egypt

Saturday June 16 2013
Guinea..........(1) 1-0 (0)....Zimbabwe
Mozambique (0) 0-1 (1)........... Egypt
Sunday September 8 2013
Zimbabwe ....(1) 1-1 (0) Mozambique
Tuesday September 10 2013
Egypt............(1) 4-2 (1)........ Guinea

Group H

	P	W	D	L	F	A	GD	Pts
Algeria	6	5	0	1	13	4	9	15
Mali	6	2	2	2	7	7	0	8
Benin	6	2	2	2	8	9	-1	8
Rwanda	6	0	2	4	3	11	-8	2

Saturday June 2 2012
Algeria..........(2) 4-0 (0)........Rwanda
Sunday June 3 2012
Benin............(1) 1-0 (0) ...... Mali
Sunday June 10 2012
Mali..............(1) 2-1 (0).......... Algeria
Rwanda........(0) 1-1 (0)........... Benin
Sunday March 24 2013
Rwanda..........(1) 1-2 (0)............. Mali
Tuesday March 26 2013
Algeria..........(1) 3-1 (1)............ Benin
Sunday June 9 2013
Benin............(1) 1-3 (2).......... Algeria
Mali..............(0) 1-1 (1).......Rwanda
Saturday June 16 2013
Mali..............(1) 2-2 (2)........... Benin
Rwanda ....(0) 0-1 (0)......... Algeria
Sunday September 8 2013
Benin............(1) 2-0 (0)........Rwanda
Tuesday September 10 2013
Algeria..........(0) 1-0 (0)............. Mali

Group I

	P	W	D	L	F	A	GD	Pts
Cameroon	6	4	1	1	8	3	5	13
Libya	6	2	3	1	5	3	2	9
DR Congo	6	1	3	2	3	3	0	6
Togo	6	1	1	4	4	11	-7	4

Saturday June 2 2012
Cameroon.....(0) 1-0 (0).....DR Congo
Sunday June 3 2012
Togo ....(1) 1-1 (1)............ Libya
Sunday June 10 2012
DR Congo .....(1) 2-0 (0)...........Togo
Libya ....(1) 2-1 (1).... Cameroon
Saturday March 23 2013
Cameroon.....(1) 2-1 (1)...........Togo
Sunday March 24 2013
DR Congo .....(0) 0-0 (0)........... Libya
Friday June 7 2013
Libya ....(0) 0-0 (0).....DR Congo
Sunday June 9 2013
Togo ....   0-3 ..... Cameroon
Match awarded
Friday June 14 2013
Libya ....(2) 2-0 (0).............Togo
Saturday June 16 2013
DR Congo .....(0) 0-0 (0)..... Cameroon

Sunday September 8 2013
Cameroon.....(1) 1-0 (0)............ Libya
Togo ....(1) 2-1 (0)....DR Congo

Group J

	P	W	D	L	F	A	GD	Pts
Senegal	6	3	3	0	9	4	5	12
Uganda	6	2	2	2	5	6	-1	8
Angola	6	1	4	1	7	5	2	7
Liberia	6	1	1	4	3	9	-6	4

Saturday June 2 2012
Senegal ....(1) 3-1 (1)..........Liberia
Sunday June 3 2012
Angola..........(1) 1-1 (0)........ Uganda
Saturday June 9 2012
Uganda ....(0) 1-1 (1)........ Senegal
Sunday June 10 2012
Liberia ....(0) 0-0 (0)......... Angola
Saturday March 23 2013
Senegal ....(1) 1-1 (0)......... Angola
Sunday March 24 2013
Liberia ....(1) 2-0 (0)........ Uganda
Saturday June 8 2013
Angola..........(0) 1-1 (1)........ Senegal
Uganda ....(1) 1-0 (0)........Liberia
Saturday June 15 2013
Uganda ....(0) 2-1 (0)........ Angola
Saturday June 16 2013
Liberia ....(0) 0-2 (1)........ Senegal
Saturday September 7 2013
Angola..........   3-0 ....Liberia
Match awarded
Senegal ....(0) 1-0 (0)........ Uganda

Senegal miss out on the finals

Round 3
Saturday October 12 2013
Ivory Coast ...(2) 3-1 (0)........ Senegal
Burkina Faso .(1) 3-2 (0)......... Algeria
Sunday October 13 2013
Ethiopia ....(0) 1-2 (0)........ Nigeria
Tunisia..........(0) 0-0 (0).... Cameroon
Tuesday October 15 2013
Ghana...........(3) 6-1 (1)........... Egypt
Saturday November 16 2013
Senegal ....(0) 1-1 (0)...Ivory Coast
Agg: 2-4
Nigeria ....(1) 2-0 (0).........Ethiopia
Agg: 4-1
Sunday November 17 2013
Cameroon.....(2) 4-1 (0).........Tunisia
Agg: 4-1
Tuesday November 19 2013
Algeria..........(0) 1-0 (0).Burkina Faso
Agg: 3-3. Algeria won on away goals
Egypt............(1) 2-1 (0).........Ghana
Agg: 3-7

There were few surprises in Asia, with the nations ranked first to fourth for the third-round draw all qualifying for Brazil.

Australia, relative new to the region, reached their third successive World Cup finals, breezing through Group D in the third round before putting in a solid performance in the fourth-round group stage where they lost only once and drew home and away with group winners **Japan**.

The Japanese were rarely troubled, taking 13 of the first 16 points available in the final group stage and becoming the first nation to qualify for the final tournament when they drew 1-1 with Australia on June 4, 2013.

Jordan finished third in Group B and impressed in home wins over Japan and Australia. But 6-0 and 4-0 defeats in Saitama and Melbourne highlighted weaknesses that would be exposed by Uruguay in the intercontinental play-offs.

South Korea and **Iran** failed to convince in Group A and only a final-day victory in South Korea moved Iran into top spot and fended off the challenge of an Uzbekistan side who missed out by just one goal.

Top scorers	P	Gls
Shinji Okazaki (Japan)	14	8
Cong Vinh Le (Vietnam)	4	7
Hassan Mahmoud (Jordan)	10	7
Younis Mahmoud (Iraq)	14	7
Ahmad Ibrahim (Jordan)	18	7
Park Chuyoung (S Korea)	7	6
Javad Nekonam (Iran)	14	6
Hao Junmin (China)	6	5
Joshua Kennedy (Australia)	6	5
Nassir Al Shamrani (S Arabia)	8	5
Keisuke Honda (Japan)	6	5
Lee Keunho (S Korea)	12	5
Hassan Maatouk (Lebanon)	15	5
Ibrahim Khalfan (Qatar)	15	5
Amer Khalil (Jordan)	17	5

Format 43 participating teams, 4.5 qualify. **Round 1** 16 teams, 8 two-legged knockout ties **Round 2** 30 teams, 15 two-legged knockout ties **Round 3** 20 teams, 5 round-robin home-and-away groups of 4. Group winners and runners-up advance **Round 4** 10 teams, 2 round-robin home-and-away groups of 5. Group winners qualify for World Cup. Third-placed advance **Round 5** 2 teams, 1 two-legged knockout tie. Winners qualify for intercontinental play-off against South America

Round 1

Wednesday June 29 2011
Afghanistan ..(0) 0-2 (1)...... Palestine
Bangladesh...(2) 3-0 (0)....... Pakistan
Cambodia......(0) 4-2 (1)............ Laos
Malaysia.......(1) 2-1 (0)Chinese Taipei
Mongolia......(0) 1-0 (0)......Myanmar
Nepal...........(1) 2-1 (0)....Timor-Leste
Sri Lanka......(1) 1-1 (0).... Philippines
Vietnam........(3) 6-0 (0)..........Macau

Saturday July 2 2011
Timor-Leste ...(0) 0-5 (1)........... Nepal
Agg: 1-7

Sunday July 3 2011
Chinese Taipei(2)3-2 (2)...... Malaysia
Agg: 4-4

Laos..............(2) 6-2 (1)....Cambodia
AET Agg: 8-6
Macau ....(0) 1-7 (4)....... Vietnam
Agg: 1-13
Myanmar......(0) 2-0 (0)..... Mongolia
Agg: 2-1
Pakistan........(0) 0-0 (0).. Bangladesh
Agg: 0-3
Palestine ......(1) 1-1 (0)...Afghanistan
Agg: 3-1
Philippines ....(2) 4-0 (0)...... Sri Lanka
Agg: 5-1

Round 2

Saturday July 23 2011
China............(1) 7-2 (2)............. Laos
Iran...............(1) 4-0 (0)...... Maldives
Iraq...............(1) 2-0 (0)........ Yemen
Jordan ....(4) 9-0 (0).......... Nepal
Kuwait..........(1) 3-0 (0)... Philippines
Lebanon ....(2) 4-0 (0).. Bangladesh
Oman .... 3-0 ....Myanmar
Match awarded
Qatar ....(1) 3-0 (0)....... Vietnam
Saudi Arabia .(2) 3-0 (0)...Hong Kong
Singapore .....(4) 5-3 (1)...... Malaysia
Syria .... 0-3 .... Tajikistan
Match awarded
Thailand ....(1) 1-0 (0)..... Palestine
Turkmenistan (1) 1-1 (1)..... Indonesia
UAE ....(2) 3-0 (0)............ India
Uzbekistan....(1) 4-0 (0)...Kyrgyzstan

Thursday July 28 2011
Bangladesh...(0) 2-0 (0)....... Lebanon
Agg: 2-4
Hong Kong ...(0) 0-5 (1).Saudi Arabia
Agg: 0-8
India ....(0) 2-2 (1)............ UAE
Agg: 2-5
Indonesia......(3) 4-3 (0) Turkmenistan
Agg: 5-4
Kyrgyzstan....(0) 0-3 (0)... Uzbekistan
Agg: 0-7
Laos..............(0) 1-6 (2).......... China
Agg: 3-13
Malaysia.......(0) 1-1 (0).....Singapore
Agg: 4-6
Maldives.......(0) 0-1 (1)............. Iran
Agg: 0-5
Myanmar........ A-A ....Oman
Match abandoned Agg: 0-4

Nepal............(0) 1-1 (0).........Jordan
Agg: 1-10
Palestine ......(1) 2-2 (1)....... Thailand
Agg: 2-3
Philippines....(1) 1-2 (0)...... Kuwait
Agg: 1-5
Tajikistan ...... 3-0 ....Syria
Match awarded Agg: 6-0
Vietnam........(0) 2-1 (1)..........Qatar
Agg: 2-4
Yemen ....(0) 0-0 (0) .... Iraq
Agg: 0-2

Round 3

Group A

	P	W	D	L	F	A	GD	Pts
Iraq	6	5	0	1	14	4	10	15
Jordan	6	4	0	2	11	7	4	12
China	6	3	0	3	10	6	4	9
Singapore	6	0	0	6	2	20	-18	0

Friday September 2 2011
China............(0) 2-1 (0).....Singapore
Iraq...............(0) 0-2 (1)........Jordan

Tuesday September 6 2011
Jordan ....(0) 2-1 (0) .... China
Singapore .....(0) 0-2 (0) .... Iraq

Tuesday October 11 2011
China............(0) 0-1 (1)............. Iraq
Singapore .....(0) 0-3 (1)........Jordan

Friday November 11 2011
Iraq...............(0) 1-0 (0).......... China
Jordan ....(1) 2-0 (0)....Singapore

Tuesday November 15 2011
Jordan ....(1) 1-3 (0) .... Iraq
Singapore .....(0) 0-4 (1).......... China

Wednesday February 29 2012
China............(1) 3-1 (0)....Singapore
Iraq...............(4) 7-1 (0).......Jordan

Group B

	P	W	D	L	F	A	GD	Pts
S Korea	6	4	1	1	14	4	10	13
Lebanon	6	3	1	2	10	14	-4	10
Kuwait	6	2	2	2	8	9	-1	8
UAE	6	1	0	5	9	14	-5	3

Friday September 2 2011
S Korea.........(2) 6-0 (0).......Lebanon
UAE ....(0) 2-3 (1)...... Kuwait

Coach Alberto Zaccheroni gets a soaking as Japan become the first nation to qualify for the finals

Tuesday September 6 2011
Kuwait..........(0) 1-1 (1) ....S Korea
Lebanon ....(1) 3-1 (1) ....UAE
Tuesday October 11 2011
Lebanon ....(1) 2-2 (0) ....Kuwait
S Korea ....(0) 2-1 (0) ....UAE
Friday November 11 2011
Kuwait..........(0) 0-1 (0) ......Lebanon
UAE ....(0) 0-2 (0) ....S Korea
Tuesday November 15 2011
Kuwait..........(0) 2-1 (1) ....UAE
Lebanon ....(2) 2-1 (1) ......S Korea
Wednesday February 29 2012
S Korea ....(0) 2-0 (0) .... Kuwait
UAE ....(2) 4-2 (2) ......Lebanon

Group C
	P	W	D	L	F	A	GD	Pts
Uzbekistan	6	5	1	0	8	1	7	16
Japan	**6**	**3**	**1**	**2**	**14**	**3**	**11**	**10**
N Korea	6	2	1	3	3	4	-1	7
Tajikistan	6	0	1	5	1	18	-17	1

Friday September 2 2011
Japan.............(0) 1-0 (0) ....N Korea
Tajikistan ......(0) 0-1 (0) ... Uzbekistan
Tuesday September 6 2011
N Korea ....(1) 1-0 (0) ..... Tajikistan
Uzbekistan....(1) 1-1 (0) .... Japan
Tuesday October 11 2011
Japan.............(4) 8-0 (0) ..... Tajikistan
N Korea ....(0) 0-1 (1) ... Uzbekistan
Friday November 11 2011
Tajikistan ......(0) 0-4 (1) .... Japan
Uzbekistan....(0) 1-0 (0) ......N Korea
Tuesday November 15 2011
N Korea ....(0) 1-0 (0) .... Japan
Uzbekistan....(1) 3-0 (0) ...... Tajikistan

Wednesday February 29 2012
Japan.............(0) 0-1 (0) ... Uzbekistan
Tajikistan ......(0) 1-1 (0) ....N Korea

Group D
	P	W	D	L	F	A	GD	Pts
Australia	**6**	**5**	**0**	**1**	**13**	**5**	**8**	**15**
Oman	6	2	2	2	3	6	-3	8
Saudi Arabia	6	1	3	2	6	7	-1	6
Thailand	6	1	1	4	4	8	-4	4

Friday September 2 2011
Australia ....(0) 2-1 (1) ......Thailand
Oman ....(0) 0-0 (0).Saudi Arabia
Tuesday September 6 2011
Saudi Arabia .(0) 1-3 (1) ......Australia
Thailand ....(2) 3-0 (0) ....Oman
Tuesday October 11 2011
Australia ....(1) 3-0 (0) ....Oman
Thailand ....(0) 0-0 (0).Saudi Arabia
Friday November 11 2011
Oman ....(1) 1-0 (0) ......Australia
Saudi Arabia .(0) 3-0 (0) ....Thailand
Tuesday November 15 2011
Saudi Arabia .(0) 0-0 (0) ....Oman
Thailand ....(0) 0-1 (0) ......Australia
Wednesday February 29 2012
Australia ....(1) 4-2 (2).Saudi Arabia
Oman ....(1) 2-0 (0) ....Thailand

Group E
	P	W	D	L	F	A	GD	Pts
Iran	**6**	**3**	**3**	**0**	**17**	**5**	**12**	**12**
Qatar	6	2	4	0	10	5	5	10
Bahrain	6	2	3	1	13	7	6	9
Indonesia	6	0	0	6	3	26	-23	0

Friday September 2 2011
Bahrain..........(0) 0-0 (0) ....Qatar

Iran...............(0) 3-0 (0) ..... Indonesia
Tuesday September 6 2011
Indonesia......(0) 0-2 (1) .... Bahrain
Qatar ....(0) 1-1 (0) ....Iran
Tuesday October 11 2011
Indonesia......(2) 2-3 (1) ....Qatar
Iran...............(3) 6-0 (0) .... Bahrain
Friday November 11 2011
Bahrain..........(1) 1-1 (0) ....Iran
Qatar ....(2) 4-0 (0) ..... Indonesia
Tuesday November 15 2011
Indonesia......(1) 1-4 (3) ....Iran
Qatar ....(0) 0-0 (0) .... Bahrain
Wednesday February 29 2012
Bahrain.........(4)10-0 (0) ..... Indonesia
Iran...............(1) 2-2 (1) ....Qatar

Round 4

Group A
	P	W	D	L	F	A	GD	Pts
Iran	**8**	**5**	**1**	**2**	**8**	**2**	**6**	**16**
S Korea	**8**	**4**	**2**	**2**	**13**	**7**	**6**	**14**
Uzbekistan	8	4	2	2	11	6	5	14
Qatar	8	2	1	5	5	13	-8	7
Lebanon	8	1	2	5	3	12	-9	5

Sunday June 3 2012
Lebanon ....(0) 0-1 (0) ....Qatar
Uzbekistan....(0) 0-1 (0) ....Iran
Friday June 8 2012
Lebanon ....(1) 1-1 (1) ... Uzbekistan
Qatar ....(1) 1-4 (1) ....S Korea
Tuesday June 12 2012
Iran...............(0) 0-0 (0) ....Qatar
S Korea ....(1) 3-0 (0) ....Lebanon
Tuesday September 11 2012
Lebanon ....(1) 1-0 (0) ....Iran
Uzbekistan....(1) 2-2 (1) ....S Korea

Tuesday October 16 2012
Iran...............(0) 1-0 (0)........S Korea
Qatar.............(0) 0-1 (1)... Uzbekistan

Wednesday November 14 2012
Iran...............(0) 0-1 (0)... Uzbekistan
Qatar.............(0) 1-0 (0)....... Lebanon

Tuesday March 26 2013
S Korea..........(0) 2-1 (0)............Qatar
Uzbekistan....(0) 1-0 (0)....... Lebanon

Tuesday June 4 2013
Lebanon ....(1) 1-1 (0)........S Korea
Qatar.............(0) 0-1 (0)..............Iran

Tuesday June 11 2013
Iran...............(2) 4-0 (0)....... Lebanon
S Korea.........(1) 1-0 (0)... Uzbekistan

Tuesday June 18 2013
S Korea.........(0) 0-1 (0)..............Iran
Uzbekistan....(0) 5-1 (1)............Qatar

Group B

	P	W	D	L	F	A	GD	Pts
Japan	8	5	2	1	16	5	11	17
Australia	8	3	4	1	12	7	5	13
Jordan	8	3	1	4	7	16	-9	10
Oman	8	2	3	3	7	10	-3	9
Iraq	8	1	2	5	4	8	-4	5

Sunday June 3 2012
Japan............(1) 3-0 (0)...........Oman
Jordan ....(1) 1-1 (1)..............Iraq

Friday June 8 2012
Japan............(4) 6-0 (0)..........Jordan
Oman ....(0) 0-0 (0)......Australia

Tuesday June 12 2012
Australia ....(1) 1-1 (0)...........Japan
Iraq...............(1) 1-1 (0)...........Oman

Tuesday September 11 2012
Japan............(1) 1-0 (0)..............Iraq
Jordan ....(0) 2-1 (0)......Australia

Tuesday October 16 2012
Iraq...............(0) 1-2 (0)......Australia
Oman ....(0) 2-1 (0).........Jordan

Wednesday November 14 2012
Iraq...............(0) 1-0 (0).........Jordan
Oman ....(0) 1-2 (1)..........Japan

Tuesday March 26 2013
Australia ....(0) 2-2 (1)...........Oman
Jordan ....(1) 2-1 (0)...........Japan

Tuesday June 4 2013
Japan............(0) 1-1 (0)......Australia
Oman ....(1) 1-0 (0)..............Iraq

Tuesday June 11 2013
Australia ....(1) 4-0 (0)..........Jordan
Iraq...............(0) 0-1 (0)...........Japan

Tuesday June 18 2013
Australia ....(1) 1-0 (0)..............Iraq
Jordan ....(0) 1-0 (0)...........Oman

Round 5

Friday September 6 2013
Jordan ....(1) 1-1 (1)... Uzbekistan

Tuesday September 10 2013
Uzbekistan....(1) 1-1 (1)..........Jordan
AET Jordan won 9-8 on pens

Panama came within a whisker of causing the biggest shock of World Cup qualifying and dumping **Mexico** out of the finals. The Mexicans had struggled for form throughout qualifying but needed just a point to guarantee fourth spot in their final group game against already qualified **Costa Rica**. They lost, meaning Panama needed a home win over much-changed group winners **USA** to pip the Mexicans to a place in the play-off against New Zealand.

The shock looked firmly on with the home side leading 2-1 in Panama City as the game went into injury time, but two late USA goals broke Panamanian hearts with the Central American minnows just minutes from a shot at a first ever World Cup finals appearance.

Mexico went on to confirm their World Cup place by thrashing the Kiwis 9-3 over two legs but that intercontinental play-off performance was in stark contrast to the rest of the Mexicans' qualifying campaign.

The regional giants were comfortably outclassed by a confident **Honduras** outfit who always looked likely to repeat their World Cup qualification of 2010, while a resurgent and resilient Costa Rican side also impressed, conceding just seven goals in ten games. Los Ticos beat the USA, the dominant outfit in the section, 3-1 in San Jose and put together a perfect W5, D0, L0, F10, A2 record at home.

Top scorers

	P	Gls
Deon Mccaulay (Belize)	8	11
Oribe Peralta (Mexico)	11	10
Peter Byers (Antigua & B)	12	10
Blas Perez (Panama)	18	10
Jerry Bengtson (Honduras)	12	9
Alvaro Saborio (Costa Rica)	15	8
Clint Dempsey (USA)	14	8
Luis Tejada (Panama)	14	7
Carlo Costly (Honduras)	13	7
Richmar Siberie (Curacao)	6	6
Carlos Ruiz (Guatemala)	7	6
Osael Romero (El Salvador)	12	6

Format 35 participating teams, 3.5 qualify. **Round 1** 10 teams, 5 two-legged knockout ties **Round 2** 24 teams, 6 round-robin home-and-away groups of 4. Group winners advance **Round 3** 12 teams, 3 round-robin home-and-away groups of 4. Group winners and runners-up advance **Round 4** 6 teams, 1 round-robin home-and-away group of 6. Top 3 qualify for World Cup, 4th place qualifies for intercontinental play-off v Oceania

Round 1

Wednesday June 15 2011
Montserrat....(1) 2-5 (1)...........Belize

Saturday July 2 2011
Turks/Caicos..(0) 0-4 (2)......Bahamas

Sunday July 3 2011
US Virgin I ....(1) 2-0 (0)British Virgin I

Friday July 8 2011
Anguilla........(0) 0-2 (2).Dominican R
Aruba ....(4) 4-2 (1)........ St Lucia

Saturday July 9 2011
Bahamas.......(2) 6-0 (0). Turks/Caicos
Agg: 10-0

Sunday July 10 2011
British Virgin I(1) 1-2 (1)....US Virgin I
Agg: 1-4
Dominican R .(3) 4-0 (0)....... Anguilla
Agg: 6-0

Tuesday July 12 2011
St Lucia.........(2) 4-2 (1)..........Aruba
AET Agg: 6-6 St Lucia 5-4 pens

Sunday July 17 2011
Belize............(1) 3-1 (0)... Montserrat
Agg: 8-3

Round 2

Group A

	P	W	D	L	F	A	GD	Pts
El Salvador	6	6	0	0	20	5	15	18
Dominican R	6	2	2	2	12	8	4	8
Suriname	6	2	1	3	5	11	-6	7
Cayman I	6	0	1	5	2	15	-13	1

Friday September 2 2011
El Salvador ...(0) 3-2 (0).Dominican R
Suriname ......(1) 1-0 (0)......Cayman I

Tuesday September 6 2011
Cayman I ....(0) 1-4 (0)... El Salvador

Dominican R.(0) 1-1 (1)......Suriname

Friday October 7 2011
Cayman I......(0) 0-1 (0)......Suriname
Dominican R.(0) 1-2 (1)..El Salvador

Tuesday October 11 2011
El Salvador ...(3) 4-0 (0)......Cayman I
Suriname ......(0) 1-3 (1).Dominican R

Friday November 11 2011
Dominican R.(2) 4-0 (0)......Cayman I
Suriname ......(0) 1-3 (1)...El Salvador

Monday November 14 2011
Cayman I......(0) 1-1 (1).Dominican R

Tuesday November 15 2011
El Salvador ...(1) 4-0 (0)......Suriname

Group B

	P	W	D	L	F	A	GD	Pts
Guyana	6	4	1	1	9	6	3	13
Trin/Tobago	6	4	0	2	12	4	8	12
Bermuda	6	3	1	2	8	7	1	10
Barbados	6	0	0	6	2	14	-12	0

Friday September 2 2011
Guyana.........(1) 2-0 (0)......Barbados
Trin/Tobago..(1) 1-0 (0)...... Bermuda

Tuesday September 6 2011
Barbados ......(0) 0-2 (1).. Trin/Tobago
Guyana.........(0) 2-1 (0)...... Bermuda

Friday October 7 2011
Barbados ......(0) 0-2 (1)...... Guyana
Bermuda.......(0) 2-1 (0).. Trin/Tobago

Tuesday October 11 2011
Bermuda.......(0) 1-1 (0)...... Guyana
Trin/Tobago..(1) 4-0 (0)......Barbados

Friday November 11 2011
Bermuda.......(1) 2-1 (1)......Barbados
Guyana.........(1) 2-1 (0).. Trin/Tobago

Monday November 14 2011
Barbados ......(0) 1-2 (0)...... Bermuda

Tuesday November 15 2011
Trin/Tobago..... 3-0 .... Guyana

Group C

	P	W	D	L	F	A	GD	Pts
Panama	4	4	0	0	15	2	13	12
Nicaragua	4	2	0	2	5	7	-2	6
Dominica	4	0	0	4	0	11	-11	0

Friday September 2 2011
Dominica ......(0) 0-2 (2).....Nicaragua

Tuesday September 6 2011
Nicaragua.....(1) 1-2 (1)........Panama

Friday October 7 2011
Dominica ......(0) 0-5 (2)........Panama

Tuesday October 11 2011
Panama ....(1) 5-1 (0).....Nicaragua

Friday November 11 2011
Nicaragua.....(0) 1-0 (0)......Dominica

Tuesday November 15 2011
Panama ....(2) 3-0 (0)......Dominica

Group D

	P	W	D	L	F	A	GD	Pts
Canada	6	4	2	0	18	1	17	14
Puerto Rico	6	2	3	1	8	4	4	9
St Kitts/Nevis	6	1	4	1	6	8	-2	7
St Lucia	6	0	1	5	4	23	-19	1

Friday September 2 2011
Canada.........(1) 4-1 (1)........ St Lucia
St Kitts/Nevis (0) 0-0 (0)...Puerto Rico

Tuesday September 6 2011
Puerto Rico ...(0) 0-3 (1).........Canada
St Lucia.........(0) 2-4 (4) St Kitts/Nevis

Friday October 7 2011
Puerto Rico ...(1) 1-1 (0) St Kitts/Nevis
St Lucia.........(0) 0-7 (4).........Canada

Tuesday October 11 2011
Canada.........(0) 0-0 (0)...Puerto Rico
St Kitts/Nevis (0) 1-1 (0)........ St Lucia

Friday November 11 2011
St Kitts/Nevis (0) 0-0 (0).........Canada
St Lucia.........(0) 0-4 (2)...Puerto Rico

Monday November 14 2011
Puerto Rico ...(1) 3-0 (0)........ St Lucia

Tuesday November 15 2011
Canada.........(3) 4-0 (0) St Kitts/Nevis

Group E

	P	W	D	L	F	A	GD	Pts
Guatemala	6	6	0	0	19	3	16	18
Belize	6	2	1	3	9	10	-1	7
St Vincent/G	6	1	2	3	4	12	-8	5
Grenada	6	1	1	4	7	14	-7	4

Friday September 2 2011
Grenada ....(0) 0-3 (2)........... Belize
Guatemala....(2) 4-0 (0).. St Vincent/G

Tuesday September 6 2011
Belize............(0) 1-2 (1)... Guatemala

Thursday September 18 2011
St Vincent/G..(1) 2-1 (0) ... Grenada

Friday October 7 2011
Belize............(0) 1-4 (2)....... Grenada
St Vincent/G..(0) 0-3 (1)... Guatemala

Tuesday October 11 2011
Guatemala....(1) 3-1 (1)........... Belize

Saturday October 15 2011
Grenada ....(0) 1-1 (0). St Vincent/G

Friday November 11 2011
Belize............(1) 1-1 (1). St Vincent/G
Guatemala....(3) 3-0 (0)....... Grenada

Tuesday November 15 2011
Grenada ....(1) 1-4 (0)... Guatemala
St Vincent/G..(0) 0-2 (1)........... Belize

Group F

	P	W	D	L	F	A	GD	Pts
Antigua/Barb	6	5	0	1	28	5	23	15
Haiti	6	4	1	1	21	6	15	13
Curacao	6	2	1	3	15	15	0	7
US Virgin I	6	0	0	6	2	40	-38	0

Friday September 2 2011
Antigua/Barb (2) 5-2 (1)........Curacao
Haiti ....(3) 6-0 (0)....US Virgin I

Tuesday September 6 2011
Curacao ....(2) 2-4 (1).............. Haiti
US Virgin I ....(0) 1-8 (2) Antigua/Barb

Friday October 7 2011
Curacao .... 0-3 ..Antigua/Barb
Match awarded

US Virgin I ....(0) 0-7 (2)............. Haiti

Tuesday October 11 2011
Antigua/Barb (5)10-0(0).... US Virgin I
Haiti ....(1) 2-2 (2)......Curacao

Friday November 11 2011
Antigua/Barb (0) 1-0 (0)............. Haiti
US Virgin I ....(0) 0-3 (3)........Curacao

Tuesday November 15 2011
Curacao ....(2) 6-1 (0).... US Virgin I
Haiti ....(0) 2-1 (1) Antigua/Barb

Round 3

Group A

	P	W	D	L	F	A	GD	Pts
USA	**6**	**4**	**1**	**1**	**11**	**6**	**5**	**13**
Jamaica	6	3	1	2	9	6	3	10
Guatemala	6	3	1	2	9	8	1	10
Antigua/Barb	6	0	1	5	4	13	-9	1

Friday June 8 2012
Jamaica ....(1) 2-1 (0) ... Guatemala
USA ....(2) 3-1 (0) Antigua/Barb

Tuesday June 12 2012
Antigua/Barb (0) 0-0 (0) ....Jamaica
Guatemala....(0) 1-1 (1)..............USA

Friday September 7 2012
Guatemala....(0) 3-1 (1) Antigua/Barb
Jamaica ....(1) 2-1 (1)..............USA

Tuesday September 11 2012
Antigua/Barb (0) 0-1 (1)... Guatemala
USA ....(1) 1-0 (0) ....Jamaica

Friday October 12 2012
Antigua/Barb (1) 1-2 (1)..............USA
Guatemala....(1) 2-1 (1)........Jamaica

Tuesday October 16 2012
Jamaica ....(2) 4-1 (0) Antigua/Barb
USA ....(3) 3-1 (1)... Guatemala

Group B

	P	W	D	L	F	A	GD	Pts
Mexico	**6**	**6**	**0**	**0**	**15**	**2**	**13**	**18**
Costa Rica	**6**	**3**	**1**	**2**	**14**	**5**	**9**	**10**
El Salvador	6	1	2	3	8	11	-3	5
Guyana	6	0	1	5	5	24	-19	1

Friday June 8 2012
Costa Rica.....(2) 2-2 (1)... El Salvador
Mexico..........(2) 3-1 (0)........ Guyana

Tuesday June 12 2012
El Salvador ...(0) 1-2 (0)......... Mexico
Guyana ....(0) 0-4 (2)... Costa Rica

Friday September 7 2012
Costa Rica.....(0) 0-2 (1)......... Mexico
El Salvador ...(2) 2-2 (1)........ Guyana

Tuesday September 11 2012
Guyana.........(1) 2-3 (1)... El Salvador
Mexico..........(1) 1-0 (0)... Costa Rica

Friday October 12 2012
El Salvador ...(0) 0-1 (1)... Costa Rica
Guyana.........(0) 0-5 (0)......... Mexico

Tuesday October 16 2012
Costa Rica.....(2) 7-0 (0)........ Guyana
Mexico..........(0) 2-0 (0)... El Salvador

The first meeting between the USA and Costa Rica took place in a blizzard in Colorado

Group C

	P	W	D	L	F	A	GD	Pts
Honduras	6	3	2	1	12	3	9	11
Panama	6	3	2	1	6	2	4	11
Canada	6	3	1	2	6	10	-4	10
Cuba	6	0	1	5	1	10	-9	1

Friday June 8 2012
Cuba.............(0) 0-1 (0).........Canada
Honduras......(0) 0-2 (0)........Panama

Tuesday June 12 2012
Canada ....(0) 0-0 (0) .... Honduras
Panama ....(0) 1-0 (0) .... Cuba

Friday September 7 2012
Canada ....(0) 1-0 (0)........Panama
Cuba.............(0) 0-3 (1)..... Honduras

Tuesday September 11 2012
Honduras......(1) 1-0 (0) .... Cuba
Panama ....(1) 2-0 (0)..........Canada

Friday October 12 2012
Canada ....(1) 3-0 (0) .... Cuba
Panama ....(0) 0-0 (0) ..... Honduras

Tuesday October 16 2012
Cuba.............(1) 1-1 (0)........Panama
Honduras......(4) 8-1 (0).........Canada

Round 4

Standings

	P	W	D	L	F	A	GD	Pts
USA	10	7	1	2	15	8	7	22
Costa Rica	10	5	3	2	13	7	6	18
Honduras	10	4	3	3	13	12	1	15
Mexico	10	2	5	3	7	9	-2	11
Panama	10	1	5	4	10	14	-4	8
Jamaica	10	0	5	5	5	13	-8	5

Wednesday February 6 2013
Honduras......(1) 2-1 (1)...............USA
Mexico..........(0) 0-0 (0).........Jamaica
Panama ....(2) 2-2 (1).... Costa Rica

Friday March 22 2013
Honduras......(0) 2-2 (1) .... Mexico
Jamaica ....(1) 1-1 (0) ....Panama
USA ....(1) 1-0 (0) .... Costa Rica

Tuesday March 26 2013
Costa Rica.....(1) 2-0 (0).......Jamaica
Mexico..........(0) 0-0 (0)...........USA
Panama ....(1) 2-0 (0) ..... Honduras

Tuesday June 4 2013
Jamaica ....(0) 0-1 (0) .... Mexico

Friday June 7 2013
Costa Rica.....(1) 1-0 (0) ..... Honduras

Jamaica ....(0) 1-2 (1) ....USA
Panama ....(0) 0-0 (0) .... Mexico

Tuesday June 11 2013
Honduras......(1) 2-0 (0).......Jamaica
Mexico..........(0) 0-0 (0) .... Costa Rica
USA ....(1) 2-0 (0)........Panama

Tuesday June 18 2013
Costa Rica.....(0) 2-0 (0)........Panama
USA ....(0) 1-0 (0) ...... Honduras

Saturday September 7 2013
Costa Rica.....(2) 3-1 (1)..............USA
Mexico..........(1) 1-2 (0) ...... Honduras
Panama ....(0) 0-0 (0)........Jamaica

Sunday September 11 2013
Honduras......(1) 2-2 (0)........Panama
Jamaica ....(0) 1-1 (0) .... Costa Rica
USA ....(0) 2-0 (0) .... Mexico

Friday October 11 2013
Honduras......(0) 1-0 (0) .... Costa Rica
USA ....(0) 2-0 (0)........Jamaica

Saturday October 12 2013
Mexico..........(1) 2-1 (0).......Panama

Wednesday October 16 2013
Costa Rica.....(1) 2-1 (1) .... Mexico
Jamaica ....(1) 2-2 (2) ...... Honduras
Panama ....(1) 2-3 (0) ....USA

Top scorers

	P	Gls
G Gope-Fenepej (N Caledonia)	10	8
Jacques Haeko (N Caledonia)	8	7
Chris Wood (New Zealand)	9	7
Shane Smeltz (New Zealand)	9	5
Lorenzo Tehau (Tahiti)	8	5
Bertrand Kai (N Caledonia)	11	5
Cesar Lolohea (N Caledonia)	6	4
Roy Kayara (New Caledonia)	11	4
Alvin Tehau (Tahiti)	9	4
Benjamin Totori (Solomon I)	10	4
Jonathan Tehau (Tahiti)	10	4

Format 11 participating teams, 0.5 qualify. **Round 1** 1 round-robin group of 4 contested in Samoa. Winners advance **Round 2** Group stage of OFC Nations Cup. 2 round-robin groups of 4 contested in Fiji, winners and runners-up advance **Round 3** 1 round-robin, home-and-away group of 4. Winners advance to intercontinental play-off against Concacaf

Round 1

Standings

	P	W	D	L	F	A	GD	Pts
Samoa	3	2	1	0	5	3	2	7
Tonga	3	1	1	1	4	4	0	4
Am Samoa	3	1	1	1	3	3	0	4
Cook I	3	0	1	2	4	6	-2	1

Tuesday November 22 2011
Am Samoa....(1) 2-1 (0)..........Tonga
Cook I...........(1) 2-3 (2)..........Samoa

Thursday November 24 2011
Am Samoa....(1) 1-1 (0).......... Cook I
Samoa..........(1) 1-1 (0)...........Tonga

Saturday November 26 2011
Samoa..........(0) 1-0 (0)....Am Samoa
Tonga ....(1) 2-1 (1).......... Cook I

Round 2

Group A

	P	W	D	L	F	A	GD	Pts
Tahiti	3	3	0	0	18	5	13	9
New Caledonia	3	2	0	1	17	6	11	6
Vanuatu	3	1	0	2	8	9	-1	3
Samoa	3	0	0	3	1	24	-23	0

Friday June 1 2012
Samoa ....(0)1-10(4)............Tahiti
Vanuatu.........(0) 2-5 (1). N Caledonia

Sunday June 3 2012
Tahiti ....(3) 4-3 (0). N Caledonia
Vanuatu........(2) 5-0 (0)..........Samoa

Tuesday June 5 2012
N Caledonia..(6) 9-0 (0)..........Samoa
Tahiti ....(2) 4-1 (0)....... Vanuatu

Group B

	P	W	D	L	F	A	GD	Pts
New Zealand	3	2	1	0	4	2	2	7
Solomon I	3	1	2	0	2	1	1	5
Fiji	3	0	2	1	1	2	-1	2
Papua NG	3	0	1	2	2	4	-2	1

Saturday June 2 2012
Fiji ....(0) 0-1 (1) New Zealand
Solomon I .....(1) 1-0 (0).....Papua NG

Monday June 4 2012
Fiji ....(0) 0-0 (0).....Solomon I
Papua NG .....(0) 1-2 (1) New Zealand

Wednesday June 6 2012
Papua NG .....(0) 1-1 (1)................Fiji
New Zealand (1) 1-1 (0).....Solomon I

Round 3

Standings

	P	W	D	L	F	A	GD	Pts
New Zealand	6	6	0	0	17	2	15	18
New Caldonia	6	4	0	2	17	6	11	12
Tahiti	6	1	0	5	2	12	-10	3
Solomon I	6	1	0	5	5	21	-16	3

Friday September 7 2012
N Caledonia..(0) 0-2 (1) New Zealand
Solomon I .....(1) 2-0 (0)............Tahiti

Tuesday September 11 2012
New Zealand (2) 6-1 (0).....Solomon I
Tahiti ....(0) 0-4 (0). N Caledonia

Friday October 12 2012
Solomon I .....(1) 2-6 (2). N Caledonia
Tahiti ....(0) 0-2 (1) New Zealand

Tuesday October 16 2012
N Caledonia..(4) 5-0 (0).....Solomon I
New Zealand (1) 3-0 (0)............Tahiti

Friday March 22 2013
New Zealand (1) 2-1 (0). N Caledonia
Tahiti ....(1) 2-0 (0).....Solomon I

Tuesday March 26 2013
N Caledonia..(0) 1-0 (0)............Tahiti
Solomon I .....(0) 0-2 (1) New Zealand

Intercontinental play-off

Wednesday November 13 2013
Mexico..........(2) 5-1 (0) New Zealand

Wednesday November 20 2013
New Zealand (0) 2-4 (3) .... Mexico
Agg: 3-9

New Zealand couldn't stop Mexico in the play-off

PLAYER PROFILES

COMPLETE
PROFILE OF
EVERY PLAYER
HEADING TO
BRAZIL

CRISTIANO RONALDO

LIONEL MESSI

CRISTIANO RONALDO		LIONEL MESSI
29	Age	26
6'1"	Height	5'5"
POR	Nationality	ARG
Real Madrid	Club	Barcelona
110 - 49	Caps – goals	83 - 37
0.67	Avg league goal per game	0.88

BET SMARTER IN BRAZIL USING OUR UP-TO-DATE AND EASY TO USE
DATABASE OF STATS FOR EVERY TEAM, PLAYER, GROUND AND REFEREE

RESULTS | FIXTURES | STATS | TIPS | NEWS | BETTING

Brazil's position as hosts reduced South American qualifying to a nine-nation group in which only four teams would fail to qualify. And with Peru, Bolivia and Venezuela managing just one World Cup appearance between them since 1982, it was no surprise to see all three miss out again.

It was, however, a surprise to see Paraguay join them on the sidelines, but the 2010 quarter-finalists and 2011 Copa America runners-up failed miserably in their attempts to rebuild an ageing defence and finished bottom.

South Africa 2010 semi-finalists **Uruguay** also failed to build on their last World Cup showing, only booking a place in the intercontinental play-offs for a fourth consecutive qualifying campaign. However, La Celeste made short work of Jordan, killing the tie off early with a 5-0 win away in the first leg.

Argentina dominated the section while rarely getting out of second gear and showcased their impressive firepower by scoring 13 goals in six matches against the other top-four sides.

Chile again impressed going forward but conceded 25 goals in 16 games and took just four points from six games against the other automatic qualifiers. Fellow qualifiers **Ecuador** continued to take advantage of their altitude advantage in Quito to collect 22 of the 24 points on offer at Estadio Olimpico Atahualpa, which sits 2,850 metres above sea level. Tellingly, however, they collected just three points on the road.

Colombia were the serious movers in South America, finishing second to qualify for their first World Cup in 14 years, but the excitement that gripped the nation on qualifying turned to despair when talismanic striker Radamel Falcao suffered a serious knee injury while playing for Paris Saint-Germain that could rule him out of the finals.

South America's top scorers (anti-clockwise from top): Luis Suarez (11 goals); Lionel Messi (ten); Gonzalo Higuain and Radamel Falcao (both nine)

Top scorers

	P	Gls
Luis Suarez (Uruguay)	14	11
Lionel Messi (Argentina)	14	10
Gonzalo Higuain (Argentina)	11	9
Falcao (Colombia)	13	9
Felipe Caicedo (Ecuador)	9	7
Teofilo Gutierrez (Colombia)	11	6
Sergio Aguero (Argentina)	8	5
Jefferson Farfan (Peru)	11	5
Eduardo Vargas (Chile)	14	5
Arturo Vidal (Chile)	11	5
Jose Rondon (Colombia)	13	5
Edinson Cavani (Uruguay)	16	5

Format 9 participating teams, 4.5 qualify plus Brazil as hosts.
1 round-robin, home-and-away group of 9. Top 4 qualify for World Cup, 5th team advances to intercontinental play-off against Asia

Standings

	P	W	D	L	F	A	GD	Pts
Argentina	16	9	5	2	35	15	20	32
Colombia	16	9	3	4	27	13	14	30
Chile	16	9	1	6	29	25	4	28
Ecuador	16	7	4	5	20	16	4	25
Uruguay	16	7	4	5	25	25	0	25
Venezuela	16	5	5	6	14	20	-6	20
Peru	16	4	3	9	17	26	-9	15
Bolivia	16	2	6	8	17	30	-13	12
Paraguay	16	3	3	10	17	31	-14	12

Friday October 7 2011
Argentina .....(2) 4-1 (0) .... Chile
Ecuador ....(2) 2-0 (0) .....Venezuela
Peru ....(0) 2-0 (0) ...... Paraguay
Uruguay ....(3) 4-2 (1) .... Bolivia

Tuesday October 11 2011
Bolivia ....(0) 1-2 (0) ......Colombia
Chile..............(2) 4-2 (0) .... Peru
Paraguay ......(0) 1-1 (0) .... Uruguay
Venezuela .....(0) 1-0 (0) ..... Argentina

Friday November 11 2011
Argentina .....(0) 1-1 (0) .... Bolivia
Colombia ......(1) 1-1 (0) .....Venezuela
Paraguay ......(0) 2-1 (0) .... Ecuador
Uruguay ....(2) 4-0 (0) .... Chile

Tuesday November 15 2011
Chile ....(1) 2-0 (0) ...... Paraguay
Colombia ......(1) 1-2 (0) ..... Argentina
Ecuador ....(0) 2-0 (0) .... Peru
Venezuela .....(1) 1-0 (0) .... Bolivia

Saturday June 2 2012
Argentina .....(3) 4-0 (0) .... Ecuador
Bolivia ....(0) 0-2 (1) .... Chile
Uruguay ....(1) 1-1 (0) .....Venezuela

Sunday June 3 2012
Peru ....(0) 0-1 (0) ......Colombia

Saturday June 9 2012
Bolivia ....(1) 3-1 (0) ...... Paraguay
Venezuela .....(0) 0-2 (0) .... Chile

Sunday June 10 2012
Ecuador ....(0) 1-0 (0) ......Colombia
Uruguay ....(2) 4-2 (1) .... Peru

Friday September 7 2012
Argentina .....(2) 3-1 (1) ...... Paraguay

Colombia ......(1) 4-0 (0) .... Uruguay
Ecuador ....(0) 1-0 (0) .... Bolivia
Peru ....(0) 2-1 (1) .....Venezuela

Tuesday September 11 2012
Chile ....(1) 1-3 (0) ......Colombia
Paraguay ......(0) 0-2 (1) .....Venezuela
Peru ....(1) 1-1 (1) ..... Argentina
Uruguay ....(0) 1-1 (1) .... Ecuador

Friday October 12 2012
Argentina .....(0) 3-0 (0) .... Uruguay
Bolivia ....(0) 1-1 (1) .... Peru
Colombia ......(0) 2-0 (0) ...... Paraguay
Ecuador ....(1) 3-1 (1) .... Chile

Tuesday October 16 2012
Bolivia ....(2) 4-1 (0) .... Uruguay
Chile ....(0) 1-2 (2) .... Argentina
Paraguay ......(0) 1-0 (0) .... Peru
Venezuela .....(1) 1-1 (1) .... Ecuador

Friday March 22 2013
Argentina .....(2) 3-0 (0) .....Venezuela
Colombia ......(1) 5-0 (0) .... Bolivia
Peru ....(0) 1-0 (0) .... Chile
Uruguay ....(0) 1-1 (0) ...... Paraguay

Tuesday March 26 2013
Bolivia ....(1) 1-1 (1) ..... Argentina
Chile ....(1) 2-0 (0) .... Uruguay
Ecuador ....(1) 4-1 (1) ...... Paraguay
Venezuela .....(1) 1-0 (0) ......Colombia

Friday June 7 2013
Argentina .....(0) 0-0 (0) ......Colombia
Bolivia ....(0) 1-1 (0) .....Venezuela
Paraguay ......(0) 1-2 (1) .... Chile
Peru ....(1) 1-0 (0) .... Ecuador

Tuesday June 11 2013
Chile ....(2) 3-1 (1) .... Bolivia
Colombia ......(2) 2-0 (0) .... Peru
Ecuador ....(1) 1-1 (1) ..... Argentina
Venezuela .....(0) 0-1 (1) .... Uruguay

Friday September 6 2013
Colombia ......(1) 1-0 (0) .... Ecuador
Paraguay ......(1) 4-0 (0) .... Bolivia

Saturday September 7 2013
Chile ....(2) 3-0 (0) .....Venezuela
Peru ....(0) 1-2 (1) .... Uruguay

Tuesday September 10 2013
Bolivia ....(0) 1-1 (0) .... Ecuador
Uruguay ....(0) 2-0 (0) ......Colombia

Wednesday September 11 2013
Paraguay ......(1) 2-5 (2) .... Argentina
Venezuela .....(1) 3-2 (1) .... Peru

Friday October 11 2013
Colombia ......(0) 3-3 (3) .... Chile
Ecuador ....(1) 1-0 (0) .... Uruguay
Venezuela .....(0) 1-1 (1) ...... Paraguay

Saturday October 12 2013
Argentina .....(2) 3-1 (1) .... Peru

Wednesday October 16 2013
Chile ....(2) 2-1 (0) .... Ecuador
Paraguay ......(1) 1-2 (1) ......Colombia
Peru ....(1) 1-1 (1) .... Bolivia
Uruguay ....(2) 3-2 (2) .... Argentina

Intercontinental play-off
Wednesday November 13 2013
Jordan ....(0) 0-5 (1) .... Uruguay
Wednesday November 20 2013
Uruguay ....(0) 0-0 (0) .... Jordan
Agg: 5-0

Results include tournaments featuring teams qualified for the 2014 World Cup

Asian Cup 2011

Group A

	P	W	D	L	F	A	GD	Pts
Uzbekistan	3	2	1	0	6	3	3	7
Qatar	3	2	0	1	5	2	3	6
China	3	1	1	1	4	4	0	4
Kuwait	3	0	0	3	1	7	-6	0

Friday January 7 2011
Qatar ....(0) 0-2 (0) ... Uzbekistan
Saturday January 8 2011
Kuwait..........(0) 0-2 (0) .... China
Wednesday January 12 2011
Uzbekistan....(1) 2-1 (0) .... Kuwait
China............(0) 0-2 (2) ....Qatar
Sunday January 16 2011
Qatar ....(2) 3-0 (0) .... Kuwait
China............(1) 2-2 (1)... Uzbekistan

Group B

	P	W	D	L	F	A	GD	Pts
Japan	3	2	1	0	8	2	6	7
Jordan	3	2	1	0	4	2	2	7
Syria	3	1	0	2	4	5	-1	3
Saudi Arabia	3	0	0	3	1	8	-7	0

Sunday January 9 2011
Japan............(0) 1-1 (1)..........Jordan
Saudi Arabia .(0) 1-2 (1)............Syria
Thursday January 13 2011
Jordan ....(1) 1-0 (0) .Saudi Arabia
Syria ....(0) 1-2 (1)............Japan
Monday January 17 2011
Jordan ....(1) 2-1 (1)............Syria
Saudi Arabia .(0) 0-5 (3)..........Japan

Group C

	P	W	D	L	F	A	GD	Pts
Australia	3	2	1	0	6	1	5	7
S Korea	3	2	1	0	7	3	4	7
Bahrain	3	1	0	2	6	5	1	3
India	3	0	0	3	3	13	-10	0

Monday January 10 2011
India.............(0) 0-4 (3) ....Australia
S Korea ....(1) 2-1 (0) .... Bahrain
Friday January 14 2011
Australia ....(0) 1-1 (1)........S Korea
Bahrain.........(4) 5-2 (1)..........India
Tuesday January 18 2011
S Korea ....(3) 4-1 (1) .... India
Australia ....(1) 1-0 (0) .... Bahrain

Group D

	P	W	D	L	F	A	GD	Pts
Iran	3	3	0	0	6	1	5	9
Iraq	3	2	0	1	3	2	1	6
N Korea	3	0	1	2	0	2	-2	1
UAE	3	0	1	2	0	4	-4	1

Tuesday January 11 2011
N Korea ....(0) 0-0 (0) ....UAE
Iraq...............(1) 1-2 (1) ....Iran

Saturday January 15 2011
Iran...............(0) 1-0 (0) ....N Korea
UAE ....(0) 0-1 (0) ....Iraq
Wednesday January 19 2011
Iraq...............(1) 1-0 (0) ....N Korea
UAE ....(0) 0-3 (0) ....Iran

Quarter-finals
Friday January 21 2011
Japan.............(1) 3-2 (1)............Qatar
Uzbekistan....(0) 2-1 (0)..........Jordan
Saturday January 22 2011
Australia........(0) 1-0 (0)..............Iraq
AET 0-0 90 mins
Iran...............(0) 0-1 (0)........S Korea
AET 0-0 90 mins

Semi-finals
Tuesday January 25 2011
Japan.............(1) 2-2 (1)........S Korea
AET 1-1 90 mins. Japan won 3-0 pens
Uzbekistan....(0) 0-6 (2)......Australia

3rd/4th place play-off
Friday January 28 2011
Uzbekistan....(1) 2-3 (3)........S Korea

Final
Saturday January 29 2011
Australia ....(0) 0-1 (0)............Japan
AET 0-0 90 mins

Copa Centroamericana 2011

Group A

	P	W	D	L	F	A	GD	Pts
Panama	3	3	0	0	6	0	6	9
El Salvador	3	2	0	1	7	4	3	6
Nicaragua	3	0	1	2	1	5	-4	1
Belize	3	0	1	2	3	8	-5	1

Friday January 14 2011
El Salvador ...(0) 2-0 (0) .....Nicaragua
Saturday January 15 2011
Panama ....(2) 2-0 (0) .... Belize
Sunday January 16 2011
Belize............(1) 2-5 (2)... El Salvador
Monday January 17 2011
Panama ....(1) 2-0 (0) .....Nicaragua
Tuesday January 18 2011
Nicaragua.....(1) 1-1 (0) .... Belize
Wednesday January 19 2011
Panama ....(1) 2-0 (0)... El Salvador

Group B

	P	W	D	L	F	A	GD	Pts
Honduras	2	1	1	0	4	2	2	4
Costa Rica	2	1	1	0	3	1	2	4
Guatemala	2	0	0	2	1	5	-4	0

Saturday January 15 2011
Costa Rica.....(1) 1-1 (0) ..... Honduras
Sunday January 16 2011
Guatemala.....(0) 0-2 (0) .... Costa Rica
Wednesday January 19 2011
Honduras......(2) 3-1 (1)... Guatemala

5th/6th place play-off
Friday January 21 2011
Nicaragua .....(1) 1-2 (1) .. Guatemala

Semi-finals
Friday January 21 2011
Honduras......(0) 2-0 (0) .. El Salvador
Saturday January 22 2011
Panama ....(0) 1-1 (1) .... Costa Rica
AET 1-1 90 mins. Costa Rica 4-2 pens

3rd/4th place play-off
Sunday January 23 2011
Panama ....(0) 0-0 (0) ... El Salvador
AET 0-0 90 mins. Panama 5-4 pens

Final
Sunday January 23 2011
Honduras......(1) 2-1 (0) .... Costa Rica

Concacaf Gold Cup 2011

Group A

	P	W	D	L	F	A	GD	Pts
Mexico	3	3	0	0	14	1	13	9
Costa Rica	3	1	1	1	7	5	2	4
El Salvador	3	1	1	1	7	7	0	4
Cuba	3	0	0	3	1	16	-15	0

Sunday June 5 2011
Costa Rica.....(2) 5-0 (0) .... Cuba
Monday June 6 2011
Mexico..........(0) 5-0 (0) ... El Salvador
Friday June 10 2011
Costa Rica.....(0) 1-1 (1)... El Salvador
Cuba ....(0) 0-5 (1)........... Mexico
Sunday June 12 2011
El Salvador ...(2) 6-1 (0) .... Cuba
Monday June 13 2011
Mexico..........(4) 4-1 (0) .... Costa Rica

Group B

	P	W	D	L	F	A	GD	Pts
Jamaica	3	3	0	0	7	0	7	9
Honduras	3	1	1	1	7	2	5	4
Guatemala	3	1	1	1	4	2	2	4
Grenada	3	0	0	3	1	15	-14	0

Tuesday June 07 2011
Jamaica ....(2) 4-0 (0) .... Grenada
Honduras......(0) 0-0 (0) ... Guatemala
Saturday June 11 2011
Jamaica ....(0) 2-0 (0) ... Guatemala
Grenada ....(1) 1-7 (3) ..... Honduras
Tuesday June 14 2011
Guatemala.....(2) 4-0 (0) .... Grenada
Honduras......(0) 0-1 (1).........Jamaica

Group C

	P	W	D	L	F	A	GD	Pts
Panama	3	2	1	0	6	4	2	7
USA	3	2	0	1	4	2	2	6
Canada	3	1	1	1	2	3	-1	4
Guadeloupe	3	0	0	3	2	5	-3	0

USA goalkeeper Tim Howard warms up for the Gold Cup final

Supporters of USA and Mexico get in the mood in Pasadena

Mexico's Giovanni Dos Santos and Andres Guardado celebrate

Tuesday June 07 2011
Panama ....(2) 3-2 (0). Guadeloupe
Wednesday June 8 2011
USA ....(1) 2-0 (0).........Canada
Saturday June 11 2011
Canada ....(0) 1-0 (0). Guadeloupe
Sunday June 12 2011
USA ....(0) 1-2 (2).......Panama
Wednesday June 15 2011
Canada ....(0) 1-1 (0).......Panama
Guadeloupe ..(0) 0-1 (1)..............USA

Quarter-finals
Saturday June 18 2011
Costa Rica.....(0) 1-1 (0)..... Honduras
Sunday June 19 2011
Mexico..........(0) 2-1 (1)... Guatemala
Jamaica ....(0) 0-2 (0)..............USA
Panama ....(0) 1-1 (0)... El Salvador
AET 1-1 90 mins. Panama 5-3 pens

Semi-finals
Thursday June 23 2011
USA ....(0) 1-0 (0).......Panama
Honduras......(0) 0-2 (0)......... Mexico
AET 0-0 90 mins

Final
Sunday June 26 2011
USA ....(2) 2-4 (2)......... Mexico

Copa America 2011

Group A

	P	W	D	L	F	A	GD	Pts
Colombia	3	2	1	0	3	0	3	7
Argentina	3	1	2	0	4	1	3	5
Costa Rica	3	1	0	2	2	4	-2	3
Bolivia	3	0	1	2	1	5	-4	1

Saturday July 2 2011
Argentina .....(0) 1-1 (0)..........Bolivia
Colombia ......(1) 1-0 (0).... Costa Rica
Thursday July 7 2011
Argentina .....(0) 0-0 (0)....Colombia
Bolivia ....(0) 0-2 (0).... Costa Rica
Sunday July 10 2011
Colombia ......(2) 2-0 (0)..........Bolivia
Tuesday July 12 2011
Argentina .....(1) 3-0 (0).... Costa Rica

Group B

	P	W	D	L	F	A	GD	Pts
Brazil	3	1	2	0	6	4	2	5
Venezuela	3	1	2	0	4	3	1	5
Paraguay	3	0	3	0	5	5	0	3
Ecuador	3	0	1	2	2	5	-3	1

Sunday July 3 2011
Brazil ....(0) 0-0 (0).....Venezuela
Paraguay ......(0) 0-0 (0)........Ecuador
Saturday July 9 2011
Brazil ....(1) 2-2 (0)......Paraguay
Venezuela .....(0) 1-0 (0)........Ecuador
Wednesday July 13 2011
Paraguay ......(1) 3-3 (1).....Venezuela
Thursday July 14 2011
Brazil ....(1) 4-2 (1)........Ecuador

Group C

	P	W	D	L	F	A	GD	Pts
Chile	3	2	1	0	4	2	2	7
Uruguay	3	1	2	0	3	2	1	5
Peru	3	1	1	1	2	2	0	4
Mexico	3	0	0	3	1	4	-3	0

Monday July 4 2011
Uruguay ....(1) 1-1 (1) .... Peru
Tuesday July 5 2011
Chile..............(0) 2-1 (1) .... Mexico
Friday July 8 2011
Uruguay ....(0) 1-1 (0) .... Chile
Saturday July 9 2011
Peru...............(0) 1-0 (0) .... Mexico
Tuesday July 12 2011
Chile..............(0) 1-0 (0) .... Peru
Wednesday July 13 2011
Uruguay ....(1) 1-0 (0) .... Mexico

Quarter-finals
Saturday July 16 2011
Colombia......(0) 0-2 (1) .... Peru
AET 0-0 90 mins
Argentina .....(0) 1-1 (0) .... Uruguay
AET 1-1 90 mins. Uruguay 5-4 pens
Sunday July 17 2011
Brazil ....(0) 0-0 (0) ...... Paraguay
AET 0-0 90 mins. Paraguay 2-0 pens
Chile..............(0) 1-2 (1) .....Venezuela

Semi-finals
Wednesday July 20 2011
Peru..............(0) 0-2 (0) .... Uruguay
Thursday July 21 2011
Paraguay ......(0) 0-0 (0) .....Venezuela
AET 0-0 90 mins. Paraguay 5-3 pens

3rd/4th place play-off
Saturday July 23 2011
Peru...............(1) 4-1 (0) .....Venezuela

Final
Sunday July 24 2011
Uruguay ....(2) 3-0 (0) ...... Paraguay

Group A

	P	W	D	L	F	A	GD	Pts
Zambia	3	2	1	0	5	3	2	7
Eq Guinea	3	2	0	1	3	2	1	6
Libya	3	1	1	1	4	4	0	4
Senegal	3	0	0	3	3	6	-3	0

Saturday January 21 2012
Eq Guinea.....(0) 1-0 (0) .... Libya
Senegal ....(0) 1-2 (2) ....Zambia
Wednesday January 25 2012
Libya ....(1) 2-2 (1) ....Zambia
Eq Guinea.....(0) 2-1 (0) .... Senegal
Sunday January 29 2012
Libya ....(1) 2-1 (1) .... Senegal
Eq Guinea.....(0) 0-1 (0) ....Zambia

Group A

	P	W	D	L	F	A	GD	Pts
Ivory Coast	3	3	0	0	5	0	5	9
Sudan	3	1	1	1	4	4	0	4
Angola	3	1	1	1	4	5	-1	4
Burkina Faso	3	0	0	3	2	6	-4	0

Sunday January 22 2012
Ivory Coast ...(1) 1-0 (0)...........Sudan
Burkina Faso .(0) 1-2 (0)......... Angola
Thursday January 26 2012
Sudan...........(1) 2-2 (1)......... Angola
Ivory Coast ...(1) 2-0 (0).Burkina Faso
Monday January 30 2012
Ivory Coast ...(1) 2-0 (0)......... Angola
Sudan...........(1) 2-1 (0).Burkina Faso

Group A

	P	W	D	L	F	A	GD	Pts
Gabon	3	3	0	0	6	2	4	9
Tunisia	3	2	0	1	4	3	1	6
Morocco	3	1	0	2	4	5	-1	3
Niger	3	0	0	3	1	5	-4	0

Monday January 23 2012
Gabon ....(2) 2-0 (0)............Niger
Morocco ....(0) 1-2 (1)..........Tunisia
Friday January 27 2012
Niger ....(1) 1-2 (1)..........Tunisia
Gabon ....(0) 3-2 (1)........Morocco
Tuesday January 31 2012
Niger ....(0) 0-1 (0)........Morocco
Gabon ....(0) 1-0 (0).........Tunisia

Group A

	P	W	D	L	F	A	GD	Pts
Ghana	3	2	1	0	4	1	3	7
Mali	3	2	0	1	3	3	0	6
Guinea	3	1	1	1	7	3	4	4
Botswana	3	0	0	3	2	9	-7	0

Tuesday January 24 2012
Ghana...........(1) 1-0 (0).....Botswana
Mali...............(1) 1-0 (0)......... Guinea
Saturday January 28 2012
Botswana .....(1) 1-6 (4)......... Guinea
Ghana...........(0) 2-0 (0)............. Mali
Wednesday February 1 2012
Ghana...........(1) 1-1 (1)......... Guinea
Botswana .....(0) 1-2 (0)............. Mali

Quarter-finals
Saturday February 4 2012
Zambia ....(1) 3-0 (0)...........Sudan
Ivory Coast ...(1) 3-0 (0)..... Eq Guinea
Sunday February 5 2012
Gabon ....(0) 1-1 (0)............. Mali
AET 1-1 90 mins. Mali 5-4 pens
Ghana...........(1) 2-1 (1)..........Tunisia
AET 1-1 90 mins

Semi-finals
Wednesday Febuary 8 2012
Zambia ....(0) 1-0 (0).......... Ghana
Mali..............(0) 0-1 (1)...Ivory Coast

3rd/4th place play-off
Saturday February 11 2012
Ghana...........(0) 0-2 (1)............. Mali

Final
Sunday Febuary 12 2012
Zambia ....(0) 0-0 (0)...Ivory Coast
AET. Zambia 8-7 pens

Group A

	P	W	D	L	F	A	GD	Pts
Czech Rep	3	2	0	1	4	5	-1	6
Greece	3	1	1	1	3	3	0	4
Russia	3	1	1	1	5	3	2	4
Poland	3	0	2	1	2	3	-1	2

Camera phones to the fore as Spain set off to collect the trophy after winning Euro 2012

Friday June 8 2012
Poland ....(1) 1-1 (0) ....Greece
Russia ....(2) 4-1 (0).... Czech Rep
Tuesday June 12 2012
Greece ....(0) 1-2 (2).... Czech Rep
Poland ....(0) 1-1 (1).......... Russia
Saturday June 16 2012
Greece ....(0) 1-0 (0).......... Russia

Czech Rep.....(1) 1-0 (0) ....Poland

Group B

	P	W	D	L	F	A	GD	Pts
Germany	3	3	0	0	5	2	3	9
Portugal	3	2	0	1	5	4	1	6
Denmark	3	1	0	2	4	5	-1	3
Holland	3	0	0	3	2	5	-3	0

Saturday June 9 2012
Holland.........(0) 0-1 (1)...... Denmark
Germany.......(0) 1-0 (0)....... Portugal
Wednesday June 13 2012
Denmark.......(1) 2-3 (2)....... Portugal
Holland.........(0) 1-2 (2)....... Germany
Sunday June 17 2012
Denmark.......(1) 1-2 (1)...... Germany
Portugal........(1) 2-1 (1)........ Holland

Group C

	P	W	D	L	F	A	GD	Pts
Spain	3	2	1	0	6	1	5	7
Italy	3	1	2	0	4	2	2	5
Croatia	3	1	1	1	4	3	1	4
Rep of Ireland	3	0	0	3	1	9	-8	0

Sunday June 10 2012
Spain ....(0) 1-1 (0)..............Italy
Rep of Irex ....(1) 1-3 (2)......... Croatia
Thursday June 14 2012
Italy...............(1) 1-1 (0)......... Croatia
Spain ....(1) 4-0 (0)..... Rep of Ire
Monday June 18 2012
Croatia..........(0) 0-1 (0)............Spain
Italy ....(1) 2-0 (0)..... Rep of Ire

Group D

	P	W	D	L	F	A	GD	Pts
England	3	2	1	0	5	3	2	7
France	3	1	1	1	3	3	0	4
Ukraine	3	1	0	2	2	4	-2	3
Sweden	3	1	0	2	5	5	0	3

Monday June 11 2012
France...........(1) 1-1 (1)........England
Ukraine.........(0) 2-1 (0)........Sweden
Friday June 15 2012
Ukraine.........(0) 0-2 (0)......... France
Sweden ....(0) 2-3 (1)........England
Tuesday June 19 2012
England ....(0) 1-0 (0)....... Ukraine
Sweden ....(0) 2-0 (0).......... France

Quarter-finals
Thursday June 21 2012
Czech Rep.....(0) 0-1 (0)....... Portugal
Friday June 22 2012
Germany.......(1) 4-2 (0).........Greece
Saturday June 23 2012
Spain ....(1) 2-0 (0)......... France
Sunday June 24 2012
England ....(0) 0-0 (0)..............Italy
AET 0-0 90 mins. Italy 4-2 pens

Semi-finals
Wednesday June 27 2012
Portugal........(0) 0-0 (0)............Spain
AET 0-0 90 mins. Spain 4-2 pens
Thursday June 28 2012
Germany.......(0) 1-2 (2)..............Italy

Final
Sunday July 1 2012
Spain ....(2) 4-0 (0)..............Italy

Group A

	P	W	D	L	F	A	GD	Pts
Costa Rica	3	2	1	0	4	1	3	7
Belize	3	1	1	1	2	2	0	4
Guatemala	3	0	3	0	2	2	0	3
Nicaragua	3	0	1	2	2	5	-3	1

Friday January 18 2013
Guatemala....(0) 1-1 (1).....Nicaragua
Saturday January 19 2013
Costa Rica.....(0) 1-0 (0)........... Belize
Sunday January 20 2013
Belize............(0) 0-0 (0)... Guatemala
Monday January 21 2013
Costa Rica.....(1) 2-0 (0).....Nicaragua
Tuesday January 22 2013
Nicaragua.....(0) 1-2 (1)........... Belize
Wednesday January 23 2013
Costa Rica.....(1) 1-1 (0)... Guatemala

Group B

	P	W	D	L	F	A	GD	Pts
Honduras	2	0	2	0	2	2	0	2
El Salvador	2	0	2	0	1	1	0	2
Panama	2	0	2	0	1	1	0	2

Saturday January 19 2013
Honduras......(0) 1-1 (0)... El Salvador
Sunday January 20 2013
El Salvador ...(0) 0-0 (0)........Panama
Wednesday January 23 2013
Panama ....(1) 1-1 (1)..... Honduras

5th/6th place play-off
Friday January 25 2013
Guatemala....(0) 1-3 (1)........Panama

Semi-finals
Friday January 25 2013
Honduras......(0) 1-0 (0)........... Belize
Saturday January 26 2013
Costa Rica.....(0) 1-0 (0)... El Salvador

3rd/4th place play-off
Sunday January 27 2013
El Salvador ...(0) 1-0 (0)........... Belize

Final
Sunday January 27 2013
Costa Rica.....(1) 1-0 (0)..... Honduras

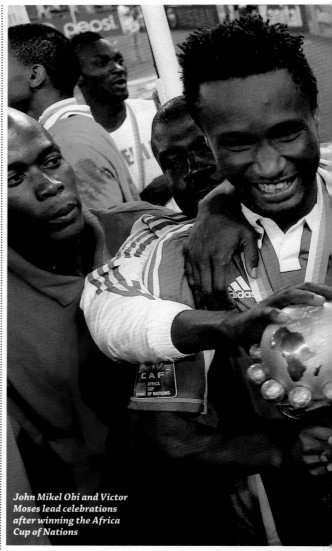

John Mikel Obi and Victor Moses lead celebrations after winning the Africa Cup of Nations

Group A

	P	W	D	L	F	A	GD	Pts
South Africa	3	1	2	0	4	2	2	5
Cape Verde I	3	1	2	0	3	2	1	5
Morocco	3	0	3	0	3	3	0	3
Angola	3	0	1	2	1	4	-3	1

Saturday January 19 2013
South Africa..(0) 0-0 (0).Cape Verde I
Angola..........(0) 0-0 (0).......Morocco

Wednesday January 23 2013
South Africa..(1) 2-0 (0)......... Angola
Morocco ....(0) 1-1 (1).Cape Verde I
Sunday January 27 2013
Morocco ....(1) 2-2 (0)..South Africa
Cape Verde I .(0) 2-1 (1)......... Angola

Group B

	P	W	D	L	F	A	GD	Pts
Ghana	3	2	1	0	6	2	4	7
Mali	3	1	1	1	2	2	0	4
DR Congo	3	0	3	0	3	3	0	3
Niger	3	0	1	2	0	4	-4	1

Sunday January 20 2013
Ghana...........(1) 2-2 (0).....DR Congo
Mali..............(0) 1-0 (0)...........Niger

Thursday January 24 2013
Ghana...........(1) 1-0 (0)............. Mali
Niger ....(0) 0-0 (0).....DR Congo

Monday January 28 2013
DR Congo .....(1) 1-1 (1)............. Mali
Niger ....(0) 0-3 (2)......... Ghana

Group C

	P	W	D	L	F	A	GD	Pts
Burkina Faso	3	1	2	0	5	1	4	5
Nigeria	**3**	**1**	**2**	**0**	**4**	**2**	**2**	**5**
Zambia	3	0	3	0	2	2	0	3
Ethiopia	3	0	1	2	1	7	-6	1

Monday January 21 2013
Zambia ....(1) 1-1 (0).......Ethiopia
Nigeria ....(1) 1-1 (0).Burkina Faso

Friday January 25 2013
Zambia ....(0) 1-1 (0)......... Nigeria
Burkina Faso .(1) 4-0 (0)........Ethiopia

Tuesday January 29 2013
Burkina Faso.(0) 0-0 (0).........Zambia
Ethiopia........(0) 0-2 (0)......... Nigeria

Group D

	P	W	D	L	F	A	GD	Pts
Ivory Coast	**3**	**2**	**1**	**0**	**7**	**3**	**4**	**7**
Togo	3	1	1	1	4	3	1	4
Tunisia	3	1	1	1	2	4	-2	4
Algeria	**3**	**0**	**1**	**2**	**2**	**5**	**-3**	**1**

Tuesday January 22 2013
Ivory Coast ...(1) 2-1 (1).............Togo
Tunisia ....(0) 1-0 (0)......... Algeria

Saturday January 26 2013
Ivory Coast ...(1) 3-0 (0)..........Tunisia
Algeria..........(0) 0-2 (1)............Togo

Wednesday January 30 2013
Togo ....(1) 1-1 (1)..........Tunisia
Algeria..........(0) 2-2 (0)...Ivory Coast

Quarter-finals

Saturday February 2 2013
Ghana...........(0) 2-0 (0).Cape Verde I
South Africa ..(1) 1-1 (0)............. Mali
AET 1-1 90 mins. Mali 3-1 pens

Sunday February 3 2013
Ivory Coast ...(0) 1-2 (1)......... Nigeria
Burkina Faso .(0) 1-0 (0).............Togo
AET 0-0 90 mins

Semi-finals

Wednesday February 6 2013
Mali..............(0) 1-4 (3)......... Nigeria
Burkina Faso.(0) 1-1 (1).......... Ghana
AET 1-1 90 mins. Burkina Faso 3-2 pens

3rd/4th place play-off

Saturday February 9 2013
Mali..............(1) 3-1 (0).......... Ghana

Final

Sunday February 10 2013
Nigeria ....(1) 1-0 (0).Burkina Faso

Confederations Cup 2013

Group A

	P	W	D	L	F	A	GD	Pts
Brazil	3	3	0	0	9	2	7	9
Italy	3	2	0	1	8	8	0	6
Mexico	3	1	0	2	3	5	-2	3
Japan	3	0	0	3	4	9	-5	0

Saturday June 15 2013
Brazil ....(1) 3-0 (0) .... Japan
Sunday June 16 2013
Mexico..........(1) 1-2 (1) ....Italy
Wednesday June 19 2013
Brazil ....(1) 2-0 (0) .... Mexico
Italy ....(1) 4-3 (2) .... Japan
Saturday June 22 2013
Italy ....(0) 2-4 (1) ....Brazil
Japan............(0) 1-2 (0) .... Mexico

Group B

	P	W	D	L	F	A	GD	Pts
Spain	3	3	0	0	15	1	14	9
Uruguay	3	2	0	1	11	3	8	6
Nigeria	3	1	0	2	7	6	1	3
Tahiti	3	0	0	3	1	24	-23	0

Sunday June 16 2013
Spain ....(2) 2-1 (0) ...... Uruguay
Monday June 17 2013
Tahiti ....(0) 1-6 (3) .... Nigeria
Thursday June 20 2013
Spain ....(4)10-0(0)........... Tahiti
Nigeria ....(1) 1-2 (1) .... Uruguay
Sunday June 23 2013
Nigeria ....(0) 0-3 (1) ....Spain
Uruguay ......(4) 8-0 (0) .... Tahiti

Semi-finals
Wednesday June 26 2013
Brazil ....(1) 2-1 (0) ...... Uruguay
Thursday June 27 2013
Spain ....(0) 0-0 (0) ....Italy
AET 0-0 90 mins. Spain 7-6 pens

3rd/4th place play-off
Sunday June 30 2013
Uruguay ......(0) 2-2 (1) ....Italy
AET 2-2 90 mins. Italy 3-2 pens

Final
Sunday June 30 2013
Brazil ....(2) 3-0 (0) ....Spain

Concacaf Gold Cup 2013

Group A

	P	W	D	L	F	A	GD	Pts
Panama	3	2	1	0	3	1	2	7
Mexico	3	2	0	1	6	3	3	6
Martinique	3	1	0	2	2	4	-2	3
Canada	3	0	1	2	0	3	-3	1

Sunday July 7 2013
Canada ....(0) 0-1 (0) ... Martinique
Monday July 8 2013
Mexico..........(1) 1-2 (1) .... Panama
Friday July 12 2013
Panama ....(0) 1-0 (0) ... Martinique
Mexico..........(1) 2-0 (0) ....Canada

You don't have to be mad to support Brazil... but it helps!

Sunday July 14 2013
Panama ....(0) 0-0 (0) ....Canada
Martinique....(1) 1-3 (2) .... Mexico

Group B

	P	W	D	L	F	A	GD	Pts
Honduras	3	2	0	1	3	2	1	6
Trin/Tobago	3	1	1	1	4	4	0	4
El Salvador	3	1	1	1	3	3	0	4
Haiti	3	1	0	2	2	3	-1	3

Tuesday July 9 2013
El Salvador ...(1) 2-2 (1) .. Trin/Tobago
Haiti ....(0) 0-2 (1) ..... Honduras
Saturday July 13 2013
Trin/Tobago...(0) 0-2 (1) .... Haiti
Honduras......(0) 1-0 (0) ... El Salvador
Tuesday July 16 2013
El Salvador ...(0) 1-0 (0) .... Haiti
Honduras .....(0) 0-2 (0) .. Trin/Tobago

Group C

	P	W	D	L	F	A	GD	Pts
USA	3	3	0	0	11	2	9	9
Costa Rica	3	2	0	1	4	1	3	6
Cuba	3	1	0	2	5	7	-2	3
Belize	3	0	0	3	1	11	-10	0

Wednesday July 10 2013
Costa Rica.....(0) 3-0 (0) .... Cuba
Belize............(1) 1-6 (3) .... USA
Saturday July 13 2013
USA ....(1) 4-1 (1) .... Cuba
Costa Rica.....(0) 1-0 (0) .... Belize
Tuesday July 16 2013
Cuba..............(1) 4-0 (0) .... Belize
Wednesday July 17 2013
USA ....(0) 1-0 (0) .... Costa Rica

Quarter-finals
Saturday July 20 2013
Panama ....(2) 6-1 (1) .... Cuba
Mexico..........(0) 1-0 (0) .. Trin/Tobago
Sunday July 21 2013
USA ....(2) 5-1 (1) ... El Salvador

Monday July 22 2013
Honduras......(0) 1-0 (0) .... Costa Rica
Semi-finals
Thursday July 25 2013
USA ....(2) 3-1 (0) ..... Honduras
Panama ....(1) 2-1 (1) .... Mexico
Final
Sunday July 28 2013
USA ....(0) 1-0 (0) ....Panama

Last five U20 World Cups

Turkey 2013
Final: France beat Uruguay
Semi-finals: Ghana, Iraq
Colombia 2011
Final: Brazil beat Portugal
Semi-finals: Mexico, France
Egypt 2009
Final: Ghana beat Brazil
Semi-finals: Hungary, Costa Rica
Canada 2007
Final: Argentina beat Czech Republic
Semi-finals: Chile, Austria
Holland 2005
Final: Argentina beat Nigeria
Semi-finals: Brazil, Morocco

Last five U17 World Cups

Mexico 2011
Final: Mexico beat Uruguay
Semi-finals: Germany, Brazil
Nigeria 2009
Final: Switzerland beat Nigeria
Semi-finals: Spain, Colombia
Korea 2007
Final: Nigeria beat Spain
Semi-finals: Germany, Ghana
Peru 2005
Final: Mexico beat Brazil
Semi-finals: Holland, Turkey
Finland 2003
Final: Brazil beat Spain
Semi-finals: Argentina, Colombia